The British Political Proc

'. . . a very good introductory text which should be widely used. Everything is very clearly explained and the quality and quantity of information and analysis is very high.'

Andrew Gamble, *University of Sheffield*

The British Political Process: An introduction is an exciting new text for students which clearly and simply explains the workings of the British political system. Written by practitioners close to the political process, it provides an authoritative, up-to-date and manageable guide to understanding how British government and politics today really works. It begins by placing British politics in the context of constitutional change and, continuing with this theme, explores those areas which feature on British politics courses and which students need to know about.

Benefits to students include:

- an exploration of the key areas, including: the constitution, elections, parties, pressure groups and lobbying, media, parliament, Whitehall, the Prime Minister and ministers, the EU, devolution, and the future of British politics;
- access to official documents which give unique insights into actual political processes, as well as figures and tables which illustrate and summarise information and statistics in an accessible way;
- appendices providing useful information such as a glossary of terms, a chronology of events, a digest of facts and a guide to politics on the Internet;
- a knowledgeable and experienced team of writers who offer a unique insight into the realities of the British political process.

Tony Wright is Member of Parliament for Cannock Chase. He is also Honorary Professor of Politics at the University of Birmingham.

The British Political Process

An introduction

Edited by Tony Wright

With Rob Clements, Oonagh Gay, Janet Seaton,
Paul Seaward, Alison Weston, Barry K. Winetrobe
and Edward Wood

London and New York

First published 2000
by Routledge
11 New Fetter Lane, London EC4P 4EE

Simultaneously published in the USA and Canada
by Routledge
29 West 35th Street, New York, NY 10001

Routledge is an imprint of the Taylor & Francis Group

Typeset in Baskerville by RefineCatch Limited, Bungay, Suffolk
Printed and bound in Great Britain by
Biddles Ltd, Guildford and King's Lynn

British Library Cataloguing in Publication Data
A catalogue record for this book is available from the British Library

Library of Congress Cataloging in Publication Data
The British political process: an introduction / edited by Tony
   Wright.
      Includes bibliographical references and index.
      1. Great Britain – Politics and government.   I. Wright, Anthony.
   JN231.B72   1999
   320.441 – dc21   99–16476

ISBN 0 415 04965 2 (hbk)
ISBN 0 415 04966 0 (pbk)

Contents

9 Governing beyond the centre 287

Figures

Tables

Contributors

Rob Clements is Director of Parliamentary and Reference Services in the House of Commons Library, where he has worked since 1976. He is a member of the Council of the Royal Statistical Society.

Oonagh Gay has worked in the House of Commons Library since 1983. She is the Library specialist in electoral law, devolution and the civil service and has contributed a number of articles to specialist journals in these fields.

Janet Seaton has worked in research and reference services of the House of Commons Library since 1978, and is currently seconded to Edinburgh as Head of Research and Information Services of the Scottish Parliament. She was co-author of *Facts About the British Prime Ministers* (H. W. Wilson/Mansell, 1995).

Paul Seaward is a Clerk in the House of Commons and currently acts as the Clerk to the Select Committee on Public Administration.

Alison Weston is a former researcher in the House of Commons Library, now at the European University Institute, Florence. Her areas of interest include European foreign policy development and the politics of the European Union.

Barry K. Winetrobe has worked in the Research Service of the House of Commons Library since 1981, and is currently seconded to the Scottish Parliament Information Centre in Edinburgh. His publications include two chapters of Oliver and Drewry's *The Law and Parliament* (Butterworths, 1998).

Edward Wood is a senior researcher in the House of Commons Library. His specialisms include local government, Parliament and the constitution.

Tony Wright is Member of Parliament for Cannock Chase. The author of many books, including *Citizens and Subjects* (Routledge, 1994) and *Socialisms Old and New* (Routledge, 1996), he is Honorary Professor of Politics at the University of Birmingham, and co-editor of the *Political Quarterly*.

Preface

There are many textbooks on British politics and some justification is needed for producing another one.

With such texts becoming ever bulkier, we wanted to try to produce an introductory textbook of manageable length that would cover the essential ground in an accessible and coherent way. We wanted it to be authoritative, providing a reliable guide to how the political process works, while also raising issues and questions. We hoped that the fact that it is written by people who are close to the political process, although from different vantage points, would help in our task. It is for others to judge how far we have succeeded.

The book is a collective enterprise, although individual contributors have concentrated on the preparation of particular chapters: the editor for Chapters 1, 4 and 10; Barry Winetrobe for Chapter 2; Oonagh Gay for Chapters 5 and 8 and, with Rob Clements, for Chapter 3; Edward Wood for Chapter 6 and, with Alison Weston, for Chapter 9; and Paul Seaward for Chapter 7. Janet Seaton and Rob Clements prepared much of the material in the appendices. However, all the chapters went through many drafts in which several hands were involved. Only the editor takes responsibility for everything, especially any expressions of opinion, while all the other contributors were involved only in their personal (rather than professional) capacity.

We would like to express our thanks to the Librarian of the House of Commons and to the Clerk of the House for their support and encouragement in making a book like this possible.

Tony Wright
House of Commons, October 1999

1 The shape of British politics

This country's distinctive contribution to civilisation has been the development of stable institutions of representative government.
(*Daily Telegraph* editorial, 19 December 1997)

The British Constitution has always been puzzling and always will be.
(The Queen, early 1990s, quoted in Peter Hennessy, *The Hidden Wiring*, 1995, p. 33)

INTRODUCTION: WHY POLITICS MATTERS

'Somebody has to do it.' This is the best explanation, and justification, for politics and politicians. They may not always be nice, but they are necessary. All societies have to make policy choices, confront problems, resolve conflicts, handle disagreements, decide 'who gets what, when and how' (as one famous definition of politics put it) – and this is what politics and politicians are all about. If we all agreed about everything and had the same interests we could perhaps replace messy politics with simple administration. At the time of the Russian Revolution, Lenin argued that the communist future would be like this! In the real world, politics is part of the furniture.

This is why, from Aristotle onwards, it has often been seen as a human activity of supreme importance. In a famous essay, Bernard Crick celebrates politics as 'a great and civilising human activity . . . something to be valued almost as a pearl beyond price in the history of the human condition.'[1] This may seem far removed from the way in which politics and politicians are frequently regarded in practice – where the focus is sometimes more on swine than pearls – but it is all the more reason to remember the ideal. At its best, politics is the means whereby human beings living in societies co-operate to negotiate their conflicts, tackle their problems and pursue their goals. At its worst, it is the scene of disorder, strife, corruption and tyranny. The modern world has witnessed the full range of political experiences.

THE CONTEXT OF BRITISH POLITICS

This book is about Britain, but the shape of British politics necessarily carries the imprint of the political experience of this wider world. As we shall see, there is much that is distinctive about the British political tradition (for example, a culture of liberty that predated democracy and was rooted in the common law, and the assertion of the rights of Parliament as the result of the constitutional struggles of the seventeenth century), but there is also much that can only be understood in the wider context of the politics of the modern world. Britain both contributed to this experience and drew from it. This remains the case today. Different political systems have to confront many of the same problems and feel the impact of many of the same forces, but they are also the product of particular histories, traditions and cultures. That is why they are different. They are organised differently (compare the federal constitutions of Germany, the United States or Australia with the unitary state in Britain), operate differently (for example, coalition politics is normal in much of Europe but abnormal in Britain) and behave differently (it has been said that a disgruntled Frenchman blocks the roads, a disgruntled American goes to court, and a disgruntled Englishman lobbies his MP). Such differences define the shape, flavour and character of political systems.

The historian Eric Hobsbawm has described the shaping forces of the past two centuries in Europe in terms of a 'dual revolution' (*The Age of Revolution, 1789–1848*). One revolution was the set of ideas associated in particular with the French Revolution of 1789, which provided the modern world with its distinctive political language of rights, liberty, democracy, equality, nationhood and constitutionalism. The other revolution was the industrial one, in which Britain was the pioneer, that transformed the way in which people lived and worked. In combination, these two revolutions shaped much of the politics of western Europe (and beyond) in the nineteenth and twentieth centuries. They spawned the political ideologies, social movements, national upheavals, reforms and revolutions that are the history of this period. Yet this shared context produced very different national histories; and it included the distinctive experience of Britain. Having got their own revolutionary moment safely out of the way in the seventeenth century, the British managed to reform their way to democracy in the nineteenth and twentieth centuries.

We should not make this story sound too smooth, as there was no shortage of crises and conflicts, but it is nevertheless a story of accommodation and adaptation. An old society, with its established political institutions, had to meet the challenge of new social forces and new political demands. The fact that this happened through a process of integration and incorporation, rather than through revolutionary upheaval, means that the British political system was never pulled up by its roots and reconstructed. This is regarded by some as a great blessing; by others as a considerable curse. Whatever view is taken, it is a shaping fact of modern British politics. It explains why the institutional landscape of British politics – the monarchy, the Commons, the Lords, the civil service, the Cabinet, the Prime Minister, the procedures and the pageantry – looks so unchanging. Of course it has changed in practice, and any realistic picture of the

British political process now has to include other institutions too (notably those of the European Union), but there is also a remarkable continuity. The 'village' of Whitehall and Westminster, the small patch of central London where the key political institutions are to be found, continues to provide the hub of the political process (Figure 1.1). Even the pattern of the political year has its particular and

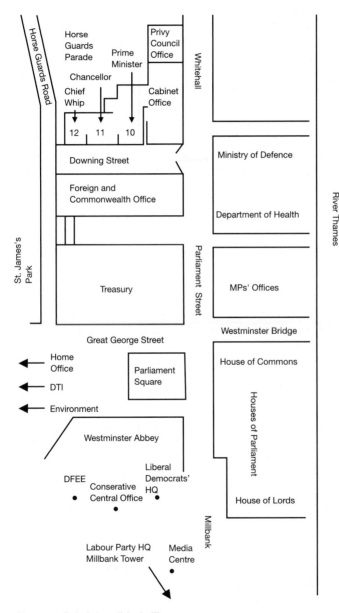

Figure 1.1 Britain's political village

distinctive shape. Individual years bring their own events and crises (when asked what were the most difficult issues facing him as Prime Minister, Harold Macmillan replied 'events, dear boy, events'), the cycle of general elections provides the larger framework – at intervals of no more than five years, but there is always the underlying annual rhythm of political life (see box below).

The British political year

Late September/early October	To the seaside, for the annual party conferences (Liberal Democrat, Labour and Conservative, in that order)
Mid-October	Parliament reconvenes to complete 'overspill' business of the session
Late October/early November	State opening of Parliament. Queen's Speech outlines the Government's legislative programme for the new session
November	Pre-Budget report by Chancellor of the Exchequer, with assessment of the economy and spending plans
December	Private members' bills announced after ballot
January	Honours list announced and public records released under 30-year rule
February	Budget preparation and lobbying
March	Chancellor delivers Budget, with its tax and spending announcements
May	Elections to local council (and, every four years, to the devolved assemblies in Scotland, Wales and Northern Ireland; and, every fifth year in June, to European Parliament)
June–July	Scramble to get legislation through all its stages before the end of the parliamentary session
Late July	Parliament goes on holiday for its long summer recess (and the 'silly season' starts in the press to fill the gap)

We can only understand what is distinctive about the British political tradition if we begin by setting it within the wider context referred to above. Britain shared in the 'dual revolution' that shaped the modern world, but did so in a particular way that reflected its own history and character. It reformed its way to democratic politics. Its industrial leadership produced a strong labour movement, but the influence of Marxism on it was much weaker than elsewhere in Europe (owing 'more to Methodism than to Marx', it was often said). Social class divisions were profound, shaping much in British society and politics, but without bringing revolutionary consequences. It was a multinational state, but – with the massive exception of Ireland – avoided the bog of nationalist conflicts. It had religious differences, but outside Ireland these were not of a scale or nature to provide the basis for a sectarian politics of religion. While sharing some of the conditions that fostered it, Britain did not succumb to the snare of fascism. These are just some leading examples of the way in which modern history has been felt in Britain in a particular and distinctive way. The same continues to be true. Globalisation and technology are transforming the world, but – just as with the dual revolution earlier – the political impact is not uniform everywhere and meets the force of local traditions. Perhaps the clearest example of this in Britain is the process of European integration, the running sore of recent British politics, which can only be understood as a political issue in terms of the legacy of a particular history.

APPEARANCE AND REALITY

Before summarising some of the features that define the modern shape of British politics, two warnings are needed. The first is about confusing appearance with reality. Things are not always what they seem. This warning is particularly neces-sary in relation to a political system which gives the appearance of such continu-ity. 'An ancient and ever-altering Constitution', wrote Walter Bagehot in the middle of the nineteenth century, 'is like an old man who still wears with attached fondness clothes in the fashion of his youth: what you see of him is the same; what you do not see is wholly altered.'[2] Institutions may look the same as ever, they may go through the same motions, they may even claim to be the same; but they may in fact have become quite different. Functions and powers may have gone else-where. Bagehot advised his readers to distinguish between the 'dignified' and the 'efficient' parts of the political system – the difference between appearance and reality – advice that should still be followed.

In looking at the political process in its various aspects in the chapters that follow, this question of appearance and reality – and how formal descriptions may be different from actual functions – is one to be kept constantly in mind. The British system of government is formally described as the 'Crown-in-Parliament', but this is not very useful as a description of how it actually works. It reflects the terms of a 300-year-old constitutional settlement between monarchy and Parlia-ment (also reflected in the words of the rarely sung but much more interesting second verse of the national anthem – *May she defend our laws / And ever give us cause / To sing with heart and voice / God save the Queen* – with its sly reminder of the conditions upon which the monarchy exists); but it tells us next to nothing about the real nature of the modern political process. Indeed, and worse still, it can work to obscure this. The monarchy has lost its political power (except in the sense, as Bagehot also observed, that symbolic and decorative institutions perform political functions too), but it is not Parliament but the executive that has now acquired this power. This was not yet true in the nineteenth century, but it has become abundantly clear with the development of disciplined party government in the twentieth. The famous doctrine of 'parliamentary sovereignty', that is supposed to be the core concept of the British political system, now obscures more than it reveals. It is not Crown-in-Parliament but Executive-in-Party that now provides the best description and efficient secret of modern British government.

CHANGE AND CONTINUITY

Then there is the second warning, in addition to the problem of appearance and reality: the issue of change and continuity, the need always to distinguish between the enduring features of the political process and those that are changing. This can often be very difficult. The environment in which the political system operates is in constant flux, at some periods dramatically so, and it is inevitable that this will reshape the political process. It is only necessary to consider some of the striking ways in which British society has changed in the period since the end of the Second World War (Table 1.1) to see that such changes will bring consequences for political life and institutions. The growth in the role of the state during the course of the twentieth century, especially in the Second World War and the post-war development of the welfare state, makes the point well (Figure 1.2). This is also a reminder of how underlying trends, external forces, inherited policies and established expectations circumscribe political life. Politicians may speak a language of new departures and bold initiatives, but this meets a reality of powerful continuities. Thus the Conservatives came to office in 1979 with a mission to cut taxes and reduce the size of the state; when they left office in 1997, taxes were 3 per cent higher as a share of GDP. Yet change there had clearly been, notably in the massive privatisation programme, and the post-war trend for the ratio of central government expenditure to GDP to increase was checked (falling from 44 per cent in 1979 to 41 per cent in 1996) and the size of the civil service reduced. The balance between change and continuity at any period is notoriously difficult to identify, as are the forces bearing down on each side, and often becomes clearer only much later.

What this means is that all generalisations about the political process in Britain should be treated with caution. The confident assertions of one generation can look like historic misjudgements to the next. Generalisations are sometimes becoming untrue just at the moment when they are being made; or they may only be true if huge exceptions and qualifications are made. This does not mean we should avoid trying to make general statements about the underlying character-istics and continuities of the political process. Sorting out the general from the particular, the enduring from the transient, is a key task for political analysis; but the health warning should not be forgotten either.

Table 1.1 Change in post-war Britain

	Early 1950s	*Late 1990s*
Expectation of life	69	77
Per thousand population		
Population aged 75+	35	72
Ethnic minority population	2	58
Cars owned	46	378
Television licences	29	368
Violent crime	0.1	4.9
Prison population	0.5	1.2
Trade union members	189	136
Church attendance [a]	58	32
Civil servants	14.9	7.8
Deaths from TB	0.25	0.01
Per thousand married population		
Divorces	2.8	13.0
Per thousand live births		
Births outside marriage	48	376
Infant mortality	28.1	5.9
Maternal deaths [b]	0.71	0.05
Per thousand dwellings/households		
Owner-occupied	310	680
Lacking WC [c]	80	2
Per thousand employed		
Women	320	448
In manufacturing	416	174
Per thousand age group		
Entering full-time higher education	52	340
Exports to EU15 as % of total	26	57
£ per head at 1995 prices		
Household disposable income	2,870	8,915
% of wealth owned by top 1%	44	19
% household spending on essentials [d]	45	30

Notes

The figures are for the United Kingdom, Great Britain, or England and Wales. Those for the early 1950s are averages of 1951 to 1953 where possible, otherwise selected years in the period. Those for the late 1990s are the latest available. They have been compiled from a wide range of sources. Some of the figures are approximate.

[a] Church of England Easter Day communicants per 1,000 population aged 15+.
[b] Per thousand live and still births.
[c] Lacking inside WC in 1996.
[d] Food, clothing, housing.

The point is best made with some examples. Britain is described as a unitary state, but the development of forms of devolved government in Scotland and Wales (and the beginnings of what may become serious regionalism in England), not to mention the fact that Northern Ireland had its own form of self-government for fifty years from 1922 to 1972, suggests a more complex picture. It

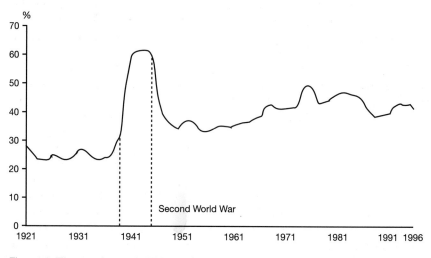

Figure 1.2 The growing state: UK government expenditure (% of GDP)
Source: Office for National Statistics.

is described as having an unwritten constitution, but much of this is nevertheless codified in some form and the trend in this direction is accelerating fast as a range of constitutional issues (such as access to information, the conduct of ministers and MPs, party funding) come under the political spotlight, while the extensive programme of political reform undertaken by the Labour Government elected in 1997 will have a major impact on the whole constitutional landscape. The doctrine of parliamentary sovereignty is described as the fundamental principle of the constitution, but – even leaving aside questions about what this means in practice – the impact of European Union law and the incorporation of the European Convention on Human Rights clearly require the doctrine to be revisited.

THE PERILS OF GENERALISATION

Nor are these the only examples of the perils of generalisation about various aspects of the political system. It used to be suggested at one time that a pendulum effect was at work that delivered periods of government alternating between the two major parties; but it was a very peculiar pendulum that could become so stuck that one party could enjoy prolonged periods in power (as the Conservatives did between 1951 and 1964, and between 1979 and 1997) while Labour had never managed to secure two full consecutive terms of office. Yet this experience in turn produced its own flawed generalisation. After the Conservatives had won their fourth consecutive election victory in 1992, there were many commentators (including some disguised as political scientists) who confidently announced that Britain had now become a single or 'predominant' party state.[3] No sooner had this been proclaimed than the fortunes of the major parties were dramatically transformed, culminating in the Labour landslide of 1997. This in turn produced new generalisations about what was happening to British politics, of a contrary kind, and likely to prove equally flawed.

The trouble comes when passing trends are confused with eternal truths. A longer and wider perspective is often needed to supply the context. Britain may be described as a classical two-party system, but this soon becomes a misdescription if it neglects the important role that has been played at different periods by a range of minor parties. It is said that Britain is characterised by strong governments formed from a single party, but not only have governments often been weakened by small majorities (Labour after 1974, the Conservatives before 1997) but over the course of the twentieth century as a whole formal or informal coalitions have been a regular feature of British politics (in the First World War, in the 'national' government of the early 1930s, in the Second World War, in the Lib-Lab pact of 1977/8, in the arrangement made by Tony Blair with the Liberal Democrats after the 1997 election and in the post-devolution Labour–Liberal Democrat coalition in Scotland). It used to be asserted as an axiom of British politics that after 1945 (though its roots were put down during the preceding war years) a 'post-war settlement' had been established that provided the basis for a broad political consensus. At its centre was said to be an agreement about the full-employment welfare state ('Keynes plus Beveridge' in shorthand) as the policy goal of governments. Yet not only was such consensus rather less complete in practice than often presented,[4] but it was blown apart in the 1970s and explicitly repudiated by the Thatcher government that was elected in 1979. The consensus model of British politics suddenly looked antiquated.

In fact, the post-1945 period that had for so long been presented as the general model of British politics began to look more like an exceptional period when set against the experience of the century as a whole. The politics of the years from the early 1960s to the mid-1970s, which shaped so many accounts of the fundamental characteristics of the British political process, now had to be set within the larger context of the years that came before and the period that came after. Taken on its own, it could be seriously misleading – even perhaps to be seen as the particular product of the boom economy of the post-war generation. Both earlier and later, other features of British politics needed to be added: for example, sharper ideological divisions, significant social and industrial conflicts, political turbulence and constitutional questioning. In the early 1960s a cross-national study famously pronounced that Britain was the model of a stable 'civic culture'; but just twenty years later another study proclaimed that the situation was so transformed that it was a case of 'Britain against itself.'[5] Nearly two decades on, a further and different analysis is clearly required. This is yet another warning about the difficulties involved in distinguishing the general from the particular and the durable from the changing, in describing the main shaping characteristics of British politics. That said, what are these shaping features?

POLITICAL CULTURE

The political culture is perhaps the most important of all, although it is also the area where the warning about the difficulties involved is most needed. Because the term is used to describe the cultural basis of politics – the whole mix of attitudes and behaviours that people bring to the political process – the danger is that it may be used to explain too much. An attempt to explain everything can too easily end up explaining little or nothing. The concept invites broad generalisations, even though detailed analysis of the elements of the political culture in Britain reveals it to be 'a baffling and contradictory phenomenon'.[6] What evidence can we turn to? It is not enough to present certain structural features about British society (for example, class patterns or regional differences) and then 'read off' from these into attitudes and behaviours. This can be seriously misleading, for the relationship between structural features and attitudes – between what we might call the 'objective' and the 'subjective' sides of politics – can be very complex. It is where this relationship can seem most puzzling (why has the Conservative Party historically drawn a substantial section of its support from the working class? Why have regional inequalities not produced a regional politics? Why has the monarchy survived in an age of democracy? Why has a European country not easily embraced a European identity?) that the most interesting and revealing insights into the political culture can often be found.

The evidence we turn to includes how people actually behave (as opposed to how they 'ought' to) and what we can learn from observation and inquiry about what they feel and believe about the political process. The study of political behaviour is more straightforward and lends itself to quantitative analysis, above all in relation to voting behaviour. We can see how many people vote and which parties they support. We can also observe whether people join political parties, participate in pressure groups, engage in direct action, display political violence, attach themselves to political extremism – and all similar measures of political behaviour. From this we might conclude that in Britain there is general support for mainstream politics, a vast network of voluntary groups for every cause and interest under the sun and involving millions of people in civic participation of some kind (for example, the membership of the Royal Society for the Protection of Birds alone exceeds the combined membership of all political parties) and a disinclination to engage in political extremism.

Yet of course there have to be instant qualifications to a general statement of this kind. Against any generalisation about the rejection of political violence is the stark fact that in one part of the United Kingdom the politics of the gun and the bomb has long been a way of life (from the beginning of the troubles in the late 1960s to the end of March 1998, 3,248 people were killed and 40,899 injured in Northern Ireland), with terrorism regularly exported to the mainland and forcing the country to live for long periods with the security requirements of a threatened state. The attachment to mainstream politics has to accommodate the fact that protest movements and direct action have also been part of British politics (sometimes dramatically so, as with the suffragettes and the General Strike in the early part of the twentieth century, but also including the protests against nuclear weapons and the Vietnam war in the 1960s and 1970s, and the anti-poll tax agitation of the early 1990s); while the development of direct action campaigning on environmental and animal welfare issues has been a notable feature of recent British politics. As for political extremism, this is notoriously difficult to define. Yesterday's extremism can be tomorrow's orthodoxy. For example, the rise of the Labour Party was accompanied by a sustained propaganda attack on the new party by its political opponents designed to portray it as un-British and extremist.[7]

None of this means that the previous broad characterisation of British political culture, based upon actual political behaviour, is not accurate. It just means that it has to be rich enough to take account of the full range of evidence. This is why some of the best descriptions of the real texture of the political culture – the complex mixture of feelings, attitudes and beliefs that people bring to the political process – come not from the raw evidence of actual political behaviour but from the insights gleaned from other sources. It might be a politician taking stock or a writer sniffing the air. 'A people so fundamentally at one that they can safely afford to bicker' was Balfour's famously comforting summary of the political culture. George Orwell gave this a radical twist: the country was 'a family, with the wrong members in control'. (Orwell was an acute observer of the particular mixture that made up the political culture, as in his remark that if there was ever a radical revolution in Britain it would 'abolish the House of Lords, but quite probably will not abolish the Monarchy' and exhibit 'a power of assimilating the past which will shock foreign observers'.[8]) Some observers have noticed how a culture of shared understandings among the political class in Britain has been more important than formal written rules (hence Sidney Low's oft-quoted remark: 'We live under a system of tacit understandings. But the understandings are not always understood'[9]). These are all rich insights, illuminating and inter-preting some of the most fundamental aspects of British politics, impressionistic not 'scientific', but perhaps all the better for it. They are not timeless truths – Bagehot's observations on the role of deference in the middle of the nineteenth century or Orwell's perceptions in the 1940s could scarcely be that, nor are they complete truths; but they are examples of what it means to try to capture the inner secrets of the political culture. The extraordinary public reaction to the death of Princess Diana in 1997, prompting a deluge of commentary on what it signified for contemporary attitudes in Britain, is a recent example of an event provoking a search for wider cultural meanings.

Another way to find out what people think and believe is to ask them. The development of survey techniques is a growth industry. What may be revealed is a gap between beliefs and behaviours, what people say and what they do. Perhaps the best example of this is the fact that during the 1980s most people told pollsters that they would prefer better public services to tax cuts, but regularly voted for the opposite. If handled with care though, survey data can be very useful in throwing light on political attitudes and how they may change over time. The annual *British Social Attitudes* survey, which started in 1983, is an authoritative source for evidence on contemporary public opinion, attitudes and values. The 1997 report was particularly interesting for its evidence that the under-30s 'Thatcher's children' generation was the group *least* likely to identify with the ideological messages of that era (with nearly 90 per cent of them believing that the gap between those with high and low incomes in Britain was too high). Any idea that the Conservative 'revolution' might have produced a permanent shift in political values was clearly not true. Nor is there any real support for the view that a generational gulf may have opened up in British politics. Where generational differences exist (for example, on interest in politics) it seems likely that younger people will correct their 'deviance' as they get older. However on some issues – attitudes to the monarchy, the claims of conscience in relation to the law, membership of the European Union – generational differences are significant and 'there is an apparent "fault-line" between those who grew up before the 1960s and those who came of age afterwards'.[10] On these issues the young will probably not fall into line as they get older, for these are the kinds of attitudes that stick, and British political culture will change to the extent that these values become those of society as a whole.

What about changing attitudes to the political process itself? Here the survey evidence suggests a decline since the 1970s in public confidence and trust in the political system. Between the early 1970s and the mid-1990s there was a sharp and progressive decline in the number of people thinking the system did not need much improvement; and an equally sharp increase in the number believing that it needed to be improved significantly. Over the same period there was also a strong downward trend in people's trust that governments would pursue national rather than party interests; and a strong upward trend in the belief that they would not (see box, p. 13). By the mid-1990s fewer than one in four people trusted British governments to put the interests of the nation above those of party – a fall of 16 percentage points over a decade (whereas the proportion had been more or less constant over the thirteen years before 1987). It is not that trust in politicians has ever been high; it is just that it clearly underwent a steep decline in this period.

If we search for explanations for this, it is likely that the prevailing allegations of assorted political misconduct played a significant part. The conduct of MPs came under scrutiny by the Nolan Committee on Standards in Public Life, set up in 1994; while the conduct of ministers was examined by the Scott Inquiry into arms sales to Iraq. In these circumstances it is not surprising if trust in the political system and in politicians was eroded. In its first report in 1995, the Nolan Committee declared that 'the erosion of public confidence in the holders of public office is a serious matter' and gave two reasons why it mattered:

> First, we in Britain have, with reason, always prided ourselves on the standards of conduct of the vast majority of our public servants; that pride must be restored. Second, experience elsewhere warns that, unless the strictest standards are maintained and where necessary restored, corruption and malpractice can become part of the way of life. The threat at the moment is not great. Action needs to be taken before it becomes so.[11]

Views of the system: Governments and politicians

The system of governing Britain (%)

	1973	1977	1991	1994	1995	1996
'Could not be improved' or 'Could be improved in small ways'	48	34	33	29	22	35
'Could be improved quite a lot' or 'a great deal'	49	62	63	69	76	63

How much do you trust British governments of *any* party to place the needs of the nation above the interests of their own political party? (%)

	1974	1986	1987	1991	1994	1996
'Just about always' or 'most of the time'	39	38	37	33	24	22
'Only some of the time' or 'Almost never'	57	57	60	63	73	75

Source: R. Jowell *et al.*, *British Social Attitudes: The 14th Report* (Social and Community Planning Research (SCPR)/Ashgate, 1997), p. 91.

How would you rate the honesty and ethical standards of the people in these different fields?

(Very high, high, average, low, or very low? The figures shown are the aggregate of 'high' and 'very high' responses, shown as a percentage.)

	1985	1995
Doctors	75	72
Police officers	55	52
Lawyers	46	34
Civil servants	20	20
Trade union leaders	9	14
Business executives	20	14
MPs	17	9
Government ministers	22	8
Journalists	10	6

Source: Gallup.

The fact that action was taken may help explain why (as the box shows) by 1996, a year before the general election, confidence in the political system had already revived significantly. The general election of 1997 seemed to carry this process further: for example, while 25 per cent of people strongly agreed that parties were 'only interested in people's votes not in their opinions' in 1996, this fell to 20 per cent during the 1997 general election campaign and then to 14 per cent after voting day. This does not mean that there has been a permanent revival of trust in politics and politicians; but it does provide a reminder that trends can be reversed.

Nor should the discussion of trends be allowed to obscure the main underlying truths about the British political culture. There may be healthy scepticism about politicians, but this does not translate into mass alienation from the political system. Indeed the evidence reveals that those who are most negative about the system are no less likely than others to take part in it (the 1997 general election saw the lowest turn-out, at 71.5 per cent, of any post-war election, but whatever the reason there is no evidence that it was because of a decline of confidence in the political system). The belief in reform – and the evidence from many surveys over recent years shows wide support for a range of constitutional reforms – indicates engagement rather than disengagement. Above all, there is not a belief in Britain (as there is in some other countries) that the political system is fundamentally corrupt and the political class equally corrupt. While there is always much enjoyment to be derived from the surveys showing that politicians are ranked even lower than estate agents in public esteem of assorted professions (though, significantly, when people are asked about their own members of parliament the response is always much more positive), the larger truth is that the political system draws on a deep reservoir of cultural support. People laugh at politics and politicians with comedians such as Rory Bremner, but it is still laughter within the family.

So nothing is more important than the political culture, even though nothing is more amorphous. Its influence touches everything. The language used by politicians is honed to hit popular cultural buttons (the 'spirit of Dunkirk' was a particular favourite with the post-1945 generation) and potent cultural symbols (such as the Union Jack) are regularly expropriated for political purposes. Even seemingly trivial matters – for example, the Labour Party's instructions to its women candidates in the 1997 general election not to wear dangly earrings, or the party's earlier replacement as its emblem of the red flag by a red rose – can be seen as reflections of larger cultural judgements. More significantly, the political culture expresses itself in the broad continuities and stabilities of British political life. There is still sufficient cultural glue in British society, even if it is weaker than it once was, to have a broadly consensual effect on political life. This does not mean the absence of party or ideological conflict, which has been robust and sharp, but it does mean that such conflict has been conducted within a framework of agreement about the 'rules of the game'.

The fact that there has been more 'game' than 'rules' in British politics is a further illustration of the political culture at work. It has been possible to conduct so much of politics on a basis of conventions rather than rules, essentially a make-it-up-as-you-go-along kind of politics, because of the underlying procedural affinities and agreements among the participants. The most important part of Parliament, rarely mentioned in the textbooks, is what is mysteriously described as the 'usual channels': this is the network of informal arrangements between party managers that effectively governs how Parliament works. Much of the British political process – in both Westminster and Whitehall – has its 'usual channels' of one kind or another, rooted in a private network of cultural understandings. It provides the basis for what Peter Hennessy has called the 'good chaps' view of British government in a 'back-of-the-envelope nation'.[12]

This is also a reminder of how, for a long period, many of those involved in governing Britain have shared a common culture rooted in the same class, the right schools, and the ancient universities (for example, between the mid-1950s and the mid-1980s, 87.1 per cent of Conservative cabinet ministers had been to public schools, 36.3 per cent to Eton or Harrow, and 72.8 per cent to Oxbridge[13]). The good chaps were literally chaps too. Women had been able to vote only since 1918, and at an equal age with men only since 1928, but parliamentary politics still remained almost exclusively a male preserve. From 1945 to the mid-1980s the number of women in the House of Commons never climbed above 5 per cent. The dramatic change came in the 1997 election, but only because the Labour Party had changed its candidate selection rules in favour of women: 120 women were elected (of whom 101 were Labour) and this produced a sudden leap in the proportion of women MPs to the giddy heights of 18.2 per cent of the total. This may be seen as an example of a changing political culture, with consequences for the character of British politics.

Although political culture is fundamental, because it captures the attitudinal basis of politics, it does not exist in a vacuum. The attitudes and behaviours that people bring to the political process are themselves shaped by history and experience. This is the context of politics – historical, social, economic, territorial, international – within which attitudes form and behaviour develops. In the case of Britain, there are aspects of this context that have been particularly significant for its political life and continue to be so. The most important aspects may be summarised briefly in the following three propositions about society, history and territory:

Three propositions: society, history and territory

British society exhibits a high degree of integration and homogeneity, despite major social divisions

The stability of British politics clearly owes much to the absence of the sort of social cleavages – especially of religious or ethnic kinds – that often fragment and destabilise political life. Outside Northern Ireland, there have not been parties organised on religious or ethnic lines; and although there have been minority nationalist parties in Scotland and Wales they have generally played by the rules. Yet Britain has had significant social divisions. Class differences have been profound, in some respects more profound than elsewhere (it has often been remarked that in Britain it is only necessary for someone to open their mouth for their whole class position to be established, which is why so much of British television comedy has been rooted in class themes); and social class remains the best single predictor of attitude and behaviour, including political behaviour. In this sense it is true that modern British politics has been class politics. The twentieth-century party battle has been shaped by it. Yet this had an integrating effect too, as a common politics of class triumphed over other divisions. The class structure has become much more complex as occupational patterns change (in 1948 there were 800,000 miners and fewer than 100 people engaged with computers, while today there are only 17,000 people employed in mining and 370,000 people in the computer industry). Class inequality has not only persisted but widened sharply from the 1980s, while the growth of middle-class occupations and the decline of traditional working-class occupations (Table 1.2) has persuaded politicians of the need to appeal as widely as possible if they are to win majority support – with 'Middle England' as their particular target.

Nor is social class the only way in which British society is differentiated. There have been important religious differences, with a political impact on issues such as schooling in the not so distant past (and again now, as with the Muslim demand for their own schools). Regions have had their own traditions, histories and dialects. Large-scale immigration from the Commonwealth, especially in the 1950s and 1960s, introduced a significant ethnic minority population into British society (0.2 per cent in 1951, still less than 2 per cent in the late 1960s, and 5.8 per cent in the mid-1990s) and for a period was the focus of considerable racial tension and for the politics of race. Allied to the generational and lifestyle differences that have developed, bringing issues such as drugs and changing family patterns onto the political agenda, this has seen Britain become a much more pluralistic, diverse and multicultural place.

Yet the general proposition remains true. Despite Britain becoming a much more heterogeneous society during the second half of the twentieth century, this has not generated the kind of fissures that might have prised apart the political system. There were moments when this seemed possible, notably in the 1970s when government and trade unions locked horns in bloody battles, but the system held. The forces of integration have proved stronger than their opposite – and continue to do so. The underlying uniformities of British society have had a profound impact on political life. Divisions have co-existed with shared loyalties (for example, attachment to class alongside attachment to country) and the increasingly similar patterns of life in different parts of Britain have been reflected in the 'national' character of its politics. The fact that Britain has had an over-

Table 1.2 Social class in Britain (% of working population)

		1911	1921	1931	1951	1971	1981	1991
I	Professional	1	1	1	2	3	4	5
II	Managerial and technical	13	14	14	15	20	25	32
III	Skilled (manual and							
	non-manual)	37	37	35	38	39	37	34
IV	Partly skilled	39	34	35	33	25	24	22
V	Unskilled	10	14	15	12	12	11	6

Sources: G. Routh, *Occupation and Pay in Great Britain 1906–1979* (Macmillan, 1980); G. Routh, *Occupations of the People of Great Britain 1801–1981* (Macmillan, 1982); Office of Population Censuses and Surveys, *Census 1991*.

whelmingly national media system, in which the same newspapers are read and the same programmes listened to throughout the country, both reflects an integrated society and contributes to a common politics.

British history has distinctive features which have helped to shape the distinctive character of its politics

A number of key features stand out. The fact that Britain has been unconquered since 1066 is a basic ingredient of continuity. Its institutions have evolved rather than been remodelled from without by others. The lack of conquest was a particular achievement in the twentieth century, with its two world wars, when occupation and reconstruction was the common European experience. The country's island status has decisively shaped its history. The further fact that Britain had its revolution in the seventeenth century, rather than in the eighteenth or nineteenth, also set it apart: it was not remodelled from within by the social, economic and national upheavals of the modern period.

Or at least it was not remodelled in a sudden or systematic way. Change came incrementally. The tradition of common law was the legal expression of this. The balance between Crown, Lords and Commons that had been struck as a result of the constitutional struggles of the seventeenth century provided the framework within which subsequent rebalancing took place. It had a supporting ideology (that came to be known as the 'Whig view of history') of constitutionalism and liberty. It proved adaptable enough to accommodate both the shifting balance of classes as industrialism and urbanisation developed and the demand for reform as democracy developed. This compresses a complex history, but if we want to know why Britain has no written constitution, or bill of rights, or separation of powers (or much else of the same kind), then it is the continuity and adaptability of this history that provides the indispensable clue.

The impact of history is felt in other ways too. The fact that for much of the nineteenth and early twentieth century Britain was the world's leading industrial power, with a huge overseas empire, has had a massive effect on every aspect of life. Britain was manufacturer to the world (producing in the middle of the nineteenth century as much as two-thirds of the world's coal and half its iron), banker and financier to the world, and policeman of the world's seas. Empire provided raw materials, markets, military glory, escape routes – and a powerful ideology. It is scarcely surprising that the rapid collapse of this imperial and economic role during the twentieth century proved almost as significant as its previous existence.

The question that dogged and dominated British politics for much of the second half of the twentieth century was how to respond to the sudden loss of this economic and political power. The rapidity of the transition from the 'finest hour' of 1940 to the diminished realities of the post-war world was a psychic shock of traumatic proportions. It affected every aspect of British policy. Britain alone had drawn the lesson from the Second World War that the nation state was alive and well; the rest of Europe had drawn a different lesson and began the construction of a European union from which Britain stood aside. A famous remark in the early 1960s by the American statesman Dean Acheson about Britain having 'lost an empire but not yet found a role' seemed to capture the problem. The issue of 'decline', especially relative economic decline, became the haunting theme of political argument, with a supporting apparatus of comparative league tables of economic performance (still going strong – see Figure 1.3). On all sides the underlying issue seemed to be that of adjustment to dramatically changed historical circumstances. The fact that the language of politics at the end of the 1990s was still dominated by the imagery of newness and 'modernisation' suggested that the reckoning with history was still being made.

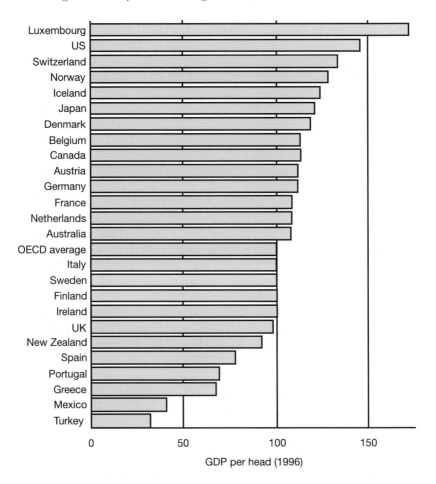

Figure 1.3 Britain in the world

Source: Department of Trade and Industry, *Competitiveness: Our Partnership with Business*, November 1997.

British territory encompasses a multinational kingdom, though one of a particular kind

Ask someone in London, Birmingham or Manchester which country they live in and the answer could be as various as England, Britain, Great Britain, the British Isles or the United Kingdom. Identity, geography and statehood are hopelessly confused (see box below). The same question asked in Edinburgh, Cardiff or Belfast would produce further additions to the list (and some deletions). Britain (the United Kingdom of Great Britain and Northern Ireland) is a unitary state but a multinational kingdom, with a more complex politics of territory than has often been recognised.

Britain: Defining terms

In law, the expression 'United Kingdom' refers to the United Kingdom of Great Britain and Northern Ireland; it does not include the Channel Islands or the Isle of Man. For purposes of international relations, however, the Channel Islands and the Isle of Man are represented by the UK government. So too are the colonies and other dependent territories of the United Kingdom overseas.

The expression 'British Islands' is defined in the Interpretation Act 1978 as meaning the United Kingdom, the Channel Islands and the Isle of Man. The British Islands do not in law include the Republic of Ireland, which is outside the United Kingdom.

The expression 'Great Britain' refers to England, Scotland and Wales: these first became a single kingdom by virtue of article 1 of the Treaty of Union between England and Scotland in 1707.

The Wales and Berwick Act 1746 provided that where the expression 'England' was used in an Act of Parliament, this should be taken to include the dominion of Wales and the town of Berwick on Tweed. But the Welsh Language Act 1967, section 4, provided that references to England in future Acts should not include the dominion of Wales. Concerning the boundary between Wales and England, a long-standing controversy was brought to an end by the Local Government Act 1972, which declared that Monmouthshire was to be within Wales.

The adjective 'British' is used in common speech to refer to matters associated with Great Britain or the United Kingdom. It has no definite legal connotation and one authority has described the expression 'British law' as hopelessly ambiguous. In legislation 'British' is sometimes used as an adjective referring to the United Kingdom, particularly in the context of nationality.

(A. W. Bradley and K. D. Ewing, *Constitutional and Administrative Law*,
12th edn, Longman, 1997, pp. 38–9)

The unitary state is rooted in the sovereignty of the Westminster Parliament. In turn this has been rooted in a set of powerful 'national' bonds involving monarchy, empire, war and class. Yet Britain was nevertheless a construct. It had been made through a process whereby England had brought the troublesome constituent nations of Britain under its wing – and consolidated the union state (see box below). This process was not uniform or smooth: Wales was incorporated, Scotland required a treaty of union, Ireland developed a powerful home rule movement which ended in secession and left only the north under the British crown. It has been argued that the idea of 'Britishness' was an eighteenth-century invention to mobilise popular Protestant opinion against the Catholic French.[14]

The union has required territorial management. Wales was most fully integrated, but nevertheless retained a separate language and distinctive religious traditions. Scotland had kept its own legal, religious and education systems, reflecting the terms of its entry into the union. Northern Ireland was most different of all, a society organised around religious tribalism. While special administrative arrangements for the government of Scotland and Wales were developed over the years (beginning with the Scottish Office in 1885 and Welsh Office in 1964), Northern Ireland enjoyed what was effectively a quasi-federal status during the half-century period of Stormont self-government between 1922 and 1972. The 'British' character of much of twentieth-century politics in the United Kingdom has obscured the issues of territorial management. Yet home rule sentiment was

---

Uniting the Kingdom

1536–42   Acts of Union integrate England and Wales administratively and legally and give Wales representation in Parliament

1603   Union of the two crowns under James VI of Scotland

1707   Act of Union unites England and Scotland

1740   British national anthem composed

1801   Act of Union unites Great Britain and Ireland; Union Jack first used in its modern form

1876   Reinvention of Queen Victoria as Empress of India

1921   Anglo-Irish Treaty establishes the Irish Free State; Northern Ireland remains part of United Kingdom

1926   British Broadcasting Company (later Corporation) (BBC) established

1948   National Health Service founded

1957   First Royal Christmas broadcast

strong in the period before the First World War (a profoundly 'British' experience, as was the Second World War) and revived again from the 1960s, while Northern Ireland embarked upon a generation of sectarian violence. An ideology of Britishness and a centralising politics of class had clearly not removed the strains of a multinational union.

It has inevitably been a lopsided union. The dominance of England (Table 1.3) has ensured that. On his best-selling travels, the American writer Bill Bryson noticed that on the grave of Asquith in an Oxfordshire churchyard the man who led Britain in its Edwardian heyday was oddly described as having been prime minister of *England*.[15] There has been lopsidedness within England too. At the beginning of the twentieth century, England had great regional cities and a flourishing provincial press, reflecting the distribution of economic and civic activity. At the end of the century, it is distinguished by political and cultural centralisation, with local government having become essentially a creature of the centre, and with the dominant position of the south-east. 'British contempt for provincialism is total', according to *Times* columnist Simon Jenkins, who added: 'Ask most readers of this article to name a principal street in Manchester, Birmingham, Newcastle, or Liverpool and they will look blank. Ask when they last visited Leeds, York, Bristol or Plymouth and most will say never, with a shudder. Crests would fall at failing such a test about Florence, Nice, Barcelona, or New York . . . To fashionable London, provincial England is a cultural swamp.'[16] All roads, it seemed, led to London and the south-east, the heart of the English establishment. England displayed marked regional inequalities (Table 1.4), but these were not matched by the regional structures and loyalties that were in evidence elsewhere in Europe.

Yet the politics of territory has emphatically returned. The nature of the union is being redefined. In referendums in 1997 Scotland voted overwhelmingly for its own parliament and Wales voted narrowly for an assembly. The votes reflected the

Table 1.3 The shape of the United Kingdom

	England	Wales	Scotland	Northern Ireland	United Kingdom
Area (thousand sq km)	130.4	20.8	78.1	13.6	242.8
Population mid-1997 (million)	49.3	2.9	5.1	1.7	59.0
Members of Westminster Parliament	529	40	72	18	659
GDP, 1997 (£billion)	578.6	27.6	56.2	15.5	677.9
GDP, 1997 (£ per head)	11,740	9,442	10,975	9,235	11,488
Government expenditure per head, 1997/98 (£)	3,897	4,586	4,772	5,450	4,051
Average weekly disposable household income, 1997/98 (£)	352	295	308	301	343
Average gross weekly pay, April 1998 (£)	390	344	350	333	383
ILO unemployment rate, Nov 1998–Jan 1999 (%)	5.9	7.4	7.5	6.7	6.1

Sources: Office for National Statistics, *Annual Abstract of Statistics*; *Population Estimates*; *Family Expenditure Survey*; *Labour Market Statistics*; *New Earnings Survey*; *Public Expenditure Statistical Analyses*.

Table 1.4 The shape of England

	North East	North West and Merseyside	Yorkshire and the Humber	East Midlands	West Midlands	Eastern	London	South East	South West
Area (thousand sq km)	8.6	14.2	15.4	15.6	13.0	19.1	1.6	19.1	23.8
Population mid-1997 (million)	2.6	6.9	5.0	4.2	5.3	5.3	7.1	8.0	4.9
Members of Westminster Parliament	30	76	56	44	59	56	74	83	51
GDP, 1997 (£billion)	24.6	72.2	51.6	45.7	56.8	62.6	102.6	107.8	54.7
GDP, 1997 (£ per head)	9,473	10,481	10,244	11,002	10,669	11,739	14,411	13,549	11,213
Average weekly disposable household income, 1997/98 (£)	285	328	299	342	335	353	394	409	347
Average gross weekly pay, April 1998 (£)	339	362	345	350	359	379	501	401	354
ILO unemployment rate, Nov 1998–Jan 1999 (%)	9.5	7.1	6.8	4.8	6.3	4.5	7.6	3.8	4.4

Sources: Office for National Statistics, Regional Trends; Economic Trends; Population Estimates; Family Expenditure Survey; Labour Market Statistics; New Earnings Survey.

different relationship of the two countries to the union (significantly, while Scotland had its own media system to debate the issue, Wales did not). These developments in turn reawakened English interest in the terms of the union, involving scrutiny of the historic over-representation of Scotland and Wales at Westminster and the funding arrangement between the different parts of the union. The first stirrings of a serious English regionalism were also heard. It was not clear where all this would eventually lead, but the complex politics of the 'periphery' was now demanding a fresh constitutional response. As ever, the most acute reminder of this continued to come from the periphery of the periphery, in Northern Ireland.

CHARACTERISTICS OF THE POLITICAL PROCESS

These three propositions – about society, history and territory – are just a way of describing some of the main factors that have shaped the political culture and political process in Britain. Each reveals a picture that is changing, though with important enduring features. Together they help to explain the particular character of the British political tradition. Subsequent chapters examine aspects of the system in more detail, but from this preliminary discussion it is already possible to identify the main characteristics of the British political process in the twentieth century in summary form (see box below).

Each item in this list requires fuller analysis; and it is evident that there is tension between a number of them. Nevertheless the broad picture is clear enough. Here is a political system which, despite periodic crises, and with the standing exception of Northern Ireland, has exhibited a remarkable stability and enjoys a deep legitimacy. Institutions have been adapted and reformed to meet the requirements

---

Characteristics of the political process in the United Kingdom

- Stability and legitimacy
- Institutional continuity/adaptability
- Uncodified constitution
- No separation of powers
- Parliamentary sovereignty
- Strong executive
- Party government
- Unitary but multinational state
- Conventions/rules of the game/flexibility
- Representative democracy
- Centralised and majoritarian
- Substantial consensus
- Informal checks and balances
- Authority versus accountability

of representative democracy. For much of the second half of the twentieth century (apart from a period in the 1970s and 1980s) there has been a wide measure of political consensus. Without a constitutional rulebook, much of the working of the political system has been governed by conventional adherence to the rules of the game. The checks and balances within the system have been informal and political rather than formal and constitutional. A unitary state has been the focus for a centralised politics, but it has also involved the territorial management of a four-nation kingdom. The absence of a separation of powers has enabled the executive to exercise routine control over the legislature, and without direct challenge in the courts, through a highly organised party system rooted in the discipline of majoritarianism. The doctrine of parliamentary sovereignty has provided the system with its underpinning ideology.

AUTHORITY VERSUS ACCOUNTABILITY?

The major tension in this picture is what is described in the list as 'authority versus accountability'. This identifies a fundamental aspect of the particular way in which the political system in Britain has developed into its modern form. It is sometimes described in terms of the difference between a 'Westminster' and a 'Whitehall', a 'liberal' or 'Tory', a 'bottom-up' or 'top-down' view of the system.[17] Whatever the terms used, they denote a system in which the inheritance of strong executive government emphasising the importance of order, authority and effectiveness meets a liberal democratic tradition with its emphasis on liberty, representation and accountability. To understand the nature and terms of the precarious balance between these different approaches is to understand much of the essential character of the British political process.

However, it has also enabled this essential character to be regarded in sharply different ways. One view of the balance was expressed by Winston Churchill in an elegy to the House of Commons at the end of the Second World War:

> If it be true, as has been said, that every country gets the form of government it deserves, we may certainly flatter ourselves. The wisdom of our ancestors has led us to an envied and enviable situation. We have the strongest Parliament in the world. We have the oldest, the most famous, the most secure, the most serviceable monarchy in the world. King and Parliament both rest safely and solidly upon the will of the people expressed by free and fair election on the basis of universal suffrage. Thus the system has long worked harmoniously, both in peace and war.[18]

The social thinker R. H. Tawney saw the balance of the system rather differently, when he wrote that Britain had accepted democracy

> as a convenience, like an improved system of telephones; she did not dedicate herself to it as the expression of a moral idea of comradeship and

equality, the avowal of which would leave nothing the same. She changed her political garments, but not her heart. She carried into the democratic era, not only the institutions, but the social habits and mentality of the oldest and toughest plutocracy in the world . . . she went to the ballot box touching her hat.[19]

Even allowing for the exaggerated rhetoric of wartime, there is no doubt that Churchill's version of the balance between authority and accountability in the British political process is the one that has been closer to the twentieth-century orthodoxy. Those searching for the clue to the stability of modern British politics could find it in a tradition of strong government, without rigid rules or formal constraints, tempered by a culture of agreed understandings and the basic accountability that came from democratic elections. It was also possible to see a happy congruence between the political culture and the political structure. If this helped to explain why it was difficult to export the system, it also explained its distinctive character. A peculiarly successful graft seemed to have been made between an old tradition of authority and a new tradition of democracy.

This was the claim that the constitutional authority, A. V. Dicey, had made for the system – describing it as 'the most flexible polity in existence'[20] – at the beginning of the twentieth century and it became the received interpretation. Just as Dicey had expressed sympathy for those poor foreigners who were unfortunate enough to have to construct other systems, the particular balance contained within the 'British model' came to be seen as the reason for its stability and success. There was wide agreement that Britain was to be seen as the model of stable, representative government: 'just as Alexis de Tocqueville travelled to America in 1831 to seek the secrets of democracy, so one might journey to England to seek the secrets of stable representative government.'[21] Especially in the generation after 1945, Britain was the familiar destination for those in search of the secrets of political stability and a well-functioning polity. Even if the nature of its political system was found to be rooted in a particular political culture, itself shaped by a distinctive society and history, enabling a special kind of balancing act between authority and accountability to be executed, this did not diminish the sense of Britain as an outstanding political success story.

THE BRITISH MODEL IN QUESTION

Yet this was soon to change. If it was still the orthodox view in the 1960s, in the 1970s and 1980s it rapidly ceased to be so. Both within Britain and outside, the political system came under sustained critical scrutiny. As the country grappled with the agonies of its relative economic decline and was rocked by bitter industrial conflicts, it was no longer possible to be so sanguine about the charmed properties of its political system. If 'What's wrong with Britain?' became the persistent question, then the nature of the political system now found itself nominated as one of the answers. Far from being the model of a well-functioning polity, it was argued that the British political process was distinguished by critical disabilities.

The argument came from a number of different directions and took various forms. Instead of a system prized for its strong authority and legitimacy, it was now found to be weak and fragile, easily overwhelmed by the demands of sectional interests and the bloated expectations of the electorate. It was crippled by 'overload' and was buckling at the knees. From another direction it was claimed that the nature of party competition in Britain was to be seen as a damaging game of 'adversary politics' in which it became impossible to get long-term agreement on key policy areas. Policy reversals produced political instability and policy failure. Less significant than the intrinsic merits of such arguments is the fact that they involved a radical revision of the traditional view of the British political process. Political decline found itself sitting alongside economic decline, even as a *cause* of economic decline, in the 'state of Britain' debate of the time.[22] The exemplar of political success had been transformed into the epitome of political failure.

In terms of the balance between authority and accountability, what was striking about the various arguments of this period was their agreement that it was the authority of the system that was in question. It was too weak to cope effectively with the relentless demands that were bearing down on it. Yet no sooner had the authority side of the balance been questioned than the system's accountability came under sustained attack too. The opening fire was from Lord Hailsham in his celebrated assault on what he described as Britain's system of 'elective dictatorship'.[23] On this view it was not the weakness but the overweening and unaccountable concentration of power in the system that was its fundamental disability.

Yet Hailsham's attack was merely a foretaste of what was to come. He was a senior Conservative politician, soon to become Lord Chancellor in Mrs Thatcher's government, writing in the late 1970s when Labour was still in office. It was not until after 1979, when it was widely alleged that the Thatcher government had demonstrated what the theory of elective dictatorship meant in practice, that the accountability side of the balance came under concerted scrutiny. This led many to conclude that there was a systemic imbalance within the political process, of the kind described by the journalist Hugo Young:

> Contrary to popular myth, and to the incantations of political leaders who can hardly afford to give the question serious study, the British do not passionately care about democracy. As long as they get a vote every few years and the children don't starve, they are prepared to put up with almost anything politicians throw at them. They do not have the habit of making life difficult for government, especially a strong government. They are prepared to be quiet accessories to mandates they never really gave. This preference, which is for strong government over accountable government, is to be found throughout the British parliamentary system.[24]

In short, there was too much authority and not enough accountability. Once politicians seriously exploited the potential of a flexible system in which there were few formal checks and balances, and disregarded the conventional restraints, the system's inherent imbalance stood out in sharp relief. The Whitehall/Tory/top-down tradition had clearly won out against its rival; and a rebalancing exercise was therefore required.

This line of argument brought the nature of the political system to the centre of political debate. It provided the basis for a reform agenda and a reform movement, of a kind not seen in Britain since the early years of the twentieth century. Between the 1970s and the 1990s, whether on grounds of authority or accountability, the British political process had clearly suffered a marked loss of legitimacy. This was compounded in the 1990s by the attention given to the assorted malpractices of politicians. It is too much to say that there was a system crisis, but there was a widespread feeling by the closing years of the twentieth century that the moment had come for review and reform. One view, the more striking because it came from a former senior civil servant, pulled no punches:

> The British system of government is an impossible one. Explaining to a visiting foreigner how business is conducted in Britain strains international relations to the limit. The eager enquirer has come to the fount of democratic government, the mother of Parliaments, the home of free speech and all the rest of the theory. They find themselves listening to a description of a system with, by most standards, very few rules, no visible constitution, a system of bendable conventions and a great deal of custom and practice. But try to explain the present party system to someone from Eastern Europe and they will have no difficulty in understanding what happens, they are just surprised that it still goes on and astonished that it goes on here.[25]

The Labour government elected in 1997 arrived with a bold programme of political reform. What this would mean for the future shape and balance of the political system was a matter for lively argument. This is an issue that will be discussed further in the final chapter. Before that we need to look more closely at how the political system works.

NOTES

1 B. Crick, *In Defence of Politics*, 2nd edn (Penguin, 1982), pp. 15, 17.
2 W. Bagehot, *The English Constitution* (1867, Oxford University Press edn, 1928), p. 1.
3 A. King, 'The implications of one-party government', in *Britain at the Polls*, 1992, ed. A. King (Chatham, NJ: Chatham House, 1992); G. Alderman, *Britain: A One Party State?* (Helm, 1989); H. Margetts and G. Smyth (eds), *Turning Japanese? Britain with a permanent party of government* (Lawrence and Wishart, 1994).
4 D. Kavanagh and P. Morris, *Consensus Politics from Attlee to Thatcher* (2nd edn, Blackwell, 1994); D. Kavanagh, *The Reordering of British Politics* (Oxford University Press, 1997).
5 G. Almond and S. Verba, *The Civic Culture* (Princeton, NJ, 1963); S. Beer, *Britain against Itself* (Faber, 1982).
6 M. Moran, *Politics and Society in Britain*, 2nd edn (Macmillan, 1989), p. 58.
7 On Conservative Party propaganda, one study observed: 'Few democratic political parties can have so systematically and ruthlessly called into question the integrity, the

devotion to the institutions of the country, and the patriotism of its opponents' (R. McKenzie and A. Silver, *Angels in Marble*, Heinemann, 1968, p. 49).

8 G. Orwell, *The Lion and the Unicorn* (1940) in *Collected Essays, Journalism and Letters*, vol. 2 (Penguin, 1970), pp. 125–6.

9 Sidney Low, *The Governance of England* (Fisher Unwin, 1904).

10 R. Jowell *et al.*, *British Social Attitudes: The 14th Report* (Ashgate/Social and Community Planning Research, 1997), p. 18. This report is the source of the figures cited here.

11 Committee on Standards in Public Life, *First Report*, Cm. 2850, 1995, p. 17.

12 P. Hennessy, *The Hidden Wiring* (Gollancz, 1995).

13 M. Burch and M. Moran, 'The changing British political elite, 1945–1983: MPs and Cabinet Ministers', *Parliamentary Affairs*, vol. 38, 1985.

14 L. Colley, *Britons: Forging the Nation 1707–1837* (Yale University Press, 1992).

15 B. Bryson, *Notes from a Small Island* (Black Swan, 1996), p. 160.

16 S. Jenkins, *The Times*, 17 January 1998.

17 A. H. Birch, *Representative and Responsible Government* (Allen and Unwin, 1964).

18 House of Commons Debates, fifth series, vol. 410, 15 May 1945, cols. 2305–7.

19 Quoted in R. Terrill, *R. H. Tawney and His Times* (Harvard University Press, 1973), p. 173.

20 A. V. Dicey, *Introduction to the Study of the Law of the Constitution* (10th edn, Macmillan, 1959), p. 91.

21 R. Rose, *Politics in England* (5th edn, 1989), p. 1.

22 The debate is reviewed in A. Wright, 'British decline: political or economic?', *Parliamentary Affairs*, vol. 40, 1987.

23 Lord Hailsham, *The Dilemma of Democracy* (Collins, 1978).

24 *Guardian*, 15 September 1988.

25 Kate Jenkins, 'Effective government and effective accountability', *Political Quarterly*, vol. 70, no. 2, 1999.

FURTHER READING

For general understanding of the British political tradition, S. Beer, *Modern British Politics* (2nd edn, Faber, 1969) and A. H. Birch, *Representative and Responsible Government* (Allen and Unwin, 1964) remain indispensable. Recent political history can be traced in D. Childs, *Britain Since 1945: A Political History* (4th edn, Routledge, 1997); and an ambitious interpretation in B. Harrison, *The Transformation of British Politics 1860–1995* (Oxford University Press, 1996). There is much of interest in D. Marquand and A. Seldon (eds), *The Ideas that Shaped Post-War Britain* (Fontana, 1996) and P. Hennessy and A. Seldon (eds), *Ruling Performance: British Governments from Attlee to Thatcher* (Blackwell, 1987). Good overviews of recent trends are L. Robins and B. Jones (eds), *Half a Century of British Politics* (Manchester University Press, 1997) and B. Coxall and L. Robins, *British Politics Since the War* (Macmillan, 1998). An excellent account of the social basis of British politics is M. Moran, *Politics and Society in Britain* (Macmillan, 2nd edn, 1989). To this can be added A. Adonis and S. Pollard, *A Class Act: The Myth of Britain's Classless Society* (Hamish Hamilton, 1997). D. Kavanagh, *Thatcherism and British Politics: The End of Consensus?* (2nd edn, Oxford University Press, 1990) explores an important period; while P. Hennessy, *The Hidden Wiring* (Gollancz, 1995) is an exuberant and illuminating treat. Constitutional argument can be found in T. Wright, *Citizens and Subjects: An Essay on British Politics* (Routledge, 1994) and M. Foley, *The Politics of the British Constitution* (Manchester University Press, 1999). Some of the best recent books on British politics have come from journalists: W. Hutton, *The State We're In* (Cape, 1995), S. Jenkins, *Accountable to None* (Hamish Hamilton, 1995) and A. Marr, *Ruling Britannia* (Michael Joseph, 1995).

2   The constitutional context

> The constitution is what happens . . . if it works, it's constitutional.
>
> (J. A. G. Griffith[1])

WHAT IS A CONSTITUTION?

What is a constitution, and what is it for? At a simple level, a constitution –
whether one document or a collection of written documents, or even 'unwritten'
or 'uncodified' as in Britain – is *the set of rules, legal and otherwise, which defines, describes
and regulates the structure and operation of the state, its institutions, activities and officials*. It
can be regarded as both the fundamental blueprint and the rule-book of the state.
In states with written constitutions, it will be both:

- the law behind the law, the legal source of legitimate political authority, and
- the higher law of the state, superior to other laws.

Yet descriptions such as these cannot adequately describe the essential political
and ideological nature of most constitutions. Former communist states such as the
old Soviet Union provide obvious examples of overtly ideological constitutions.
But other written constitutions will also reflect, to some degree, the political situation (in its widest sense) of a state and its government at the time of its creation.
Such a constitution may describe, for example,

- the background to its making (e.g. revolution, independence, union of states)
- the essence, purpose and form of the state (e.g. religious, secular, democratic,
  republican)
- such matters as its framers deem to be fundamental objectives or aspirations
  (such as the references in the Republic of Ireland's constitution to the whole
  island of Ireland).

Many constitutions also embody the primacy of either 'the state' or 'the
people'. One strand of constitutional thought in modern western liberal democratic systems primarily concerns the rights of citizens as individuals, and so a

main aim of constitutions in such systems is the protection of the citizen from the potential and actual power of the state. This is to be achieved partly through concepts such as the 'rule of law' and the 'separation of powers', concepts which are considered later in this chapter. This approach is often defined as constitutionalism or limited government.

While the (mainly English) common law – the law developed over the centuries by judges through cases and precedent – has traditionally been concerned with private, individual rights and duties rather than with collective action and entities, the historical trend of British constitutional development may more usefully be seen as 'top-down' rather than 'bottom-up'. The democratisation of central state power has been caused by pressure from 'the people' (or various influential and powerful classes or groups of people) rather than being an expression of their inherent 'sovereignty'. This tension between the 'legal sovereignty' of the centre (or apex) of the state and the 'political/democratic sovereignty' of the people at large pervades British constitutional thinking. It can be seen, for example, in the relative novelty of human rights law in the domestic British legal system, or the current debate over a statutory bill of rights.

No modern and stable constitutional order can be based solely on either the rights of the citizen or the powers of the state. Both considerations are implicit in modern constitutions, though a difference in fundamental emphasis can affect the nature of a constitution, as Ian Loveland has described:

> Different evaluations may be forthcoming if one's preliminary assumption is that the constitution is about what government may do in the light of the rights possessed by its citizens rather than about what rights citizens possess in the light of the powers wielded by their government.[2]

The traditional top-down and state-centred British approach is closer to the latter assumption.

There are almost as many forms of constitution as there are countries in the United Nations (and many sub-national tiers of government, especially in federal states, will have their own constitutional documents). They may be relatively succinct documents, either because they are written in the language of broad statement and principle, or because many detailed issues are left to be settled by ordinary legislation. They may be lengthy documents, if many such detailed issues – electoral laws, governmental functions, citizenship provisions and the like – are included. Many of these features may reflect the reasons for the creation of a particular constitution in the first place, or political realities at that time. A good example of this is contained in Article I Section 2(3) of the American constitution which apportions political representation and taxes by population. This is defined:

> by adding to the whole Number of free persons, including those bound to Service for a Term of Years, and excluding Indians not taxed, three fifths of all other Persons.

This is a clear expression not only of the existence of slavery in 1787, but also of the position of native Americans in the constitution in the new republic, two political realities which had profound effects on the later history of the United States.

If a constitution establishes the 'higher' law of a state, then its provisions will be beyond the reach of the ordinary executive and legislative authorities of that state, except in so far as is provided for, or permitted by, the constitution, or by way of valid amendment to the constitution itself. Generally the constitutional amendment route is made intentionally difficult (at least notionally) so that its provisions cannot easily be tinkered with by temporary majorities or powerful leaders, perhaps in the heat of the political moment or in reaction to a particular crisis. For example, special majorities in legislatures and/or in popular referendums may be required, or the right to initiate amendments may be restricted. The further the provisions of a constitution extend outward from the minimal institutional framework of the state into what may be regarded as matters of public policy, the more these matters become ones for the courts and less ones for the ordinary political organs of the state. If these are some of the general features of constitutions, it is clear that, when we look at Britain, we are dealing with a different and distinctive case.

DOES BRITAIN HAVE A CONSTITUTION?

Asking whether Britain has a constitution may seem a strange question. However, an attempt to answer it is essential for understanding the country's system of government in general, and the present proposals for constitutional reform in particular. The form of the answer will be very different from an analysis of the same matters in the systems of many other countries. A study of their constitutions and political systems may well follow the order of the articles of their constitutional document – starting, perhaps, with:

- the basic identity of the state (its name, ideological purpose, structure, changes to its territory and so on)
- the form and powers of the various tiers and organs of government (executive, legislative and judicial powers, within a federal, unitary or other structure; including means of their election/appointment, powers, accountability and so on)
- the rights and duties of the people (a 'bill of rights')
- methods of constitutional amendment.

Standard comparisons of the architecture of constitutional documents concentrate on such matters as

- whether they are
    - written or unwritten

- – contained in one or in a number of 'constitutional' documents
- – 'flexible' or 'rigid' in terms of the (formal and practical) ease of amendment of their provisions;
- • whether they provide for
  - – presidential or parliamentary government
  - – monarchical or republican government
  - – federal, quasi-federal or unitary state
- • the method of their creation and adoption.

Not surprisingly, most accounts of British constitutional arrangements focus on such classifications, often as part of an attempt to prove the existence of something called 'the British constitution' as a politico-legal system, different in form from, but equal in its 'constitutionalness' to, the generality of constitutions around the world. In this, British constitutionalists are often particularly concerned with the first group of distinguishing characteristics noted above, given the unwritten nature of much of British constitutional law and the effect of the doctrine of parliamentary sovereignty on its creation, amendment and repeal. A picture of the British constitution can be put together which allows its main features to be compared and contrasted with the generality of constitutions (see box below).

The British constitution: Its main features

- • A unitary state, in which power is concentrated at Westminster
- • Rules which are unwritten or at least uncodified
- • The legislative supremacy of Parliament
- • The political supremacy of the executive
- • The flexibility and ease of change of its provisions
- • The breadth and importance of its conventional elements

Answering the question posed in the title of this section about the existence of a 'British constitution' therefore depends on what is meant by a 'constitution'. Britain does not have a single document (or set of documents) which can been held up as 'The Constitution', and the traditional doctrine of parliamentary sovereignty precludes the notion of a class of 'higher constitutional law'. However, we clearly have rules (statutory or otherwise) about most of the matters which are generally dealt with in typical written constitutions. They may not be written down, although many are (such as laws on representation and elections) – this is why the British constitution is more properly described as 'uncodified' rather than 'unwritten' – and they may have no specially protected status in relation to ordinary laws.[3] They do answer the question about whether Britain really does have a constitution at all. The real question is what *kind* of constitution it has. This becomes clear when explored further.

MAIN FEATURES OF THE BRITISH CONSTITUTION

The main reason why Britain is almost the only country in the world without a written constitution is that it has not, for nearly three hundred years, been subject to the kind of fundamental constitutional upheavals which have normally given rise to the creation of constitutions in other countries. We have not had to break away from the rule of a foreign power, as the United States of America did at the end of the eighteenth century, nor make a fundamental break with our past as the West Germans did after the Second World War. This suggests that we do not have a written constitution because the appropriate or compelling opportunity has not arisen to construct one, rather than there being any deliberate political, legal or cultural reason for its absence.

Yet a constitution of sorts exists, even if not in the sense of a written document or documents as understood by the rest of the world. It is also an extremely flexible constitution, in the sense that 'constitutional' laws and practices can be amended or repealed in the same way as any other legal rules. The downside of this flexibility is often highlighted by reformers, who claim that there is therefore no constitutional protection against the arbitrary or undemocratic actions of a majoritarian government. There would be nothing in law, for example, to stop a government using its parliamentary majority to

- extend its own existence by abolishing elections or disenfranchising its opponents
- discriminate against citizens with red hair or blue eyes, or for some other irrelevant ground
- alter the laws of science, such as making $2 + 2 = 5$.

That such arbitrary legislation is not enacted or even sought by governments is due more to political and cultural restraints rather than legal prohibition. Reformers wish to provide that legal prohibition by way of a written constitution or, at least, an enforceable 'bill of rights'.

On the other hand, such flexibility means that the British constitutional system can change and evolve in reaction to developments, even if not always intentionally or coherently. Some changes may well be subtle and scarcely visible, especially if apparently accommodated within traditional constitutional structures and nomenclature. If they are made through administrative rather than legislative means, their constitutional significance may not be immediately apparent, even though their implications may be profound. Examples include the effect on traditional notions of accountability inherent in recent forms of patronage, such as the growth of quangos and executive agencies, and alterations in the structure of government. The dramatic switch from a vast public sector of nationalised industries and public corporations controlled by Whitehall through statutory powers, to a system of privatised companies, accountable to the market and to various forms of statutory regulation, also represents major constitutional change.

Thus the British constitution has been subjected to apparently contradictory criticisms, that it is both

- too simple to alter, and
- too unresponsive to change.

In fact, these are two sides of the same coin.

Perhaps the main difference between the British constitution and most other constitutions to be found around the world is not that the former is 'unwritten' or 'uncodified', but that whereas other constitutions tend to establish the basic institutions of the state (executive, legislature, judiciary and so on), British 'constitutional' laws tend to deal with pre-existing institutions. The monarchy, Parliament, the courts, ministers and Prime Minister and the rest were not originally established by statute or other formal device, but have developed by custom, practice and convention, and then by recognition in common and statute law. In this sense, whereas we can describe constitutional law in other countries as *creational*, much of British constitutional law is best described as *regulatory*. It seeks to regulate what exists, rather than establishing what should exist.

The rest of this chapter examines some key constitutional concepts and doctrines, and their importance in the present and developing British constitution. These concepts are the code which explains the constitution in the absence of fundamental rules of interpretation provided by some form of written document. Concepts such as the sovereignty of Parliament are of particular importance; so much so that this doctrine has been described as containing all 'the constitution' this country really has, as it identifies the hierarchy of laws applicable to constitutional (and other) situations. This can be illustrated by comparing the United Kingdom and the Unites States, and by examining who has 'the last word' on laws relating to matters of fundamental human liberty or values, especially in controversial social or ethical fields such as abortion, contraception, capital punishment and gun control.

In the United States of America, the constitution (including its amendments) is the supreme law of the land, whereas in Britain, Acts of the Westminster Parliament are the ultimate expression of supreme law. Thus, if controversial matters of public policy such as those just mentioned are clearly within, or can be brought within (through judicial interpretation) the terms of the American constitution, that interpretation will prevail over any conflicting statute, even one passed overwhelmingly by the democratically elected Congress. On the other hand, in Britain, Parliament can (subject to any applicable European law) pass any law concerning such matters and, if properly enacted, such a law would have to be accepted and applied by the courts. Thus we can say that, whereas in Britain ultimate policy choices rest with the democratic legislature, in the United States (and other countries with similar constitutional arrangements) it may rest with the unelected courts.

A good example of this difference is the issue of gun control, which – prompted by various tragic events – has been the focus of much legislative attention on both sides of the Atlantic in recent years. In the United States the Second Amendment to the constitution states:

> A well regulated Militia being necessary to the security of a free State, the right of the people to keep and bear Arms shall not be infringed.

This has been the cornerstone of the case against forms of gun control, and especially against any attempt at prohibition, by shooters and their supporters. Yet the clause also exhibits the common problem of sweeping declaratory provisions in that its interpretation, and application to particular situations of legislative or executive action, is by no means clear. The most obvious ambiguity is in relation to the meaning and effect of the opening words of the provision, and the extent to which they qualify the apparently absolute right set out thereafter. In other words, is the need for 'a well regulated militia' simply the justification for what exists as an absolute right, or does it qualify it to the extent that the people's right to bear arms can only be constitutionally protected when it is in the context of providing a 'well regulated militia'? Representatives of shooters, such as the National Rifle Association, will naturally wish to emphasise the former interpretation, whereas proponents of gun control will tend to prefer the latter. The consequence is that laws which seek to regulate possession and use of firearms may well be upheld as constitutional by the courts, whereas outright prohibitions may well be struck down as contrary to the Second Amendment.

Now contrast the position in the United Kingdom, where in the absence of any 'higher' law on firearms, the legislation enacted by Parliament on the subject will be good law, enforceable by the courts. This has allowed the Westminster Parliament to pass a series of laws in recent years, in response to tragedies such as the Hungerford and Dunblane shootings, providing for ever-tighter gun control and effectively for prohibition in the most recent enactments, as the Home Office press release (see box, p. 36) describes.

Supporters of shooters' rights tried, unsuccessfully, to deploy 'constitutional' arguments akin to those applicable in the United States, in an attempt to prevent schemes of prohibition and surrender of weapons. They sought to invoke provisions in the (English) Bill of Rights 1688, especially articles 7 and 12:

> *Subject's arms* – That the subjects which are protestants may have arms for their defence suitable to their conditions and as allowed by law.
> *Grants of forfeitures* – That all grants and promises of fines and forfeitures of particular persons before conviction are illegal and void.

However, their protests were in vain because they confused different traditions and ran up against the rock of parliamentary sovereignty.

HOME OFFICE 342/97   **27 November 1997**

TOTAL BAN ON HANDGUNS BECOMES LAW

A new law banning all remaining handguns received Royal Assent today.
The Firearms (Amendment) (No. 2) Act 1997 will extend the ban on
large-calibre handguns, introduced earlier this year, to small-calibre
handguns.

Handgun owners, dealers and clubs will be required to lawfully dispose
of their small-calibre handguns during February 1998. The Government
will shortly put before Parliament a compensation scheme for all those who
choose to surrender their weapons to the police rather than export or
deactivate them.

Welcoming the new law, Home Office minister Alun Michael said:

'Britain now has some of the toughest gun laws in the world. The banning of all handguns is a major victory for the Government in its drive to
improve public safety following the terrible events in Dunblane and
Hungerford.

'The hand-in period for owners and dealers of small-calibre handguns
will take place during February 1998. Over 26,000 small-calibre handguns
have already been voluntarily surrendered during the large-calibre handgun
surrender. All remaining small-calibre pistols must now be surrendered by
the end of February.

'Everyone who surrenders a small-calibre handgun during the hand-in
period will receive fair compensation to cover its value under a scheme for
which Parliament's approval will be sought shortly.

'The Government has shown its commitment to ensuring maximum public safety by banning all handguns.'

Notes For Editors

The Firearms (Amendment) (No. 2) Act was introduced in May 1997. The
Firearms (Amendment) Act 1997, which dealt with large-calibre handguns,
received Royal Assent on 27 February 1997.

The Government's estimate of compensation payable for small-calibre
pistols and ancillary equipment surrendered is £31 million.

CONSTITUTIONAL CONCEPTS

Sovereignty and the supremacy of Parliament

Sovereignty is one of the most complex and debated of constitutional concepts, but it is absolutely central to an understanding of the British constitution (and to any discussion of 'constitutional reform'). Part of the complexity, and even confusion, arises because of the variety of interrelated meanings it has in modern political debate. This often results in arguments where the antagonists can be talking at cross-purposes because they each have their own view of 'sovereignty'. On one side, in relation to a state and its government, is the notion of *political* or *actual sovereignty*, the degree to which there exists the power of independent, autonomous action without interference from external (or internal extra-governmental) forces of whatever kind. Many nominally independent states in history have had the outward attributes of sovereignty, recognised for some or all purposes as such in international law, but in reality have been under some form of external or internal military, financial, criminal, economic, religious or other influence or control. On the other side, there is the notion of *legal sovereignty*, the formal, constitutional degree of independence of a state, recognised as such in domestic and international law, through membership of international organisations such as the UN or EU and in other ways. Within a state, legal sovereignty describes where the ultimate source of law-making power lies over the whole state for all purposes or, in a federal or devolved system, in parts of a state or for some purposes.

The sovereignty of Parliament (which, in this legal rather than political sense, is really the 'Queen in Parliament', that is, Monarch, Lords and Commons) is the expression of legal sovereignty in the United Kingdom. The doctrine was described as 'the very keystone of the constitution' by A. V. Dicey, the Victorian jurist most associated with its classic statement. His formulation in 1885 (see box below) remains the starting-point for much modern discussion of sovereignty:

Dicey on sovereignty

The principle of Parliamentary sovereignty means neither more nor less than this, namely, that Parliament thus defined has, under the English constitution, the right to make or unmake any law whatever; and further that no person or body is recognised by the law of England as having a right to override or set aside the legislation of Parliament.

(A.V. Dicey, *Introduction to the Study of the Law of the Constitution*, 10th edn, 1959, pp. 39–40)

In fact, several doctrines about legal sovereignty, or as it is often described the *legislative supremacy* of Parliament, fundamental to the modern UK constitution, can be derived from Dicey's definition. The sovereignty of Parliament is *a legal rule, a description of the relationship between Parliament and the courts.* The courts are bound to accept, and to give effect to, any law duly effected by Parliament (that is, Commons, Lords and Monarch) and an Act of Parliament is the ultimate expression of law (not necessarily so in states with written constitutions). No law enacted by Parliament can have its validity questioned by any court; there is no 'judicial review' by any supreme or constitutional court. Thus, the courts have ruled (or confirmed?) that the legislative supremacy of Parliament is not limited by international law; territorial boundaries (even the granting of independence to former colonies); fundamental civil liberties; or any form of so-called 'higher law' such as natural law, law of God or natural justice. In its simplest terms, sovereignty means that Parliament stands unchallenged as far as law-making is concerned, and this position of supremacy is recognised and applied by the courts.

The doctrine of sovereignty also means that *no Parliament can bind its successors.* This inability of Parliament to prevent any law from being altered or repealed by a subsequent Parliament means that, in principle, no scheme of constitutional change can be *entrenched* (that is, made secure to some degree) in the legal order against amendment or repeal. Recent schemes by proponents of Scottish devolution and of some form of a bill of rights demonstrate how difficult, perhaps impossible, it is to reconcile formal, legal entrenchment (as opposed to 'political-moral' entrenchment) with conventional sovereignty, when reform involves some attempt permanently to reorder the structures of government. In this sense all constitutional change is provisional and temporary.

This Diceyan doctrine of the legal supremacy of Parliament is essentially an English concept developed over a period of more than three hundred years. There is a powerful legal argument put forward by some, mainly Scottish, jurists that challenges the conventional conception of the British constitutional order as the product of many centuries of unbroken legal development. They argue that the various treaties and Acts which have made the modern United Kingdom are fundamental constitutional documents which *precede* and *create* the present UK Parliament. This is often known as the 'born unfree' argument, and usually centres on the 1707 Union between England and Scotland. The Union legislation declared that the two kingdoms of England and Scotland 'shall . . . for ever after be united into one kingdom by the name of Great Britain' (Article I) and 'that the United Kingdom of Great Britain be represented by one and the same Parliament of Great Britain' (Article IV). Thus, as the Union was, in law, effected by treaty between two sovereign states and enacted by Acts of the Parliaments of *both* England and Scotland, the argument is that this Union *precedes and creates* the Parliament and therefore is, in relation to it, its constituent and ultimate document authoritatively defining and limiting its powers. On this view, the inherent sovereignty of the English Parliament up to 1707 did not necessarily carry over into the legal power of the new Parliament and thus had no legal effect after the Union, either at all or at least not in relation to those Scottish provisions of the Union expressly entrenched against amendment or repeal.

There are, however, contrary arguments, concentrating on the lack of legal effect of statutory forms of purported entrenchment both before 1707 (such as the 1688 Bill of Rights) and after. There have been a number of statutory provisions since 1707 which have apparently 'breached' the Union's terms. Perhaps a more powerful argument is one which concentrates on the geo-political realities of the early eighteenth century, and the dominance of England over its northern neighbour. While a new state of Great Britain was clearly created at that time, the notion that a totally new Parliament was born with no characteristics of the pre-Union English Parliament is, in political terms, not credible. Even the Union legislation itself, in its provisions on Scottish representation for example, implicitly acknowledges that the reality corresponded more to a continuation of the Westminster Parliament, enlarged and renamed by the Union. The 1800 Union with Ireland, in different political circumstances, as a political absorption into an existing state rather than the legal creation of a totally new state, is an even clearer demonstration of the gap between constitutional theory and political reality.

Some attempts have been made over the years to place this question before the Scottish courts, in relation to the title of the present Queen in 1953 and, more recently, in terms of the validity of the legislation on the community charge ('poll tax'). The real test would be if and when Parliament ever legislated directly contrary to a core Scottish provision of the Union by, say, abolishing the Court of Session or interfering with the established status of the Protestant religion and the Presbyterian church. There are some judicial opinions in the Scottish courts which do not expressly rule out the possibility of their rejecting the validity of such legislation,[4] but this view is not reflected by the English judiciary.

Another challenge to the traditional doctrine of parliamentary sovereignty has come from a different direction. Because of the legal strength of the sovereignty argument, opponents of absolute sovereignty tend to deploy arguments *within* the existing framework. This 'new view' concentrates on the 'manner and form' of legislation, arguing that the acceptance of the rule that Acts of Parliament must be accorded ultimate authority means that the courts are entitled, or even required, to ensure that the purported legislation is a validly enacted expression of the legal sovereign, the 'Queen-in-Parliament'. In other words, courts can look at alleged non-compliance with rules governing the composition of the sovereign authority and the procedure for enactment of its legislation. This argument can be used, for example, to overcome the 'Parliament cannot bind its successors' rule, or to examine allegations that an Act was not enacted in the proper form or by the correct procedure.[5]

So the courts are not bound to give legal effect to mere resolutions of a House of Parliament as if they were Acts of Parliament, but they have not (or not yet) accepted the 'manner and form' argument in its more controversial sense. Thus they will not question the legislation process within Parliament, a matter of privilege, nor overturn the doctrine of 'implied repeal' of earlier Acts by later Acts covering the same ground.

Despite the fact that it has been argued that if the courts adopted the 'manner and form' argument they would actually be protecting rather than diluting Parliament's legislative supremacy from abuse by other bodies – in Geoffrey Marshall's words, 'they would not be in any way derogating from Parliamentary sovereignty but protecting Parliament's sovereignty from usurpation by those not entitled for the purpose in hand to exercise it'[6] – the fact that the courts have continued to adhere to traditional Diceyan doctrine means that, at present, these arguments cannot be used directly to assist the purported entrenchment of, say, bill of rights or devolution legislation, and this has a profound effect on constitutional reform. This is considered below.

Legal and political sovereignty

The above discussion may seem somewhat academic, but it demonstrates how important it is to distinguish between 'legal' and 'political' sovereignty. Dicey himself regarded the Queen-in-Parliament (that is, the legal body comprising the two Houses and the monarch) as the legal sovereign and the electorate as the political sovereign. This latter point is the British version of what in many other constitutions is the idea of 'the people' as the true sovereign, a political concept which is often invoked to confer upon the constitution moral authority and binding force as the supreme source of legal power. Perhaps the most famous example of this is in the constitution of the United States ('We the people . . .'), and it has been much deployed in the Scottish constitutional debate.

Constitutional commentators have noted this contrast between the United Kingdom and much of the rest of the world on the matter of the sovereignty of a state residing with, or flowing from, its people (see box below).

Sovereignty: People or Parliament?

Britain never developed this idea of popular sovereignty in constitutional terms, even if we sometimes talk of the sovereignty of the electorate in political terms. Even if the latter were true it would merely allow the people to choose their government: it does not base the governmental order, the British 'constitution', on their authority and thus only gives them half their right. (Moreover, since a parliamentary majority can change that order, prolong its own life, alter the franchise or reform the electoral system, even the political rights of the electorate depend on Parliament.) What we have instead is the sovereignty of Parliament. Parliament determines – and alters – the country's system of government. If we ask where that power comes from, the answer is broadly that Parliament claimed it and the courts recognised it. The people never came into the picture. The liberal (middle-class) democracies established in Europe had, despite their generally limited franchise, to base their constitutions on the principle that ultimate authority was vested in the people. Britain seems to be the sole exception to this democratic path.

(F. F. Ridley, 'There is no British constitution: a dangerous case of the Emperor's clothes' (1988), *Parliamentary Affairs*, vol. 41, p. 345)

The more frequent resort to the referendum device from 1975 onwards (and its contemporary application to a variety of constitutional issues from devolution to electoral reform to European developments) also raises the notion of 'the people' as the ultimate *political* sovereign in the United Kingdom, especially where issues involving the fundamental structure and independence of the country are believed to be raised. There is tension between a pluralist view that power can and should be shared and a view of sovereignty that holds that it is concentrated. There is a further tension between a view of the legal sovereignty of Parliament and the political sovereignty of the people. These tensions are much in evidence in modern constitutional debates in Britain.

Sovereignty and Europe

The greatest modern crisis for the Diceyan tradition, and the area where the constitutional argument between legal and political sovereignty is most pronounced, is in relation to Europe. The legal relationship since the early 1970s between the United Kingdom and the European Community/Union is not simply one of conventional international law between sovereign entities. The European legal order is unique in its supranational quality and its effect on the domestic law of member states. It should be borne in mind in this respect that Diceyan sovereignty grew out of the English common law tradition, whereas the European civil law tradition can lead to a different form of legal reasoning that produces different results when determining the hierarchy of laws in a territory. The European Court of Justice has developed a more activist, purposive approach to its case law to entrench (or create?) the supremacy of the central legal order over that of the various member states. From the point of view of domestic law, Community law was incorporated by the European Communities Act 1972, as subsequently amended.

For many years the British courts managed to avoid having to pronounce directly and unequivocally on the supremacy or otherwise of Community law in relation to traditional Diceyan sovereignty. Some early case law even suggested that the doctrine of 'implied repeal' still applied, so that later UK statutory provisions would prevail over inconsistent Community law after 1972. Generally though, potential conflicts between UK and Community law were reconciled and resolved through techniques of statutory interpretation and construction, although this approach had its limits if the conflict was apparently irreconcilable. This point came to widespread public and parliamentary attention in the series of *Factortame* cases since 1989 concerning Spanish-owned fishing vessels, where the House of Lords appeared unequivocally to accept the supremacy of European law in appropriate cases.

The power of the concept of 'sovereignty' in its political sense is beyond doubt in relation to European matters. It was much invoked in the 1990s in the context of the Maastricht Treaty, and the political battle for its ratification. The opponents of ratification, who included the remaining outright opponents of British membership of the European Community itself, claimed that the provisions of the treaty, with its ultimate aim of economic and monetary union, meant the end of British sovereignty. That this was regarded as a legitimate and serious mode of argument (whether or not it is accepted) is shown by the form of response adopted by supporters of the treaty and the political developments implied by it. Generally, they did accept that the Maastricht process could mean a loss of sovereignty, but used phrases such as 'pooled sovereignty' or 'shared sovereignty' (which may well be, strictly speaking, a reasonably accurate description) to bypass or defuse what they saw as being, in the British context at least, a highly potent argument.

The rule of law

The doctrine of the rule of law, when applied to the constitution, is both simple and complex. Put simply, it requires those in authority to act in accordance with the law, rather than in some arbitrary fashion dictated by their own preferences, whims or discretion. As such, it is an unexceptionable, even self-evident, statement of the British constitutional system. It had an obvious importance in the historical replacement of a ruling monarchy by a democratic political executive. Wider applications of the proposition, as with the issue of parliamentary sovereignty, often stem from the formulation of A. V. Dicey (see box, p. 43).

While propositions that law, rather than arbitrary power or force, should be the basis of relations between the individual and the state are widely accepted, Dicey's determination that the state should not operate under special laws granting it privileges, immunities and powers not available to ordinary citizens (a situation he believed to exist under continental systems of administrative law) has clear echoes of modern political arguments about the role and size of the state and its relationship with its citizens. The growth of systems of administrative bureaucracy with their decision-making tribunals and scope for wide official discretion along with centralised control and direction of private property and conduct which are implicit in the modern welfare state, has given rise to concerns among those opposed to such developments. These concerns are often described in 'rule of law' terms, by those who seek to reduce the size and power (allegedly arbitrary or discretionary) of the state, and who object to the development of special machinery beyond the ordinary law and courts.

Many twentieth-century theorists have criticised Dicey's *laissez-faire* approach as confusing different or special treatment of the state and its officials with greater privilege and elevated status as compared to the ordinary citizen, and failing to recognise or accept the necessary or desirable powers of public authorities (including powers of discretion) for the benefit of all citizens. Jennings in particular analysed the essentially political nature of the notion of the rule of law, describing it as 'rather an unruly horse. If it is only a synonym for law and order, it is characteristic of all civilised States. . . . If it is not, it is apt to express the political views of the theorist and not to be an analysis of the practice of government.'[7]

At a constitutional level, such objections often follow Dicey in believing that personal liberty and personal property, held to be a precondition of liberty, are

Dicey on the rule of law

It means, in the first place, the absolute supremacy of regular law as opposed to the influence of arbitrary power, and excludes the existence of arbitrariness, of prerogative, or even of wide discretionary authority on the part of the government. Englishmen are ruled by the law, and by the law alone; a man may with us be punished for a breach of law, but he can be punished for nothing else.

It means, again, equality before the law, or the equal subjection of all classes to the ordinary law of the land administered by the ordinary law courts; the 'rule of law' in this sense excludes the idea of any exemption of officials or others from the duty of obedience to the law which governs other citizens or from the jurisdiction of the ordinary tribunals; there can be with us nothing really corresponding to the 'administrative law' *(droit administratif)* or the 'administrative tribunals' *(tribunaux administratifs)* of France. The notion which lies at the bottom of the 'administrative law' known to foreign countries is that affairs or disputes in which the government or its servants are concerned are beyond the sphere of the civil courts and must be dealt with by special and more or less official bodies. This idea is utterly unknown to the law of England, and indeed is fundamentally inconsistent with our traditions and customs.

The 'rule of law,' lastly, may be used as a formula for expressing the fact that with us the law of the constitution, the rules which in foreign countries naturally form part of a constitutional code, are not the source but the consequence of the rights of individuals, as defined and enforced by the courts; that, in short, the principles of private law have with us been by the action of the courts and Parliament so extended as to determine the position of the Crown and of its servants; thus the constitution is the result of the ordinary law of the land.

(A. V. Dicey, *Introduction to the Study of the Law of the Constitution*, 10th edn, 1959, pp. 202–3)

best protected by ordinary laws rather than special laws such as bills of rights or written constitutions. However, supporters of such constitutional devices will argue the opposite: that such special methods are necessary to preserve and protect the rule of law, to prevent the deliberate or casual loss of liberty through the legislation and actions of majoritarian governments buttressed by parliamentary legislative supremacy. In other words, it is the 'ordinary law' basis of liberty that is the risk to the rule of law in Britain, the fact that it has no special protection and that there is no special category of 'constitutional' law.

It can be seen, even from this brief and simplified overview of the rule of law, that it is a concept which, once developed, enters into the heart of the political arena. It becomes part of the vocabulary of the collective versus individual debate concerning the relationship between the citizen and the state, which is at the centre of constitutional theory and political argument. Indeed, it can sometimes seem that the concept of the rule of law is capable of being used in so many different ways that it is in danger of meaning, in constitutional terms, almost anything and nothing.

The separation of powers

The concept of a 'separation of powers' is an important one in constitutional thinking. Again it is a concept which has a superficial simplicity but also a deeper complexity, not least because it has both a descriptive and a prescriptive element. The idea has a long history in political thought right back to Aristotle, through Locke and Montesquieu. The conscious adoption of 'separation of powers' principles by the framers of the American constitution in the late eighteenth century ensured its importance in subsequent constitution-making.

It is based on the idea that there are three classes of governmental function, each carried out by a distinct organ of government. In descriptive terms, these are the:

- *executive* function, carried out by the Executive (government)
- *legislative* function, carried out by the Legislature (parliament, assembly), and
- *judicial* function, carried out by the Judiciary (the courts).

The normative or prescriptive element has two parts to it:

- the three functions should be operated by three organs of government, and
- to allow some (or, on some views, any) mixing of the three functions and, in particular, the three organs is a threat to liberty.

There is obviously a wide range of ways in which the doctrine can be applied (or not) in a constitution. At one extreme there could be a complete mixing of all the functions in one organ or person, such as an absolute monarch or dictator. At the other extreme is the idea of absolute separation, with no overlapping of functions or persons. A constitution which seeks to apply the latter idea may well, as in the example of the United States, incorporate various 'checks and balances' to ensure that no single arm of the government can reign supreme over the others (while also providing for some interdependence to ensure the effective operation of government by the various organs notwithstanding the strict theoretical separation).

Between these two extremes there is the idea of the *mixed* or *balanced* constitution, as the UK constitution is often described, where there is some degree of mixing and overlap of functions and organs of government, either deliberately or by accidental historical development. In an unwritten or uncodified constitution, such as that of the United Kingdom, the boundaries of powers may be difficult to identify. The 'Westminster model' of parliamentary government was classically described by Bagehot (see box, p. 45).

Bagehot on the Westminster model of parliamentary government

The efficient secret of the English Constitution may be described as the close union, the near complete fusion, of the executive and legislative powers. . . . The connecting link is the *Cabinet*. . . . A Cabinet is a combining committee – a *hyphen* which joins, a *buckle* which fastens, the legislative part of the State. In its origin it belongs to the one, in its functions it belongs to the other.

(Walter Bagehot, *The English Constitution* (1867), Fontana edn, 1993, pp. 67–70 (extracts))

This model of government is nearly the antithesis of pure 'separation of powers' theory, with almost the whole political executive being members of the legislature. The idea of 'mixed government' is that it is the degree of connection, rather than separation, that itself provides the 'checks and balances' necessary to prevent governmental tyranny and preserve individual liberty. As such, both 'separation of powers' and 'mixed' government are predicated primarily on a 'limited government' approach to the state as a potential threat to liberty rather than primarily as a positive force for collective action.

Nevertheless, using 'separation of powers' language not only serves to illuminate some of the central features of the UK system, such as the executive's dominance of Parliament, but also because some of the central figures, such as the judges, claim to operate within the terms of the doctrine. So, although the idea of separation is negated in the operation of the executive and legislative arms of British government, it is maintained in relation to law and the courts.

The judiciary's attitude is of particular interest in this respect. The development of judicial review (especially in England) is based on the notion of judicial supervision of the legality of administration (including delegated legislation made by executive bodies), rather than of primary legislation. This kind of judicial review does not involve a challenge to Parliament's legislative supremacy, but is a way of challenging how these laws are implemented and administered. Its rapid development in the last thirty years, and the willingness of the courts to tackle issues of high political importance and controversy – from deportations and other immigration and nationality issues to the operation of major public schemes such as social security, child support and criminal injuries compensation – has often thrust judicial review and the judiciary to the forefront of political discussion. In 1987 the government responded to the growth of judicial review cases[8] by producing a guide for Whitehall called *The Judge over Your Shoulder*.

Judges who frequently deal with English judicial review cases also tend to be contributors to the wider constitutional debate, perhaps because of their experience of European jurisprudence through EU and European Convention on Human Rights cases. The judicialisation of highly controversial political and social issues can often be seen to put the judges 'in conflict' with ministers and Parliament, testing the boundary lines between Parliament and the courts. In some cases the judges will step back and state that a particular matter should be settled not by the courts but by political means. There they will often employ 'separation of powers' language to explain or justify their decision, especially when it is a matter of statutory interpretation. A good example is provided by the steel strike case (see box below).

Separation of powers: The steel strike case (1980)

A union sought to increase pressure on the British Steel Corporation by extending strike action to private sector companies not directly party to its dispute. These companies sought injunctions to stop such action. The case turned on the wording of the industrial relations legislation concerning the 'furtherance of a trade dispute'. The Court of Appeal granted the injunctions, Lord Denning being concerned about the 'disastrous effect on the economy and well-being of the country'. However, the House of Lords was clearly alarmed at the lower court's reasoning, based not so much on statutory interpretation as on extraneous political/social motives. Lord Diplock declared:

'At a time when more and more cases involving the application of legislation which gives effect to policies that are the subject of bitter public and parliamentary controversy, it cannot be too strongly emphasised that the British Constitution, though largely unwritten, is firmly based on the separation of powers: Parliament makes the laws, the judiciary interpret them. When Parliament legislates to remedy what the majority of its members at the time perceive to be a defect or a lacuna in the existing law (whether it be the written law enacted by existing statutes or the unwritten common law as it has been expounded by the judges in decided cases), the role of the judiciary is confined to ascertaining from the words that Parliament has approved as expressing its intention what that intention was, and to giving effect to it. Where the meaning of the statutory words is plain and unambiguous it is not for the judges to invent fancied ambiguities as an excuse for failing to give effect to its plain meaning because they themselves consider that the consequences of doing so would be inexpedient, or even unjust or immoral. In controversial matters such as are involved in industrial relations there is room for differences of opinion as to what is expedient, what is just and what is morally justifiable. Under our Constitution it is Parliament's opinion on these matters that is paramount.'

(*Duport Steels v Sirs* [1980] 1 All ER 529)

However, it might be noted that the use of the word 'Parliament' in this context, strictly accurate in constitutional theory, can perhaps mask the political reality that legislation is usually that of the government of the day, rather than of some 'autonomous' body called Parliament. The courts' 'dispute' therefore is, in practical terms, often with the political executive, rather than with 'Parliament' as such. Moreover, in the modern age of party discipline, the legislature has become ever more a creature of the executive. Constitutional doctrine can sometimes conceal political reality. There is argument about the extent to which the courts should concern themselves with strict constitutional theory or with the realities of political practice.

Constitutional conventions

No constitution nor any law, however detailed, can hope to provide for each and every situation which may arise in practice. Some balance between 'flexibility' and 'rigidity' is necessary to allow for organic change. New laws may be enacted to deal with novel circumstances, but often this avenue is difficult or impractical; and successful amendment to a constitution generally requires deliberately oner-ous legislative procedures to be surmounted. The more informal ways in which politicians and others will behave in particular situations, if accepted as a model for future similar occurrences (and not declared unlawful by the courts), may be described as *constitutional conventions*. Political reality and practice may indeed develop so far by these means as to transform fundamental aspects of a consti-tutional system. The American constitution, for example, written in the late eight-eenth century, did not envisage or describe the dominance of the presidency or of the federal government in modern American politics.

The 'unwritten' nature of the UK constitution, where there are no consti-tutional 'higher laws' and no universally agreed set of constitutional enactments, inevitably provides significant scope for the operation of conventions. Indeed, the role of conventions is central to the British system, for they describe, at any point in time, the practical workings of the political and governmental system, and the actual, rather than the theoretical, distribution of power among the various organs of the state. Perhaps the clearest example is the role of the sovereign who, in strict theory, appears to wield as much legislative and administrative power as an 'absolute monarch'. Through the exercise of the royal prerogative, the sover-eign can dissolve Parliament; appoint or dismiss governments, ministers and prime ministers; and refuse to assent to bills passed by Parliament. In reality the sovereign wields no such power, at least not personally, except perhaps in the most exceptional circumstances. The practical operation of the government of the United Kingdom rests in the hands of elected ministers and their officials, acting under a mixture of law and a residue of the royal prerogative. This has become the established convention.

Conventions are, therefore, those informal 'rules' or practices which relate the formal theory of the constitution to the practical realities of the day, perhaps by modifying the strict law, or by expanding it. In the vivid phrase of Sir Ivor Jennings, they 'provide the flesh which clothes the dry bones of the law'.[9] There is no accepted definition of the term 'constitutional convention', and indeed some authorities do not like the term, preferring alternatives such as 'non-legal constitutional rules'.

Perhaps the most elegant and informative description is that of Le May: 'the general agreements among public men about the "rules of the game" to be borne in mind in the conduct of political affairs'.[10] In broad terms, then, a convention is

- a binding but non-legal rule, that is, something that is different from a rule of law enforceable in the courts
- created and amended (or even rejected) by politicians by means other than legislation or common law
- a practice which is generally accepted by those affected by it and relies for its enforcement on political rather than legal sanctions
- not normally put into writing.

Thus a convention is more than a mere political fact (such as the existence of parties) or an ethical standard, but it is not a 'law' in the sense of a rule which must be enforced by the courts or Parliament. The importance of conventions in our constitutional arrangements means that the methods by which they are created or identified are inevitably of crucial importance. So what are these methods? Conventions may

- result from a *series of precedents*
- be *deliberately created* either by unilateral pronouncement (usually by the Government or Prime Minister) or by agreement
- be the articulation of *general underlying principles*.

Some key conventions in the British constitutional system, other than the position of the sovereign, mentioned above, include:

- *Majorities, whether in Parliament, local government or elsewhere, should not use their potentially unlimited power in an oppressive way in relation to minorities.* So, in Parliament, for example, the Opposition are granted representation in committees, debating time in the Chamber and so on.
- *Government ministers are accountable to Parliament for their policies and actions.* This convention of ministerial responsibility means that it is elected politicians, ultimately accountable to the public through Parliament, and not professional officials who have to explain and defend policy and, where necessary, accept the blame for errors and failures.
- *The centrality of the Prime Minister and Cabinet in the political system.* Even the very existence of the Prime Minister and the Cabinet is largely a matter of convention rather than law, and their key position is preserved by conventions such as the Prime Minister's power to set the date for general elections by seeking the dissolution of Parliament, and by collective Cabinet responsibility which unites and binds the whole government together behind common policies.

Other important conventions are the impartiality of the House of Commons

Speaker; the practice that it is only Law Lords, and not lay peers, who hear House of Lords appeal cases; the relationship between the two Houses of Parliament; the relationships between states within the Commonwealth, and the practice of government consulting relevant interest groups before implementing policies or introducing legislation affecting them.

Conventions, in this sense, provide the vital constitutional checks and balances in Britain that are often more explicit in systems with written constitutions. When such understandings are thought to have broken down to some degree, there may need to be legislation (as with certain local government practices) or written guidance (as with public appointments and codes of conduct). A good recent example is the resolutions passed by both Houses of Parliament just before the 1997 election (following episodes such as the 'arms to Iraq' affair and the subsequent Scott Report) setting out what had been recognised as the main conventions of ministerial responsibility and accountability to Parliament.

Jennings (see box below) suggested a series of tests for identifying conventions which, although not universally accepted, provides a useful working definition.

Identifying conventions

We have to ask ourselves three questions: first, what are the precedents; secondly, did the actors in the precedents believe that they were bound by a rule; and thirdly, is there a reason for the rule? A single precedent with a good reason may be enough to establish the rule. A whole string of precedents without such a reason will be of no avail, unless it is perfectly certain that the persons concerned regarded them as bound by it. And then, as we have seen, the convention may be broken with impunity.

(Sir Ivor Jennings, *The Law and the Constitution*, 5th edn, 1959, p. 135)

Conventions are crucial to the nature and operation of the unwritten British constitution, because their enforceability rests on political rather than legal foundations. There is no settled consensus on which areas of the British political system are truly 'constitutional', in the sense of being regarded as specially protected from 'routine' legislative or other change. During the 1980s some local government legislation was criticised as 'unconstitutional'. The 'constitutionality' of party leadership elections affecting the position of Prime Minister is sometimes questioned, as in 1976, 1990 and 1995. Conventions change and evolve; and are the most flexible parts of a flexible constitution.

Because conventions are not directly enforceable in the courts, judges have also tended to distinguish the effects of a breach of convention and a breach of law. An action may be described as 'unconstitutional' if it is in breach of a recognised convention, but that will not make it unlawful (although the convention can assist in the formulation of a judicial decision – for example, by aiding statutory interpretation). This was clearly demonstrated in a 1968 case following the unilateral declaration of independence by the Southern Rhodesian government in 1965. The Judicial Committee of the Privy Council had to balance the UK Parliament's right to legislate for the rebel colony against Rhodesia's substantial degree of self-government and autonomy from the United Kingdom before 1965, which had formally been recognised by the United Kingdom in 1961 as an established convention. In his judgment, Lord Reid accepted that this 'was a very important convention but it had no legal effect in limiting the legal power of Parliament', and went on:

> It is often said that it would be unconstitutional for the United Kingdom Parliament to do certain things, meaning that the moral, political and other reasons against doing them are so strong that most people would regard it as highly improper if Parliament did these things. But that does not mean that it is beyond the power of Parliament to so such things. If Parliament chose to do any of them the courts could not hold the Act of Parliament invalid. It may be that it would have been thought, before 1965, that it would be unconstitutional to disregard this convention. But it may also be that the unilateral Declaration of Independence released the United Kingdom from any obligation to observe the convention. Their Lordships in declaring the law are not concerned with these matters. They are only concerned with the legal powers of Parliament . . .
>
> (Lord Reid, *Madzimbamuto v Lardner-Burke* [1969] 1 AC 645)

By not being 'law' in the strict sense, conventions can be 'breached' or ignored by those affected by them. This may be regarded in some circumstances as valuable flexibility, but in others as arbitrary and capricious. The effect of a breach of a convention may involve political consequences for an individual (such as the resignation of a minister, MP or other public figure) or other consequences for general political behaviour, where one party feels no longer bound by a convention breached by another. A breach or breakdown of a convention may sometimes trigger legislation or other formal guidelines to reinforce the position. This was the case with the Parliament Act 1911, introduced to formalise the relationship between the Commons and the Lords in circumstances when the conventions had not proved adequate.

Conventions change as political life changes. A good example of this is the way democratic requirements altered assumptions about the recruitment of prime ministers (see box, p. 51).

To sum up, conventions are essential in the working of any constitution, even those written in apparently comprehensive detail, as no constitution can hope to deal with or even contemplate all eventualities that will arise in political society during its lifetime, even if regularly subject to formal amendment. The uncodified nature of the British constitution means that conventions are particularly necessary to the effective operation of the political system. In fact, one can see the notion of conventions in many ways, such as their generally unwritten form, their flexibility and (depending on one's view) the need to codify them, as a metaphor for the British constitution itself.

Constitutional conventions: an example

'A Prime Minister cannot nowadays operate from the House of Lords'

This is settled constitutional practice, and some would extend its scope to other senior ministers such as the Chancellor and the Home Secretary (although the Foreign Secretary has been in the Lords twice in recent times: Home in 1960–63, Carrington in 1979–82). The three major occasions since the departure of Lord Salisbury in 1902 when a peer was in contention for the premiership illustrate not only how the convention has developed, but also how political practice can depend on factors other than simple adherence to convention. As all major parties now elect their leader, such occasions are virtually impossible nowadays.

1923 Lord Curzon: Following the retirement through ill-health of Bonar Law, the succession lay between the Chancellor, Stanley Baldwin, and the Foreign Secretary, Lord Curzon, the latter being the initial favourite. The former prime minister, Arthur Balfour, advised Buckingham Palace that the Prime Minister must be in the Commons. The necessity for the Prime Minister to be able to face the Leader of the Opposition, Ramsay MacDonald, whose Labour Party had at that time no members in the Lords, appeared to be decisive in the King's choice of Baldwin. Labour even announced that if a peer was chosen, it would use 'every political device to precipitate a dissolution'.

1940 Lord Halifax: When Neville Chamberlain resigned in May 1940, the choice of successor was between Lord Halifax, the Foreign Secretary, and Winston Churchill, the maverick First Lord of the Admiralty. As the aim was the creation of a coalition government, Halifax, though a peer, was not thereby regarded by the Labour opposition as necessarily 'disqualified' (they were more immediately concerned to ensure Chamberlain's departure). The tide swung in Churchill's favour, which Halifax accepted, citing the 'difficult position of a Prime Minister unable to make contact with the centre of gravity in the House of Commons'. For Halifax this was a practical as well as a constitutional point, as he feared that, with a powerful deputy like Churchill in the Commons, he would be 'a more or less honorary Prime Minister, living in a kind of twilight just outside the things that really mattered.' Unsuccessful attempts were made by the King and Chamberlain to get round the peerage handicap in view of the national emergency, by putting the peerage in abeyance, by a special Act of Parliament, or by the Commons granting him the privilege of participating in its proceedings.

1963 Lords Home and Hailsham: When Harold Macmillan felt compelled to resign through ill-health, the situation concerning peers as potential premiers had dramatically altered because the Peerage Act, which had been passed a few months previously, allowed peers to disclaim their titles and seek election to the Commons. It was recognised in Parliament at the time that this could have an effect on the succession to Macmillan, though Hailsham was then the supposed potential beneficiary, rather than Home, and neither was the front-runner. The battle for the leadership was then played out on partisan rather than constitutional grounds, where the peerages of the two candidates were not regarded as a disqualification, *once disclaimed* and the ex-peer then in the Commons. Macmillan had advised the Queen that Home, if he accepted the commission, should disclaim and seek election immediately. One practical difficulty was that the start of the new session of Parliament had to be delayed for a time to allow Home time to disclaim his peerage and fight and win a by-election so that he could face Parliament as a duly elected MP as well as Prime Minister.

CONSTITUTIONAL REFORM

> 'Reform! Reform! Aren't things bad enough already?'[11]

The word 'reform' generally means not just change, but change for the better. However, like the term 'electoral reform', 'constitutional reform' has become a well-recognised and much used term to mean 'deliberate constitutional change'. Sometimes constitutional reform has come to mean in recent years not just *ad hoc* changes to particular areas of our existing constitution, but production of a written document, or set of documents, dealing comprehensively with all fundamental constitutional issues. This would bring Britain into line with virtually every other country, although in itself this would not be a sufficient reason for such a major change.[12] However, it is possible to argue that a number of the major constitutional changes currently proposed could or should be made only as part of a comprehensive reform package because of the inter-related nature of the UK constitution. For example, reforming the House of Lords has implications for the Commons, and devolution has implications for the rest of the United Kingdom. Changing one part of the system inevitably has implications for other parts.

The constitutional reforms being proposed or implemented by the Labour government include[13]:

- devolution for Scotland, Wales, Northern Ireland and (possibly) the English regions
- incorporation of the European Convention on Human Rights
- reform of the House of Lords, initially by the removal of the hereditary peers
- freedom of information legislation
- a referendum on changing the voting system for House of Commons elections
- changes to the voting system for elections to the European Parliament
- restoration of a form of London-wide local government
- changes to the law affecting political parties, including registration and funding.

It is clear that Britain is experiencing a period of major constitutional change. Why are we in such a period now? Part of the answer is that there has been a coming together at the present time of a number of distinct (sometimes conflicting) trends of political thought, which include:

- reaction against the 1970s period of government with a very small or no majority seeking to implement radical, controversial policies and generally act as if it had a clear electoral mandate;
- reaction against the long 1980s period of government with a huge majority (albeit on a minority of the popular vote) using it to implement fundamental changes in the existing political and social system, apparently contrary, in many cases, to the wishes of the majority of the public;

- greater support for a number of separate constitutional changes, such as devolution, proportional representation and a bill of rights;
- support on the left for the notion of 'positive rights' rather than simply legal immunities as a way of implementing and maintaining 'progressive' policies;
- fears in some parts of the left for a long period in the 1980s and early 1990s that Labour might never return to government, and that therefore there was a need for constitutional checks and balances to limit the power of non-Labour governments;
- increased involvement in political systems (such as the European Union) where different constitutional arrangements are more the norm, demonstrating in the eyes of reformers that Britain is 'out of step';
- belief that the constitution, like other parts of the British social, political and economic system, requires regular modernisation.

So we can see that there are a number of interlinked issues under the deceptively simple heading of 'constitutional reform', from ambitions for fundamental change in the nature of British society to more pragmatic or partisan concerns to alter specific 'rules' of the political 'game' which may be disadvantageous to particular groups or parties. There will always also be a streak of 'objective fairness' criteria in some demands for reforms. 'Fairness' is a significant component, for example, of arguments for 'electoral reform' or for 'more democratic' representation in both Houses of Parliament. In practice, partisan and objective considerations tend to get mixed up together in arguments about constitutional reform. Another relevant factor in the current debate is that, while enthusiasts for reform may see such changes (for example, to the voting system or devolution) as a precondition for other social and economic reforms, opponents of reform often regard constitutional debate as irrelevant to, or a time-consuming diversion from, more concrete concerns.

The existence of the doctrine of the supremacy of Parliament puts substantial obstacles in the way of certain constitutional reforms, such as the adoption of either a bill of rights or a written constitution. On these issues there is a mixing of 'sovereignty' and 'separation of powers' language, really two sides of the same coin, for what is at stake is the relationship between the courts and a parliamentary majority, as to the source of supreme law-making. The present Lord Chancellor, Lord Irvine of Lairg, has emphasised the Government's desire for its constitutional reforms to take place *within* the existing framework of constitutional theory and practice (see box, p. 54), and not to precipitate a more fundamental constitutional revolution. This shaped the way in which the European Convention on Human Rights (ECHR) was legislated for,

- by permitting the judges simply to declare, in appropriate cases, that Acts of Parliament are incompatible with ECHR rights, but not to declare such Acts invalid, and
- by empowering Parliament to enact 'remedial legislation' by a 'fast-track' legislative procedure.

'Bills of rights' and traditional constitutional theory and practice

The British Constitution is firmly based on the separation of powers. It is essential that incorporation is achieved in a way which does nothing to disturb that balance. It is for Parliament to pass laws, not the judges. It is for the judges to interpret these laws and to develop the common law, not for Parliament or the executive. It is also for the courts to ensure that the powers conferred by Parliament on the executive and other bodies are neither exceeded nor abused but exercised lawfully. That will continue to be so after the European Convention becomes part of our domestic law. . . .

Incorporating basic human rights into our domestic law will be a major new departure. It will offer new challenges. What is critical is that the form of incorporation sits comfortably with our United Kingdom institutions. It must not disturb the supremacy of Parliament. It should not put the judges in a position where they are seen as at odds with Parliament. That would be a recipe for conflict and mutual recrimination. It is vital that the courts should not become involved in a process of policy evaluation which goes far beyond its allotted constitutional role. In a democratic society, compromises between competing interests must be resolved by Parliament – or if Parliament so decides, by Ministers.

(Lord Irvine, speech to a Bill of Rights conference,
University College London, 4 July 1997)

But how in law could such a constitutional protection for rights be created, and how could it be accepted as a special or higher form of law, not simply as an ordinary Act of Parliament? In legal language this is known as the problem of 'entrenchment'. There have been many schemes of varying ingenuity suggested in recent years to overcome this apparently insuperable difficulty of reconciling a desire to make 'basic' constitutional laws with a doctrine of parliamentary sovereignty which can make or unmake all laws, and under which no Parliament can bind its successors. Devices suggested have included the election of a special constituent assembly, separate from Parliament, which would draw up the new constitutional document, along with public endorsement through a referendum requiring a special majority. A special majority was required in the Scottish and Welsh devolution referendums in 1979, which was not met in the event, resulting in the failure of the proposals.

Some constitutional reformers, especially lawyers, wish to use the precedent of the acknowledgment by the British courts of the supremacy of European Community law as a way of further undermining the British courts' otherwise complete adherence to the traditional doctrine of parliamentary sovereignty. They see the judges as the key to reform, on the grounds that they believe that the sovereignty of Parliament as a legal rule exists only because it is recognised as such by the courts. Therefore, for them, what is needed is for the judges to declare that the enactment of constitutional provisions has fundamentally altered the basic constitution of the United Kingdom, and that they will no longer be bound by the doctrine of parliamentary sovereignty. This radical shift would allow the courts for the first time in the modern age to question the validity of Acts of Parliament, and declare them to be in breach of the higher law of the written constitution or bill of rights. Such judicial power is known technically as 'judicial review' (not to be confused with the limited kind of judicial review currently exercised in British courts) and is applied in this constitutional sense most famously by the US Supreme Court. As the British courts have already adjusted traditional doctrines in the context of EC law, a shift in judicial attitudes of even this magnitude could not now be discounted. This would be more likely if it was clear from the enactment process that the new provisions were explicitly intended to have a higher place in the hierarchy of laws.

However, such a role for the British courts raises fundamental political and constitutional questions about the nature of democracy and the relationship between the judiciary and the elected government and Parliament. Should unelected judges have the power to interpret such fundamental issues as the operation of the political system and the nature of civil liberties? Should the courts be able to set aside the will of the elected Parliament, which is, theoretically at least, expressing the will of the people? Should, in essence, the judges as well as Parliament make law? Can the judges do this and remain neutral and impartial?

Even without such drastic powers over the validity of legislation itself, judges already have a significant impact in public affairs, through interpretation of existing legislation or of more general concepts such as 'the public interest' or 'the interests of the state'. They can even alter long-standing relationships between the three branches of government. This was seen, for example, in the case of *Pepper v Hart* (1992) in which the House of Lords significantly weakened the existing rule that the courts could not resort to what was said within Parliament as an aid to statutory interpretation. This new freedom has apparently become accepted by all three branches (that is, the executive, the legislature and the judiciary), and it has affected ministerial and parliamentary practice, as well as the judicial process, to some degree.

But far more radical alteration to the relationship between the branches of government would come from a written constitution and a bill of rights: it would make judges even more overtly key constitutional actors. As in the United States, the system of judicial appointment (individually and in terms of the overall balance of any constitutional court) could well become a more transparent part of the political process, with greater attention focused on the judges' political and social views. Just as important a factor is the judges' attitude to the interpretation of constitutional laws, whether in effect they adopt a restrictive, narrow interpretation (which tends to favour 'traditional'/'conservative' outcomes) or a creative, broad interpretation (which tends to accommodate 'progressive'/'liberal' decisions).

This question of judicial involvement has been one of the main reasons why some on the left have traditionally opposed written constitutional documents. They point to cases where radical policies of Labour (and Conservative) governments and local authorities, such as legislation in the fields of public spending, employment or equal opportunities, have been thwarted by the courts. This shows, they argue, that the judges are not suited by background, political outlook or training to be trusted to interpret constitutional documents in the proper, constructive spirit. A key proponent of this approach is J. A. G. Griffith (see box below).

Griffith on the political role of the judges

. . . judges in the United Kingdom cannot be politically neutral because they are placed in positions where they are required to make political choices which are sometimes presented to them, and often presented by them, as determinations of where the public interest lies; that their interpretation of what is in the public interest and therefore politically desirable is determined by the kind of people they are and the position they hold in our society; that this position is part of established authority and so is necessarily conservative not liberal.

(J. A. G. Griffith, *The Politics of the Judiciary*, 5th edn, 1997, p. 336)

At the same time many of those on the right have opposed judicial interference on the grounds that it conflicts with the traditional constitutional doctrine of parliamentary sovereignty (in its political and legal senses), which in practice also means the power of a strong executive. There is also a general fear about the consequences of bringing judges and the courts into the centre of the political arena. The arguments about whether Britain should have its own Bill of Rights raise all these issues (see box, p. 57).

The act of writing a constitution itself throws into relief the purpose(s) of constitutional change. Such change can either be *formal* (substantially the codification of existing arrangements) or *substantive* (the enactment of new arrangements). In general the results of exercises based on either motive will be the same in law, although motivation may be important for the 'entrenchment' and interpretation by the courts of the written document(s). The more radical the changes, the more likely perhaps the judiciary will be to recognise and accept that a new constitutional legal order has been established.

It is not yet clear whether the range of constitutional reforms being proposed and implemented in Britain will lead to some form of comprehensive written constitution. The Labour government has insisted that its plans for substantial reform do not include, nor will require, such a revolutionary step. On the other hand, those such as the Liberal Democrats, who have long supported a written constitution, regard it as an inevitable and desirable outcome of present developments. It may be that the piecemeal nature of the various changes being proposed and implemented since 1997 may throw up such unforeseen problems and consequences as to require some form of comprehensive settlement to meld them together in a coherent and effective way. What is clear, though, is that

---

A British bill of rights: some arguments pro and con

Pro

- Brings the United Kingdom into line with most other countries
- ECHR procedures are too slow and bring bad publicity to British human rights 'failings'
- Transfers decisions on important matters from foreign to domestic judges
- Flexible and adaptable tool, and an opportunity for developing domestic law and practice more speedily
- Necessary following devolution of legislative powers to sub-national assemblies
- Major educative force

Con

- 'Un-British' way of doing things
- Unnecessary as human rights adequately protected in Britain
- Unsuitable for a modern, complex society
- Too much power to unelected, untrained judges, for example, to decide what is 'necessary in a democratic society', and would 'politicise' the judiciary
- Entrenchment provisions would restrict Parliament's freedom to legislate in the light of prevailing circumstances, such as emergencies
- Bill of rights cases would clog an already overloaded court system, especially with frivolous litigation
- A bill of rights would require elaborate enforcement machinery, for relatively little result

    (derived from M. Zander, *A Bill of Rights?*, 4th edn, 1997, pp. ix–x)

---

constitutional issues are now at the centre of political debate in a country which has long been accustomed to take its constitutional arrangements for granted.

NOTES

1 J. A. G. Griffith, 1963, *Public Law*, 402, editorial.
2 I. Loveland, 'Labour and the constitution: the "Right" approach to reform?' (1992), *Parliamentary Affairs*, vol. 45, p. 173.
3 An illustration of this is the fact that there is no fixed definition of a 'constitutional bill' in terms of any special treatment in the parliamentary legislative process. See J. Seaton and B. Winetrobe, 'The passage of constitutional bills in Parliament' (1998), *Journal of Legislative Studies*, vol. 4, pp. 33–52.
4 Perhaps most famously by Lord President Cooper in *MacCormick v Lord Advocate* 1953 SC 396.

5 See for example R. F. V. Heuston, *Essays in Constitutional Law* (2nd edn, 1964), especially ch. 1.
6 G. Marshall, *Constitutional Theory* (1971), pp. 42–3.
7 Sir I. Jennings, *The Law and the Constitution*, 5th edn, 1959, p. 60.
8 As an illustration, there were 506 applications for leave to apply for judicial review against the Home Office on immigration matters alone in 1991, 1,220 in 1995 and 1,748 in 1996 (parliamentary written answer, 16 July 1997, House of Commons Debates vol. 298, cols. 177–8w). See generally L. Bridges *et al.*, *Judicial Review in Perspective*, 2nd edn, 1995.
9 Sir I. Jennings, *The Law and the Constitution*, 5th edn, 1959, p. 81.
10 G. Le May, *The Victorian Constitution*, 1979, p. 1.
11 Astbury J. (1860–1939), attributed.
12 Some reformist organisations, such as the Institute for Public Policy Research, have produced their own drafts of a written constitution for Britain (*A Written Constitution for the United Kingdom*, 1995).
13 In addition, there may well be other developments, including those coming from Europe, which could have implications for the British constitutional system.

FURTHER READING

Good, readable introductions to the British constitution include Colin Turpin's *British Government and the Constitution*, 3rd edn (Butterworths, 1995) and Peter Madgwick and Diana Woodhouse, *The Law and Politics of the Constitution*, (Harvester Wheatsheaf, 1995). Those wishing to burrow more deeply into constitutional theory and practice should consult texts such as Jeffrey Jowell and Dawn Oliver's collection of essays, *The Changing Constitution*, 3rd edn (Clarendon Press, 1994), Colin Munro's *Studies in Constitutional Law* (Butterworths, 1987) and the works of Geoffrey Marshall, such as his *Constitutional Conventions* (Clarendon Press, 1984). A useful recent overview is Eric Barendt, 'Is there a United Kingdom constitution?' (1997) *Oxford Journal of Legal Studies*, vol. 17, p. 137.

Judicial contributions to the constitutional debate generally and to the courts' role in particular have proliferated in recent years. See for example Sir Stephen Sedley, 'The sound of silence: constitutional law without a constitution' (1994) *Law Quarterly Review*, vol. 110, p. 270; Sir John Laws, 'Judicial remedies and the constitution' (1994) *Modern Law Review*, vol. 57, p. 213 and 'Law and democracy' (1995) *Public Law*, p. 72, and Lord Woolf of Barnes, 'Droit public – English style' (1995) *Public Law*, p. 57. A critical and influential study of the judicial role in the constitutional and political system is John Griffith's *The Politics of the Judiciary*, 5th edn (Fontana, 1997).

There has been a wealth of material on constitutional reform. Much detailed work has been published by bodies such as Charter 88 and the Constitution Unit, and in the Institute for Public Policy Research's *A Written Constitution for the United Kingdom* (Mansell, 1993). See also Vernon Bogdanor, *Politics and the Constitution* (Dartmouth, 1996) and *Power and the People: A Guide to Constitutional Reform* (Victor Gollancz, 1997); Rodney Brazier, *Constitutional Practice* (Clarendon Press, 2nd edn, 1994) and *Constitutional Reform: Reshaping the British Political System*, 2nd edn (Oxford University Press, 1998), and Anthony Barnett, *This Time: Our Constitutional Revolution* (Vintage, 1997).

A pro-reform Conservative perspective can be found in Ferdinand Mount, *The British Constitution Now* (Heinemann, 1992) and Robert Alexander, *The Voice of the People: A Constitution for Tomorrow* (Weidenfeld & Nicolson, 1997). Contrary views can be found in Andrew Lansley and R. Wilson, *Conservatives and the Constitution* (Conservative 2000 Foundation, 1997).

3 Elections and electors

Every man who is not presumably incapacitated by some consideration of personal unfitness or of political danger is morally entitled to come within the pale of the constitution.

(William Gladstone, May 1864)

We regard it as important for the health of the democratic and political system that participation in the electoral process be as high as possible.

(Home Affairs Select Committee, *Electoral Law and Administration*, HC 768 1997–8, paragraph 8)

INTRODUCTION

Elections are the essential underpinning of British politics. They determine party strengths in Parliament and the political make-up of the government. The rules under which elections are run are therefore crucial to the political process. This chapter outlines the shape of current electoral law, now subject to rapid change following the introduction of new forms of election for the devolved assemblies in Scotland and Wales and for the European Parliament, and assesses the significance of voting patterns in recent elections. There are also proposals for electoral reform for Westminster which may have an irreversible effect on the shape of British politics and these are discussed too.

THE FRAMEWORK OF ELECTIONS

The rules governing elections might seem to be a subject with little immediate relevance, but electoral law and procedures provide the framework for the wider political process. The mechanics of elections in Great Britain owe much to the historical background of the nineteenth century, where the right to be included in the political nation was extended gradually from the political elite of the eighteenth century to the respectable working men of the nineteenth. The nature of British democracy today cannot be understood without reference to the continuing influence of this evolutionary route to democracy (see box, pp. 60–1).

Milestones in electoral law

The Great Reform Act 1832
Added small landowners, tenant farmers and shopkeepers to the franchise, taking the proportion of the enfranchised adult population to about 5 per cent. Introduced principle of registration of electors.

Second Reform Act 1867
Added smaller agricultural tenants, artisans and some town labourers to the franchise, since all occupiers of rated dwellings and more prosperous lodgers were enfranchised in the boroughs. The electorate increased to 13 per cent of the adult population and one in three of adult males.

Ballot Act 1872
Introduced secret voting, thus helping to undermine the practices of bribery, intimidation and patronage.

Corrupt and Illegal Practices Act 1883
Successfully tackled the problems of bribery and corruption which had been rife in UK electoral practice, and imposed a maximum limit on expenditure.

Third Reform Act 1884
Added agricultural labourers and others in rural areas to the franchise, with the introduction of a uniform householder and lodger qualification. The total number of voters increased to 28 per cent of the adult population and two in three of adult males.

Redistribution of Seats Act 1885
Created the principle of equal electoral districts and marked a move towards single-member constituencies.

Representation of the People Act 1918
Enfranchised women aged 30 and over and virtually all settled adult males, increasing the percentage of voters to 74 per cent of the adult population. The introduction of a franchise primarily based on residence made the registration of voters more inclusive – before 1914 only an estimated 60 per cent of adult eligible males had been registered.

Representation of the People (Equal Franchise) Act 1928
Enfranchised women aged 21 and over, increasing the proportion of electors in the eligible population to 97 per cent.

House of Commons (Redistribution of Seats) Act 1944
Created permanent boundary commissions for each of the four constituent parts of the United Kingdom and established a set of broad rules for the regular redistribution of seats to create constituencies of roughly equal size.

continued

Representation of the People Act 1948
Abolished additional votes for university graduates and those owning business premises, so achieving the principle of one person, one vote. Abolished university seats. A simplified registration procedure was created by removing the requirement for a period of residence.

Representation of the People Act 1969
Lowered the minimum voting age to 18. Candidates still had to be 21 or over.

Representation of the People Acts 1985 and 1989
Introduced the principle of voting for British citizens resident abroad for up to five years hitherto reserved only for merchant seamen and service personnel. The 1989 Act extended the length of time to twenty years, increasing the potential overseas electorate to over 2 million.

NB References to adult population refer to Great Britain and Ireland until 1922, but only Northern Ireland is included after this date.

The British electoral system is extremely simple to understand, for the candidate in each constituency with the most votes wins. This is generally known as first past the post (FPTP) or plurality voting. A margin of one is sufficient and the results of the 659 individual constituencies are relayed nationwide so that twenty-four hours after the election the party with most seats takes office. There is no independent electoral commission to give an official result or to declare a particular party the winner; instead the Queen simply sends for the leader of the party with most seats.

Occasionally results are very close and the outgoing Prime Minister may try to reach an accommodation with a minority party, as the Conservative leader Edward Heath did in February 1974. The leader of the then Liberal Party, Jeremy Thorpe, refused a coalition and the Labour leader, Harold Wilson, went to Buckingham Palace on the Monday following the election to be made Prime Minister. The Queen's personal advisers and Cabinet Office staff act as guardians of the constitution in advising the monarch to act according to precedent when election results are inconclusive. Incumbent governments have the advantage of choosing the date of the next election; the only rule being that a single Parliament cannot last more than five years.

In contrast, local elections take place at fixed intervals; and although FPTP is used there are often 2–3 councillors for a local ward. The framework of local electoral law is closely based on that for parliamentary elections; and one effect of over-precise drafting is that experiments with new techniques such as electronic voting or mobile polling booths have been prevented.

The proportional representation (PR) systems now being introduced in Scotland and Wales and for the European Parliament elections bring entirely new concepts into the tradition of British elections, such as the formal acceptance of parties as an integral part of the democratic process. Although elections to Westminster will be largely unaffected, at least for some years, there may well be changes over the longer term, if there is a majority for change in the promised referendum on a new voting system for Westminster.

THEORIES OF REPRESENTATION

Who and what are MPs representing in Parliament? The House of Commons was originally a house of separate local *communities*, and echoes of this territorial representation still resonate. The Conservative politician, Enoch Powell, asserted that: 'The House [of Commons] is a geographical representation of the Kingdom. We come here sent from our respective places.'[1] Such communities have been overtaken by the realities of urban life and the idea of *functional* representation gained ground in the nineteenth century, with MPs increasingly seen as representing interest groups and social organisations, such as trade unions and agriculture. *Radical* representation theories argue that MPs are there as delegates to represent the views of their electors and not to make personal judgements about issues. In modern elections this means recognising that it is the party which puts candidates into Parliament, and that MPs are necessarily constrained by party discipline. This view of *party* representation has not totally overcome an earlier approach asserting the right of an MP to exercise individual discretion, as famously set out in Edmund Burke's *Speech to the Electors of Bristol* in 1774, and *individual* representation survives in the practice of free (non-party) votes on moral issues such as abortion and the death penalty. No single theory of representation has established hegemony in British politics, and MPs like to declare that they represent all their constituents (even, or perhaps especially, when they have been voted for by only a minority of them).

WHO CAN VOTE?

Rules about who can (and cannot) vote are basic to the electoral system (see box, p. 63). The historical baggage of British electoral law is demonstrated in the right of Irish and Commonwealth citizens to vote in UK elections as long as they are resident there. The Representation of the People Act 1918 established that only British subjects (that is, those owing allegiance to the Crown) could register to vote, and with the independence of former British colonies the inclusive nature of this concept was retained. As we move into the twenty-first century the nature of this qualification can seem bizarre, but the practical difficulties and political sensitivities of disqualifying Commonwealth and Irish citizens are evidently too great to be seriously contemplated. An additional layer of qualification has grown with UK membership of the EU. European Union citizens who are resident in Britain can now vote in European Parliament and local elections but not Westminster ones. One simple solution to all this confusion would be to enfranchise all residents of Britain regardless of nationality, especially if there was a more clearly defined test of residence – perhaps a twelve-month qualifying period for non-British citizens.

Voters

Voters have to be

- 18 or over
- registered as a voter on the electoral register maintained by independent electoral registration officers
- a British, Irish or Commonwealth citizen (or EU citizen for local, European Parliament or devolved assemblies' elections).

Who cannot vote:

- peers – who are disqualified from voting in parliamentary elections only, since they sit in the House of Lords
- convicted prisoners
- people convicted of a corrupt or illegal electoral offence within the last five years
- bankrupts
- those falling within the imprecise common law categories of mental illness and impairment. In practice it is rare for people to be excluded in these categories, but those in institutions have often experienced difficulty in registering to vote.

RESIDENCE

Identification with a particular locality lies deep within the culture of British democracy. In order to be registered, electors need to demonstrate that they are resident somewhere: this can cause problems in an increasingly mobile society for those at either end of the income scale. Since the leading case (*Fox v Stirk 1970*) it has been possible to convince a registration officer that a voter has two residences if a considerable degree of permanence has been demonstrated. The voter can then select a constituency in which to vote. It might be more sensible to make electors select a single electoral residence in line with current tax law, so that contests in highly marginal seats were not affected by possible tactical voting.[2]

But it is people who lack a settled residence who are the greatest losers in British electoral law. Although a legal case established that residence was not dependent on bricks and mortar, nor on the legal nature of occupancy, Home Office guidance on registration of rough sleepers remains cautious. Under-registration of the insecurely housed will continue to disenfranchise many in the foreseeable future.

While registration should merely be an administrative process for allocating voters to constituencies, it can often be seen as an additional qualification for the right to vote itself.

The right of British citizens resident abroad to vote in general elections up to twenty years after they have left the country also attracts criticism. It seems at odds with the emphasis on the representation of communities. In 1997 only 23,600 expatriates actually registered to vote, compared with 34,500 in 1991, and although the major parties have increased their targeting of overseas voters, this hardly seems worth the effort in political terms.

REGISTRATION

Registration is carried out by electoral registration officers (EROs) who are independent officials based in local authority areas, with the Home Office providing national guidance through circulars and practice notes. This system worked well in times of a stable and culturally homogeneous population, but it has several drawbacks for a more varied and mobile society. Compiling the electoral register involves collecting information from every household about residents who are eligible to vote. Voting is voluntary but registration is effectively compulsory since giving false information to an ERO is an offence. Only those on the current annual register, which runs from 16 February each year, can vote in the relevant constituency. People who move into the constituency after the qualifying date of 10 October (or 15 September in Northern Ireland) are not added to the register but can vote in their old constituency either in person or by postal or proxy vote.

By contrast, Australia has a 'rolling' register which is continuously updated and available in an electronic form so that electors can vote at the polling station of their choice. This system is naturally more expensive and until recently there has been little political pressure in the United Kingdom to increase expenditure on registration. Many voters do not realise that they are not on the register until after the election is called, but by then it is often too late to apply.

The electoral register is also used for jury service, and for calculating the electorate for the purposes of redistributing constituencies, as well as for certain local government grants (and it also acts as a check for residence for hire purchase, credit agreements, and so on). In October 1998 both the Neill Committee on the funding of political parties and the Independent Commission on the Voting System recommended the creation of an electoral commission to supervise electoral law, including registration. Following the election, the Home Office set up an internal working party to look at the feasibility of introducing rolling registration, simplifying postal voting, and introducing mobile polling stations in supermarkets, and so on. This may lead to changes in the way elections in Britain are organised. There is also pressure from the Department of the Environment, Transport and the Regions to use such methods to revitalise local democracy.

ELECTORAL REGISTRATION AND TURNOUT

A combination of under-registration and relatively low turnout of those who are registered, especially among young people, means that the numbers who actually vote are considerably lower than the numbers eligible to do so. There has been increasing concern at the apparent level of alienation from mainstream political life of young people, prompting a number of initiatives to promote citizenship, such as the Advisory Group on Education for Citizenship and the Teaching of Democracy chaired by Professor Bernard Crick, which reported in 1998 (see box below).

Citizen or cynic?

We aim at no less than a change in the political culture of this country both nationally and locally: for people to think of themselves as active citizens, willing, able and equipped to have an influence on public life and with the critical capacities to weigh evidence before speaking and acting. . . . There are worrying levels of apathy, ignorance and cynicism about political and public life and also involvement in neighbourhood and community affairs.

(*Final Report of the Advisory Group on Education for Citizenship and the Teaching of Democracy in Schools* (the Crick Report), September 1998)

Studies of the level of electoral registration in 1951 and 1966 found that 3 or 4 per cent of those eligible were not registered. The level of non-registration grew to 6.5 per cent by 1981 and to 7.1 per cent in 1991. These official estimates are actually underestimates as they are based on census data which themselves under-estimate the population. Taking that into account, the level of non-registration in private households in 1991 was between 7.4 per cent and 9 per cent. There is wide variation between areas and particular groups in the extent of non-registration: the proportion not registered in inner London was more than 20 per cent in 1991; men were more likely not to be registered than women; and young people, ethnic minorities, new Commonwealth citizens and those in private rent-ed accommodation were particularly under-registered.[3]

The limited evidence that is available suggests that the overall situation has not changed significantly since 1991, despite campaigns by the National Union of Students and others to improve registration levels especially among young people.[4] Moreover, the existence of an annual register, drawn up in the autumn but not coming into force until February, means that by the time the register has come into force, some people will have died and others will have moved from their place of registration. The register therefore becomes increasingly inaccurate. The level of non-registration at the qualifying date in October is already higher when it comes into force in February and, by the end of its life the following February, may be twice as much.[5]

The inaccuracies of the register, coupled with the fact that there are numerous legitimate dual entries on it, mean that calculating turnout at elections is a far from exact science. The 'official' turnout at the 1997 general election – those voting as a proportion of the number of registered electors, adjusted to take into account the number reaching the age of 18 between the date of the register and the election – was 71.6 per cent in Great Britain. If under-registration, dual registrations and those who have died or moved house are taken into account, it can be estimated that the turnout was just over 75 per cent (see Table 3.1).[6]

There were around 4.9 million people aged 18 to 24 in Great Britain at the time of the 1997 election. It is likely that just under 4 million of these were on the electoral registers. Early evidence from the British Election Study suggests that the level of turnout among this age group was between 85 and 90 per cent of the overall level, with the implication that only about 2.5 million in this age group actually voted. It is likely, in other words, that nearly half the 18–24-year-olds in Britain did not vote in 1997. There are clearly implications here both for education in citizenship and participation, and for the procedures of electoral registration.

The question of making electors vote is sometimes raised, most recently by the Home Affairs Select Committee, which called for a public debate on the issue. A number of European and Commonwealth countries, including Belgium, Italy and Australia, place a legal obligation on voters, but it is generally thought too foreign an idea for the British voter to accept.[7]

Table 3.1 Turnout in general elections in Great Britain since 1950 (%)

	Reported	*Adjusted*[a]
1950	84.1	86.9
1951	82.6	91.7
1955	76.9	81.5
1959	79.0	87.6
1964	77.2	85.7
1966	76.1	79.3
1970	72.0	77.0
1974 (Feb)	79.1	81.7
1974 (Oct)	73.0	81.0
1979	76.2	80.8
1983	72.7	77.8
1987	75.6	80.9
1992	77.9	82.0
1997	71.6	75.4

Source: D. Denver and G. Hands in P. Norris and N. Gavin (eds), *Britain Votes 1997*, p. 213.

Note
[a] Estimates to take account of age of electoral register.

CANDIDATES

In contrast to the emphasis on connection with locality associated with the franchise, candidates need not be resident in the United Kingdom at all to qualify for parliamentary elections. There are separate residential qualifications for local elections. The main qualification is to be a British, Irish or Commonwealth citizen (EU citizens may stand for local, European or devolved assemblies' elections if resident here). The nineteenth-century roots of electoral law are evident in the statutory provisions concerning the adoption of candidates, and one of the few new requirements of the twentieth century is the introduction of a deposit (currently £500) in the 1918 Act to deter frivolous candidates. If a candidate gains less than 5 per cent of the vote the deposit is forfeit – a rule which has a disproportionate effect on minority parties (such as the Greens).

The parties have their own rules and procedures (generally not subject to legal regulation) for selecting prospective candidates well in advance of an election. There is no statutory requirement for internal party democracy, which means that it has been possible for candidates to be selected by very small numbers of political activists. Procedures are now being overhauled by the parties to deal with the different requirements of new electoral systems in Scotland, Wales and European Parliament elections, and to respond to greater pressure for involvement from ordinary party members. The usual practice is for the local constituency association to select the candidate, who is then approved nationally. Legal processes have begun to intrude, for example with the initiative by the Labour Party to introduce women-only shortlists being defeated by an industrial tribunal after a disappointed male candidate applied for a ruling on the application of the Sex Discrimination Act 1975. The attempt by Labour to twin constituencies, thus ensuring the selection of equal numbers of men and women, has also been threatened with legal challenge at the elections in Wales.

A candidate, even if elected, may still be excluded from a seat in Parliament. Most exclusions relate to membership of Parliament, rather than acceptance as candidates – in other words, who can sit rather than who can stand. Those excluded include peers, Church of England (and Ireland) and Roman Catholic priests (even if they have resigned the priesthood), convicted prisoners, bankrupts and those guilty of electoral offences. The list urgently requires an overhaul as the disqualification of certain categories of clergy is no longer related to current circumstances and has already been abandoned in the legislation for the new devolved assemblies. The other main disqualifications are set out in the House of Commons (Disqualification) Act 1975 and include the holding of a wide range of public offices.

There are sometimes disputes where candidates change their name to cause confusion, as at the 1983 election when a man changed his name to Margaret Thatcher and attempted to stand against her in her constituency. A party label may be adopted by an individual which is similar to that of another party, as in the European elections in 1994 when a Literal Democrat stood against a Liberal Democrat; the Conservative candidate won and a subsequent appeal to the election court failed when it was confirmed that political parties were not registered and could not claim copyright to the name. During the 1997 general election there were many candidates identified as using misleading descriptions, and various legal avenues were explored to prevent this. Registration of parties under the Registration of Political Parties Act 1998 (see box, p. 122) is largely expected to deal with the problem, although it will not prevent the adoption of misleading personal names.

This area of electoral law is changing rapidly, since at the 1999 European elections voters were, for the first time in Britain, only able to vote for a party, rather than an individual candidate (unless an independent). There was much speculation about whether the change would affect the already low turnout for European Parliament elections. In Scotland, Wales and London voters also have a second vote which has to be cast e.g. for a party, with the party being responsible for drawing up a list of candidates in order of priority. This process is not necessarily less democratic than for Westminster elections, since under FPTP the party candidates are in effect a closed list of one. Some variants of list systems allow the elector an opportunity to reorder the list, but so far the government has not been willing to accept these forms of 'open list' on the grounds that the ballot paper would become too complex.

POLLING DAY

Polling day for parliamentary elections is customarily a Thursday, although this is not a statutory requirement. The custom dates from the 1930s and is out of step with other European countries, which vote at weekends. The introduction of new electoral systems for elections to the European Parliament, the Scottish Parliament, Welsh National Assembly and Assembly for London will require adaptations in electoral law, and it is likely that some central notification of results will be developed for all elections. Electronic voting is also under consideration, but it may be difficult to convince voters to trust entirely electronic methods, with no hard-copy ballot papers.

For parliamentary elections the returning officer (usually the chief officer of a local council) endorses the election writ sent to him by the Clerk of the Crown and gives the name of the successful candidate. An official document entitled *Election Expenses*, submitted to the Commons about one year after the election, gives details of the candidates in each constituency and the number of votes cast (including postal votes and spoilt ballot papers). The media perform instant analyses in the immediate aftermath of the count and academics publish comprehensive surveys of the results. Once an election result has been declared an election petition is required if the result is to be challenged. This is heard before a special election court presided over by a high court judge; but petitions are expensive with an uncertain outcome and major parties fear the possibility of tit-for-tat challenges. At Winchester in 1997 the Conservative candidate, who had lost by just two votes to a Liberal Democrat, brought and won a petition because some ballot papers had not been stamped with an official mark. The election was re-run but the result was that the Liberal Democrat won by more than 21,000 votes.

SPENDING ON ELECTIONS

Nowhere is the irrelevance of nineteenth-century legislation clearer than in its application to election expenditure, concerned as it is with problems of bribery and corruption in the Victorian era, even though the main issue has now become the cost of national campaigns. The Neill Committee on Standards in Public Life has recently conducted an inquiry into election expenses and party funding at both the national and local level[8] and substantial changes are under way.

Current electoral law creates a series of corrupt and illegal practices, such as the payment of money to convey electors to the poll or the treating of the cost of a meal, and expenditure above a specified limit in each constituency is illegal. Each candidate must appoint an agent who is responsible for the proper conduct of the campaign, and through whom all expenditure is channelled, so that other supporters of the candidate cannot inadvertently breach the limits through expenditure on the candidate's behalf. Therefore outsiders, or third parties, cannot spend money promoting the campaign of a particular candidate during the election period.

Candidates can send a postal communication without charge and have the free use of school halls for meetings. Major parties will qualify for election broadcasts without an access fee and these subsidies help to cut the cost of elections to some extent.

The system of local expenditure limits (see box below) is under challenge following a case at the European Court of Human Rights where Mrs Bowman, on behalf of the anti-abortion group SPUC, successfully argued that the prohibition

---

Election expense limits for parliamentary constituencies

Constituencies are designated either county or borough and higher amounts for county constituencies reflect the heavier expenses of reaching rural constituents, while by-elections attract national attention.

- County constituency: £4,965 plus 5.6p for every entry in the electoral register
  Borough constituency: £4,965 plus 4.2p for every entry in the electoral register
- The maximum permitted spend, based on average 1997 electorate per constituency: £8,941 for a county and £7,825 for a borough constituency
- By-elections: £19,863 plus 22.2p (county) and 16.9p (borough) for every entry in the electoral register

on spending by third parties breached the right to free expression. She had distributed leaflets in the 1992 election setting out each candidate's position on abortion and had been charged with illegally incurring election expenses, only escaping prosecution. The court concluded that a third party should be able to spend more than £5 per constituency. The Neill Committee has recommended a limit of £500 instead, and this may prove to be an acceptable compromise.

The legal position of computers, databases and telephone canvassing from outside the constituency can be unclear in terms of election expenses, and there are some well-used methods of circumventing the rules, such as purchasing stationery long before the election or hiring equipment at a nominal sum.[9] A series of cases have confirmed that the expenditure limits apply only in individual constituencies and not nationally, so the amount national parties spend is entirely unregulated. Arguably the limits for individual constituencies should be increased significantly, which would assist smaller parties with limited national resources. The candidate's agent is required to detail the expenses incurred in the constituency and these are published after the election. The accounts are open to challenge and there are occasional prosecutions.

National campaigning is now the major activity of parties, and television has supplanted newspapers as the key medium. Nevertheless, advertisements on billboards still form a vital part of the campaign strategy and these do not count as constituency expenditure. Party supporters, such as trade unions and business interests, will also advertise in this way. The Advertising Standards Authority exempts political advertising from its requirements on truth and accuracy. Direct mail looks set to be the growth area of the years ahead, with the electorate in target seats as the main recipients. Sophisticated use of data can enable parties to identify key undecided groups and target their concerns. It is not surprising that the whole issue of election spending has come under review.

The Neill Committee proposed maintaining a system of local limits but allowing greater expenditure by third parties, such as pressure groups, trade unions or voluntary groups. Its most radical recommendation was for national limits on each party of £20m, with one-tenth of that figure allowable for third-party spenders. The recommendation has attracted some criticism, due to the difficulty of policing the limit effectively.

The main Neill recommendations on electoral expenditure were:

- a limit of £20 million on national campaign expenditure by each political party contesting at least 600 seats (including benefits in kind) in addition to the maintenance of local limits;
- a lower proportional limit for the seats contested for elections to devolved assemblies: £1.5 million for Scotland, £600,000 for Wales and £300,000 for Northern Ireland. Local limits were recommended for constituency members;
- a national limit on expenditure on elections to the European Parliament of £3.5 million, with no separate limits on candidates or regional lists;
- limits on spending by third-party groups, such as pressure groups, which

would have to register if they wished to incur expenditure on elections or referendums;

- revision of the Representation of the People Act 1983 to contain a full and up-to-date list of expenditure items;
- an independent electoral commission which would scrutinise expenditure by political parties, among other duties;
- new limit of £100,000 for by-elections.

The government accepted these proposals in outline and legislation is expected before the next general election. The main change is to apply controls on expenditure by separate periods of time, dependent on which elections take place in each period.[10]

SETTING THE BOUNDARIES

Establishing where the boundaries of constituencies should fall is of crucial importance to politicians. Just how crucial is shown by the fact that at the 1997 election over 400 of the seats being fought had new boundaries. But this process of redistribution cannot be left to the political parties, as each could seek to redraw the boundaries to its own advantage.

The present electoral system, FPTP, evolved from the medieval roots of the House of Commons when each community sent its local representative to Westminster. What reform there has been has concentrated on the need to ensure that constituencies are of roughly equal size. The first step came with the Great Reform Act 1832 which at least ensured some representation of populous areas such as Manchester and Liverpool, but it was not until 1944 that permanent machinery was established to review constituency size consistently in the form of boundary commissions.

The system has been subject to change in the fifty years since then, for there is a basic conflict between the disruption to local ties which redistribution brings and the need to ensure numerical equality. The most recent amendment was under the Conservatives in 1992,[11] when the process of review was speeded up to ensure reviews under way were completed by 1995. This gave rise to comment that the motive was to ensure that the reviews were implemented before the following general election, as reviews generally favour the Conservatives because of the trend of population movement. However, the 1992 Act also reduced the timescale for future reviews, which seems sensible given the increasing mobility of the population.

Although the boundary commissioners themselves are recognised as strictly impartial, the process over which they preside is deeply party-political. How boundaries are determined has a major effect on electoral outcomes. The commissioners are bound by a set of general rules which require them to take account of local ties while also achieving numerical equality. The broad framing of the rules and their internal inconsistency has allowed the commissioners considerable discretion. The normal procedure in England is to consider each county and

London borough separately and to publish provisional recommendations; if objected to, there is a public inquiry, after which the provisional recommendations are either confirmed or modified. The inquiry is normally presided over by a barrister, who is appointed an assistant commissioner. The political parties and other interested groups will argue about the provisional recommendations in terms of local ties, disruption or numerical equality and will present counter-proposals. Political considerations are never raised overtly, since these are inadmissable factors, but are implicit in the cases put by the parties.

The importance of the local inquiry in modifying the original proposals is well established, and the party which organises a coherent national strategy in relation to the review process is likely to benefit, as did the Labour Party in the most recent review completed in 1995. A good example of this is provided by Leicestershire, where an extra seat had provisionally been recommended for the south of the county. A Labour counter-proposal successfully set the agenda at the subsequent inquiry and opposition from Conservative representatives tended to be piecemeal rather than strategic. The assistant commissioner accepted the counter-proposal on the basis that it caused minimal disruption and achieved reasonably balanced sizes.[12] In the last review the commissioners tended to prefer a 'doughnut' shape, differentiating between urban and rural areas, over a 'sandwich' shape, incorporating both town and rural hinterland, so constituencies with an urban (Labour) core were created undiluted by outlying (Conservative) villages.

Fifty years ago there was an electoral bias towards the Conservatives because rural seats were smaller than those in the cities where Labour had its base. The balance has now changed, with average electorates in urban areas smaller than in rural areas. The result is that, if Labour and Conservative had received an equal share of votes at the 1997 election, Labour would still have won the election by 82 seats.

The internal contradictions of the rules have led to problems for the commissioners, as there is an in-built mechanism which tends to increase the number of seats at each review.[13] An electoral 'quota' is established by dividing the number of electors by the number of constituencies in each separate part of the United Kingdom; and the commissioners then try to draw boundaries which will bring each constituency as close as possible to the quota. At successive redistributions the divisor used to calculate the quota has increased, since each review has recommended more seats; and this, combined with the tendency to round up the number of seats to fit within county boundaries and the allocation of some seats on geographical grounds (such as in the Highlands and Islands) inevitably produces a steady rise in the number of seats. The rules themselves arose from a series of political compromises made at the Speaker's Conference in 1944 and their illogicality has been compounded by subsequent modifications and differing interpretations by the four separate commissions (for England, Wales, Northern Ireland and Scotland). In addition the rules allow Scotland and Wales to be over-represented in terms of seats per population (see box, p. 73).

Pressure has grown for a fresh look at the whole system and there are proposals for an independent electoral commission with responsibility for all aspects of electoral organisation and conduct. Any major change is likely to be brokered by

---

Representation in the constituent parts of the United Kingdom

The average constituency electorates in 1997 in the four countries were:

England	69,577
Wales	55,563
Scotland	55,339
Northern Ireland	66,122

The United Kingdom average was 67,077.

If each country had an average electorate at the UK average, the number of seats would be:

England	549	(compared with 529 at present)
Wales	33	(compared with 40 at present)
Scotland	59	(compared with 72 at present)
Northern Ireland	18	(the same as now)

If each country had an electorate at the *English* average, the number of seats would be:

England	529
Wales	32
Scotland	57
Northern Ireland	17

The total size of the House of Commons would be 635.

---

the political parties, with or without an independent electoral commission. A start has already been made in Scotland, where the next review must use the electoral quota for England when calculating numbers of seats, and this will have the effect of reducing the number of Scottish seats by up to ten. However, such piecemeal reform does not resolve the major problem, which is the built-in inflation in the number of seats (see Table 3.2). A solution might come if proportional representation were to be introduced for Westminster elections, as this would require a radical restructuring of constituencies. The Jenkins Commission has already called for a complete review of the boundary commission rules and procedure, and the introduction of a UK electoral quota.

ELECTORAL BEHAVIOUR: HOW PEOPLE VOTE

Having looked at how elections in Britain are organised, we can now turn to how people behave in them. Those who study post-war elections in the United

Table 3.2 Seats in the House of Commons, 1945–97

	England	Wales	Scotland	Northern Ireland	United Kingdom
1945	510	35	71	12	640[a]
1950	506	36	71	12	625
1955	511	36	71	12	630
1974 (Feb)	516	36	71	12	635
1983	523	38	72	17	650
1992	524	38	72	17	651
1997	529	40	72	18	659

Note
[a] Includes 12 university seats. These were abolished subsequently.

Kingdom tend to divide the period into two. The period from 1950 to 1970 is regarded as an era of *alignment*, during which the electorate was divided into two large groups which gave stable and reliable support to the Conservative and Labour parties at every level of politics in Britain. During this period the Liberal Party was relatively weak, as can be seen from its general election performance. On the whole, voters tended to identify themselves with a particular party – generally Labour or Conservative – and, even though their votes might have sometimes changed from election to election, that party link remained. This identification is known as *partisan alignment*. Such strength of party identification obviously had an effect on electoral behaviour: those who identify strongly with particular parties are more likely to vote for the party with which they identify, to vote for the same party over time, and to turn out and vote at all.

Many different factors can influence the way people vote, and the way they align themselves with particular political parties. During the 1950s and 1960s, the most important factor found to influence party choice was social class. As Peter Pulzer memorably put it at the time: 'Class is the basis of British party politics; all else is embellishment and detail.'[14] Four-fifths of middle-class voters regularly voted Conservative and some two-thirds of the working class supported Labour. While other factors – for example, age, gender, area of residence and religion – clearly had an effect both on longer-term alignment and on voting in particular elections, every survey and study of voting found that class was the overwhelmingly most important influence. Electoral change did, of course, take place. This was mainly due to the influence of relatively small numbers of 'floating voters' changing their votes and others who switched between voting and not voting (or vice versa) at successive elections. The influences on such electors were many, but tended to include short-term factors such as the state of the economy or perceptions of the performance of the parties.

The period since 1970 has been rather different. Although the dominance of Conservative and Labour has been maintained in the House of Commons, that has been at least in part the result of the first-past-the-post British electoral system. The long-standing foundations of the dominant two-party system have been progressively undermined. This has been particularly obvious in local government, where since 1995 there have been considerably more Liberal Democrat than Conservative councils. At the same time, the nationalist parties have become more successful in Scotland and Wales and, in general, electoral volatility has replaced the stability of the previous two decades. In short, a process of *dealignment* appears to have taken place.

Surveys such as the British Election Study continue to show that the majority of electors continue to identify with a particular party, but that the strength of that identification has become progressively weaker. In the 1960s, for example, more than 40 per cent of electors said that they were 'very strong' party supporters; by the 1990s, fewer than 20 per cent regarded themselves as such. At the same time, there is evidence to show that the extent to which voters identify themselves with either the Labour or Conservative parties has also fallen. In other words, the core support for the two main parties, on which they used to be able to rely from year to year, is now much smaller.

A range of reasons for this progressive weakening in party identification (or *partisan dealignment*) has been put forward. One is that voters have become more politically aware and, as a result, have been more able to make up their own minds on the relative merits of political parties whereas in the past a straightforward identification with a particular party simplified a complex political world for the individual elector. There has certainly been increased access to education over the last three decades and there is some evidence to show that those with more education at higher levels tend to identify less with a particular party. There has also been greatly increased ownership of televisions coupled with greater coverage of politics on television, contrasting with a progressive reduction in coverage of proceedings in Parliament in the national press. This is likely to have increased political awareness in general and exposed partisans to alternative views and may also, paradoxically, have contributed to the growing distrust of politicians, who came to seem less Olympian than those of a previous generation.

Another factor that may help to explain partisan dealignment is the way in which governments are perceived to have performed in practice. Relative economic decline, with governments blown off course as they struggled to cope with the demands of a global economy, created a legacy of policy failures and reversals. Survey evidence confirms the electoral effect of this: typically more than 40 per cent of electors approved the record of the government (of either political persuasion) in the 1950s and early 1960s, while by the 1990s this proportion had fallen to 30 per cent or less and in the (perhaps exceptional) period from 1992 to 1997 averaged just 15 per cent. In parallel with the process of partisan dealignment, there seems also to have been at least some process of *class dealignment*. This has not been confined to the United Kingdom: as one study put it, 'almost all of the [fourteen] countries we have studied show a decline during our period in the ability of social cleavages to structure individual voting choice.'[15] There has been a lengthy, if inconclusive, academic debate about the extent of class dealignment and its impact on voting patterns[16]: while there have undoubtedly been considerable changes in the social structures of the United Kingdom since 1945, the extent to which these changes have affected voting behaviour is much less certain. What is more certain is that the British electorate is now less rigidly aligned with specific parties than it once was, although there remain important social influences on the ways in which people vote – with class still the most important. While some of these influences, such as age and gender, may be less important than in the past, others (such as region and locality) remain influential, while new factors have also emerged. For example, all the available evidence suggests that ethnic minority voters strongly support the Labour Party.

A further factor which appears to some extent to have filled the gap left by the decline of stable party identification is *issue voting*. Voters have become more aware of and responsive to political debate, often on particular issues such as the government's handling of the economy, and form opinions and make electoral judgements on that basis. In other words, electors have become more rational and instrumental in their voting behaviour, increasingly aware of individual issues and, as a result, less habitually loyal to one of the two main parties, more willing to support other parties, change their vote, or even to switch from voting to not voting or vice versa.

The Conservative victories in four successive elections from 1979 to 1992 cannot, however, simply be explained by issue-voting overcoming the effects of a dealigned electorate. In 1987 and 1992, at least, Labour led on most of the most salient issues. Other factors clearly played their part. These include, in different ways, the degree of personal economic optimism, the popularity of the respective party leaders, general perceptions of the parties and the strong support for the Conservatives in the majority of the national press during the period. Such factors seem to have over-ridden the longer-term effects of partisan and class dealignment which might otherwise have been expected to produce more frequent changes in governments. In this sense the stability in electoral outcomes during the period concealed the underlying development of a much less stable electorate, more prone than before to be influenced by a range of short-term factors. Seen in this way, the landslide reversal of electoral fortunes in the 1997 general election – paradoxically occurring when the economic situation alone would have suggested a different result – confirms this trend rather than confounds it.[17]

THE 1997 GENERAL ELECTION

Among the reasons for the dramatic results in the 1997 general election was that those factors that had worked to the Conservatives' advantage in previous years had changed. Following the 1992 election, the party lost its reputation for economic competence, lost the support of much of the national press and faced a new Labour leader who was more popular than their own. Between 1992 and 1997, the electorate behaved in a typically 'dealigned' manner, with high levels of volatility in opinion polls and elections at all levels. The 1997 election saw Labour elected with the highest swing and the largest majority in the House of Commons since the Second World War. The Conservative share of the vote was the party's lowest since 1832 and their 165 seats the party's fewest since 1906. The Conservatives won no seats at all in Wales or Scotland and the vast majority of the seats they won in England were rural or suburban. The Liberal Democrat vote was lower in 1997 than in 1992, but the party more than doubled its representation in the House of Commons. The level of turnout was the lowest since 1935.

The results are summarised in Appendix 3 (Tables A.2–4). The swing from Conservative to Labour (in Great Britain) was 10.2 per cent. Swing, the term used for the average of one party's gain and another's loss of share of vote between two elections,[18] remains a commonly used measure of electoral change, but it has limitations. Swing is essentially a two-dimensional concept, useful when a political system is dominated by just two parties but less useful when three or more parties feature strongly. It cannot take into account flows of the vote between the two major parties and minor parties, nor between the minor parties themselves, nor between voting and non-voting. With the increasing electoral success of the Liberal Democrats, and the nationalist parties in Scotland and Wales, it has become more useful to examine aggregate electoral change by looking at changes between two elections in each party's share of the vote.

Labour's share of the vote in Great Britain rose by 9.1 per cent between 1992 and 1997. It rose by most in the south of the country, where Labour has traditionally had little success outside the conurbations. In Greater London it rose by 12.4 per cent and in the rest of the South East by 11.1 per cent. By contrast it rose by only 9.3 per cent in the North West and 7.6 per cent in Yorkshire and Humberside, though it did increase by 10.3 per cent in the northern region. In Scotland it rose by 6.6 per cent and in Wales by 5.5 per cent. The Conservatives' loss of votes mirrored these changes in many ways: their share fell by 14.1 per cent in London and 13.2 per cent in the rest of the South East, but by 10 per cent in Yorkshire and Humberside, 10.7 per cent in the North West, 8.1 per cent in Scotland and 9.0 per cent in Wales.

The Liberal Democrat share of the vote fell by a small amount in all regions. The nature of the British electoral system and the effects of tactical campaigning and tactical voting are well illustrated by the Liberal Democrats. In the South West region, where they are the second party in terms of votes, their share fell by 0.1 per cent but they more than doubled their number of seats in the region from six to fourteen. In Greater London the party's share of the vote fell by 1.3 per cent but the number of seats it won rose from one to six, while in the rest of the South East, with no seats in 1992, the party won eight despite a fall in its share of the vote from 23.3 per cent to 21.4 per cent.

The exit polls carried out among people leaving polling stations are the basis for an analysis of individual voting patterns in 1997. What they reveal is shown in Table 3.3.

Some features of voting patterns in 1997 are particularly interesting. For many years there has been a gender gap at British elections, with a larger proportion of women voting Conservative than men. The Harris/ITN exit polls carried out between 1979 and 1992 show the difference to be between 2 and 4 per cent: in 1979, for example, 43 per cent of men but 46 per cent of women voted Conservative

Table 3.3 The 1997 general election: How people voted

	Voting in 1997 (%)			Change from 1992 (%)		
	Lab	*Con*	*Lib Dem*	*Lab*	*Con*	*Lib Dem*
Gender						
Men	45	31	17	+8	−11	0
Women	45	32	17	+11	−12	−2
All	44	31	17	+9	−11	−1
Age						
18 to 29	56	22	18	+18	−19	+1
30 to 44	49	26	17	+15	−15	−5
45 to 64	43	33	18	+9	−14	+1
65 and over	34	44	17	−1	−3	+1
Social grade						
AB	31	42	21	+11	−14	0
C1	47	26	19	+15	−15	−4
C2	54	25	14	+13	−13	−4
DE	61	21	13	+15	−16	−2

Source: P. Kellner, *Parliamentary Affairs*, October 1997.

Note
Data from BBC/NOP exit polls, adjusted to match the election result.

while 39 per cent of men and 36 per cent of women voted Labour. In 1997 the gender gap seems finally to have disappeared, in an election with an increasing focus on women candidates and which resulted in a doubling of the number of women elected.

There is a clear correlation between age and voting for the two main parties, though the Liberal Democrats draw support equally from all age groups. The strong preference for Labour among younger voters has not always been evident – indeed, the Conservatives led Labour in this age group in 1983 and 1987. The swing in 1997 from Conservative to Labour among 18–29-year-olds was 19 per cent, and Labour finished with a margin of 34 per cent over the Conservatives in this age group. In older groups, the Conservatives held decisive leads in elections from 1979 to 1992 (with the one exception of 1992 when the two parties were neck and neck in the 30–44 age group), but Labour led among all those of working age in 1997. A Conservative lead was only to be found among pensioners and even this is not confirmed by pre-election surveys: MORI's aggregate campaign polls showed a 5 per cent Labour lead among the over-65s.

It can also be seen from the table that there remains a clear social class-related gradient in voting patterns for all three main parties, albeit shallower than in the past, but there was little difference between the social grades in terms of swing since 1992. Nonetheless, the electorate's judgements about issues, the Government's record, feelings about the parties and the ability of the party leaders all played their part too. While the changes from 1992 to 1997 demonstrate that

Britain has a dealigned electorate, it is clear that shorter-term influences play an increasingly important role. This makes the explanation of voting behaviour, never an exact science, ever more difficult.

THE ELECTORAL SYSTEM

The issues at stake

It is central to our approach to argue that the issues at stake between different sorts of electoral systems are not primarily technical ones, but rather raise some of the deepest questions about the nature of representation, the role of parties and the nature and scope of assemblies and parliaments.

(*Interim Report of the Working Party on Electoral Systems* (Plant Report) for the Labour Party in 1991)

Britain has always used the first-past-the-post system for elections. However, one of the earliest proponents of proportional representation (PR) – designed to match votes cast with seats won as closely as possible – was the distinguished British thinker John Stuart Mill, who wanted in the 1860s to introduce the single transferable vote (STV), the system traditionally supported by the Liberal Democrats and many electoral reformers today. The advent of a mass electorate in the nineteenth century seems to have been the main force behind the consideration of alternative electoral systems (see box, p. 80), as representation of different groups in society seemed more appropriate than merely territorial representation, and as fears grew about the rejection of independent-minded MPs by powerful party machines.

Prompted by growing party realignment and political tension, a royal commission in 1909–10 advocated the alternative vote (AV) for the Commons while a Speaker's Conference of 1917 recommended STV in constituencies returning between three and seven MPs and AV in single-member constituencies. In 1917 and 1930 government bills were passed by the Commons which would have introduced AV into British elections, but both failed to reach the statute book because of intra-party splits and tactical opposition from the Lords. Interest in electoral reform only revived in the 1970s and 1980s, when the two-party dominance began to be challenged by a resurgent Liberal Party and nationalist parties. Following the Troubles in Northern Ireland, proportional representation was introduced in its STV form for Assembly and local elections there from 1973 and for the European Parliament from 1979. STV had also been used for elections to university seats in Britain until their abolition from 1950.

The creation of the Social Democratic Party (SDP) in 1981 and its subsequent alliance with the Liberals focused attention on electoral reform, while the demand for devolution in Scotland led to intense debate about appropriate forms of

Electoral systems: The main options

First past the post (FPTP)

MPs represent geographical constituencies and each constituency elects its own representative to Parliament in contests in which the candidate with the most votes wins. The rise of party government has undermined the rationale behind FPTP but its defenders argue that it helps to create effective government since voters are offered clear alternatives, rather than simply registering a party preference. Its detractors claim that many votes are wasted since electors voting for a party in a particular area cannot affect the overall result if they are outnumbered by supporters of a different party in that constituency and seats won are not proportional to votes cast. It is used in the United Kingdom, United States, Canada and India, among others.

Alternative vote (AV)

The alternative vote is an attempt to overcome one of the main drawbacks of FPTP, that a candidate may be elected on a minority of votes. AV demands that the candidate elected must have a majority of the votes cast. The voter lists preferences, and the candidate with least votes is eliminated and the second preference votes are distributed. The process continues until one candidate reaches an absolute majority. Variations are 1) the *supplementary vote* (SV), where only two preferences are allowed and all but the top two candidates are eliminated, and 2) the *second ballot*, where there is a first round, with a gap of some days before the second round when electors vote again, with all but the leading candidates having been eliminated.

AV retains the constituency link, but encourages alliances between parties and does little to counteract the effects of uneven geographical distribution of electoral support, which disadvantages parties such as the Liberal Democrats whose support is spread relatively evenly through the country. It can have a capricious effect in four-party systems, such as Scotland. It can also be highly disproportional. AV is used in Australian House of Representatives elections, and a second ballot is used for French Assembly and presidential elections. SV will be used for the London Mayor elections.

Additional member system (AMS)

Electors have two votes at one ballot. A proportion of seats are constituency seats where the members are elected through FPTP and the elector votes for an individual, and a proportion are grouped either regionally or nationally and electors vote for parties on a list. Each time a party gains enough votes to be allocated a seat, the candidate at the top of the relevant list is elected. The votes are counted first for the constituency seats and then the additional list seats are allocated in a way that corrects for disproportionality (with the aim of ensuring that a party which had a 30 per cent share of the vote in a particular region should gain 30 per cent of all that region's seats, whether constituency or list). AMS therefore retains a constituency link while injecting some proportionality, since all votes count. Its opponents argue that this system can hand power to a small party of the centre, since voters can use their second vote to select a coalition partner for their party of choice (as occurred with the Free Democrats in Germany until 1998), and that the party bureaucracy is given too much power through manipulation of the lists of candidates. AMS has been chosen for the Scottish Parliament, the Welsh Assembly and the Assembly for London elections, in order to prevent new assemblies being otherwise dominated by a single party. AMS has been used in Germany since the Second World War and was introduced into New Zealand in 1996 (but is known there as mixed member proportional (MMP)).

Single transferable vote (STV)
This system is designed to give the voter maximum freedom of choice, since the elector lists candidates in order of preference in a multi-member constituency. A candidate is elected once their votes reach the relevant quota and any excess votes over this quota are then transferred, according to the second preferences of the voters, so that other candidates can reach the quota. Candidates with insufficient votes are eliminated and their preferences transferred until all the seats in the constituency are filled. Voters can choose between candidates of the same party as well as between those of different parties; and STV turns all seats into marginal seats, which may increase the responsiveness of MPs. However, it needs multi-member constituencies to operate and tends to create factions in larger parties. It can also encourage MPs to concentrate on local politics since no seats are safe. It is used in Irish Dail elections, for the Australian Senate and in Northern Ireland local, Assembly and European Parliament elections.

Party list systems
This requires multi-member constituencies where the voter chooses between the lists of different parties, but cannot normally reorder the list of candidates (although some variants exist, as in Belgium, where preference for individuals can be given). Seats in the constituency are allocated between the parties according to their share of the vote. Whenever a party wins a seat, the highest candidate on the list is elected. It gives great power to the party, and is most commonly used in continental Europe, where the constituency link is considered less important than in Britain. The formula used to distribute the seats is important as it can be weighted to encourage larger or smaller parties. Opponents claim that party lists can encourage each strand of opinion to be represented in a different party, resulting in fragile coalitions, although many countries using the system have enjoyed long periods of stable government. It was used for the British elections to the European Parliament in 1999, on the grounds that this body does not have major executive functions and that nearly all EU states use a variant of party lists.

electoral systems. The Scottish Constitutional Convention, a wide coalition of supporters of devolution, eventually supported the additional member system (AMS) for a Scottish Parliament, and this was implemented in the Scotland Act 1998. Labour representatives accepted AMS as a way of calming fears about domination of the Parliament by their party, as occurs with the Scottish seats at Westminster. Similar arrangements have been made for Wales, though without a preceding political consensus.

The key to change on this whole issue has been internal debate within the Labour Party. Having been out of power since 1979, it considered with a new seriousness the possibility of change in many constitutional areas and drew conclusions from arguments about the fragmentation of the anti-Conservative vote. In 1990 Labour set up a working party on electoral reform under Raymond Plant, a professor of politics at Southampton University (see box, p. 79). It produced an initial document, *Democracy, Representation and Elections*, which identified relevant issues and discussed alternative voting systems, without coming to any firm conclusions beyond the fact that all systems had their attractions and difficulties for different purposes. Its final report in 1993[19] recommended by a narrow majority the supplementary vote (SV) for the Commons, and regional list systems for a second chamber replacing the Lords, and for the European Parliament.

During the 1992 election Labour was neutral on electoral reform but there was an important development soon afterwards. Once its National Executive Committee had considered the Plant report, John Smith – as the new leader – publicly committed the party to a referendum on the future of the electoral system for Westminster in the first Parliament of a Labour government. John Smith was personally unconvinced of the need for change, a stance shared by his successor, Tony Blair, who told the *Economist* in September 1996 that: 'it is not, as some claim, a simple question of moving from an 'unfair' to a 'fair' voting system. An electoral system must meet two democratic tests: it needs to reflect opinion, but it must also aggregate opinion without giving disproportionate influence to splinter groups. Aggregation is particularly important for a parliament whose job is to create and sustain a single, mainstream government.'[20]

Nevertheless, Tony Blair reaffirmed the commitment to a referendum after becoming party leader in 1994 and the Labour/Liberal Democrat joint consultative committee on constitutional change which reported in March 1997 proposed a referendum in the first Parliament after the general election, preceded by an electoral commission which would recommend an appropriate proportional alternative to FPTP that would provide the choice in the referendum.

In December 1997 an independent advisory commission on the voting system was duly announced, headed by Lord Jenkins of Hillhead, a founder of the Social Democratic Party and a prominent Liberal Democrat. There were also Conservative and Labour representatives, together with non-aligned figures. Emphasis on a constituency link and stable government in the terms of reference established the parameters of the systems on offer. To some, the terms of reference appeared difficult, if not impossible, to reconcile (see box, p. 83).

The reform agenda

The Commission shall observe the requirement for broad proportionality, the need for stable government, an extension of voter choice and the maintenance of a link between hon Members and geographical constituencies.

(Extract from the Terms of Reference of the Jenkins Commission, given in Cmnd. 4090, October 1998)

Apart from setting up the Jenkins Commission, the Labour government had already begun to adopt new electoral systems for other types of parliaments and assemblies, even while reserving its position on Westminster (see Table 3.4).

The Scottish Parliament has 129 members initially, with 73 elected under first past the post and 56 under regional party lists. The Welsh Assembly has 60 members with 40 under FPTP and 20 under regional party lists. AMS is also being used for elections to the Assembly for London, but this has only 14 constituency and 11 list members. The new Assembly for Northern Ireland uses STV as part of the deal brokered between the different parties there.

The arguments put forward by the Government in support of AMS in Scotland, Wales and London might also seem to resonate for Westminster: wider and more consensual representation of opinions and parties, and greater opportunities for the election of women and minorities. Supporters of the Scottish Parliament have already begun to examine the arguments for PR in local councils as an opportunity to end local one-party states. It seems likely that the arguments and examples from Scotland and elsewhere will have an impact on the debate about Westminster elections.

The government has introduced a different form of electoral system for elections to the European Parliament – in the form of the regional list, which removes any single-member constituency element. This presents voters with a novel kind of ballot paper (see Figure 3.1).

There is a long history of attempts within the European Community/Union to develop a uniform system of elections to the European Parliament, something vigorously opposed by Conservative governments. A commitment to change was made by Labour in 1993, and activated in 1997, even though the party was likely to be the main loser under the new system in the 1999 elections (under FPTP there is a disproportionate benefit in numbers of seats for the party with the highest percentage of the vote, which worked to Labour's advantage in the previous election of 1994).

The regional list system has been criticised for allowing too much power to political parties, which allocate the order of candidates on the list, but it is argued that this is defensible for a body such as the European Parliament which does not have executive powers and which has not placed value on constituency links. Claims that a new system for European Parliament elections does not create a precedent for Westminster therefore have more validity than the equivalent

Table 3.4 New electoral systems in the United Kingdom

	Scottish Parliament	Welsh Parliament	European Parliament	Northern Ireland Assembly	London mayor	London Assembly
Franchise	Local	Local	Parliamentary and peers and EU citizens	Local	Local	Local
System	AMS	AMS	Regional list (STV in Northern Ireland)	STV	SV	AMS
No. of seats	Constituency 73 List 56 Total 129	Constituency 40 List 20 Total 60	71 England (9 regions) 8 Scotland 5 Wales 3 Northern Ireland	108 (6 seats for each of 18 Parliamentary constituencies)	1	Constituency 14 List 11 Total 25
Date of election	6 May 1999	6 May 1999	10 June 1999	22 May 1998	4 May 2000	4 May 2000
Deposit	£500 per candidate in constituency £500 per list 5% threshold	£500 per candidate in constituency £500 per list 5% threshold	£5,000 per list 2.5% threshold	5% threshold	£10,000 deposit with 330 signatures 5% threshold	£1,000 per candidate in constituency 5% threshold £5,000 per list 2.5% threshold

Election for the European Parliament

SOUTHWEST REGION ■ 7 SEATS

You vote for a party or an independent, not for individual candidates.

Parties win seats according to the share of votes they get. Names are taken from the top of each party's list to fill their seats.

You have <u>one</u> vote.

Mark an ☒ in one box.

☐ 🦅	☐ 🦅	☐ 🌻	☐	☐ 🌹	☐	☐
Conservative party	**Liberal Democrats**	**Green party**	**Cornish Alliance**	**Labour party**	**Independent: No federal Europe**	**Independent: Socialist**
Lord Plumb MEP	Robin Teverson MEP	Colin Anderson	Jack Cowan	Ian White MEP	Clive Kitchen	Rosie Kane
Bryan Cassidy MEP	Graham Watson MEP	Richard Smith	Ian Fraser	Peter Jackson		
Sheila Jones	Mark Peters	Patrick Annerley	Euan Hazlitt	Helen Jones		
Giles Chichester MEP	Sheila Johnson	Jason Fisher		Nigel Ely		
Caroline Jackson MEP	Margaret Isherwood			Fraser Tyndale		
Peter Wiley	Sonia Hallett			John Hanna		
Justin Fletcher	Richard Pascoe			Rachel Kelmscott		

Figure 3.1 Sample ballot paper for European elections in 1999

Source: Constitution Unit, January 1999.

argument in respect of the changes for Scotland and Wales. However, the accept-ance of proportional systems and increased familiarity with their use seems to electoral reform supporters to be undermining the case for FPTP. The fact that Labour has approved the supplementary vote (SV) for the election of a mayor for London can only intensify the arguments in SV's favour for the election of MPs. Whatever happens, a programme of voter education will be required to familiarise electors with the various new systems.

ELECTORAL REFORM: THE ARGUMENTS

The long-running debate on electoral reform entered a new phase when the Blair government set up an independent electoral commission to devise the form of electoral system to be tested against FPTP in a referendum. However, politicians remain divided on the issue, and surveys indicate that the public is not convinced of the need for change. Supporters of reform are faced with the task of persuad-ing people that such a major upheaval is necessary to improve British political life, for a desire to experiment with electoral systems as an end in itself is unlikely to win wide support. In New Zealand, for example, the additional member system (AMS) was voted for by an electorate which had become disenchanted with the two major parties and wanted a break with the recent past but polls taken a year after its first use in the 1996 election indicated that most electors would like to change back to FPTP.

Supporters and opponents of reform tend not to address each other's argu-ments, as they do not necessarily accept each other's premises. For example, supporters of FPTP tend to favour strong governments as good in themselves, whereas advocates of reform express fears about an over-mighty executive in a Parliament dominated by a single party. Reformers deploy arguments about Par-liament's role in reflecting public opinion (an 'input' argument), whereas pro-ponents of FPTP emphasise its role as the place where governments are formed (an 'outcome' argument). The main issues at stake concern fairness, the constitu-ency link, effective government and effective representation: let us look briefly at each of these in turn.

Fairness

Fairness is a central theme for supporters of proportional representation, who seek to match seats to votes. It subsumes arguments about wasted votes (votes not necessary for a candidate to win and votes given to losing candidates), and about the discrimination against smaller parties which are not concentrated in particular geographical areas. The statistical evidence about FPTP's lack of proportionality or fairness can be illustrated by the 1997 election (see Table 3.5).

It can be seen that Labour's landslide victory in 1997 was only a landslide because its 44 per cent share of the vote delivered 65 per cent of the seats. Elections which produce obviously disproportionate results usually encourage

Table 3.5 Unfair? Votes and seats in 1997

	Vote share (%)	Seats	Seat share (%)	Seats if proportional
England				
Lab	43.5	328	62.0	231
Con	33.7	165	31.2	178
Lib Dem	18.0	34	6.4	95
Ref	2.9	–	–	15
Other	1.9	2	0.4	10 [a]
Wales				
Lab	54.7	34	85.0	22
Con	19.6	–	–	8
Lib Dem	12.3	2	5.0	5
PC	9.9	4	10.0	4
Ref	2.4	–	–	1
Other	1.0	–	–	–
Scotland				
Lab	45.6	56	77.8	33
Con	17.5	–	–	13
Lib Dem	13.0	10	13.9	9
SNP	22.1	6	8.3	16
Ref	1.0	–	–	1
Other	0.9	–	–	–
Great Britain				
Lab	44.3	418	65.2	286
Con	31.5	165	25.7	199
Lib Dem	17.2	46	7.2	109
PC/SNP	2.6	10	1.6	20
Ref	2.7	–	–	17
Other	1.8	2	0.3	10 [a]

Note
[a]   Assumes for illustrative purposes that 'others' are a single party.

public support for changes in the voting system. This is compounded on those occasions when the disproportionality is combined with a failure of any party to achieve an overall majority of seats, as in February 1974, thereby undermining the claim of FPTP to produce strong governments.

However, supporters of FPTP argue that strict proportionality is not required, for the will of the people is broadly represented in the party which has developed a strategy to win the largest number of seats. It is the party which must adapt to the requirement of the electoral system, as opponents of PR in Labour's Plant commission noted: 'if [Labour's] policies have not been found to be acceptable in certain areas and regions of the country or, say, in rural constituencies, then it is to our policies, our organisation and our presentation that we should turn, rather than to an alteration of the electoral system'. On this view, the party's ability to win the 1997 general election vindicates this argument.

The constituency link

Supporters of FPTP emphasise the importance of the link between individual MPs and their constituencies. It is claimed that, once elected, MPs represent all their constituents. However, as one former MP puts it: 'what little empirical evidence there is suggests that MPs have grossly inflated ideas about their impact on the constituency.'[21] Nevertheless, the strong tradition of a personal relationship with a defined geographic area and the fact that MPs themselves would need to approve any alternative, has led some supporters of electoral reform to advocate either AV or AMS because they retain that link – and this condition was built into the terms of reference of the Jenkins Commission. By contrast, STV depends on multi-member constituencies, and Irish politics is often used to illustrate the danger of MPs in the same constituency competing against each other through excessively local activity. On the other hand, this might suggest that STV and multi-member constituencies produce more responsive representatives and greater voter choice than FPTP.

Effective government

Strictly speaking, outcome arguments are irrelevant to those who want greater 'fairness' in representation, but supporters of change nevertheless have to address the practical consequences of change. Supporters of FPTP place much of their emphasis on the need to ensure an effective government. They dislike the idea of coalitions and argue that proportional systems actually give disproportionate power to small parties when it comes to forming governments. Some evidence of this comes from a study which 'replays' the 1997 election under different electoral systems, using survey evidence about second preference votes and assumptions about how existing constituencies would be grouped (Table 3.6).

It is clear that different systems can produce substantially different results, both in terms of the balance between the two main parties and in the strength of smaller parties (which gain from every alternative to FPTP). Under these assumptions, the alternative vote system would have produced a result *more* disproportionate in 1997 than FPTP, while a classic additional member system, with half the seats elected proportionately, would not have produced a majority government at all.

In the 1970s, when there appeared to be sharp ideological differences between the Labour and Conservative parties, political scientists such as S. E. Finer[22] argued that the need to define themselves to the voters pushed the parties in 'adversarial' two-party systems further apart, leading to frequent and damaging policy changes. In the early 1990s, however, other commentators suggested that the need to appeal to as much of the electorate as possible led the two parties to strive for the centre ground and to form broad coalitions of interests and opinions,

Table 3.6 Election replay: The 1997 election under different voting systems

	Lab[a]	*Con*	*Lib Dem*	*Other*	*Labour majority*
Supplementary vote	436	110	84	29	213
Alternative vote	436	110	84	29	213
Actual (first past the post)	419	165	46	29	179
AV plus – 85% locally elected	378	160	89	32	97
AV plus – 80% locally elected	359	175	91	34	59
AMS – 83% locally elected	354	190	82	33	49
Single transferable vote	342	144	131	42	25
Pure proportionality	286	199	109	65	−87

Sources: P. Dunleavy, H. Margetts and S. Weir, *Making Votes Count 2*, Democratic Audit, 1998: P. Dunleavy and H. Margetts, *The Performance of the Commission's Schemes for a New Electoral System*, LSE Public Policy Group/Birkbeck Policy Centre, September 1998.

Notes
Simulated results for SV plus are the same as for AV plus.
[a] Includes Speaker where appropriate.

rather than representing a narrower strand. Much seems to depend on the particular political culture of the time as to which theory is most appropriate. Electoral systems are just one element in a much larger picture.

For example, FPTP does not necessarily create stable single-party government; eight of the past twenty-six election results have been indecisive and if FPTP started to produce a consistent string of indecisive results its basic rationale might be thought to disappear. Equally, PR is strongly associated with coalition governments, but countries such as Spain and Portugal have formed majority governments using party lists. Supporters of FPTP argue that coalitions are managed by parties, not voters, with inevitable compromises over policies resulting in actions never endorsed by the electorate and with a loss of clear accountability. Supporters of PR counter this by arguing that parties should bargain with the true variety of opinion in the country as accurately represented, and that voters can be presented with likely coalition partners before an election. What all this reveals is that arguments about multi-party versus two-party systems tend to be highly subjective and depend on different views of what makes for effective government. Moreover, there might well be a very similar range of policy options available in practice under a coalition as under single-party government.

Effective representation

Proponents of PR stress the importance of representing the nation effectively in its parliament, and consider the under-representation of groups such as women and ethnic minorities as anti-democratic. There have only ever been thirteen MPs from ethnic minorities. Nine were elected in 1997, all from the Labour Party. The first woman MP was elected in 1918, but the total of 120 women elected at the 1997 general election was almost double the previous record (see Figure 3.2).

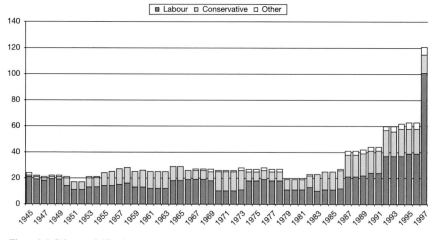

Figure 3.2 Women MPs since 1945

However, the effects of a change in the electoral system on the representation of different sections of the population may be difficult to disentangle from wider cultural developments. Ireland has a small proportion of women MPs despite STV, but list systems in Europe have tended to promote greater representation of women. There is some evidence that in single-member constituencies local selectors have tended to 'play safe' (which has often been thought to mean picking a man).[23] However, determined efforts by parties to ensure a more representative spread of candidates can produce change, as Labour demonstrated in 1997. Supporters of FPTP would not oppose greater representation of minorities, but might argue that cultural change is the way it will come – and that anyway Parliament need not be an exact mirror of the electorate for it to be representative.

JENKINS AND AFTER

The report of the Independent Commission on the Voting System was an elegantly crafted attempt to balance the requirements of broad proportionality against the constituency link. Its proposals were designed to tempt all but the most committed opponents of electoral reform; unlike other pro-PR reports, it made a virtue out of designing an electoral system which would produce single-party government more often than a coalition. However, its opponents seized on the need for large-scale redrawing of constituency boundaries, and on the undefined role of the top-up MP to declare its impracticality. One of the Commission's members, Lord Alexander of Weedon, a Conservative peer, dissented from the recommendation on AV, preferring a straight AMS system with FPTP in the constituency element. Lord Jenkins accepted in the report that the scheme could not be introduced until after another general election (see box, p. 91).

A new electoral system? The main aspects of the Jenkins proposals

- 80–85 per cent of the Commons to be represented by constituency MPs, elected by AV; this will involve redrawing the boundaries of constituencies
- 15–20 per cent of seats to be in the form of regional lists – the 'top-up' seats
- Top-up areas to be based on cities and counties in England, and in the electoral areas for AMS in Scotland and Wales. Northern Ireland to have AV-plus as well, rather than STV
- 1–3 seats per top-up area with a semi-open list system; voters can either tick a party box or choose a candidate from the party's list
- Electoral commission to oversee electoral administration and independent commission to run the referendum on voting systems, following the Neill recommendations on impartiality

(Report of the Independent Commission on the Voting System,
Cmnd. 4090, October 1998)

Labour reaction was cautious; while Tony Blair indicated his overall support, the Home Secretary, Jack Straw, emphasised the practical difficulties of implementation and the need to consider the recommendations in the overall context of the constitutional reform package hastily put together in the first year of the Labour government. There were immediate hints that Cabinet collective responsibility might have to be suspended for the referendum, given that up to two-thirds of the Cabinet were opposed to the Jenkins scheme. Electoral reform campaigners, including the Liberal Democrats, rallied to the commission's support, and the Conservatives expressed their immediate opposition. The proposals were most likely to cause dissension within Labour, of all the parties, and yet if a Lib-Lab alliance could endure, Labour stood to gain the prize of long-term power due to the electoral benefit of the preferential voting system which Jenkins offered.

CONCLUSION

The recent experience of New Zealand, which has been widely cited in debates in Britain, indicates that the introduction of a form of PR does not automatically bring widespread acceptance. New Zealand moved from FPTP to mixed member proportional (MMP), a form of AMS, after two referendums, but following the first MMP election in 1996 a maverick political figure, Winston Peters, held the balance of power and formed a coalition with the National (conservative) Party, despite indications before the election that his New Zealand First Party would support Labour. Recent polls there indicate that public support for PR has fallen away. Several states, notably France, have frequently changed their electoral system for party advantage. This can heighten public cynicism about politicians and suggests that any change needs to be prefaced by an informed public debate and considerable realism about the likely effects.

In making a decision in a referendum, people may well feel that they are being asked to weigh in the balance the relative importance of broad proportionality and firm government, a choice that reflects the characteristics of the British political culture. There will also, inevitably, be considerations of party advantage (or disadvantage) that will come into play. Whatever the outcome of a referendum on this pivotal issue, the general shape of British elections is set to change significantly in the years ahead. The registration of parties will eventually prompt a long overdue overhaul of electoral law; the process of boundary reviews may also undergo major modifications and there are likely to be new rules on the funding and conduct of elections. The only certainty in all of this is that voter behaviour will continue to surprise both the pundit and the politician.

NOTES

1 House of Commons Debates, vol. 69, 10 December 1985, col. 783.
2 There was speculation before the 1977 election that key university marginals could be swung by student voters, depending on where they chose to vote.
3 Stephen Smith, *Electoral Registration in 1991* (Office of Population Censuses and Statistics, 1993).
4 *Electoral Statistics 1997*, Office of National Statistics.
5 Eleven per cent in 1981, compared with 6.5% at the qualifying date. Jean Todd and Bob Butcher, *Electoral Registration in 1981* (Office of Population Censuses and Statistics, 1982).
6 David Denver and Gordon Hands in *Parliamentary Affairs*, vol. 50, no. 4, October 1997, p. 721.
7 Home Affairs Select Committee, *Electoral Law and Administration*, HC 768, 1997–8.
8 *The Funding of Political Parties: The Fifth Report of the Committee on Standards in Public Life*, Cmnd. 4057, October 1998.
9 A recent unsuccessful prosecution of Fiona Jones MP on the charge of overspending has highlighted the uncertainties of the current legislation.
10 *The Government's Proposals for Funding of Political Parties in the United Kingdom*. Cmnd. 4413, July 1999.
11 Boundary Commissions Act 1992.
12 Michael Thrasher and Colin Rallings, 'The Parliamentary Boundary Commissions: Rules, Interpretations and Politics' in *Parliamentary Affairs*, vol. 47, no. 3, July 1994.
13 Iain McLean and David Butler (eds) *Fixing the Boundaries: Defining and Redefining Single-Member Electoral Districts* (Dartmouth, 1996).
14 Peter Pulzer, *Political Representation and Elections in Britain* (Allen and Unwin, 3rd edn, 1975), p. 102.
15 Mark Franklin, Tom Mackie, Henry Valen *et al.*, *Electoral Change* (Cambridge University Press, 1992), p. 385.
16 For a concise summary of the debate, see David Denver, *Elections and Voting Behaviour in Britain*, 2nd edn (Harvester Wheatsheaf, 1994).
17 A brief and helpful summary of the issues affecting voting behaviour in this period is David Denver's chapter entitled 'The British electorate in the 1990s' in Hugh Berrington (ed.), *Britain in the Nineties* (Frank Cass, 1998).

18 Swing is defined as $((C2 - C1) + (L1 - L2))/2$ where C1 is the percentage share of the vote polled by the Conservatives at the first election and C2 their percentage at the second. L1 is Labour's share at the first election and L2 its share at the second.

19 *Report of the Working Party on Electoral Systems* (Labour Party, 1993).

20 *Economist*, 14 September 1996, 'Blair on the Constitution'.

21 *The Politics of Electoral Reform* (Electoral Reform Society, 1991).

22 S. E. Finer, *Adversary Politics and Electoral Reform* (Antony Wigram, 1975).

23 Pippa Norris and Joni Lovenduski, *Political Recruitment: Gender, Race and Class in the British Parliament* (Cambridge University Press, 1995).

FURTHER READING

For a comprehensive survey of electoral law, see *The Electoral System in Britain* (St Martin's Press, 1995) by Robert Blackburn. For material on voting behaviour see *Elections and Voting Behaviour in Britain*, 2nd edn (Harvester Wheatsheaf, 1994) by David Denver. *Critical Elections: British Parties and Voters in Long-Term Perspective* (Sage, 1999), eds Geoffrey Evans and Pippa Norris is a good overview of long-term change in British electoral politics. A guide to the various PR systems is offered in *Comparing Electoral Systems* (Prentice Hall/Harvester Wheatsheaf, 1997) by David M. Farrell. *Fixing the Boundaries* (Dartmouth, 1996), ed. Iain McLean and David Butler, sets out details on the redistribution of parliamentary boundaries. *Electoral Change since 1945* (Blackwell, 1997) by Pippa Norris looks at trends in elections and parties. Each general election is the subject of a number of studies, some of which also look at longer term issues. One of the most authoritative is the latest in a long series of Nuffield election studies: *The British General Election of 1997* by David Butler and Dennis Kavanagh (Macmillan, 1997). Among the other useful studies are *Labour's Landslide* (Manchester University Press, 1997), eds Andrew Geddes and Jonathon Tonge; *New Labour Triumphs* (Chatham House, 1998), eds Anthony King *et al.* and *Britain Votes 1997* (Oxford University Press, 1997), eds Pippa Norris and Neil Gavin. Another useful regular source is the annual *British Elections and Parties Review*, published by Frank Cass.

4 Parties and the party system

I know nothing about Whips.
(The Speaker, House of Commons, 15 December 1954; cited in G. Marshall and
G. Moodie, *Some Problems of the Constitution*, 1959, p. 105)

It is impossible to understand the political process in Britain without understanding the role of party. The political parties are the engine-room of British politics, driving the process on and providing its inner momentum. British government is party government, even though this central fact has not been formally recognised in the past. It is only necessary to consider some of the crucial functions that the parties perform to see why this is so:

- they are the recruitment agencies for politicians
- they provide the package of political choices for voters
- they represent opinions and interests
- they enable people to participate in the political process
- they organise election campaigns
- they generate a continuous flow of political argument and information
- they develop policies on a whole range of issues
- they sustain governments and oppositions.

These are important functions in any political system, which is why political parties exist almost everywhere, but they are especially important in Britain because of the strength and dominance of the party system. Sometimes it is suggested that the grip of party in the British political process is too tight, that too little room is left for independent thought and action, but the fact is that the parties are what make the wheels of politics turn. This can be seen by looking a little more closely at the functions that the parties perform.

POLITICAL RECRUITMENT

The parties are the gatekeepers to political office. Where the number of major parties is very small, as in Britain – with its two-and-a-half-party system across most of the country – this gatekeeping role is crucially important. Political leadership, which of course includes the government of the country, is drawn from the narrow slice of people who have passed through the party gates. From local councillors to cabinet ministers, political careers are overwhelmingly rooted in party. The electorate decides which candidates win; but the party's 'selectorate' decides who the candidates are in the first place. As elections are routinely determined by party choice rather than candidate choice, the latter function might seem much more significant than the former. Tony Blair became Prime Minister in May 1997 because of the result of the general election; but also, and indispensably, because of his original selection as a candidate (against the odds) by the eighty-three-strong selectorate of the safe Labour constituency of Sedgefield just three weeks before the 1983 general election.[1]

Politics in Britain is a bleak place for those who eschew party. Independent candidates have been uniformly unsuccessful. Those who have broken with or been rejected by their parties and have gone on to ask the electorate for their continued support have all failed, usually immediately, always eventually. The 1997 general election did produce an 'independent' member of parliament in the shape of the former BBC reporter Martin Bell, who won the safe Conservative seat of Tatton on an anti-corruption platform, but both his candidature and success were only secured by the support of Labour and the Liberal Democrats. Although uncommon, it has proved rather easier to change parties and survive. A junior minister in John Major's Conservative government had once been a Labour minister; and a junior minister in Tony Blair's Labour government had once been a Conservative minister. It has been more usual, though, for party refugees to fade into oblivion (or at least into the House of Lords).

If we think of parties as political recruitment agencies, we can consider how – and whom – they recruit. It is not surprising that issues about candidate selection (and deselection) have been very important. In all the major parties candidates are selected by the local party organisations, but this can sometimes cause difficulties for the parties nationally. Labour's exercise of its reserve power to approve (or reject) candidates has periodically provoked controversies; while the lack of such powers in the Conservative Party caused it considerable embarrassment in relation to certain candidates involved in 'sleaze' allegations in the run-up to the 1997 general election. A major factor in the rise of the Labour Party in the early years of the twentieth century was the refusal of local Liberal organisations to select working-class candidates from the labour movement, so stimulating the cause of separate Labour representation. Similarly, the Conservative Party has long suffered from a reluctance on the part of local party associations to select women candidates.

One attribute of a political career is that it requires no formal entry qualifications, beyond an ability to win the approval of the party gatekeepers. Because

candidate selection belongs to the local parties, it is difficult for the party leadership or the national party machines to influence the process directly (and it is often
resented if they try). Both the Labour leadership in the 1980s and the Conservative leadership in the 1990s found life very troublesome because the candidate
selection process had produced parliamentary parties that were difficult to lead
coherently. Labour introduced new selection rules to give all party members a
vote in candidate selection, as well as provisions for all-women shortlists in enough
seats to ensure a dramatic increase in the number of women members of parliament in 1997. Issues about how representative the political recruitment process by
party is – both ideologically and socially – are central.

If we look at the kind of people now produced by this recruitment process, it
shows the extent to which politics has become an occupation of the professional
classes. This is apparent from an analysis of the candidates in the 1997 general
election. Labour has a bias towards public sector professionals, the Conservatives towards business and the law, but university graduates dominate all parties.
The number of Labour MPs from manual working backgrounds reached its
lowest-ever level of 13 per cent (compared with 28 per cent when Labour last
won an election in October 1974). Although the number of old Etonians on the
Conservative benches also reached an all-time low (of 9 per cent), there
remained twice as many old Etonians in the Commons as members of ethnic
minorities; and 66 per cent of Conservative MPs had still been to public schools
(Table 4.1). The parties have expressed a concern with improving the 'quality'
of candidates, but this raises issues about central control over the recruitment
process. As different electoral systems are developed for different purposes,
including a party list system for the European Parliament election in 1999
in which electors vote not for candidates but for parties, and for the Parliament and Assembly elections in Scotland and Wales, this gives a much greater
role for the party machines in the process of candidate selection and political

Table 4.1 Recruiting politicians: Some characteristics and backgrounds of party candidates
elected in the 1997 general election

	Labour	*Conservative*	*Liberal Democrat*
Lawyers	29 (7%)	29 (18%)	6 (13%)
Teachers/lecturers	111 (27%)	8 (5%)	7 (15%)
Company directors/executives	16 (4%)	53 (32%)	9 (20%)
Manual workers	54 (13%)	1 (1%)	1 (2%)
Political professionals	40 (10%)	15 (9%)	5 (11%)
Women	101 (24%)	13 (8%)	3 (7%)
Black/Asian	9 (2%)	0 (–)	0 (–)
University educated	275 (66%)	133 (81%)	32 (70%)
Oxbridge	61 (16%)	84 (51%)	15 (33%)
Old Etonians	2 (–)	15 (9%)	1 (2%)
Public school	67 (16%)	109 (66%)	19 (41%)

Source: D. Butler and D. Kavanagh, *The British General Election of 1997* (Macmillan, 1997).

recruitment. As today's candidates are tomorrow's cabinet ministers, or at least form the small pool from which they are drawn, this whole issue of candidate selection is clearly fundamental.

PACKAGED CHOICE

The parties provide voters with the political package deals from which to choose. Without referendums on every single issue (which, even if technically possible, would produce contradictory results), some method is required for putting individual policies into larger programmes that can be presented to the electorate for their choice. This process of 'aggregating' is what parties do (and what pressure groups do not have to do). This can have an integrating effect on political life, in so far as all the demands made on the political system have to be negotiated and processed through the packaging process performed by the parties.

In Britain, because of the small number of major parties, the packages are very broad. Unlike those systems where parties know that they are assembling only part of a larger coalition, which means that their ideological focus can be quite narrow, the major British parties are bidding to govern alone – and this means a programmatic base capable of supporting a majority of voters. Sometimes this process can be carried too far, as it was by Labour in the early 1980s when some in its ranks thought that an electoral majority could be constructed by putting together a 'rainbow coalition' of group demands (a strategy that produced 'the longest suicide note in history', as the party's manifesto for its disastrous 1983 general election campaign was famously described). Voters make judgments about the balance and coherence of whole packages, not merely compile an inventory of their parts.

The packages are presented as election manifestos and victory on the basis of them is described as a mandate to implement their contents. The language of manifesto and mandate forms an essential part of British party politics. The practice for parties to issue ever more detailed policy manifestos has developed during the second half of the twentieth century, replacing an earlier practice of making broad appeals for support. The contents of manifestos are exhaustively scrutinised and debated during election campaigns and the actions of governments are constantly examined in terms of the extent to which manifesto commitments are being delivered or broken. The more precise the commitment, then the more conspicuous becomes the issue of delivery. In the 1997 general election, Labour distilled its manifesto into a credit-card-like listing of five key delivery pledges, presented as its 'contract' with the voters. This proved highly effective, but it also made the Blair government vulnerable when at least one of these pledges (on NHS waiting lists) proved more difficult than anticipated to deliver.

In practice, of course, a mandate can never be like a contract. It might suit a government to claim that it has a mandate for a particular policy because it was in its manifesto, or an opposition to claim that a government lacks a mandate because a policy was not in its manifesto, but both claims are really spurious.

Because parties offer package deals, it is impossible to disaggregate the package and establish the amount of approval (or disapproval) for its constituent parts. All we know is that a package has been supported or rejected. For example, in the 1997 general election, one person may have voted Labour because they liked the party's policy on the minimum wage even though they disliked its policy on Europe, while another may have voted Conservative because they liked the party's policy on Europe even though they disliked its policy on the minimum wage. The only real mandate that a winning party can claim is a mandate to govern.

It is as if supermarkets only sold their goods in pre-filled trolley loads, with customers choosing the trolley that best seemed to meet their tastes and needs. This may be less satisfactory than pick-'n'-mix, especially when there are only two or three trolleys from which to choose, but it does organise political choice in a reasonably effective way. The political parties may have selected the contents of the trolleys, but they have usually done so with a careful eye on the tastes of voters and with the aim of putting together an attractive package. They also know that, if the goods disappoint, a different trolley may well be chosen next time.

OPINIONS AND INTERESTS

The parties are the political representatives of interests and opinions that exist in society. This is why it is not enough to present them simply in the language of political consumerism, as if they were merely marketing agencies. They need to appeal to the broad mass of the electorate, if they want to secure majority support and form a government, but they do so from a basis of beliefs and interests of their own. This means being responsive and persuasive at the same time, which can sometimes prove a difficult enterprise.

A party might turn in on itself and lose touch with the wider electorate. This is the general verdict on the Labour Party in the 1980s, when the representation of party activists seemed to take precedence over the electoral need to be more widely representative, resulting in the loss of four general elections in a row. The party was divided and in turmoil (one of the unwritten laws of British politics is that voters turn away from divided parties, as the Conservatives also learned in the 1990s) and seemed not even to represent its own membership or natural supporters. There began a long period, starting after the 1987 general election, and intensifying after the 1992 general election, during which the party struggled to renew and modernise itself. It involved change on many fronts – policy, ideology, organisation, presentation – designed to give the party a wider appeal. This is the story of the making of New Labour, which culminated in the party's sweeping election victory in 1997 (see box, pp. 99–100). After its crushing defeat in this election, the Conservative Party also embarked upon a similar process of internal reconstruction.

When parties adapt in this way, the question is naturally asked if it means that they are ceasing to represent the interests and opinions in society that they once represented – or if they are merely responding to the changing nature of such

The making of New Labour 1987–97

1987 Third consecutive general election defeat, despite slick campaign (and replacement of red flag with red rose as party emblem). Launch of comprehensive policy review by party leader Kinnock with aim of getting more voter-friendly policies, supported by extensive opinion research. Changes to candidate selection to reduce power of local activists.

1988 Publication of *Democratic Socialist Aims and Values* as ideological framework for policy review. National membership scheme introduced. Constituencies encouraged to use one-member-one-vote (OMOV) in leadership elections. More responsive party signalled by 'Labour Listens' campaign. Kinnock crushes Benn in leadership election.

1989 Main policy review document *Meet the Challenge, Make the Change* is produced, and approved by party conference. Unpopular policies on tax, defence, public ownership and trade unions are changed, while market economy is embraced. Big gains for party in Euro elections.

1990 Policy review proposals given more popular and accessible form in *Looking to the Future*, and linked to presentational initiatives. Dramatic victory for party in Mid-Staffordshire by-election, but replacement of Thatcher by Major dents Labour's poll lead.

1991 Labour backs Gulf war. Two Militant-supporting Labour MPs are expelled. Conference approves *Opportunity Britain*, the final product of policy review process.

1992 Fourth consecutive general election defeat. Kinnock resigns and John Smith becomes leader. Commission on Social Justice established as arm's-length think-tank. Labour strategists observe Clinton's campaign techniques in US presidential election. Reduction of trade union block vote at party conference agreed.

1993 Trade union block vote abolished for party leadership elections. A version of one-member-one-vote (OMOV) narrowly approved by party conference for parliamentary candidate selection (after stirring last-minute speech by John Prescott), so reducing the influence of the unions. All-women shortlists proposed.

1994 Death of John Smith. Tony Blair elected as leader. Big Labour gains in local council and Euro elections. Record poll lead. Blair declares intention to change Clause IV of party constitution and accelerate party modernisation. Launch of 'New Labour, New Britain' theme at party conference.

continued

1995   Special party conference votes for new Clause IV by 3 to 1 majority, redefining what the party stands for. Blair tightens control of party organisation, including appointment of chief whip instead of selection by MPs. Campaign and media centre established at Millbank Tower, with a Rapid Rebuttal Unit, presided over by Peter Mandelson. Big investment in market research.

1996   Draft manifesto *The Road to the Manifesto* (in which the word 'new' appeared 107 times) approved in ballot of party members. Identified key policy pledges. Gordon Brown pledges no income tax increases and fiscal discipline. Draft manifesto published as *New Labour, New Life for Britain*. Party membership reaches thirty-year high of 420,000, reversing long decline and overtaking Conservative membership.

1997   Gordon Brown pledges to stick to Conservative spending plans for two years. Party's general election campaign reaches new heights of discipline and efficiency. Massive Labour victory, the biggest two-party swing since 1945 and the biggest majority since 1935, giving Labour more seats than at any time in the party's history. Before entering Number 10, Blair says he has run as New Labour and will govern as New Labour.

interests and opinions. The Labour and Conservative parties have dominated British politics since adult male suffrage was fully and finally secured in 1918; and twentieth-century politics in Britain has been structured by the different social and economic interests represented by these parties (with the Liberal Party as a casualty of this process). The parties have stood on opposite sides of the class divide that has run through the centre of twentieth-century British politics. On one side, the Conservative Party has been seen as the representative of business, property and wealth; the Labour Party, on the other side, as the representative of organised labour, the propertyless and the poor. Of course all kinds of qualifications are required to this broad picture. Politics has not just been about class interests. Party ideologies have embraced other themes. There has been substantial cross-class voting (the Conservative Party has traditionally depended upon working-class votes for as much as half of its electoral support, while the 1997 general election saw a dramatic rise in middle-class support for Labour). Party support in Britain continues to reflect a pattern of class representation, but the class–party link has weakened considerably. Both these facts are evident from an analysis of how Britain voted in the 1997 general election – and from longer-term trends (Figure 4.1).

In so far as British society is composed of different (and often competing) interests, it remains the role of the political parties to give expression and representation to them. Yet the nature of these interests changes, while the link between interests and opinions can be complicated. Although it is easy to show

Figure 4.1 Party and class
(a) Voting by social grade in 1997

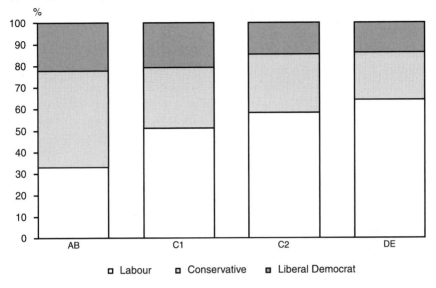

□ Labour   □ Conservative   □ Liberal Democrat

(b) Class voting in decline, 1964–97

	Absolute class voting index	*Relative class voting index*		*Absolute class voting index*	*Relative class voting index*
1964	76	6.4	1979	52	3.7
1966	78	6.4	1983	45	3.9
1970	64	4.5	1987	44	3.5
1974 (Feb)	64	5.7	1992	47	3.3
1974 (Oct)	59	4.8	1997	29	1.9

Note
Absolute index = the difference in non-manual votes between Conservatives and Labour added to the difference in manual votes between Labour and Conservative.
Relative index = the ratio of non-manual votes for Conservative and Labour in relation to the ratio of manual votes for Conservative and Labour.
Source: D. Sanders in A. King *et al.*, *New Labour Triumphs: Britain at the Polls* (Chatham House, 1988), p. 220.

that the two dominant parties in Britain have reflected distinct patterns of class representation, this is not an adequate account of the way in which the parties represent interests and opinions. The broad interest blocs that sustain the parties are themselves full of internal tensions and divisions. The changing occupational class structure has produced a much more differentiated electorate. Many contemporary political issues do not fit easily (or at all) into the traditional moulds and demand representation from the parties: the striking difference in the voting patterns across the age range in the 1997 general election, much more significant than class for young voters, can be seen as an expression of this.

All this requires a response from the parties if they are to assemble broad constituencies of support. The development of 'new' Labour, explicitly designed to extend the range of the party's appeal while retaining its core support, is the leading example of such a response. It has involved a deliberate attempt to become the party of 'business' as well as the party of 'labour' and to cultivate wide cross-class support. This has raised many questions, not least about the connection between the interests that parties represent and the opinions they articulate. It can be misleading to wrap interests and opinions up together in a neat bundle. The Labour Party was founded upon an uneasy mixture of trade union interest and socialist opinion; and doubts have been raised at different times about the extent to which the party has accurately reflected the opinions and beliefs of those who support it. As for the Conservative Party, its negative attitude to a European single currency sits uneasily alongside the more positive attitude of many of the business interests with which the party has traditionally been associated. Interests and opinions form a complex mixture – and parties are regularly engaged in trying to square circles.

POLITICAL PARTICIPATION

The parties provide an important channel through which people are able to take part in political life. People participate in political life in a whole variety of ways – for example, voting, discussing, joining a pressure group – but membership of a political party brings a direct connection to the central functions in the political process that the parties perform. It gives a role in the selection of candidates for local councils and for Parliament. It enables views on policy to be expressed. It brings direct contacts with political leaders. More passively, it enables financial support to be expressed through the membership subscription and a symbolic identification with the party to be affirmed.

Yet party members form a tiny percentage of the electorate; and even among party members only a minority are politically active. Accurate figures on party membership have always been difficult to collect. Labour Party membership was traditionally inflated by the affiliation of millions of trade unionists. Conservative Party membership has been buried in the black hole of the local party associations. However, certain generalisations are possible. First, party membership as a whole probably peaked in the 1950s and has been in decline since, part of a trend in the decline of mass parties that has been a general feature of modern political life in the West. Second, the Conservative Party has historically enjoyed the largest number of individual members, part of the larger story about the party's long record of political success. Third, the mid-1990s saw a reversal of both of these trends. Labour gained substantial numbers of new members as part of its drive to reform and modernise itself, while the Conservatives suffered a decline in membership and an associated collapse in local organisation as part of the party's general political difficulties. It remains to be seen whether these developments prove to be a temporary phenomenon or an enduring trend.

A best estimate, at the end of the 1990s, would indicate that the Conservative

Party has around 330,000 members and Labour around 390,000 members, while the Liberal Democrats have 90,000. A wide-ranging survey of the members of the Conservative and Labour parties in the early 1990s (and so before the significant developments that came later) revealed some interesting information, not least the fact that the average age of a Conservative member (62) was fourteen years more than that of a Labour member. In most respects, though, this comprehensive survey of Labour and Conservative party members showed what might have been supposed: that members of the rival parties disagree on the issues they would be expected to disagree on, that party membership is now a predominantly middle-class activity, and that party activists are more likely to be strongly partisan.[2]

Most party members are not activists. Although a majority in both main parties (66 per cent of Labour and 57 per cent of Conservative members) believe they 'can have a real influence in politics if they are prepared to get involved,' most do not translate this belief into active involvement. A majority of Labour members (51 per cent) and an overwhelming majority of Conservative members (76 per cent) give no time at all to party activity in the average month; while 42 per cent of Labour members and 66 per cent of Conservative members had not attended a party meeting during the previous year. Taken alongside other measures of political participation (see box below) it is clear that party membership merely provides the opportunity for such participation. Oscar Wilde famously remarked that the trouble with socialism was that it took up too many evenings; and this view of

---

Participation of party members

Party members (%) who, during the last five years, have

		Labour	Conservative
Displayed election poster	*Not at all*	9.6	48.9
	Occasionally	21.8	31.8
	Frequently	68.6	19.3
Donated to party funds	*Not at all*	9.7	14.9
	Occasionally	51.0	55.3
	Frequently	39.3	29.8
Delivered party leaflets	*Not at all*	17.6	61.1
	Occasionally	27.1	16.9
	Frequently	55.3	22.0
Attended party meetings	*Not at all*	21.5	50.8
	Occasionally	40.7	32.6
	Frequently	37.8	16.6
Canvassed voters	*Not at all*	36.9	74.9
	Occasionally	31.2	14.7
	Frequently	31.9	10.4

Source: P. Seyd, P. Whiteley and J. Parry, *Labour and Conservative Party Members 1990–92* (Dartmouth, 1996), pp. 337–8.

political activity seems to be widely shared by the members of both main parties in Britain.

Yet party membership and participation matter. The political scientist Robert McKenzie, whose *British Political Parties* (1963) is a classic text, once advised the revolting students of the London School of Economics in the late 1960s that, instead of merely attacking the Labour Party, they could effortlessly take it over. What he meant was that it was possible for very small numbers of party activists, who might not be representative of the wider party membership – let alone of party supporters and the general electorate – to exercise substantial political power. The troubled history of the Labour Party in the 1980s turned on just this issue. It eventually prompted the party leadership to take steps to enfranchise the whole party membership – in selecting candidates, in choosing a party leader, in approving key policy statements – in order to make decisions more representative. The new Conservative leader, William Hague, adopted a similar approach in 1998 when he balloted the party membership (although less than a third of them actually voted) on his package of party reforms. The parties clearly want to enthuse and energise their largely passive memberships.

ELECTION CAMPAIGNS

The parties organise and run election campaigns. Much of the life of political parties is taken up with preparing for and running elections, both locally and nationally. In 1999 the parties were faced with the daunting task of running election campaigns for the local councils, the Scottish Parliament and Welsh Assembly, and for the European Parliament. It is a striking fact that it was not until 1969 that the party affiliations of candidates in elections were allowed to be printed on ballot papers, a belated acknowledgement that modern elections were not really about the representation of areas by individuals but the representation of interests by parties. In practice, if not in constitutional theory, every aspect of the modern electoral process is dominated by party machines, from the selection of candidates to the conduct of campaigns. Even the arrangements for broadcasting during elections are strictly controlled to ensure party balance and key aspects (notably party election broadcasts) are agreed in private meetings between the broadcasting organisations and the parties.

At the local level, elections bring the parties into top gear. There are leaflets to be printed, envelopes to be addressed, streets to be tramped, doors to be knocked, canvass returns to be logged, postal votes to be organised, poster sites to be found, loudspeakers to be wired up, cars to be prepared, money to be raised, workers to be mobilised – and all the other ingredients of electioneering to be put into shape. The number of people involved may often be very small, but the activity can be frenetic. Local activists are sometimes heard to complain that their national parties only see them as electoral machines, to be revved up when required, and there is no doubt that electoral activity defines much of the life of local parties. Inside parties, elections also provide a folk history of great victories and painful defeats, through which the story of the party is told.

Does all this local activity make a difference to the outcome of elections? The answer is not as straightforward as it might appear. It would seem obvious that effective local campaigning has at least some impact on the result and there are studies that claim to have established a positive correlation of this kind.[3] Yet in the 1997 general election the results in the 'key seats' to which Labour had devoted concentrated organisational effort showed no greater swing than in non-targeted seats (although an even more concentrated attention on certain seats by the Liberal Democrats did produce a significant gain in seats despite a fall in the party's total vote). There was also speculation about the impact of the collapse of local Conservative organisation in many areas. The difficulty lies in separating out the effect of local campaigning in elections that have become dominated by the national campaigns. In close contests differential local effort might well prove significant. That this was not so in 1997 was summed up by the remark of one defeated Conservative: 'my result would have been exactly the same if I had spent six weeks in the South of France (provided this was not public knowledge of course).'[4]

What is not in doubt is that election campaigning is overwhelmingly run by the central party machines, that it has the media as its focus, and that it reaches ever more dizzying heights of professionalism. Local party campaigning is increasingly orchestrated from the centre, while the national campaigns mounted by the parties grow slicker, costlier and tighter. Direct mail and telephone canvassing (sometimes from afar) are prominent among the new campaign techniques, some of which – such as the 'instant rebuttal' teams – are deliberate imports from the United States. The repertoire of modern party campaign techniques is most vividly displayed in key by-elections, when voters find themselves besieged at all times, in all places and from all angles by parties determined to maximise their 'contact rate' with them. Computer technology makes it easy to assemble target lists of subsets of the electorate – from animal lovers to single parents – and to deliver specific campaign messages to them.

It used to be the case that the Conservatives were seen as having the most effective campaign organisation, with the Liberal Democrats as the specialists in by-election campaigning. In recent years, however, it is the Labour Party that has taken campaign skills to a new level of professionalism and established a formidable reputation for the party in this respect.[5] Its organisational and media centre at Millbank has become synonymous with campaign professionalism. If the 1997 general election 'will be remembered as one where the techniques of controlled electioneering took a quantum leap forward',[6] then Labour deserves most of the credit. Whether controlled electioneering has much to do with public enlightenment is another matter.

ARGUMENT AND INFORMATION

The parties generate a continuous flow of political argument and information. In part, this is because election campaigning is now a permanent activity, not confined only to election periods but a continuing process. Parties are engaged in a constant campaign to win trust and support for themselves and to undermine it in their opponents. In this way a general identity is established with the electorate, not in the few weeks of an election campaign but in the preceding years. The reason why public opinion seemed so immovable during the long general election campaign of 1997 was that it had been formed and fixed much earlier.

What this means is that, day by day, the parties are engaged in an unending war of position. Statements are made, press releases issued, figures compiled, speeches delivered, interviews given: all in a continuous round of propaganda activity designed to attack other parties and to promote one's own. From the *Today* programme at dawn to the *Newsnight* studio at night, the rival party protagonists slug it out. The tabloids are courted with populist spin and the broadsheets solicited with joined-up arguments. Members of parliament take up the battle locally, conveniently provided by their parties with press releases on which they may be required only to insert their name. The party troops are armed by their leaders with the messages that are to be deployed in the unceasing battle for public opinion.

This shows the extent to which political argument in Britain is structured by the party battle. The parties provide a constant supply of material for the political process. Political debate is typically organised as an encounter between the representatives of rival parties (a format encouraged by the political balance requirements of the public service broadcasting system). Programmes such as *Question Time* replicate the party battle. Information compiled and released by the parties forms an important part of the daily political and media agenda. Charges and counter-charges are made. Leading party figures dominate political debate. The daily parliamentary battle forms just one part of this wider struggle.

In all of this activity, the parties perform an important function for the political system. They ensure that there is continuous political discussion, with information supplied and arguments exchanged. It may seem to be an elaborate game, but (rather like the arguments between barristers in a court of law) it is a game that has to be played if the political process is to be sustained. It means that issues are debated, leaders examined and arguments tested. If the parties were not promoting this on a daily basis, the operation of the political process would be very different. Yet there are also dangers in the party domination of political argument. Other voices and issues may find themselves excluded; while the routine predictability of party exchanges can stultify genuine political debate.

POLICY DEVELOPMENT

The parties develop policies across the whole range of issues. They present these to the electorate and promise to implement them if elected. It is expected that parties will have a policy on every issue (except on issues of 'conscience', such as abortion, where traditionally there is no party line) and the party manifestos have become ever more detailed documents. Even parties which have no chance of forming a government at Westminster or only one fundamental policy (such as the nationalist parties in Scotland and Wales) have felt obliged to produce a full policy portfolio. Pressure groups can confine themselves to particular policy areas, but parties are expected to have a policy on everything. An interesting exception to this rule was Sir James Goldsmith's Referendum Party, which contested the 1997 general election on the single issue of Britain's relations with Europe. It spent a vast sum of money, contested no less than 547 seats, averaged 3.1 per cent of the vote in constituencies where it stood (the strongest performance ever by a minor party in Britain), but was not a 'proper' party in its focus on a single issue.

The main parties have traditionally approached the task of policy-making in sharply different ways. In the Conservative Party, policy development has been a responsibility of the leadership (indeed, of the leader), with no formal involvement of the wider party membership or organisation. By contrast, the Labour Party was founded upon principles of internal party democracy and this involved an assumption that policy would be made by the party and transmitted to the leadership. The different nature of the annual party conferences has reflected the contrasting styles of policy-making: Conservative conferences listened to leaders announcing policies, while Labour conferences engaged in intense policy debate and voted on policy resolutions. In practice, of course, the contrast was less dramatic. Conservative policy-making had to take account of sentiment within the party, as variously expressed, while Labour policy-making incorporated devices and conventions designed to blunt the edge of direct party democracy. More recently, as will be seen shortly, both parties have made radical changes to the way in which policy is made and approved.

Policy development is a continuing activity for the parties. It takes place in a number of settings and draws upon a variety of sources: the party leader's office, the party's parliamentary spokespersons on particular areas, outside experts and think-tanks (particularly influential during the Thatcher government in the 1980s), the party's own research staff and party groupings of various kinds. There is a policy-making cycle, broadly corresponding to the electoral cycle, culminating in the policy package that is contained in the party's election manifesto. Election defeat can prompt policy revision, while repeated election defeats can prompt fundamental policy review (as with Labour after 1987). Sometimes policies are deliberately crafted and adjusted in an effort to reconcile conflicting opinions within a party, as with Conservative policy on Europe in recent years. Policies that are popular with party opinion may not always be those that are popular with public opinion.

There is also the matter of devising policies that work. This may seem an obvious point, but a policy that is designed to reflect an ideological position, or unite a party, or appeal to voters may not necessarily be workable in practice (or consistent with other policies). It is when a winning party encounters the civil service machine that such difficulties come under scrutiny. The Blair government was elected in 1997 on a very precise set of policy proposals that were emphasised as deliverable; whereas Mrs Thatcher's government came into office in 1979 with major policy areas (notably, the privatisation programme) still underdeveloped. It is sometimes asked whether party policies really 'make a difference' anyway[7] compared with the underlying trends, external events and shaping forces within which they are set. The short answer is probably that they do, but not nearly as much as politicians like to claim.

SUSTAINING GOVERNMENTS AND OPPOSITIONS

The parties sustain the operation of government and opposition in Britain. Although this function is listed last, it is by far the most important in explaining how the Westminster system works. There is a paradox here. In formal terms the traditional position has been that 'the law of the constitution does not regulate political parties and indeed barely acknowledges their existence';[8] yet the reality is that the operation of the political parties determines the nature of government and politics at Westminster. Members of parliament are referred to by their constituencies and formal references to parties have only occurred in 'housekeeping' provisions about such matters as payments of salaries to the Leader of the Opposition and opposition whips and financial assistance to opposition parties, and in procedural arrangements for allocation of time and membership of committees. What this has concealed is the comprehensive way in which the party system rules at Westminster.

The government is drawn from the majority party, while the largest minority party forms the Official Opposition. The function of the parties is to sustain this institutional adversarialism, rooted in the long dominance of a two-party system and reflected in the shape and organisation of the House of Commons. Members of parliament are members of rival parliamentary armies, supporting their respective commanders and engaging in a permanent political campaign on behalf of their parties. It can even be misleading to refer to 'Parliament' as if it was an independent or collective entity, when it is really just the place where Government and Opposition meet to engage in continuous political battle. Appeals to 'the House' in parliamentary speeches are no more than rhetorical flourishes. When ministers declare that a policy has been 'approved by Parliament', it sounds better than saying that it is the product of the routine majority of the governing party.

All the essential features of the House of Commons are structured by the realities of party. Above everything else, members of parliament are members of parties. Their only indispensable obligation is to serve their party by voting for it in the division lobbies, an obligation identified in the printed 'whip' circulated to MPs every week and enforced daily and in person by the party's whips. The business of the Commons is arranged by the 'usual channels' of the party managers. Appointments to committees are in the hands of the whips and committee proceedings routinely run on party lines. Lacking an independent career structure of its own, promotion within Parliament is measured in terms of government or opposition office-holding and this gives enormous patronage power to the party leadership (and can put as much as a third of a governing party effectively on the 'payroll' vote, with much of the rest hoping to be).

Of course, this picture needs qualifications. Many MPs are not just slaves of the whips and bring other considerations to their role. There are dissidents and mavericks. Issues can divide the unity of parties, sometimes severely (as with the group of 'whipless rebels' in the Conservative Party who caused so much difficulty on the issue of Europe for John Major's government in the mid-1990s). Parties have internal groupings and factions and these can cause problems for party management: in the past the Labour Party in particular has been rife with organised factionalism of various kinds. Opinions have to be listened to and accommodations made. Yet when all this is said, the fact of party as the underlying truth of Westminster politics is undented. It is what makes the Westminster world go round. Most MPs are willing servants of their party, to which they owe their political existence, not reluctant conscripts. The role of the whips is not the cause, but the consequence, of the dominance of party.

The growth in party discipline is part of the story of modern British politics. Organised party whipping and voting in the House of Commons grew rapidly in the generation after 1867 (see box below) and routine party discipline became the twentieth-century norm.

Growth of whipping and party cohesion

(a) divisions (%) in a session when a party in government put on its whips and (b) the percentage of members voting with the party in those divisions.

	Whipped votes	*Party cohesion*
1836	48.9 (Liberals)	
1850	68.3 (Liberals)	
1860	66.9 (Liberals)	58.9 (Liberals)
1871	82.1 (Liberals)	75.5 (Liberals)
1881	96.6 (Liberals)	83.2 (Liberals)
1883	78.2 (Liberals)	
1890	79.7 (Conservatives)	
1894	90.2 (Liberals)	89.8 (Liberals)
1899	85.7 (Conservatives)	97.7 (Conservatives)
1903	86.5 (Conservatives)	
1906	92.2 (Liberals)	96.8 (Liberals)
1908	95.7 (Liberals)	94.9 (Liberals)
1945	100.0 (Labour)	99.9 (Labour)

Source: S. Beer, *Modern British Politics*, 2nd edn (Faber, 1969, pp. 257, 262–3).

Some 'dissidence' always remains, varying from period to period and influenced by issues and circumstances,[9] but the central context is clear. Nor should it be imagined that there was once a golden age of robust independence before party discipline arrived. In fact, during the period in the middle of the nineteenth century when a fluid Commons could make or break ministries, there were lamentations about the loss of party direction. Bagehot in 1867 proclaimed that the alternative to party was 'impotence' in which 'there will be 657 amendments to every motion, and none of them will be carried or the motion either'; and Salisbury in 1857 deplored the way in which 'selfish or sectional ends' had replaced 'the old fidelity to a party banner'. Now the primary role of party is to sustain government and Opposition. As Riddell puts it, 'Parliament without party would be unpredictable chaos'[10]; although a Parliament that was only about party would carry its own dangers.

THE CHANGING PARTIES

It is clear from this account of the main functions performed by the political parties in the British political process that, in significant respects, the way in which they perform their role is changing. There seems also to be a development towards 'constitutionalising' at least some aspects of what parties do: the Blair government has made explicit legislative provision for parties in its proposals for a regional party list electoral system for European Parliament elections and for the voting system for the new assemblies in Scotland and Wales, has introduced legislation on the registration of political parties, and referred the whole issue of party funding to the Committee on Standards in Public Life as a prelude to legislation. Having been for so long the informal secret of British politics, the parties are increasingly being brought within the pale of the constitution. Against this background, it is useful to look briefly at three areas where the parties are currently experiencing significant changes: in ideology, structure and funding.

Ideology

Ideology is about what parties 'stand for' in a general sense, not just which policies they advocate (although a connection between these would clearly be expected). Because of the broad character of parties in a predominantly two-party system, each of the major parties is really an internal coalition and therefore encompasses a wide range of ideological opinion. Moreover, opinions and ideas may change over time, in the light of events and circumstances. There is the further difficulty that the ideological language traditionally used by the parties – notably, the language of 'left' and 'right' – may not correspond with the more complex and variegated beliefs of voters. A survey conducted during the 1997 general election campaign categorised voters in terms of their attitudes as conservative (36 per cent), libertarian (19 per cent), socialist (18 per cent), authoritarian (13 per cent) and centrist (15 per cent). Labour was the first choice of all ideological groups except for conservatives; although for every four conservatives planning to vote Conservative, two were planning to vote Labour.[11] It is also widely suggested that the era of traditional ideological politics, the basis of much of twentieth-century party politics, may now be over.

In the last quarter of the twentieth century, both the Labour and Conservative parties were the scene of dramatic ideological change. Labour swung sharply to the left, before swinging more slowly back to the centre as it struggled to learn the lessons of successive electoral defeats. The Conservatives swung emphatically to the right after Mrs Thatcher became leader in 1975 and were not required to engage in further ideological stocktaking until after their devastation at the polls in 1997. The minor parties, notably the Liberal Democrats, had to make their own adjustments in response to this changing ideological environment. Within a generation the answer to the question about what the parties 'stood for' had significantly altered.

Traditionally, the Conservative Party had eschewed ideology, priding itself on its adaptability and flexibility. Presenting itself as a 'national' party, its main purpose consisted in being in power (an enterprise in which it was remarkably successful). It managed to combine different traditions – order with freedom, land with trade, capitalism with 'one nation' social concerns – and this enabled it to adapt to changing circumstances, as it did by accepting (and presiding over) the post-war consensus established by the 1945–51 Labour government. However, as that consensus began to crumble in the 1970s, a more robust and ideological conservatism – the 'new right' of Thatcherism – gained ascendancy in the party. It embraced markets, wanted to roll back the state, denounced notions of equality and social justice, and aimed to unscramble the post-war 'settlement' in which the Conservative Party had been an accomplice. 'It was only in April 1974 that I was converted to Conservatism,' wrote Sir Keith Joseph, Mrs Thatcher's principal lieutenant; 'I had thought I was a Conservative, but now I see that I was not really one at all.'[12]

Although detaching itself from elements of its own tradition, this 'new' conservatism combined a liberal emphasis on markets with a Tory emphasis on order. The mixture of 'free market and strong state' proved a potent combination. Above all, it turned Conservatives into the radical ideologists of British politics, whose ideas were shaping the intellectual and political agenda. 'Since 1979 Conservative governments have moved forward like ice-breakers, ploughing their way through the frozen wastes of state control': this was the proud boast of the Conservative thinker and politician, David Willetts, at the time of the 1997 general election.[13] However, after the election, his ice-breakers had turned into demolition squads as he recalled a lesson learned on an election doorstep: 'The lady who answered the door used to vote for us but now, she said, "I call you Conservatives the demolition squad". That is an absurd position for the Conservative Party to have got itself into.'[14] Whether this kind of analysis will eventually produce a rebalancing of Conservative ideology is still unclear. Much will depend upon whether it can resolve the issue of Europe, the permanent battlefield for the party's divergent ideological traditions.

Much more will depend upon whether Tony Blair's Labour Party consolidates its hold on middle opinion in Britain. Founded on a mixture of trade union interest and socialist belief, Labour had always been an ideological 'broad church' – though often with warring factions. As a party of the left, it stood for a collectivist politics that involved using the state to remedy what it saw as the injustices and inefficiencies of a capitalist market economy. What this meant in practice was endlessly disputed, especially as society and the economy changed. It responded to the breakdown of the post-war settlement in the late 1970s by moving leftwards, just as the Conservatives moved rightwards, embracing a radical programme of public ownership, planning and redistribution. This threw the party into turmoil, produced a breakaway of some members into a new Social Democratic Party, and kept the party in the political wilderness throughout the 1980s.

As it sought to claw its way back, under the leadership first of Neil Kinnock and then of John Smith, the party set about redefining its identity. The election of Tony Blair as leader in 1994, an event as significant as Mrs Thatcher's election as Conservative leader in 1975, gave this process a dramatic new twist. His ambition was to create nothing less than a new party of the 'radical centre.' The extent of this ambition was signalled by his successful campaign to replace Labour's traditional statement of its core doctrine – the Clause IV commitment to public ownership – with a new statement of broad ethical values (see box, p. 113). The party's association with trade union interests, state intervention, and high levels of taxing and spending was replaced with an emphasis on consumers, financial prudence, and public action to create pathways of opportunity for individuals. Old ideological antagonisms were pronounced obsolete.

Yet Blairism aims to be the ideology for the age that has shed ideologies. It claims to be neither 'old left' nor 'new right,' but something distinctively different – a 'third way' that rejects the choice between free markets and state collectivism.[15] It argues that it is possible to combine a dynamic market economy with social inclusion. In 1988 Mrs Thatcher told the Conservative conference that her ideas had become 'the common ground of British politics'; but a decade later Mr Blair could plausibly make the same claim. Whether British politics has really entered new ideological territory will, as ever, only be clear much later.

Structure

It is a period of great change in the organisation of the major political parties in Britain, requiring a revision of traditional accounts. The Labour Party was rooted in a tradition of internal party democracy, with the sovereignty of the annual conference at its apex. In practice, the parliamentary leadership tended to get its way (sustained by the conference voting power of the big trade unions), but the process was often fractious and difficult to manage. For a period in the early 1980s, an attempt was made to close the gap between theory and practice in the way the party was run by a left-wing campaign to 'democratise' key parts of its structure. This produced procedures for the de-selection of MPs and for the selection of party leaders by a party 'electoral college' rather than by the parliamentary party alone. However, it also produced civil war within the party, claims that power was passing to unrepresentative activists, and electoral disaster.

The next decade saw Labour engaged in a continuous process of internal party

Revising Clause IV

Clause IV of Labour's constitution sets out what the party stands for. The replacement of the original 1918 version with a new version in 1995 was seen as central to the party's modernisation. The key sections are these:

1918 version

To secure for the workers by hand or by brain the full fruits of their industry and the most equitable distribution thereof that may be possible upon the basis of the common ownership of the means of production, distribution, and exchange, and the best obtainable system of popular administration and control of each industry or service. Generally to promote the political, social and economic emancipation of the people, and more particularly of those who depend directly upon their own exertions by hand or by brain for the means of life.

1995 version

The Labour Party is a democratic socialist party. It believes that by the strength of our common endeavour we achieve more than we achieve alone, so as to create for each of us the means to realise our true potential and for all of us a community in which power, wealth and opportunity are in the hands of the many not the few, where the rights we enjoy reflect the duties we owe, and where we live together, freely, in a spirit of solidarity, tolerance and respect.

To these ends we work for:

A dynamic economy, serving the public interest, in which the enterprise of the market and the rigour of competition are joined with the forces of partnership and cooperation to produce the wealth the nation needs and the opportunity for all to work and prosper, with a thriving private sector and high quality public services, where those undertakings essential to the common good are either owned by the public or accountable to them;

A just society, which judges its strength by the condition of the weak as much as the strong, provides security against fear, and justice at work; which nurtures families, promotes equality of opportunity and delivers people from the tyranny of poverty, prejudice and the abuse of power;

An open democracy, in which government is held to account by the people; decisions are taken as far as practicable by the communities they affect; and where fundamental human rights are guaranteed;

A healthy environment, which we protect, enhance and hold in trust for future generations.

reform, as it sought to blunt the edge of these earlier changes and move the party towards a new constitutional settlement. The power of activists was trumped by the introduction of one-member-one-vote (OMOV) in candidate and leadership elections, the trade union vote was reduced and reformed, and the central party machine was strengthened. In 1997, as the party prepared for government, a further package of reforms was introduced. These were set out in a document, *Labour into Power*, which declared: 'There is always a challenge when political parties come to power, namely how to reconcile the requirements of two aspects of democracy: the democracy of the country and the democracy of the political party in question.' The answer to this challenge was a new 'partnership' in which the composition of the party's national executive committee was broadened and the policy-making by the party conference was set within the framework of a rolling programme presided over by a new policy committee and national policy forum. Along with other measures to strengthen central control over candidates and MPs, it was hoped that the traditional disputes between a Labour government and the party would become a thing of the past.

If the 1990s saw Labour becoming more controlled and streamlined, the Conservative Party seemed to be moving in the opposite direction. This was a reversal of roles as far as traditional accounts of the parties were concerned. The 'democratic' Labour Party discovered discipline, while the 'undemocratic' Conservative Party discovered dissent. The party conferences reflected this role reversal as Labour's became more stage-managed and the Conservatives' more disputatious. If this was a remarkable change for the Labour Party, it was even more remarkable for the Conservatives. A top-down, leader-dominated party that had traditionally relied on loyalty and eschewed internal democracy found itself in organisational trouble as arguments about Europe and general demoralisation revealed the party's inability to function effectively. This was exposed to full view in the 1997 general election, as policy disarray and a failure to deal with errant candidates cost the party dear.

After the party's crushing electoral defeat, its new leader, William Hague, initiated sweeping changes to the way the party was organised and run. The document setting out the proposals (*Our Party: Blueprint for Change*) was stark in its description of the state of the Conservative Party: 'Electoral defeat has laid bare the extent of decline in our organisation and membership over the last twenty years. This decline is structural, not cyclical.' The prescription was as radical as the analysis: a single governing board for the party in place of the separate wings; election of the party leader by the members instead of by MPs; a national membership list; more control over constituency associations; and a new disciplinary procedure. The effect was to create a single Conservative Party for the first time, able to identify its membership and operate consistent procedures. When the reform package was approved in the spring of 1998, *The Times* declared: 'The Conservative Party as an organisation has been transformed in the past 12 months. Democracy has finally entered its soul' (30 March 1998). The party claimed to have reformed itself more in eight months than Labour had done in eighteen years. Yet the party was in such a reduced condition that its organisational revolution was scarcely noticed at the time.

What pattern emerges from the way in which both the major parties have been changing how they are run? Two features stand out. First, there is a growing similarity between the parties on key aspects of structure and organisation, despite their very different histories and traditions (Table 4.2). The Liberal Democrats may be included here too, with their own structure a product of the amalgamation of the old Liberal Party with the Social Democratic Party that had broken away from Labour in the early 1980s. They claimed to be the most democratic of the parties in their organisation (an example of which was the vote at the party's spring conference in 1998 to attach conditions to the leadership's co-operation with Labour), but they also combined – sometimes uneasily – the more top-down approach of the SDP with the bottom-up tradition of the Liberals. If all the parties have now begun to share the same organisational characteristics, it is because they all have to grapple with the same organisational issues.

This highlights the second feature in what is happening. In his classic study, *British Political Parties* (1955, revised 1963), R. T. McKenzie argued that internal party democracy would necessarily lose out to the demands of parliamentary politics. His focus was on the Labour Party, but the argument was a general one. Do the recent changes in party structures vindicate this analysis? Yes and no. The paradox is that they involve both more central control and more democratic involvement. They combine the requirements of leadership and legitimacy. Parties are developing the centralised command and control structures necessary for effective campaign organisations, but they are also developing the procedures for membership ballots on leaders and key programmes in order to sustain democratic legitimacy. It is no doubt the case that the emphasis on effective leadership comes first, and that plebiscites of party members can be seen as providing a democratic veneer to the reality of central control, but the combination of leadership and democratic legitimacy nevertheless distinguishes the recent changes in party organisation and provides their common thread.

Funding

On 12 November 1997 Prime Minister Tony Blair wrote to Lord Neill, chairman of the Committee on Standards in Public Life, extending the committee's remit so that it could undertake a study of the funding of political parties. The terms of reference for the study were: 'To review issues in relation to the funding of political parties, and to make recommendations as to any changes in present arrangements.' Behind these words was an issue with far-reaching implications not just for the parties but also for many aspects of British politics. Like so much else in the British political process, change had been triggered by crisis and controversy.

Parties now spend huge sums of money, especially in fighting elections, and this means that they have to raise equivalent sums (Table 4.3). The money-spending and the money-raising activities of the parties have therefore attracted increasing attention. Part of the sleaze that enveloped the final years of Conservative rule

Table 4.2 Structures: The parties compared

	Conservative Party	Labour Party	Liberal Democrat Party
How is the leader elected?	MPs nominate a shortlist of two candidates to the wider party electorate. The members are then balloted on a basis of OMOV.[a]	A candidate with the support of 12.5% of the PLP[b] may stand in a full leadership election, in which an electoral college of one-third MPs, one-third party members and one-third trade unionists are balloted on the basis of OMOV.	Leader elected on the basis of OMOV. Candidates must first secure the support of 200 party members in at least 20 local parties. Election conducted on the basis of AV.[c]
How is the leader removed?	A vote of no confidence is triggered if 15% of MPs write to the 1922 Committee. 51% of MPs need to back the leader in order to avoid a leadership contest. If this is not achieved MPs hold a parliamentary 'primary' to select two candidates to be put to the full party membership.	20% support for a challenger within the PLP triggers a full membership ballot preceded by a 'first round' ballot of conference if in government. A simple majority either way is required in both cases. MPs must re-elect the leader annually to avoid a challenge.	If the leader loses either a vote of no confidence (a majority of MPs) or the support of 75 local parties a full membership ballot is triggered. The leader is automatically reinstated every year if there is no challenge.
Who chooses the parliamentary candidates?	Conservative Central Office produces a list of candidates who apply directly to Local Associations, whose executive narrows a shortlist down to two and then ballots the membership.	CLPs[d] can select locally nominated candidates and ones approved by the NEC[e] for their shortlist. The CLP then votes on the basis of OMOV, with ratification by the NEC. The NEC determines the shortlist at by-elections.	Local constituency membership is balloted after the English, Scottish and Welsh parties have produced a list of candidates from which they may choose, again using the AV election system.
What disciplinary mechanisms exist for members (including MPs?)	Ethics and Integrity Committee set up to provide a mechanism by which members and officers can be disciplined.	The NEC can report members to the NCC[f] and suspend members pending inquiry. Alternatively CLPs can report direct to the NCC on disciplinary matters.	MPs are disciplined by the parliamentary party. For members this is done at the local level. Appeal mechanisms are located at the regional, national or ultimately federal level.

How are members represented: Locally?	Constituency Associations provide organisation and campaigning at local level. They also contribute to national funds.	CLPs involve members and representatives of other affiliated organisations in activities on behalf of the party in a specific area.	Local parties provide members with a voice in the local governance of the party.
Nationally?	The annual conference provides national representation for party members and a forum in which to debate national policy.	The annual party conference provides a forum in which rank and file members and trade unionists can influence national policy.	The Federal Conference provides UK-wide representation and gives representatives a chance to determine national policy.
How is policy made?	The new Conservative Policy Forum supported by Regional Policy Congresses allows members to formulate policy ideas with the leadership. This is facilitated by the party's new unified status.	A National Policy Forum considers and revises policy overseen by a Joint Policy Committee which is controlled by the parliamentary leadership and chaired by the leader.	The Federal Policy Committee commissions working groups to look at policy. It then consults the national parties and associated organisations and reports to conference.
Who has the final say on policy?	The leadership retains almost complete control over party policy. However, members are now able to vote on certain 'crucial' policy issues, such as the European single currency in 1998.	Conference is the sovereign body for overall policy-making. However, the conference agenda is now largely controlled by the National Policy Forum.	The Federal Conference is the party's sovereign policy-making body. Composed of representatives from every local party. Meets twice a year.
Who controls the content of the manifesto?	The party leadership retains almost complete control over the party's election manifesto.	The NEC and the Cabinet or (in opposition) the parliamentary committee of the PLP determine the manifesto's content. In 1996 it was put to a ballot of the membership for approval.	The National Policy Committee in consultation with the parliamentary party determines the content of the manifesto.

Table 4.2 continued

	Conservative Party	Labour Party	Liberal Democrat Party
Overall, where does power lie?	Power in the party is exercised almost exclusively by the national leadership, with some ratification by member ballots.	Power now rests largely with the national (parliamentary) leadership, with some ratification by member ballots.	More devolved than other major parties. Conference decisions become party policy. Can produce tensions with parliamentary leadership.

Notes
a OMOV – one-member-one-vote.
b PLP – Parliamentary Labour Party.
c AV – alternative vote.
d CLPs – Constituency Labour Parties.
e NEC – National Executive Committee.
f NCC – National Constitutional Committee.

Table 4.3 Party election spending: General election expenditure since 1983 (£m)

Election year	Conservative	Labour	Alliance/Lib Democrat
1983	3.6	2.2	1.9
1987	9.0	4.4	1.9
1992	11.2	10.2	1.8
1997	28.3	26.0	2.1
Total	52.1	42.8	7.7
Total change, 1983–97 (at 1997 prices)	+329%	+550%	−40%

Source: Committee on Standards in Public Life (Neill Committee), *Fifth Report: The Funding of Political Parties in the United Kingdom*, Cmnd. 4057, October 1998, p. 43.

involved the party's refusal to identify its donors, reports that major donations came from wealthy foreigners (especially in the Far East), charges that honours and access were linked to funding – and the Conservative government's refusal to allow the Committee on Standards in Public Life to examine party funding. When the new Labour government found itself caught in controversy about lobbying access on cigarette advertising granted to a motor racing entrepreneur who was also a major Labour funder (with the party handing back a million pounds), it was clear that the whole issue of party funding needed urgent attention.

The anti-corruption legislation of 1883 had largely cleaned up constituency electioneering and put a ceiling on how much candidates could spend. More than a century later, its provisions are still in place; but they have nothing to say about the rise of the party machines that have come to dominate political spending and campaigning in the twentieth century. Thus the cap on constituency spending is not matched by an equivalent cap on national spending at elections. A series of *ad hoc* arrangements have been devised to deal with particular aspects of spending and funding. For example, political broadcasting has been provided free to the parties; while a special fund ('Short money') was set up to assist the parliamentary work of the parties. Various inquiries and committees have examined party funding issues over the years – notably the Houghton Report (1976) which recommended state funding, and the Home Affairs Select Committee (1994) which split on party lines – but no serious or agreed action followed.

However, the pattern of party funding has also changed in recent years, making action even more necessary. The key factor has been the rise of the major individual donor. This is true of both main parties, each of which has seen its traditional funding pattern change as institutional donors have become less important and individual donors more important. Apart from membership income, the Conservative Party relied heavily on support from business while Labour was dependent upon the trade unions. The change on both fronts has been dramatic. It is estimated that company donations to the Conservatives have declined from 60 per cent of the party's central income in the 1970s to about 20–25 per cent now; while trade union funding of Labour has fallen from around 80 per cent of total income in the mid-1980s to some 35–40 per cent now. The rise of major personal donors has taken up the slack, but whereas company and trade union donations are readily identifiable this is not the case with individual donors – with the result that the problem of secrecy has become central to the whole question of party funding.

This was the background to the Neill Committee's inquiry. The Labour government had already announced its intention to require public disclosure of all donations over £5,000 and to ban foreign donations, but the committee's inquiry was required to examine the whole issue. This meant confronting a number of key questions. Should there be a national cap on party election spending? Should there be a cap on the size of individual donations? Should all donations above a certain figure be disclosed? Should there be more state funding of political parties? Should there be a new regulatory body to police this area? Behind such questions were complex issues both of principle and practice. In its report in October 1998, the Neill Committee noted that 'something of an arms race' had developed in party funding and set out a series of proposals to ensure public disclosure of significant donations and to set a limit on total campaign spending (see box, p. 121).

There were also proposals for an independent electoral commission to police the new arrangements; and for fair funding rules for the conduct of referendums. The Neill Committee believed that this package of measures would 'contribute to the health of political parties and of democracy in the United Kingdom'. By putting a regulatory framework around the whole issue of party funding, the intention was to halt the spending arms race and to strengthen public confidence in how the parties operated. The government has announced that there will be legislation to implement the Neill Committee's proposals.

WHAT KIND OF PARTY?

All these changes – in ideology, structure and funding – raise questions about the kind of party that is developing in Britain; and also about the place of party in the political system. Britain has moved rapidly from a position in which parties were scarcely recognised by the constitution to one in which their existence is made explicit, their status formalised and their activities increasingly regulated. The parties have come in from the cold.

There is already legislation on the registration of political parties, so that parties can register and protect their names (and emblems) against 'spoiler' candidates (see box, p. 122). This legislation was a major constitutional innovation in terms of the place of parties in the constitution. The electoral systems for the new assemblies in Scotland and Wales involve a party list element and this has both required the registration of parties and involved the central party machines in devising procedures for candidate selection. The adoption of proportional representation through regional party lists for the European Parliament elections has also centralised party control of candidate selection. The mayor and assembly for

Reforming party funding: The Neill Committee proposals (1998)

Our proposals consist of various elements. These include:

- Clear rules on full public disclosure of donations (including benefits in kind) to political parties – of £5,000 or more nationally and of £1,000 or more in a constituency – in any one financial year, from any one person or source
- An end to blind trusts
- Donations to political parties to be allowed only from a 'permissible source' (defined so as effectively to ban foreign donations)
- A ban on anonymous donations to political parties in excess of £50
- A limit of £20 million on national campaign expenditure in a general election (including benefits in kind) by a political party
- Clear rules on the preparation and auditing of a political party's annual accounts and national expenditure on an election
- No new state funding, but tax relief on donations up to £500, to encourage small donations to political parties
- Wider scrutiny by an Honours Scrutiny Committee of all proposals where there might be or be perceived to be a connection between the honour and a political donation
- A review of the arrangements for financing opposition parties in the House of Commons and House of Lords, with a recommended increase in funding to enable them to discharge their roles more effectively
- Controls on the activities of organisations and individuals (other than a political party) spending more than £25,000 nationally on political activity during a general election, with registration and reporting requirements, a ban on foreign donations and both national and local expenditure limits
- Maintenance of free access to television and radio for party broadcasts
- Maintenance of the ban on political advertising on television and radio
- Shareholder consent for company donations.

Source: Committee on Standards in Public Life (Neill Committee), *Fifth Report: The Funding of Political Parties in the United Kingdom*, Cm. 4057, October 1998, pp. 2–3.

London has raised similar issues. If we add to this the proposed new package of measures to regulate the funding of political parties, backed by a powerful regulatory commission, it is clear that parties can no longer be regarded as outside the pale of the constitution.

There is lively argument about the significance of what is happening. Some see the development of professional and centralised party bureaucracies as a threat to the vitality of parties, even when referendums of members are held to legitimate

Registration of Political Parties Act 1998

An Act to make provision about the registration of political parties.

[19th November 1998]

B E IT ENACTED by the Queen's most Excellent Majesty, by and with the advice and consent of the Lords Spiritual and Temporal, and Commons, in this present Parliament assembled, and by the authority of the same, as follows:-

The register of political parties

The register.   **1.** - (1) There shall be a register to be known as the register of political parties.

(2) The register shall be maintained by the registrar or other officer who performs the duty of registration of companies in England and Wales under the Companies Act 1985.

Registration

Applications for registration.   **2.** (1) A party may apply for inclusion in the register by sending to the registrar-
(a) an application which complies with the requirements of Schedule 1, and
(b) a declaration that the party intends to have one or more candidates at a relevant election.
(2) The following elections are relevant for this purpose-
(a) parliamentary elections,
(b) elections to the European Parliament,
(c) elections to the Scottish Parliament,
(d) elections to the National Assembly for Wales,
(e) elections to the New Northern Ireland Assembly,
(f) local government elections, and
(g) local elections in Northern Ireland.

Grant of applications.   **3.** (1) The registrar shall grant an application by a party under section 2 unless in his opinion it proposes a registered name which-
(a) would be likely to result in the party's being confused by voters with a party which is already registered,
(b) comprises more than six words,
(c) is obscene or offensive,
(d) includes words the publication of which would be likely to amount to the commission of an offence,
(e) includes any script other than Roman script, or
(f) includes any word or expression prohibited by order made by the Secretary of State.
(2) An order under subsection (1)(f) may except the use of a word or expression from the prohibition in specified circumstances.

Entries in the register.   **4.** The registrar shall include in an entry in the register the particulars, apart from home addresses, given in the party's application in accordance with paragraphs 2 to 7 of Schedule 1.

Emblems.   **5.** (1) A party's application under section 2 may include a request for the registration of up to three emblems to be used by the party on ballot papers.
(2) The registrar shall grant a request under this section in relation to an emblem unless in his opinion it-
(a) would be likely to be confused by voters with an emblem which is already registered for another party,
(b) is obscene or offensive,
(c) is of such a character that its publication would be likely to amount to the commission of an offence, or
(d) includes a word or expression prohibited under section 3(1)(f).
(3) A registered emblem shall be a black and white representation of the emblem shown in the application.

decisions. While some welcome the moves to put a framework of public interest regulation around the activities of parties, others stress the voluntary and private nature of parties and argue that 'the state should be kept at a distance'.[16] More generally, it has been suggested that the traditional model of the mass party may represent 'merely a phase of democratic development that is passing away',[17] increasingly replaced by other devices and organisations; but this view is not shared by those who continue to see the political party as a key feature of civic life in a democratic society. On this view, the task is to rejuvenate the parties and to give them a new lease of life.[18] Whatever view is taken, there is no doubt that recent developments in the role and status of political parties in Britain represent an important ingredient in a changing political system.

THE PARTY SYSTEM

The final question to be asked is whether the party system itself is changing. On one view, it looks remarkably stable and intact. The traditional description of a 'strong' or 'classical' two-party system reflects the fact that in the entire period since 1945 either the Conservative Party or the Labour Party has been in government. The two parties have exercised a duopoly on power. When Tony Blair and William Hague confront each other today over the despatch box in the House of Commons, the scene is essentially the same as that following Labour's last landslide victory in 1945 when Clement Attlee and Winston Churchill squared up to each other.

Although there have been some years over this long period when governing majorities have been fragile or even non-existent, single-party government by one or other of the two main parties has been maintained. Many parties have contested elections (over thirty in 1997 – from the Natural Law Party to the Monster Raving Loony Party), but only two parties have formed governments. They have not won in equal measure (while the Conservatives enjoyed two long periods of uninterrupted power in 1951–64 and 1979–97, Labour never secured two full consecutive terms of office in the whole period between 1945 and 1997), but between them they have dominated the roles of Government and Opposition. In turn this has sustained the organised adversarialism that is a fundamental feature of British political life at Westminster.

On another view, though, this picture of stability and continuity in the party system looks rather different. For example, it is argued that if a much longer perspective than the post-1945 period is taken, then this particular period can seem more like an exception than the rule. Familiar assumptions about a British tradition of strong single-party government in a two-party political system are dented by a history peppered with coalitions, cross-party arrangements, minority rule and tenuous majorities. In its report on the electoral system in October 1998, the Jenkins Commission summarised this line of argument:

> It is therefore the case that in only 64 of the past 150 years has there prevailed the alleged benefits of the FPTP [first-past-the-post] system, the production

of single-party government with an undisputed command over the House of Commons. On the factual record it clearly cannot be sustained that . . . there is anything shockingly unfamiliar to the British tradition about government depending upon a broader basis than single party whipped votes in the House of Commons.[19]

However, the main grounds for challenging an over-simplistic account of the British party system are not to be found in the period before 1945, but in the period since the early 1970s. For a generation after 1945 Britain was as close to a classical two-party system as it was possible to get. In this period more than 90 per cent of voters routinely cast their vote for the two big parties (with a peak of 97 per cent in 1951); and between 1945 and 1966 in half of all the seats only Labour and the Conservatives fielded candidates. From whatever angle this period is surveyed and the evidence assembled, two-partyism is emphatically the order of the day.

After 1970 this picture changes rapidly and radically. It might continue to look the same on the surface, with governments still formed by one or other of the two big parties, but the underlying picture had changed. What remained true of the system of government was no longer true of the wider political system and its electoral basis. The nature and extent of the change can most clearly be seen in the sharply reduced share of the vote at general elections taken by the two parties (Table 4.4). From 90 per cent in 1966, this figure had dropped to under 77 per cent by 1974 (and hit a low of only 72 per cent in 1983). In the landslide of 1997, it remained at under 76 per cent. Labour reached its nadir in 1983 (with 28 per cent, only just in front of the alliance of Liberals and Social Democrats), while the Conservatives dived to 31 per cent in 1997. In the period between the 1970s and 1990s elections were won on votes that would have ensured defeat in the generation after 1945.

Table 4.4 Labour/Conservative share of the vote in general elections, 1945–97 (Great Britain) (%)

1945	88.4
1950	89.8
1951	97.1
1955	96.6
1959	93.4
1964	87.7
1966	90.3
1970	90.1
1974 (Feb)	76.8
1974 (Oct)	76.9
1979	82.7
1983	71.8
1987	74.8
1992	78.0
1997	75.8

What had happened? There were more players on the field and old allegiances had weakened. The Liberals (helped by the Social Democratic split from Labour in the early 1980s) increased their electoral support, while the nationalist parties advanced in Scotland and Wales. From 1974 onwards all seats at general elections were contested by three or more parties (and increasingly by many more). At a local level, change was even more marked and did more damage to the two-party duopoly: the number of Liberal Democrat councillors quadrupled between the 1970s and the 1990s and 'hung' councils became more common. Yet at Westminster, despite all this fragmentation, two-partyism remained intact. Even when the combined two-party vote was only 70 per cent in 1983, this still produced 93 per cent of the seats in the Commons. The effect was that the House looked the same, even though its electoral foundations were crumbling.

In short, the two-party system had been saved by the electoral system. Its high 'breakthrough' threshold meant that it was difficult for competitors to get in (though once beyond this level a party could rapidly transform its fortunes, as Labour did in replacing the Liberals as one of the two big parties in the early part of the twentieth century). From the 1970s it was possible to identify a mismatch between the continuing strength of the two-party system at Westminster and its fragmentation elsewhere, such that 'this impressive continuity and stability rests in the end on one very narrow base – the electoral system'.[20] This poses problems for the way in which the party system should properly now be described.

It is scarcely accurate to go on using the 'two-party' label in the way that this was appropriate in the period from 1945 to the early 1970s. Even its extension to 'two-and-a-half-party system' only captures part of the reality. In Scotland and Wales, for example, there is a four-party system (while Northern Ireland has a separate party system of its own). In the 1970s and early 1980s the demise of the two-party system was much discussed and widely predicted, with the arrival of a 'multi-party' system heralded as its replacement. Although this captured the changing pattern of party support in the electorate, it was at odds with the continuity at Westminster. It was particularly at odds with the way in which a single party seemed to have consolidated its hold on government in the period after 1979. This experience therefore produced new terms – such as 'predominant' party system – to describe what seemed to be happening. When this 'predominant' party was itself blown out of the water in 1997, further revision was clearly required. Norris provides a sensible summary: 'Britain has not become a multi-party or predominant system. Rather Britain has evolved from a *dominant* two-party system to a *declining* two-party system during the last fifty years.'[21]

The congruence between two-party domination of Westminster and of the electorate, characteristic of the post-1945 generation, no longer exists. Yet continuity at the centre, in Parliament and in government, does persist. Nine out of ten seats are still held by the two main parties and single-party majoritarian government remains the norm. The Northern Ireland parties aside, in addition to the Liberal Democrats the only minor parties to have any representation at all in the House of Commons are the two nationalist parties of Scotland and Wales. There is room for endless debate about the lack of 'fit' between the party system at Westminster and the political world outside. Does it matter? Some argue that it has kept government strong and stable, protected against fragmenting tendencies outside, and that this makes for coherent and accountable policy-making. Others argue that it makes governments less representative, fosters a sterile adversarialism, and damages both the legitimacy and continuity of the policy process. Behind these competing perspectives lies the stuff of much recent political debate in Britain.

What of the future? The perils of previous predictions about the evolving shape of the party system suggest the need for caution. Even a declining two-party system exhibits a remarkable resilience. Having survived the fragmenting pressures of recent decades, it would be foolish to expect its necessary demise. A less attached electorate can still deliver landslide victories. The breakthrough threshold for minor parties remains as high as ever. The major parties can dip to perilous levels of electoral support (Labour in 1983, the Conservatives in 1997) and still retain enough seats to keep out other contenders and provide a base from which to mount a recovery. There is life in the two-party system yet.

However, there are also new challenges. A less attached electorate is also a more fickle one. What is given can just as easily be taken away; and this may lower the barriers to entry. Devolution will almost certainly have a fragmenting effect on the party system, no longer centralising all efforts on Westminster but stimulating distinctive political systems that will require a party system to match. But the real joker in the pack is electoral reform. Any serious move towards a more proportional electoral system would transform the party system at a stroke (and with it much else in the British political system). In framing its recommendations, the Jenkins Commission on the voting system was careful to devise a system that would retain high entry barriers and continue to allow for the possibility of single-party governments. However, this could not disguise the fact that its only certain effects would be to increase Liberal Democrat representation and make coalition government more likely. It would be the final end of the two-party system. No doubt this is why the response from both main parties has been less than enthusiastic.

NOTES

1 J. Sopel, *Tony Blair* (Michael Joseph, 1995), pp. 62–7.
2 P. Seyd, P. Whiteley and J. Parry, *Labour and Conservative Party Members 1990–92* (Dartmouth, 1996).
3 D. Denver and G. Hands, 'Measuring the intensity and effectiveness of constituency campaigning in the 1992 general election' in D. Denver *et al.* (eds), *British Elections and Parties Yearbook, 1993* (Harvester Wheatsheaf, 1993).
4 D. Butler and D. Kavanagh, *The British General Election of 1997* (Macmillan, 1997), p. 210.
5 A revealing insider's account is P. Gould, *The Unfinished Revolution: How the Modernisers Saved the Labour Party* (Little Brown, 1998).
6 D. Butler and D. Kavanagh, *The British General Election of 1997* (Macmillan, 1997), p. 243.

7 R. Rose, *Do Parties Make a Difference?*, 2nd edn (Macmillan, 1984).
8 C. Turpin, *British Government and the Constitution*, 2nd edn (Weidenfeld, 1990), p. 545.
9 P. Norton, 'Parliamentary behaviour since 1945', *Talking Politics*, vol. 8, no. 2 (1996), pp. 107–14.
10 P. Riddell, *Parliament under Pressure* (Gollancz, 1997), p. 24.
11 Beyond Left and Right: The New Politics of Britain (Institute of Economic Affairs/MORI, 1997).
12 K. Joseph, *Reversing the Trend* (Centre for Policy Studies, 1975), p. 4.
13 D. Willetts, *Why Vote Conservative?* (Penguin, 1997), p. 1.
14 D. Willetts, 'Conservative renewal', *Political Quarterly*, vol. 69, no. 2 (1998).
15 T. Blair, *The Third Way*, Fabian Society, 1988.
16 P. Seyd, 'In praise of party', *Parliamentary Affairs*, vol. 51, no. 2 (1998), p. 204.
17 V. Bogdanor in D. Butler and A. Ranney (eds), *Referendums around the World* (Macmillan, 1994), p. 97.
18 For example, M. Pinto-Duschinsky, 'Parties need their anoraks', *The Times*, 6 October 1998; and M. Leonard, 'You can't get away from the party', *New Statesman*, 24 July 1998.
19 *Report of the Independent Commission on the Voting System*, Cm. 4090, HMSO, October 1998, pp. 13–14.
20 I. Budge, 'Great Britain: a stable, but fragile, party system?', in P. Pennings and J. Lane (eds), *Comparing Party System Change* (Routledge, 1998), p. 126.
21 P. Norris, *Electoral Change since 1945* (Blackwell, 1997), p. 62.

FURTHER READING

The classic study by R. McKenzie, *British Political Parties* (2nd edn, Heinemann, 1963) is still well worth reading. Useful recent texts include J. Fisher, *British Political Parties* (Prentice Hall/Harvester Wheatsheaf, 1996) and R. Garner and R. Kelly, *British Political Parties Today* (2nd edn, Manchester University Press, 1998). P. Norris, *Electoral Change since 1945* (Blackwell, 1997) also covers party change, while D. Butler and D. Kavanagh, *The British General Election of 1997* (Macmillan, 1997) is indispensable for the recent past. Important studies of party membership are P. Seyd and P. Whiteley, *Labour's Grass Roots* (Oxford University Press, 1992) and P. Whiteley, P. Seyd and J. Richardson, *True Blues: The Politics of Conservative Party Membership* (Oxford University Press, 1994). Books on the Labour Party include M. Smith and J. Spear (eds), *The Changing Labour Party* (Routledge, 1992), E. Shaw, *The Labour Party since 1979* (Routledge, 1994) and S. Fielding, *Labour: Decline and Renewal* (Baseline, 1995). On the Conservatives there is P. Norton (ed.), *The Conservative Party* (Prentice Hall/Harvester Wheatsheaf, 1996), S. Ludlam and M. Smith (eds), *Contemporary British Conservatism* (Macmillan, 1996) and S. Ball, *The Conservative Party since 1945* (Manchester University Press, 1998). Beyond the two main parties, there is J. Stevenson, *Third Party Politics since 1945* (Blackwell, 1993). On party ideas, L. Tivey and A. Wright (eds), *Party Ideology in Britain* (Routledge, 1989) is useful, along with I. Adams, *Ideology and Politics in Britain Today* (Manchester University Press, 1998). Good insights into current party debate can be found in the three Penguin specials produced for the 1997 general election: D. Willetts, *Why Vote Conservative?*, T. Wright, *Why Vote Labour?* and W. Wallace, *Why Vote Liberal Democrat?* (Penguin, 1997).

5 Pressures and publics

Westminster and Whitehall are evolving separately from the rest of the nation, like some fascinating but isolated evolutionary backwater, a political Galapagos islands full of living political fossils and shambling tortoises meditatively chewing familiar foliage while the real business is going on elsewhere.

(Chris Rose, Campaign Director, Greenpeace 1996[1])

INTRODUCTION

There are a number of ways in which the citizen (or bodies acting on behalf of citizens) can register protests, pursue complaints, apply pressure or make comments about government in Britain. In the traditional model of British politics, the MP was seen as the major channel of communication between the governed and the governors. But other mechanisms have developed, in the process undermining this traditional role, although strengthening the means by which government can be influenced and monitored. Paradoxically this has occurred at the same time as MPs themselves have become more skilled at attending to the concerns of constituents, supplanting the role of local councillors and so tending to undermine accountability in local government. The information revolution is also poised to offer new ways of communication between citizens and the state.

This chapter looks at some of the main channels, beyond the traditional machinery of Parliament, by which government can be influenced and held to account. These include: individual routes of complaint and redress, such as the ombudsman and judicial review; then information and regulation, with reference to performance indicators, regulatory bodies and freedom of information. Finally, attempts to influence policy by pressure groups and lobbyists are reviewed, as well as other forms of communication between government and governed such as referendums, opinion polls and new forms of participation, including focus groups and 'electronic' democracy.

COMPLAINT AND REDRESS

The ombudsman

The first ombudsman in Britain was the Parliamentary Commissioner for Administration, established in 1967 as a new type of public official who could investigate complaints of citizens about maladministration by government officials. What 'maladministration' included, in the words of cabinet minister Richard Crossman when introducing the legislation in 1966, was: 'bias, neglect, inattention, delay, incompetence, ineptitude, perversity, turpitude, arbitrariness and so on'.[2] At the time the new office was attacked as a constitutional innovation which could not be reconciled with ministerial accountability to Parliament, and which usurped an MP's traditional role of pursuing the grievances of constituents. Therefore the new scheme required that all complaints were to be channelled through MPs who could pass them on to the ombudsman. This 'MP filter' is criticised for reducing the visibility of the Parliamentary Ombudsman, since in a public survey commissioned by his office in 1996 only 14 per cent had heard of the post. MPs also vary in the number and type of cases which they refer and this introduces an element of lottery for the individual complainant.[3]

Several types of ombudsman now exist, either in statutory form, as in health, local government and housing, or in non-statutory form, as self-regulatory devices for particular industries. The newer types of ombudsmen may undertake mediation and dispute resolution in addition to the formal investigation of complaints. They have also developed into information providers and regulators of codes of practice. In the last two decades there has been a huge growth in ombudsman schemes of all kinds not only in Britain but throughout the world – and the European (Union) Ombudsman was established in 1995 (see box below).

Selected ombudsman schemes

Statutory

Parliamentary Ombudsman and Health Services Ombudsman
Independent Housing Ombudsman
Local Government Ombudsman
Pensions Ombudsman
Adjudicator for Inland Revenue, Customs and Excise and Contributions Agency

Non-statutory

Funerals Ombudsman
Prisons Ombudsman
Banking Ombudsman
Buildings Societies Ombudsman
Ombudsman for Corporate Estate Agents
Insurance Ombudsman

The National Consumer Council publication *A–Z of Ombudsmen* gives a comprehensive list.

The Parliamentary Ombudsman is independent of government and Parliament and has access to all government papers, except Cabinet and Cabinet committee papers. A select committee monitors his work as Parliamentary and Health Services Ombudsman, since one official combines both posts. It is the select committee which asks departments to explain the shortcomings set out in the ombudsman's reports. Although ombudsman findings and recommendations are not binding, in only two instances have departments refused to put right the maladministration found. In general the ombudsman's decision is final, but recent cases have confirmed that his recommendations are subject to judicial review. There are now separate parliamentary ombudsmen schemes for devolved matters in Northern Ireland, Scotland and Wales.

As Table 5.1 shows, nearly a quarter of all complaints in 1997–8 were about the Child Support Agency, with the Benefits Agency next. Three-fifths of all complaints referred are rejected as unsuitable for investigation, often because they do not concern administrative actions. Fewer than one in six results in a full investigation, though in most of these the complaint is upheld either in full or in part.

Significant delays occur in investigating complaints – the average throughput time in 1996 was ninety-nine weeks, though this was partly due to an accumulation of very old cases – and long delays are also common for the Local Government and Health Services ombudsmen. Although what is sometimes described as a 'Rolls Royce' service is offered to the individual complainant, the process can be lengthy and bureaucratic. As a response to such criticism, more use is being made of the 'fast-track' procedures pioneered by the Northern Ireland Ombudsman to resolve individual complaints quickly, but this may conflict with the larger (and longer) task of investigating administrative failure.

A further issue is whether more could be done by public sector ombudsmen to publicise best or worst practice so that standards of administration are improved. Innovations in the 1990s include the booklet *The Ombudsman in Your Files*, explaining the role of the Parliamentary Ombudsman to government departments, and the publication of special ombudsman reports on certain cases – such as those involving the Child Support Agency – because of the particular issues of redress and administrative practice raised. The Local Government Ombudsman now issues guidance to councils on such matters as devising complaints procedures.

The Parliamentary Ombudsman has no power to conduct audits of the administrative practices of government bodies (a power which has been suggested by the Centre for Ombudsman Studies at Reading University), with some arguing that such a power would detract from his central role of responding to individual complaints. The number and range of public bodies subject to the ombudsman is also believed to require overhaul. The large number of complaints rejected by him as inappropriate for investigation illustrates confusion about his role and remit. There may now be too many different ombudsmen with entirely separate jurisdictions so that a more collegiate approach might be sensible – with citizens having a common access point to put a complaint – and the task of allocating the appropriate avenue for redress falling on the ombudsmen. More radical still,

Table 5.1 The Parliamentary Ombudsman at work, 1997–8

	Total complaints[a]	Not suitable for investigation	Resolved without full investigation	Full investigation: reports completed	Reports upheld in full or part	Cases carried forward
DSS – Child Support Agency	578	308	11	114	112	145
DSS – Benefits Agency	468	261	47	75	71	85
DSS – Contributions Agency	38	13	2	17	17	6
Inland Revenue	217	147	1	43	37	26
Department of the Environment, Transport and the Regions	161	116	3	20	17	22
Legal Aid Board	147	89	5	19	17	34
Department for Education & Employment	115	70	6	18	18	21
Lord Chancellor's Department	98	73	3	10	10	12
HM Customs & Excise	33	12	–	14	13	7
Others	696	480	32	46	39	138
Total	2,551	1,569	110	376	351	496

Source: Parliamentary Ombudsman, *Annual Report 1997–8*.

Note

[a] Includes complaints brought forward from previous year.

should a single ombudsman be responsible for complaints about all types of public service?

Judicial review and public inquiries

Judicial review – legal challenge to government decisions – has grown enormously in the last fifteen years. There has been a greater awareness of the feasibility of challenging the decisions of many different types of statutory bodies, or private bodies carrying out public functions. In 1981 there were 558 applications for leave to apply for judicial review in England and Wales; there were 3,848 in 1997.[4] Most of the increase is accounted for by immigration and homelessness cases, but the reforming zeal of successive Conservative governments in areas of public policy encouraged opponents to use all available obstacles, including the courts: 'The pursuit of contentious policies by the governments of the 1980s undoubtedly stimulated increased litigiousness on the part of both public bodies and individuals affected by them.'[5] The incorporation of the European Convention on Human Rights into British law will also extend the role of the courts in scrutinising and challenging administrative decisions (this is discussed further in Chapter 2).

Decisions affecting benefit claimants, the homeless, the mentally ill, prisoners, health service users, and those affected by planning decisions are all potentially within the scope of judicial review. Judicial review is not an appeal on the merits of a decision but a process which asks whether a correct legal basis was used to reach that decision (for example, whether the body had the power to make the decision, or whether it had taken irrelevant factors into account). Recent cases have had a profound impact on legislation and illustrate how powerful the courts can be in determining the exercise of executive power, notwithstanding the principle of parliamentary sovereignty. For instance, the challenge by the Fire Brigades Union to the use of prerogative (executive) powers forced the Home Secretary to introduce legislation to underpin the new tariff scheme of criminal injuries compensation in 1995. Government has responded to the growth of judicial review by attempting to make 'judge-proof' laws, and by issuing the guidance *The Judge over Your Shoulder*, which warns civil servants to think more carefully about the prospect of facing a legal challenge to their administrative decisions.

Independent tribunals already adjudicate on disputes over social security, taxation and employment rights, including racial, sexual and disability discrimination. There are some 2,000 administrative tribunals dealing with over 1 million cases a year. These tribunals are independent of the government and are set up under statutory powers governing their constitution, procedures and functions. The machinery of the courts is not suited to solving every dispute arising out of the work of government, as the issues involved are specialist, and tribunal procedures are intended to be informal and cost-effective. However, each type of tribunal is subject to different rules and the lack of coherence can be confusing to the ordinary citizen. As with ombudsmen, a common access point might give citizens an easier way into the system.

Public inquiries of various kinds also play a role in holding government to account. They may be set up to establish the facts of a particular incident (such as the Dunblane massacre). They take evidence and make recommendations, for example in cases of child abuse where wider lessons could be drawn. They can also be used to make decisions, such as on planning applications. In particularly serious cases a tribunal of inquiry can be set up under the Tribunals of Inquiry (Evidence) Act 1921 to conduct hearings, one of the most recent being that established to investigate the events of Bloody Sunday. Such inquiry reports usually have a major impact on policy-making (see box below). It is increasingly common for judges to head politically sensitive inquiries, for a variety of reasons:

> rightly or wrongly judges are held to have the reputation of being immune to political bias and special interest pleadings and this means that politicians who have got into a hole are easily tempted to conclude that it will help them to get out of this unenviable situation if they can cite the findings of a judicial personage in favour of what they propose to do.[6]

Some recent inquiries

- Inquiry into the causes of BSE announced in December 1997, chaired by Lord Justice Phillips. There is no statutory basis to the enquiry
- Bloody Sunday inquiry (events of 30 January 1972 in Londonderry), announced January 1998 and chaired by Lord Saville under the 1921 Tribunals of Inquiry (Evidence) Act
- Death of Stephen Lawrence inquiry announced in July 1997, and chaired by Sir William MacPherson under S.49 of the Police Act 1996
- Southall Rail Accident Inquiry announced in September 1997, and chaired by Professor John Uff QC under S14(2)(b) of the Health and Safety at Work etc. Act 1974

Appropriate sources of advice are also essential for citizens in pursuit of redress. The citizens advice bureaux (CABs), set up in the Second World War following a massive extension of the role of the government, deal with around 6.5 million enquiries a year. CABs rely mainly on local authority funding, as do independent law centres, but this is often inadequate for the growing demands on their services. Redress mechanisms are only effective if people know how to access them.

PERFORMANCE, REGULATION AND INFORMATION

The Citizen's Charter

The Citizen's Charter was launched in July 1991 as a ten-year programme to improve the standard and efficiency of public services and to be at the heart of government policies in the 1990s. Its founding white paper declared: 'Through the Citizen's Charter the government is now determined to drive reforms further into the core of the public services, extending the benefits of choice, competition and commitment to service more widely.'[7] The Prime Minister John Major identified himself personally with the charter, which was to be administered through a special Cabinet Office Unit.

The initiative drew together a number of different strands in the Conservative Party's public service reform programme – market testing of public services, provision of information about performance, delegation of responsibility, and greater responsiveness to customers. The charter was more about consumer rights and managerial performance than citizen participation. A key emphasis was the availability of more information through the publication of service standards and performance figures, thus empowering the consumer. The Labour Party claimed that it was the true begetter of the charter, pointing to local experiments carried out at York (which launched its own charter in 1989) and other Labour-controlled councils.

The charter initiative is not party-political and the Blair government has relaunched the initiative under the title of 'service first', setting out nine principles of public service delivery and focusing on the themes of responsiveness, quality, effectiveness and working together. In November 1997 there were 40 national charters and over 10,000 local charters which are not centrally controlled. This means that most public services now have their own charters, such as the Patient's Charter in the National Health Service (see box, p. 135).

The charter initiative has been criticised on the grounds that the standards of service specified are too vague to be meaningful, that consumer rights are not legally enforceable, that there is inadequate compensation and redress, that there is no independent audit of the charters, and that consumers are not involved enough. However, the Citizen's Charter programme has undoubtedly had a significant impact on the operation and culture of central government and its agencies. For example, the Passport Agency reduced the maximum time for processing passport applications from ninety-five working days in 1989 to ten in 1995/6 – and there are similar examples of increased efficiency in other services. But the introduction of privatisation and the contracting out of services through the 'Competing for Quality' programme within the public sector alongside the charter confused its impact. The perception was that improving public services had become mixed up with privatising them (or controlling their cost). The Blair government has now dropped privatisation of service delivery as a policy objective for the programme. But the Public Service Select Committee found in 1997 that public recognition of the Citizen's Charter programme remained patchy and

---

The Patient's Charter (extract)

GP SERVICES
You have the **right** to be registered with a GP.

* You can **expect** your local Family Health Services Authority (FHSA) to find you a GP within two working days. **The NHS now achieves this standard fully**.

You have the **right** to change your GP easily and quickly.

* You can **expect** your local FHSA to send you a list of doctors within two working days together with details of how to change doctors.

If you have changed GP, you can **expect** your local FHSA to send your medical records to your new GP quickly. This means within two working days for urgent cases and six weeks for all other cases.

The NHS now meets this standard in eight out of ten urgent cases and in over seven out of ten routine cases.

(*Patient's Charter*, December 1996)

---

that, in the absence of systematic surveys of people's views over time, firm conclusions could not be drawn on its success.[8]

Audit, inspection and regulation

The provision of public services is audited for its value for money by a growing number of bodies on behalf of the taxpayer. The oldest – dating from the nineteenth century – is the National Audit Office which scrutinises projects funded by central government. There is also the Audit Commission (and its Scottish equivalent, the Accounts Commission), established by the Thatcher government in the 1980s to achieve the 'three Es' – economy, efficiency and effectiveness – in local government and the NHS. It appoints local auditors, specifies indicators of performance and produces general value-for-money studies. Its reports can sometimes have a devastating effect on perceptions of government policy; for example, its *Misspent Youth* report on youth justice provision, published in November 1996, was highly critical of government policy, and was influential in encouraging the policy change embodied in Labour's Crime and Disorder Act 1998.

A host of new regulators such as Oftel and Ofgas inspect the privatised utilities and deal with public complaints about them. These regulators are independent of government and Parliament and are often seen as unaccountable, subject to no general statutory requirements to consult or to give reasons for decisions. Yet far more information is now made available about the performance of utilities than before privatisation. Given discretion to balance social and consumer considerations alongside economic efficiency concerns, the regulators have developed into powerful but independent public officials, as a 'deregulating' government created a far-reaching regulatory regime. They have been at the forefront of pressures to increase competition, deploying their statutory powers to the full and breaking with previous patterns of policy-making.[9]

There has also been a massive expansion in the regulation of the public sector in the last twenty years, with one study finding no fewer than 136 separate bodies regulating the British public sector at national government level in 1995, costing £766m to run.[10] Regulation is growing as the number of public sector employees is declining. Bodies such as Ofsted and the Housing Corporation have set increasingly complex targets, but there has been criticism that the need to meet these has led to procedural overload and an explosion of controls. The profusion of regulators brings the danger of confusion. A single access point, particularly at local level, would be useful to make the mass of information now published on performance available to the citizen. One recent study concluded that 'there is no central monitoring of the monitors. Nobody inspects the inspectors to make sure that they are giving the public value for money.'[11] No single body oversees this growing regulatory industry to ensure best practice. There appears to be duplication and lack of scrutiny – the very faults which regulators are supposed to remedy in the regulated.

Freedom of information

Access to official information is a powerful instrument for obtaining redress and influencing policy; and after a long campaign a freedom of information (FOI) bill is likely to become law by the turn of the century. In his 1996 report on arms exports to Iraq, Sir Richard Scott saw information as the most powerful method of accountability to Parliament, making FOI a central recommendation. Under pressure for legislation, John Major's government had introduced a non-statutory Code of Practice on Access to Government Information, with extensive exemptions, and with appeals to the Parliamentary Ombudsman. This suffered from lack of publicity and requests for information under the code were infrequent, with only thirty cases going to the Parliamentary Ombudsman in 1997. There was a general feeling that a non-statutory code was a poor substitute for comprehensive FOI legislation, a view supported in a Commons select committee report of 1996.[12] Labour and the Liberal Democrats had for many years been committed to FOI and a white paper was issued by the new Labour government in December 1997, with legislation to follow (see box, p. 137).

The white paper promised a presumption in favour of openness and legally enforceable rights to seek both official information and documents from a wide range of public bodies, including local authorities, quangos and even private bodies contracted to carry out public functions. Seven exemptions were proposed, familiar from FOI overseas, and covering areas such as foreign affairs, information supplied in confidence, and cabinet and ministerial policy-making. Crucially,

Ending secrecy?

Unnecessary secrecy in government leads to arrogance in governance and defective decision-making. The perception of excessive secrecy has become a corrosive influence in the decline of public confidence in government.

(*Your Right to Know*, white paper, December 1997)

the exemptions were *contents* rather than *class* based: this meant that a particular document, in itself releasable without harm but falling within a category covered by an exemption, could still be released, unless the public body was able to demonstrate 'substantial harm' as a result, outweighing any public interest in disclosure. The only area where the test was reduced merely to 'harm' in the government's proposals was for policy documents, including Cabinet and Cabinet committee papers. Certain areas, such as the intelligence services and public sector employment records, were excluded altogether. A subsequent white paper in 1999 made some substantial changes, reintroducing some class-based exemptions and limiting the release of policy advice (Freedom of Information: Consultation on Draft Legislation. Cm. 4355, May 1999).

The Blair government has chosen the device of an Information Commissioner to police the new legislation, broadly on the lines of the current Data Protection Registrar. The commissioner will not be responsible to Parliament, on the grounds that local authorities and other public bodies within the scope of FOI are not directly accountable to MPs. There will be no select committee formally linked with the work of the commissioner and the legislation, unlike the traditional ombudsman model, with MPs no longer seen as the essential or unique mediators between the government and the governed. Experience overseas indicates that the most frequent use of FOI legislation is by people checking personal data held on them, rather than for scrutiny of government policy. In this sense, FOI can simply be another mechanism for individual redress, but open government in its widest sense should be a valuable way of decreasing the distance between those within the policy circle and those outside. The white paper promises that a whole range of government information could be made available over the internet, and already there have been rapid developments in electronic access to official documents. The whole issue of citizen access to the wealth of official information available through new technology and the ability to make comments on it is increasingly central.

Data protection legislation also gives individuals rights in relation to those who record and use computerised personal information, including the right to see personal information about oneself and, if necessary, have it corrected. All data users must comply with eight data protection principles designed to ensure that data is obtained and used fairly and lawfully. The Data Protection Commissioner considers complaints about breaches of these principles and takes enforcement action against users. Individuals can obtain compensation if they have been damaged by inaccurate data or its unauthorised disclosure. The new Data Protection Act 1998 will gradually extend these rights to some data held in manual records. Much of the impetus on data protection law in Britain has come from international pressures, especially the EU, but there has been no similar enthusiasm from this quarter for FOI.

INFLUENCE AND PRESSURE

Pressure groups

A more familiar and traditional way in which citizens try to influence policy is through pressure groups. They are not a new phenomenon. The nineteenth century was a golden age of such groups, with the Anti-Corn Law League in the 1840s successfully linking popular pressure with an organised elite to force change on a divided government and open up agriculture to free trade. Earlier successful examples include the Anti Slavery Association and Daniel O'Connell's campaign for Catholic emancipation in the 1820s, which had made Ireland ungovernable. His mass subscription associations meant that funding from the elite was no longer necessary to sustain organised pressure, while his objective was clear and achievable, and already accepted by a minority of the political class, unlike the Chartists' demands of a decade later. Leaders of successful pressure groups have learned over the years that objectives must always be clear and the strategy achievable.

Pressure groups can be categorised in a number of ways. A familiar distinction is between a *cause* group which promotes issues not directly connected with the interests of its members and which anyone can join (such as the Society for the Protection of the Unborn Child (SPUC) or the Campaign for Freedom of Information) and an *interest* group which focuses on the common interests of its members, notably trade unions, employers' groups and professional associations (such as the British Medical Association (BMA) and the Law Society). Clearly there can be overlap between these broad types and it would be difficult to categorise Daniel O'Connell's campaigns so neatly.

The other main distinction is between *insiders* and *outsiders*. Governments need to consult when drawing up policies to establish their feasibility and to receive information about practical issues which only those working in an area can provide. Even a government determined not to rule by consensus, like Mrs Thatcher's in the 1980s, needs insider groups to communicate with. Under her premiership the relationship between government and groups was placed deliberately under stress so that the balances of power could be disturbed, but there was no attempt to curtail their right to be consulted.[13] Interest groups are more likely to be consulted than cause groups and groups which are routinely consulted are known as insider groups.[14] Perhaps the best example of an insider group is the National Farmers Union's relationship with the Ministry of Agriculture (MAFF), but the BMA and the Department of Health and teacher unions and the Education Department also come into the same category. Local government went from outsider to insider in the new Blair government but insider status does not guarantee success in achieving desired policy goals, as the Local Government Association found.

Some cause groups may gain access through expertise, such as the Campaign for Freedom of Information and the RSPCA, but they are unlikely to be true insiders as they promote different objectives from those of the government and exert external pressure in pursuit of those objectives. Some relationships between interest groups and government are so close that part of the government machine can be seen to be 'captured' by the pressure group, routinely promoting its interests. A new minister, or change in the structure of government may be necessary to break the hold. This consideration was a factor in the decision by the Blair government to make changes to the Ministry of Agriculture, involving the creation of an independent Food Standards Agency.

Whether insider or outsider, authority is a key aim for any pressure group. To bargain effectively with government it is necessary to be able to organise members, threaten sanctions or offer indispensable expertise. Greenpeace's credibility was damaged by the apparent lack of scientific evidence supporting its position in the Brent Spar oil rig incident in 1995.[15] However, a group which achieves insider status may need to make compromises and respect confidences as a result. There is a danger that a group may lose credibility through too close a connection with government and be outflanked by others with a more robust approach. RADAR lost credibility in the area of disability rights with the growth of the Disability Income Group in the 1980s. It may sometimes be more productive to be a principled outsider than a compromised insider.

Different methods are used by groups to pursue their objectives. Insider groups are more likely to use influence in Whitehall and Westminster and resort to external protest only when their voice is not being heard. Outsider groups and cause groups are more likely to be dependent on the media and the public to sustain their authority and spread their message as well as to raise their funds. Pressure groups commonly produce material in the form of leaflets and pamphlets and mobilise support in the form of strikes, demonstrations and mass lobbies, all with varying degrees of success. When insider interests combine with popular pressure (as with the successful campaign by the financial services industry in 1998 to change government proposals on tax-exempt savings schemes), the political impact can be particularly effective.

Groups rise or fall as issues change and public concerns move on. The Campaign for Nuclear Disarmament (CND) has seen a sharp decline in support in recent years, for example, while environmental and animal welfare groups have grown in size and significance. The pressure group world is a dynamic one. The relationship between organised groups and the political parties is particularly interesting. The parties like to win group support, although picking fights with unpopular groups (as Mrs Thatcher did with the trade unions) can sometimes be useful. Groups are usually wary of seeming too close to political parties, although there are times when one group may decide that converting a party to its cause is the best way to achieve its objectives. The animal welfare movement in recent years has deliberately associated itself with the Labour Party for this reason, and

Labour was glad to have this support. When the Labour government did not immediately move to ban fox-hunting (partly under pressure among a rival 'countryside' movement that had begun to exercise itself energetically), this provoked considerable disappointment among the anti-hunting pressure groups (Figure 5.1).

There have been close links in the past between the Conservative Party and business interests and between the Labour Party and trade unions. However, these historic attachments have been called into question by the deliberately 'inclusive' ambitions of Tony Blair's New Labour, with its wooing of business and message to the trade unions that 'fairness not favours' was now the nature of the relationship. Many commentators consider that New Labour is more likely to listen to the Confederation of British Industry (CBI) than the unions.

There has been much discussion about the value or otherwise of pressure groups to the political process. In the 1960s and 1970s the rise and fall of 'tripartism' – collaborative decision-making between government, trade unions and employers – provoked criticisms that producers and not consumers were in control of the state. When the TUC and the CBI eventually proved unable to control their members, Mrs Thatcher reaped the advantage and her pursuit of different economic priorities shut the trade unions – and, to a lesser extent, the employers – out of their insider status. Other insider groups suffered too, as changes in health and education disturbed the position of the professional interest groups. Other interest or cause groups prospered, however, and certain think-tanks such as the Institute of Economic Affairs were given direct access to government. In fact, the number of pressure groups grew in the 1980s as a response to Thatcherite

As one of your constituents, I am writing to express my extreme disappointment that the Wild Mammals (Hunting with Dogs) Bill may fail to become law because a handful of MPs are being allowed to thwart the will of Parliament and the people.

Please will you do everything you can to ensure the Bill becomes law in this session of Parliament.

Comments:

I HOPE LABOUR WILL GET THIS PASSED

From: *DANIEL HAYES*
        BOLTON

P.S. I realise you are busy and there is no need for you to reply to this card.

LEAGUE
WORKING FOR WILDLIFE   Produced by League Against Cruel Sports Ltd (0171) 403 6155

To: *RUTH KELLY*   MP

House of Commons

London

SW1A 0AA

Figure 5.1 Putting on the pressure: Postcard campaign to MPs organised by the League Against Cruel Sports, 1998

policies. The role of media moguls such as Rupert Murdoch also came into prominence and can be regarded as interest group activity. Indeed, there was much discussion after Labour came to power about the nature of the relationship between the Blair government and the Murdoch interest.

Government is inoperable without the co-operation of professional interests and this is reflected in the way policy is made. Although the 1980s was character-ised by a whole series of deliberate policy challenges to entrenched groups in education, health, law and industry, only partly prompted by funding issues, mat-ters stabilised in the 1990s and the Blair government shows no sign of rejecting the policy networks which have flourished since Victorian times.

Indeed, despite its huge majority, the Blair government has sought to combine the pursuit of its policy objectives with a deliberately consensual style. It claims to be a 'people's government', pursuing public interest goals and not special inter-ests, but this has not prevented it from seeking to find the widest agreement for its policies. On contentious manifesto commitments, such as the minimum wage and trade union recognition, it has gone to elaborate lengths to find common ground between major interest groups – usually the CBI and the TUC – which have different stances. An extensive programme of policy reviews has also been established to enable wide consultation to take place.

Lobbying

Lobbying is an imprecise term, sometimes with pejorative overtones. Different kinds of activity are associated with the term, and the definition given by Michael Rush to the Select Committee on Members' Interests inquiry into lobbying in 1991[16] identified four types:

1   professional lobbyists or consultants
2   organisations outside Parliament and government which seek to lobby, whether professional groups or voluntary bodies
3   MPs, journalists and others who have direct access to Parliament, and receive some kind of remuneration to represent the interests of an outside body
4   MPs and other individuals with direct access to Parliament who have non-pecuniary interests in policy areas but make representations on behalf of outside bodies.

It is normally types (1) and (3) which excite concern.

If pressure group behaviour arouses concern that issues are being manipulated for the benefit of sectional groups in society, the proliferation of professional lobbying companies is seen as confirmation that an insidious process is at work, one that denies representation to those without financial power. Yet lobbying companies are used by 'cause' groups as well as by more traditional commercial clients, because the expertise which these organisations provide can be seen as essential to promote a group's objectives.

The practice of lobbying has deep roots in British society but the creation of firms whose sole business is to lobby is a much more recent development. One study found that around sixty such firms had been created by 1993, with dramatic growth in the 1980s.[17] Various factors can explain their growth, including the use of more sophisticated techniques by pressure groups, the 'Americanisation' of politics and, perhaps most important, the increasing centralisation of power in Whitehall in the 1980s. Britain remains at present a unitary state, with weakened local government and as yet no real regional tier. Governments in the 1980s enjoyed large majorities in Parliament, accentuating the lack of alternative power bases and contributing to the centralisation of the media in London. There is little point in lobbying at a local or regional level and therefore attention is focused on Whitehall where generalist civil servants, with little experience of the professions which they are administering, are often willing to listen to specialist advice and opinion, while also being aware of the pressures which Parliament exerts on ministers.

What this means is that Whitehall is the real target of successful commercial lobbying, although this is rarely advertised. Instead concern is mainly expressed about Parliamentary lobbying. In the 1990s links between MPs and lobbying companies came under increasing scrutiny. Michael Lee noted in 1991[18] that about 180 MPs, nearly one-third of the total, declared in the *Register of Members' Interests* that they were political consultants to private firms. Lee noted the professionalisation of backbench life, as MPs became full time and gained privileged access to information through the Commons library, ministerial contacts or parliamentary questions. He believed that 'MPs have been drawn systematically into the realms of public relations and corporate entertainment.' Yet the clients of professional lobbyists had only a basic understanding of the policy process and gave Westminster a much greater importance than it merited. Lobbying firms could massage egos and attract clients by arranging entertainment with MPs, despite their lack of policy clout.

Concentration on the activities of lobbying companies at Westminster is also due to the fact that they are at least semi-visible there. The *Register of Members' Interests* requires MPs to list consultancies, following a number of cases linking MPs with lobbying companies in the 1992–7 Parliament. The Committee on Standards in Public Life was appointed under a judge, Lord Nolan, and in May 1995 made recommendations designed to restrict MPs from having direct links with lobbying companies (see box below).

MPs for hire?

We would consider it thoroughly unsatisfactory . . . if a Member of Parliament, even if not strictly bound by an agreement with a client to pursue a particular interest in Parliament, was to pursue that interest solely or principally because payment, in cash or kind, was being made.

(The Committee on Standards in Public Life First Report,
Cmnd. 2850, May 1995)

The post-Nolan reforms implemented by the Commons prohibit paid advocacy by MPs altogether. Nolan had backed away from this prohibition, preferring to ban work merely for multi-client consultancies, but, as a parliamentary committee[19] noted, it was logically the activity of advocacy for payment rather than for whom the work was done which was the problem. The select committee's recommendations received the support of the House on a free vote. Many MPs were concerned to repair the damage to the reputation of Parliament that the much publicised 'cash for questions' scandals had brought about.

Significantly, though, the corporate entertainment aspect of the lobbying industry, such as the use of private dining rooms within the Palace of Westminster, was left untouched by the reforms and MPs may still provide advice to lobbying firms. Information-giving activities are in reality often much more important to lobbying firms than the tabling of parliamentary questions, which are unlikely to elicit much genuinely new information.

The advent of a new generation of politicians since the 1997 election is likely to diminish the more disreputable aspects of parliamentary lobbying. Most MPs paid by lobbying firms in the 1992–7 Parliament were Conservatives, although lobbying firms have been careful to recruit on to their staff Labour and Liberal Democrat activists as well and some former Labour insiders have set up their own lobbying companies. It remains to be seen whether, after a few years of Labour government, former ministers and underemployed backbenchers will find attractions in lobbying companies, but this is probably unlikely after the taint of sleaze in the 1990s and the new prohibitions. There has been loose talk by some former Labour policy advisers about the nature and extent of their influence on the Blair government (exposed in a newspaper story in the summer of 1998)[20] but this was vehemently disputed by ministers who have taken extra care to avoid perceptions of sleaze by distancing themselves from these former advisers turned lobbyists.

Lobbyists may therefore intensify their focus on Whitehall, which remains the submerged aspect of the lobbying issue. Civil service corruption is very rare in Britain, even with the contracting-out initiatives of the 1990s, but it cannot be discounted. What lobbying firms achieve in their contacts with the civil service is unreported, as civil servants do not brief publicly on the factors influencing a change in policy. Some lobbying successes are recorded – the defeat of the Shops Bill at second reading in 1986 is often cited – but lobbying firms do not advertise their successes with anonymous civil servants. The former special adviser Cliff Grantham has noted one exception to this rule; in 1987 the lobbyists Westminster Strategy claimed a success when the Government decided not to proceed with plans for a levy on blank tapes, but in his view this victory was due more to a change of minister at the Department of Trade and Industry than the cogency of lobbying. Civil servants are known to have altered briefs when they have been persuaded by the arguments. These changes of policies tend to be at the margins, yet it is precisely those details which prompt the commercial interests to hire consultancies. The most important asset of a professional lobbying firm is knowledge of the policy network, and the point at which to apply pressure.

The present Labour government is considered to be relying more on its own policy networks, rather than on the guidance of the senior civil service. This produces new challenges for lobbying firms, which need to establish the appropriate contacts. There is a danger that lobbying may become even less visible if it is not being monitored within the civil service. The government was soon criticised for an alleged susceptibility to lobbying, especially where the lobbyist had financial connections to the party (as with Bernie Ecclestone and allegations of private lobbying over an exemption from the ban on tobacco advertising for Formula One motor racing in 1997). Lobbyists have called for codes of conduct and monitoring procedures for their industry to ensure against the purchase of access or influence but so far this has been resisted, for fear that a register of lobbyists, would seem to confer recognition on selected firms. However, new guidance was issued by the Cabinet Office in 1998 to regulate civil service contacts with lobbyists, which is allowable only 'where this is justified by the needs of Government'.

The most important stage for effective lobbying is the pre-drafting stage of legislation. It is only a last-ditch attempt to effect change when backbench amendments are tabled at the committee stage of a bill. Nevertheless, ministers are more susceptible to pressure once the fundamentals of policy are not in danger. Is the fact that lobbyists and consultancies can achieve success a threat to the political process? It is an open question and the case is not proven. Lobbyists argue that they improve the efficiency of the policy-making process by explaining the tight timetable of legislation to clients and the need to apply pressure at the right place. They can also give MPs, especially opposition MPs, the hard information they need and cut through postbags filled with unfocused lobbying material, while offering ministers an alternative source of advice during policy formulation and civil servants the specialist knowledge they would otherwise lack. Richardson and Jordan give an example from the 1970s of a lobbyist explaining how he helped exclude ship-repairing from the shipbuilding nationalisation legislation, by briefing a civil servant that the bill would otherwise be hybrid, and so run into insuperable parliamentary procedural difficulties.[21]

Yet the fact remains that the expertise of lobbying firms is only available to those who can pay for it. Would Daniel O'Connell have needed a consultant? It is sometimes possible for single-interest groups to cut through the need for consultants by acquiring the appropriate knowledge of Westminster and Whitehall themselves. The gay rights group Stonewall is a good example of a new group that built up expertise quickly in these areas without generous amounts of funding. Many cause and interest groups employ parliamentary officers, and professional consultants may only be necessary for special campaigns. One way to lessen the influence of lobbyists would be to explain more fully the real nature of the policy process. Parliament itself lacks an effective educative body which could set out the pattern of legislation and provide a guide to effective pressure points. The domination of the legislature by the executive is unlikely to encourage a move in this direction though, since governments by nature do not wish to advertise potential obstacles to their control of the policy-making process.

PARTICIPATION AND POLLING

Referendums

Referendums are devices for obtaining extra legitimacy for specific policy proposals or for mitigating internal party disputes over policy alternatives. They tend to replace the normal role of Parliament and are a form of direct democracy, which is why they are included here, although initiation comes from the government not the governed. In some other countries, such as the United States, Switzerland and Italy, citizens have the right to call a referendum if there is sufficient popular support.

Labour entered the 1997 election with commitments to several referendums, and four were carried out in its first year of office – in Scotland, Wales, London and Northern Ireland. This is an indication of the growing frequency of the use of referendums as a way of legitimising policies or appealing to the public beyond divided party structures. What was once seen as an 'unBritish approach', inconsistent with parliamentary sovereignty, has rapidly established itself as a central part of the British political process (see box, p. 147).

The constitutional lawyer A. V. Dicey was the first major advocate of the referendum in British politics in the early years of the twentieth century, as a method of mobilising popular opposition to home rule for Ireland – which illustrates how political expediency is often behind the promotion of the device. The inter-war experiences of Hitler's stage-managed plebiscites discredited the idea and led Clement Attlee in 1945 to reject a proposal from Churchill for a referendum to determine whether the wartime coalition should continue until the end of the Japanese war.

The referendum idea did not emerge again until the 1970s, when intra-party divisions over membership of the EEC led rebels from both the Conservative and Labour parties to call for the people's voice to be heard. The border poll of 1973, to legitimise the constitutional arrangements of Northern Ireland, was the first example of a referendum in the United Kingdom and a divided Labour Shadow Cabinet took up Tony Benn's proposal for a referendum throughout the United Kingdom on membership of the EEC. Benn argued that 'a referendum would get it out of our system and leave the party united; the party was divided at this stage and we should accept the fact that this would resolve it.'[22]

Once the Labour Party had been elected to government after the two 1974 elections, the practical problems of a referendum had to be tackled. The ensuing white paper summarised the constitutional issues in a single paragraph:

> The referendum is to be held because of the unique nature of the issue which has fundamental implications for the future of this country, for the political relationship between the United Kingdom and the other member governments of the Community and for the constitutional position of Parliament.[23]

The reference to 'unique' is interesting in view of subsequent developments.

This referendum, held in 1975, was considered to be advisory only; under the doctrine of parliamentary sovereignty, the result could not bind Parliament. Yet the decisive expression of public opinion clearly could not be ignored by the Government. As Ted Short, Lord President of the Council and Leader of the House, said before it was held: 'The Government will be bound by its result, but Parliament of course cannot be bound.' This was constitutionally correct, but politically implausible.

The 1975 referendum remains, so far, the only United Kingdom-wide one, although Labour has promised to hold them on both voting reform and on entry to a single currency. Margaret Thatcher, as the new Opposition leader at the time, dwelt at length in the first major Commons debate on the referendum on the constitutional difficulties and the danger of establishing a precedent without sufficient thought. Nevertheless a Referendum Act was passed quickly and the result was decisive, with 67.2 per cent in favour of continued membership of the EEC. The issue was settled for nearly twenty years, until the Maastricht Treaty provided another opportunity for party dissidents to attempt to play the referendum card. Ironically, it was Mrs Thatcher in late 1990, now the ousted Conservative leader, who was the first major figure to call for a referendum on the Maastricht proposals which strengthened the powers of the EU.

The Major government successfully resisted attempts by backbenchers to secure a referendum during the passage of the European Communities (Amendment) Act 1993, the core of the government case being the threat to a parliamentary style of democracy. However, by 1996 John Major sought to achieve party unity by promising a referendum on UK entry into a single currency in the next Parliament if the Cabinet supported entry. Conservative backbenchers also introduced private members' bills to provide for referendums on EU membership and the single currency; but although their main concern was to uphold parliamentary sovereignty, the conventional view of referendums is that they undermine such sovereignty.

The debate over Europe illustrates well how referendums can be the product of political expediency, even if they are presented in terms of democratic principle. In the 1997 election the Liberal Democrats, Conservatives, SNP and Labour all had pledges to hold a referendum on the single currency. An entire party, the Referendum Party, was set up to campaign for a referendum on European political integration (see p. 107). It is clear that parties have come to see referendums as a way to defuse potentially divisive and explosive issues.

Referendums on devolution to Scotland and Wales were forced on the 1974–9 Labour government by backbench pressure arising from internal party dissent. If these earlier referendums were the product of divisions, the referendums of 1997 in Scotland and Wales were based on different considerations. The commitment to hold them came from Tony Blair, who had imposed them on reluctant Scottish and Welsh Labour parties in the summer of 1996 as a way of circumventing parliamentary opposition to devolution legislation and to help entrench any devolution settlement. There was much criticism of the pre-legislative nature of the proposed referendums: essentially the people were to decide on the basis of

Referendums in the United Kingdom

Northern Ireland Border Poll, 8 March 1973

Do you want Northern Ireland to remain part of the United Kingdom?   98.9%
Do you want Northern Ireland to be joined with the Republic of Ireland
outside the United Kingdom?   1.1%
Turnout   58.7%

UK membership of the EEC, 5 June 1975

Do you think that the United Kingdom should stay in the European Community
(the Common Market)?
Yes 67.2%   No 32.8%   Turnout 64.0%

Devolution for Scotland, 1 March 1979

Do you want the provisions of the Scotland Act 1978 to be put into effect?
Yes 51.6%   No 48.4%   Turnout 63.6%
Not less than 40 per cent of the electorate had to vote yes for devolution to be put
into effect; only 32.8 per cent of the electorate voted yes.

Devolution for Wales, 1 March 1979

Do you want the provisions of the Wales Act 1978 to be put into effect?
Yes 20.3%   No 79.7%   Turnout 58.8%
Not less than 40 per cent of the electorate had to vote yes for devolution to be put
into effect; only 11.9 per cent voted yes.

Scottish devolution, 11 September 1997

I agree that there should be a Scottish Parliament   74.3%
I do not agree that there should be a Scottish Parliament   25.7%
I agree that a Scottish Parliament should have tax-varying powers   63.5%
I do not agree that a Scottish Parliament should have tax-varying powers   36.5%
Turnout   60.2%

Welsh devolution, 18 September 1997

I agree that there should be a Welsh Assembly   50.3%
I do not agree that there should be a Welsh Assembly   49.7%
Turnout   50.1%

Greater London Authority, 7 May 1998

Are you in favour of the Government's proposals for a Greater London Authority,
made up of an elected mayor and a separately elected assembly?
Yes 72.0%   No 28.0%   Turnout 34.0%

Northern Ireland agreement, 22 May 1998

Do you support the Agreement reached at the multi-party talks in Northern Ireland
and set out in Command Paper 3883?
Yes 71.1%   No 28.9%   Turnout 81.0%

white paper proposals rather than (as in 1979) on the detailed legislation. But pre-legislative referendums were an essential part of the political strategy to overcome parliamentary opposition and win support for the proposals. As Ron Davies, then Shadow Welsh Secretary of State, put it: 'If the Welsh people say yes, as I am confident they will, let the Tories accept the will of the people and do not stand in the way of legislation.'[24] At this stage, long parliamentary battles were anticipated, on the precedent of the 1977–8 Scotland and Wales Bills.

What was seen as the constitutional weakness of the pre-legislative referendums was seized upon by opponents, such as the anti-devolutionist MP Tam Dalyell, who argued that a post-legislative referendum would also be required to allow for changes during the parliamentary passage of the bill, following detailed debate. As William Hague put it: 'If it is possible to amend the bill, how will voters know what they are voting on?'[25] In the event, the overwhelming defeat of the Conservatives in 1997 meant that the issue of a pre-legislative referendum did not receive the attention it probably deserved. The result of the Welsh referendum was extremely close, and there might well have been closer scrutiny of whether this really represented a popular endorsement of devolution if the parliamentary arithmetic had not been so heavily weighted towards pro-devolution parties. Both the Scotland Bill and the Government of Wales Bill emerged substantially unamended more because of lack of parliamentary opposition than because of popular will, although the size of the yes vote in Scotland undoubtedly helped to underpin the measure.[26] If the vote in Scotland had been as narrow as in Wales, it is unlikely that the proposal (or the Secretary of State) would have survived.

These referendums were held only in parts of the United Kingdom, but Londoners voted on the principle of a mayor and assembly in May 1998, and a referendum in Northern Ireland in the same month allowed the population to give its verdict on the Belfast peace agreement. Labour also has plans for nation-wide referendums on the single currency and on electoral reform; and in a second term of a Labour government referendums have been mooted for people in English regions to indicate whether they want a regional assembly. At local level there is also a commitment to ballot parents in feeder schools connected with individual grammar schools about the future of those schools and suggestions that local ballots have a role to play in the future shape of local government.

This plethora of referendum commitments has inevitably raised questions about common principles. The Labour Party policy statement *New Politics, New Britain* in September 1996 set out the philosophy behind the use of referendums: 'we know that people want more of a direct say in the issues facing the country. That is why we will make use of referenda to seek the public's explicit approval for major constitutional change.' However, there were no proposals to hand over the administration of referendums to an independent commission. The ability of a government to decide which issues warrant a referendum, the timing of the poll, the nature of the question(s) to be asked, the identity of the electorate, issues of conduct and finance and even the basis for the count were not to leave govern-ment control. Yet it can be argued that they should, if referendums are to become an integral part of the British political process.

The independent Constitution Unit joined forces with the Electoral Reform Society in 1996 to produce a *Report of the Commission on the Conduct of Referendums*. This report was careful not to offer opinions on the desirability or otherwise of referendums, but argued that the conduct of such polls should be 'entrusted to a statutory independent body, accountable to Parliament, in order to ensure maximum confidence in the legitimacy of the results.'[27] A generic Referendum Act was recommended as a statutory framework for the efficient, fair and consistent conduct of referendums, and it proposed twenty guidelines in areas such as campaign expenditure and public information. The Conservative Opposition has also recently called for some form of statutory framework for referendums (no doubt with the referendums on electoral reform and European Monetary Union in mind). Rather unexpectedly, the Neill Committee report on party funding[28] used some trenchant language in proposing an independent commission to oversee the conduct of referendums and core funding for yes and no umbrella groups. The government was also advised not to use the civil service machine in putting forward its case to the electorate. This seemed to the government a step too far, but the Neill Committee report raised the profile of the case for an impartial presentation of the issues. In response, a white paper in 1999 proposed overall expenditure limits for campaigning groups, limited funding for umbrella organisations and a ban on campaigning literature published by the government for 28 days before the poll (*The Government's Proposals for Funding of Political Parties in the United Kingdom*, Cm. 4413, July 1999).

It is clear that detailed matters of this kind are of considerable importance. The 1975 referendum was the only poll to date where the campaign organisations received public funding to put across their case and only £125,000 (about £580,000 at 1998 prices) was allocated to each side. Yet if voters are to be able to assess the issues properly, the opposition to the government position needs sufficient resources to explain its argument to the public and to have access to the media. This point has recently been accepted in the Republic of Ireland where referendums are a precondition for constitutional change. The funding in 1975 was prompted by political expediency, designed to reconcile the pro- and anti-marketeers within the Labour Party.[29] Calls since then for further public funding on the same lines have always been rejected. In any case, the pro-marketeers in 1975 spent far more than the antis (£1,850,000 against £133,630) and it has been estimated that the Scottish 'vote yes' campaign spent three times as much as its opponents in the 1997 referendum. The use of public money in support of government campaigns to 'explain' the issues can also be controversial, as it is the Government Information and Communication Service which drafts summaries of the policies to be voted upon. This is one area where the Neill Committee felt it necessary to redraw the boundaries.

Control over who forms the electorate can also have significant repercussions. In both referendums for Scotland and Wales, in 1979 and 1997, there were demands for the electorate to extend to the whole of Britain, as a devolution settlement would affect England as well. There have been similar demands in respect of a referendum on the constitutional position of Northern Ireland, as in the border poll of 1973, where one option was to join the Republic of Ireland. A further difficulty is that the electorate in Northern Ireland is divided culturally, with any peace settlement needing significant support from both sides of the community. Whether such cross-community support has been attained is difficult to measure since separate electoral registers for Protestants and Catholics are politically impossible.

The 1979 referendums were dominated by the question of thresholds. A threshold is a qualified majority designed to confirm clear public support for a policy. In the referendums in 1979, 40 per cent of all those eligible to vote in Scotland and Wales had to vote yes for the legislation implementing devolution to come into effect, a hurdle that was not crossed. Scottish public opinion considered that the result had been manipulated since the majority required was extraordinarily high, based as it was on the total electorate and not on those who had voted. Yet the threshold device has some attractions. A number of states use a threshold for constitutional issues, on the principle that such change needs something more than a simple plurality vote. However, when a government decides to hold a referendum it generally wishes to win it – and is unlikely to choose to put what Donald Dewar has called 'fancy franchises' in its way.

The government also decides the question to be asked and would normally wish to retain this power. This can lead to apparent inconsistencies, such as imposing a second question on a tax-varying power for the Scottish Parliament, but refusing pressure for a second question on an assembly-only option for the Greater London Authority referendum. Ideally a referendum should be constructed in such a way as to enable voters to exercise a choice that mirrors as closely as possible their personal view of the issue under consideration. It should also not be constructed to force those with diametrically opposed views to vote the same way.[30] In the Scottish referendum in 1979 supporters of independence and alternative forms of devolution had to choose to vote yes for a particular version of devolution or to vote no and risk losing the whole policy. Lord Home is said to have swayed Conservative pro-devolutionists in 1979 by urging a no vote on the grounds that a Conservative government would promote a better scheme. In the event Mrs Thatcher had no truck at all with devolution, and no developments occurred for eighteen years. In 1973 Nationalist voters in Northern Ireland boycotted the border poll on the grounds that it was inherently flawed, for a question on whether voters wished to remain in the United Kingdom was always bound to receive a majority while other options, such as an involvement of the Republic short of sovereignty, were not considered.

For these reasons, the possibility of multi-option referendums (or 'preferendums') has been suggested. New Zealand held one in 1993 to decide between different forms of electoral system, but the results can be confusing and even contradictory. Voters are not forced to make a choice between real options, but can merely express an opinion about ideal types. Alternatively, when a dynamic process of change is under way, a series of referendums at each particular stage could be held. Yet such developments are unlikely to occur while governments retain their present power over the initiation and conduct of referendums.

A final issue concerns the way in which referendums are counted. In the 1973 border poll and the 1998 Belfast Agreement referendum the count was conducted as a single exercise for the whole of Northern Ireland, making it impossible to identify officially the views of the population in more local areas such as counties or constituencies. The government resisted amendments to allow local counting for fear that it would reopen the issue of the border between the Republic and the United Kingdom. Similarly in 1975 the government initially sought a national count on the basis that it was impossible for an individual part of Britain to leave the European Community, but during the passage of the Referendum Act an amendment for county (but not constituency) voting was carried on a free vote. This precedent was used for the 1979 and 1997 referendums (regions were used in Scotland), thereby avoiding direct constituency counts which might reveal MPs at odds with the views of their constituents.

Referendums have now become an accepted mechanism in Britain for deciding on constitutional issues. However, earlier arguments about their constitutional validity and the wisdom of using them are likely to continue. In particular, the practice of pre-legislative referendums raises new arguments about the legislative process and the extent to which MPs, acting as legislators, can amend or refine the wishes of the electorate. During the passage of the Government of Wales Bill and the Scotland Bill in 1998, the government repeatedly refused amendments on the details of the legislation, such as the type of electoral system, on the grounds that the electorate had voted for all the details of the package put before them. This may be no more than an extension of the arguments about the nature of mandates given in general elections, but it does reduce the purpose and force of parliamentary scrutiny.

Opinion polls

Opinion polling and similar techniques also provide a means by which the public can relay views to politicians and policy-makers. Polls have been a feature of public and political life for more than sixty years. British Gallup, originally known as the British Institute of Public Opinion, was founded in 1937, two years after its American predecessor. Gallup's surveys have been carried out regularly since, and it has been joined by a number of other major companies (including ones that specialise in polling in Scotland and Wales). The polls that are regularly published in the press are very much the tip of a very large iceberg. All the companies ask many more questions in their regular political polls than are published in the newspapers and conduct numerous surveys in the field of market and opinion research that are not made public at all, as part of a much larger market research industry (see box, p. 152).

Public opinion surveys have three principal functions: reporting what is happening; analysing why what is happening is taking place; and predicting what will happen. It is the last of these that attracts the most attention but which is also the least reliable. Despite the frequent claims of journalists and headline-writers, opinion polls are not predictions of a future election result, merely a snapshot of

Sample opinion poll survey questions (*extract*)

Good morning/afternoon, my name is . . . of MORI, the opinion poll company. We're carrying out a very short survey in this area. It will only take a few minutes.

Q1   How do you intend to vote in the General Election on May 1?
       IF UNDECIDED OR REFUSED AT Q1
Q2   Which party are you most inclined to support?

       Conservative..
       Labour ....
       Liberal Democrat ....
       Scot/Welsh Nationalist...
       Green Party ....
       Referendum Party..
       Other...

       Would not vote ....

       Undecided ....
       Refused ....

       ASK ALL
Q3   SHOWCARD A From this card, can you tell me how likely you are to get along to vote in the General Election?

       Certain <u>not</u> to vote ....
       Not very likely to vote...
       Quite likely to vote..
       Very likely to vote ....
       Certain to vote ....
       Don't know ....

       ASK Q4 IF PARTY NAMED AT Q1 OR Q2. IF NO PARTY GO TO Q7
Q4   How strongly do you support the . . . PARTY NAMED AT Q1 OR Q2. Do you support them very strongly, fairly strongly, not very strongly or not strongly at all?

       Very strongly ....
       Fairly strongly ....
       Not very strongly...
       Not strongly at all ....
       Don't know/no answer..

Q5   Have you definitely decided to vote for the . . . (PARTY NAMED AT Q1/Q2) party or is there a chance you may change your mind before you vote?
       Definitely decided... <u>GO TO Q7</u>
       May change mind... <u>ASK Q6</u>
       Don't know.. <u>GO TO Q7</u>

public opinion at the time the survey was carried out. The interpretation of published polls is not always easy, especially as many of the technical details can be unclear and there are various ways in which those initially answering 'don't know' are reclassified. Polls are also not safe predictors of the seats that will be won in an election, even if they are carried out close to that election. Although the projected consequences for seats in the House of Commons are often published alongside poll results, these are necessarily based on assumptions of uniform swing nationally (occasionally regionally). But there has been a considerable decline in uniform swing as a result of tactical voting and other factors; and this means that polls in marginal constituencies, rather than national polls, will increasingly be used as predictors of an election result in terms of seats.

Political polls are not simply a feature of election campaigns but serve as regular indicators of the political temperature, measuring not only how electors would vote 'if there were an election tomorrow' but also a range of views on the parties and their policies, the issues of the day, political leaders and the performance of government. Private polling is used widely by the major parties as an essential tool of planning and campaigning, though the expense involved limits the amounts that can be done. In the 1992–7 Parliament, the Labour Party commissioned regular private polls from 1993 onwards. The Conservatives also commission surveys but not in recent years at the level of the early 1990s, while the Liberal Democrats' polling has been mostly in-house.

The use of polls by the parties – and by some of the national press – has now been supplemented by focus groups. These are structured discussions with a small number of selected electors, which aim to capture in greater depth the mood of voters on issues. They are particularly used to obtain suggestions for action and can produce these very quickly. Their use stems partly from the poor performance of the polls in 1992 and also from their widespread use in campaigning in the United States, where one of Labour's key strategists, Philip Gould, had worked. From Tony Blair's election as Labour leader in 1994, he regularly met focus groups and by the time of the 1997 election had conducted 300 such sessions, with 70 more added during the campaign. The Conservatives also used focus groups, conducted by one of the polling companies, though on a smaller scale than Labour.[31]

The first general election in Britain at which polls were carried out was in 1945. Since then, they have grown steadily in number and influence, both during the life of a Parliament and especially during election campaigns. Some countries prohibit the publication of poll results during election campaigns: France, Spain, Portugal, Belgium and Luxembourg all ban publication in the last few days before an election (though the law is not always enforced). Indeed, improvements in communications (such as the internet) mean that such bans become progressively more difficult to enforce. In Britain there is no ban, though there were somewhat fewer polls in 1997 than five years previously, perhaps following the polls debacle of 1992 or – more likely – because of the apparently settled nature of the contest.

The performance of the polls as predictors of the outcome in general elections has historically been quite good: most have been within 2 per cent of the actual result. In 1951, however, the gap in the polls between the two leading parties was wrong by more than 5 per cent, in 1970 by more than 6 per cent, and in 1992 the polls' reputation was seriously damaged by a much worse performance. The four surveys published on election day showed the two main parties neck and neck, if anything with a narrow Labour lead. In the event, the Conservatives had a majority of 7.6 per cent and an overall majority of twenty-one seats in the House of Commons.

Despite the damage done by this to the polls' reputation, the national press continued to commission polls on voting intentions during the period after 1992. These showed a large Labour lead from shortly after that election but, perhaps because of the 1992 performance, the message that they carried was not always confidently accepted by either politicians or commentators, and Labour's land-slide win in 1997 therefore still came as something of a surprise. After the 1992 election, the Market Research Society convened a group of experts to carry out a post mortem to find out what had gone wrong with the polls. It concluded that there had been four main sources of error. First, there was a small swing to the Conservatives between the poll interviews and the election itself. Second, there was a 'spiral of silence' – a refusal by some voters, mainly Conservative and older, to admit their voting intention or even to be interviewed at all. Third, there was a small error due to the under-registration of mainly Labour voters, partly due to the poll tax. And fourth, the polls were themselves faultily designed. Traditionally, almost all opinion polls used *quota sampling*, in which interviews are conducted with a pre-set number of people according to factors such as age, gender, social class and employment status so that the overall sample is representative of the elector-ate as a whole. Quota sampling is criticised by many statisticians who would prefer *random sampling*, but it has been used regularly for opinion polling because it is relatively quick and cheap to carry out and has had a good record in practice. In 1992, however, the quotas set were faulty, with the result that the polled samples did not accurately reflect the national electorate. The variables chosen were not closely related to voting behaviour and the data sources used to set them were not sufficiently up-to-date.

As a result of this analysis, all the major polling companies – which hitherto had used broadly similar methods – changed the way in which they conducted their surveys. Each did so differently and in some cases there were several changes over the five-year period from 1992 to 1997. ICM first experimented with the use of secret ballots before using telephone polling. They also introduced adjustments to allow for refusals to answer and for those who said they did not know how they would vote; these were based on reports of past voting and on answers to other questions. Gallup also moved to telephone polling in late 1996 and made some small adjustments for refusals to answer. MORI, NOP and Harris continued to use quota sampling, though with improved methodology, but the latter two made small adjustments for presumed non-response while only MORI concentrated on unadjusted figures. (In fact, all polls make some adjustments to fine-tune raw data, and MORI made further adjustments to its basic results, while still using the latter for its 'headline' surveys.)

The results of forty-seven opinion polls were published during the 1997 general election campaign, fewer than in 1987 or 1992 but more than in previous elections. As ever, there was considerable variation in what they showed: polls published on successive days a week before the election showed Labour leads of 5 and 21 per cent. Labour's average lead fell somewhat during the long campaign but, overall, there was a broadly consistent picture, with four of the polling companies producing close and consistent figures for party support. The exception was ICM, whose surveys showed a consistently lower lead for Labour (probably because the adjustments used by ICM were more extensive than those employed by the other pollsters).

The final polls published by each company, with fieldwork carried out in the days immediately before the election, showed considerable variation, with leads for Labour ranging between 10 and 22 per cent. In the event, Labour won by 13 per cent. A better test of the polls' accuracy is the mean difference between each party's percentage of the vote and the poll's forecast of that share. On this measure ICM did best, with a mean score of 1.25; the other polls had scores of between 2.0 and 3.5. These results were regarded as very successful by the pollsters themselves but by historical standards their performance was at best patchy. The mean error of 2.0 in the six final polls was better than the 3.0 of 1992 but was otherwise only exceeded in 1951 and equalled in 1970. Five of the six final polls overstated Labour's actual share of the vote and four of them underestimated the Conservative share, although by smaller margins and within the accepted sampling tolerance for opinion polls of plus or minus 3 per cent. The initial verdict that this had been a successful campaign for the pollsters looks somewhat premature and it remains to be seen whether the new and divergent methodologies used by the various companies will restore their reputation in the longer term.

New forms of participation

The familiar models of representative democracy only require citizens to vote at infrequent intervals, with no more than a small minority active in political parties. But there is evidence of increasing public disengagement from this model; and, partly in response to this, more participative and deliberative forms of democracy are now being explored (see box below).

New Labour – New democracy?

It may be that the era of pure representative government is coming slowly to an end ... representative government is being complemented by more direct forms of involvement, from the internet to referenda.

(speech by Peter Mandelson, 'European Integration and National Sovereignty: Democracy and Legitimacy in Europe', 3 March 1998)

A host of initiatives for consulting the citizen, often pioneered by local government, is currently under way, all designed to reduce barriers to participation. Citizens' juries, which can offer advice on policy options, and focus groups to assess suggested proposals before implementation, are in growing use and offer a chance for ordinary citizens to get involved in issues such as local strategies for minimising drug use, or to offer government a taste of the likely response to a policy initiative. Local councils in particular have felt the need to find new ways to involve people and groups in decision-making, given the low turnout in local elections. Councillors and officers are reported to have been impressed by the informed and considered views of participants which have emerged from pilot studies of citizens' juries.[32] The Blair government has launched a People's Panel, made up of 5,000 members of the public, to find out how public service delivery could be improved. Proponents have even suggested that members of quangos and the House of Lords should be chosen by lot to bring the ordinary citizen into government. There is no shortage of interesting ideas for doing politics differently.[33]

Perhaps information technology (IT) has the most potential for opening up the internal operation of the state. Policy-makers need to be subjected to constant pressure to throw light on decision-making, so that physical attendance at a meeting or knowing which official to contact is no longer the essential requirement. Electronic responses to consultation papers or access to MPs via email really only scratch at the surface, for IT has the potential to dissolve the departmental divisions of responsibility which complicate the delivery of services. The public should be able to download and process official information and key documents at any time (such as driving licence applications or key performance indicators for local schools) from their own terminals or from public-access terminals, and communicate electronically with government by means of one-stop shops. Service providers need to create 'joined-up government', sharing files and solutions to offer a comprehensive facility. For example, Canada offers a SchoolNet which connects all schools, libraries, colleges and universities into a single network, offering online teaching, and Australia offers touch screen kiosks in 320 job centres to allow users to search instantaneously a national vacancies database. Britain is beginning to move in similar directions.

By 2002 the Blair government plans to make 25 per cent of government services available electronically under the modernising government programme (Cm. 4310, March 1999). Electronic forms for the self-employed have already been introduced in the Intelligent Forms Project launched by the Inland Revenue, Customs and Excise and Department of Social Security. There have been calls for the complete 're-engineering' of government so that it is re-packaged in relation to the 'life events' of each citizen with one point of communication at key moments, such as changing jobs. Richard Stokes, director of government business for ICL, has complained that: 'the machinery of government is organised for the convenience of government, not the convenience of the citizen.'[34] One-stop shops pioneered by local authorities have the potential to develop into fully interactive service providers; for example, Surrey County Council is working with the local

LATEST NEWS

START HERE

FREEDOM OF INFORMATION

TONY BLAIR HAS HIS SAY

NEED TO KNOW?

LATEST NEWS
BACKGROUND
WHAT'S AT STAKE?
WHO'S INVOLVED?

WHITE PAPER

IN BRIEF
WITH NOTES
TEXT IN FULL

HAVE YOUR SAY

YOUR OPINION
CHAT
SUBMISSIONS
MEET THE MINISTER
YOU, THE JURY

Picture. Keith Taylor
Cameracraft.co.uk

Keep up to date with what's on the site - enter your email address below

[   ]

Submit

Note: This address will only be used to keep you informed about our activities and unsubscribing is easy.

AN INTERNET
TOP
10
WEB SITE

"The 'Have Your Say' website is a historic opportunity for the public to play a meaningful part in the framing of new legislation by using the Internet to lobby and question a Government minister. I support this initiative to help modernise and enhance British democracy and open up Government and I hope similar consultations will be set up in future as part of the legislative process."

The Prime Minister, Rt. Hon. Tony Blair MP.

This site is no longer being regularly updated, but you can still read submissions and David Clarks' responses to site users.

Have Your Say is a UK Citizens Online Democracy production in association with AOL, GX Networks and Sun Microsystems

Figure 5.2 Citizens Online Democracy website 'Have Your Say on Freedom of Information', front page

district councils to provide an integrated service allowing consumers to obtain such items as disabled parking badges without visiting a county council office, and to register views on the efficiency of street cleansing.

The United States has pioneered tele-democracy, with online debate and electronic referendums, but the main participants have been those already familiar with IT. Drawing in new voices has so far proved elusive, as a new Demos pamphlet has found.[35] In Amsterdam's digital city, which allows users to gather information and debate in over one hundred discussion groups, the most popular debates are over lifestyle and sport, with most participants being white, male and professional; a new input into political debate has not occurred. Manchester's Information City, designed to facilitate comments on council services, has also not made a significant impact on local democracy or decision-making, despite attempts to set up links for the 'information poor'. There is a long way to go before new technology makes a real impact on the democratic process.

The Blair government has experimented with allowing access to interactive websites, such as the one illustrated in Figure 5.2, which invited responses to FOI proposals. Pressure groups have also begun to exploit the internet, but a recent Henley Centre survey found that 62 per cent of people in Britain had never even used a PC. Social exclusion from electronic services is widespread and will need government action if it is to be overcome. Leeds City Council participated in an EU-funded project called 'Equality' which provided access to the internet and a city intranet for 200 people with disabilities and found that the system rescued some from complete isolation, through the chat forum, electronic shopping and opportunities to participate in community development. The opportunities are clearly there; the task is to develop them further.

The interaction of government with the citizen is likely to deepen, whether or not it is increasingly by electronic means. Improving redress of grievances, extending participation and widening access to information are key parts of New Labour's declared aim of rebuilding trust in government. Integrating the mechanisms for access to provide a single entry point for information about government and Parliament would mark a significant step forward in this direction. The Blair government's plans for 'better government' connect with the themes discussed here, but demands for more responsive channels of communication between the government and the governed will undoubtedly be at the centre of political debate in the twenty-first century.

NOTES

1   Cited in George Lawson, *Netstate: Creating Electronic Government* (Demos, 1998).
2   House of Commons Debates, vol. 734, 18 October 1966, col. 51.
3   Select Committee on the Parliamentary Commissioner for Administration; *First Report: The Powers, Work and Jurisdiction of the Ombudsman*, HC 33, 1993–4.
4   *Judicial Statistics 1997*, Cmnd. 3980, table 1.13.
5   Neville Johnson in 'Judicial interventionism' in *Britain in the Nineties: The Politics of Paradox* (Frank Cass, 1998, ed. Hugh Berrington), p. 152.

6 Ibid., p. 155.
7 *The Citizen's Charter*, Cmnd. 1599, 1991.
8 Third Report *Public Service Committee*, HC 78, 1996–7.
9 Mark Thatcher, 'The new regulatory agencies', in *Britain in the Nineties: The Politics of Paradox* (Frank Cass, 1988, ed. Hugh Berrington).
10 Christopher Hood *et al.*, 'Regulation inside government: where new public management meets the audit explosion' in *Public Money and Management*, April–June 1998.
11 *Independent on Sunday*, 17 May 1998, 'Boom time for Britain's big brothers'.
12 Select Committee on the Parliamentary Commissioner for Administration, HC 84, 1996–7.
13 Jeremy J. Richardson (ed.), *Pressure Groups* (Oxford University Press, 1993).
14 Wyn Grant, *Pressure Groups, Politics and Democracy in Britain*, 2nd edn (Harvester Wheatsheaf, 1995).
15 See Lynn G. Bennie, 'Brent Spar, Atlantic Oil and Greenpeace' in F. F. Ridley and Grant Jordan (eds), *Protest Politics: Cause Groups and Campaigns* (Oxford University Press, 1998).
16 *Third Report: Parliamentary Lobbying*, HC 586, 1990–91. Professor Rush's evidence was published in HC Paper 518 1987–8.
17 Sebastian Barry, 'Lobbying: a need to regulate?' in Bill Jones (ed.) *Political Issues in Britain Today* (Manchester University Press, 4th edn, 1994).
18 Michael Lee, 'Westminster and professional lobbying', *Legislative Studies*, vol. 5, no. 2 (1991), p. 11.
19 *Select Committee on Standards in Public Life Second Report: Advocacy and Disclosure*, HC 816, 1994–5.
20 *Observer*, 19 July 1998, 'The American way of influence'.
21 A. G. Jordan and J. J. Richardson, *Government and Pressure Groups in Britain* (Oxford University Press, 1987), p. 270.
22 Tony Benn, *Diaries 1970–73* (Hutchinson, 1995), p. 420.
23 *Referendum on UK Membership of the European Community*, Cmnd. 5925, February 1975.
24 *Labour Wales Press Notice*, 27 June 1996.
25 House of Commons Debates, vol. 294, 15 May 1997, col. 290.
26 Colin Munro, 'Power to the people', *Public Law*, Winter 1997.
27 *Report of the Commission on the Conduct of Referendums* (1996), Briefing, p. 1.
28 *Committee on Standards in Public Life, Fifth Report*, October 1998.
29 David Butler and Uwe Kitzinger, *The 1975 Referendum*, 2nd edn (Macmillan, 1996), p. 59.
30 Barry K. Winetrobe, 'Is a referendum acceptable?', *Scottish Law Gazette*, vol. 60, no. 4 (1992).
31 David Butler and Dennis Kanavagh, *The British General Election of 1997* (Macmillan, 1997), p. 129.
32 Anna Coote and Jo Lenaghan, *Citizens' Juries: Theory into Practice* (IPPR, 1997).
33 *Lean Democracy*, Demos pamphlet, 1994.
34 *Guardian*, 30 July 1998, 'Wired for living'.
35 George Lawson, *Netscape: Creating Electronic Government* (Demos, 1998).

FURTHER READING

Who Do I Complain to? The Essential Handbook for Every Citizen (Headline, 1997) by Tony Wright offers a practical introduction. *When Citizens Complain: Reforming Justice and Administration* (Open University Press, 1993) by Norman Lewis and Patrick Birkinshaw looks at the ombudsman and the system of tribunals and inquiries. *The 1975 Referendum*, 2nd edn (Macmillan, 1996) by David Butler and Uwe Kitzinger covers the only nationwide referendum held in the UK so far and *The Referendum Experience in Europe* (Macmillan 1996), ed. Michael Gallagher and Pier Vincenzo Uleri, looks at experience abroad. *The Report of the Commission of the Conduct of Referendums* (Constitution Unit, 1996) recommends ideal 'ground rules' for referendums. *Pressure Groups, Politics and Democracy in Britain*, 2nd edn, (Harvester Wheatsheaf, 1995) by Wyn Grant surveys the role of pressure groups. *Sleaze: Politicians' Private Interests and Public Reaction* (Oxford University Press/Hansard Society, 1995), ed. F. F. Ridley and Alan Doig, looks at the Nolan Committee recommendations and public perception of politicians. Useful studies on opinion polls include David Broughton's *Public Opinion Polling and Politics in Britain* (Prentice-Hall/Harvester Wheatsheaf, 1995) and Nick Moon's *Opinion Polls: History, Theory and Practice* (Manchester University Press, 1999).

6 Campaigns and communications

Policies are like cornflakes. If they are not marketed they will not sell.
(Lord Young, former Conservative cabinet minister, quoted in *PR Week*,
16 March 1988)

INTRODUCTION: THE MASS MEDIA AND POLITICS

The term *mass media* encompasses an ever widening range of means of communication, but the focus here is on television, radio and the press because they are most central to the political process. The media are the public's main source of information about politics, and for most people it is the media which make them aware of the issues which affect them as *political* issues (from NHS waiting lists to school standards, the environment to interest rates). They also provide the primary forum for modern political campaigns. As Colin Seymour-Ure pointed out a quarter of a century ago, the mass media are 'so deeply embedded in the [political] system that without them political activity in its contemporary forms could hardly carry on at all.'[1] Most political strategies therefore feature, as an integral part, a media strategy designed to communicate the desired message to the intended audience.

Many commentators now feel, however, that the tail is wagging the dog. The content of the message, they claim, is determined by what will come across well in the media.[2] This possibility was identified many years ago by the political correspondent of *The Times*[3]:

> The real risk is that we are moving towards the day when market research, opinion poll findings, techniques of motivational persuasion and public relations, and even the analyses of political scientists would be crudely and cold bloodedly used to govern party strategies in government and out.

This might have seemed an alarming prospect in 1965, but today similar observations are commonplace as descriptions of what now happens.

In looking at aspects of campaigning and communications, we examine some of the more visible meeting-points between the political process and the media:

party political broadcasts, coverage of Parliament, the lobby system and the government's information machine. We also examine the increasing professionalism of political campaigning and ask what effect media coverage of politics has on the electorate. But we will start with a fundamental issue: the radically different approaches to bias and regulation which have been adopted by, or imposed on, broadcasters and the press.

BIAS AND REGULATION

In Britain today the broadcast media are heavily regulated, while the press is subject to virtually no statutory regulation – other than rules which apply equally to all citizens (including the prohibition of libel, blasphemy against the Christian religion, incitement to racial hatred and the breaking of official secrets). This is due in part to technical considerations. Until recently the narrow spectrum of frequencies available for television and radio meant that only a finite number of stations could operate, with the result that state regulation seemed inevitable. The different histories of the two media are also important, though. The freedom of the press became a central tenet of British political life in response to draconian censorship in Cromwellian times. The BBC, on the other hand, with its 'arm's-length' relationship with government, is clearly a creature of the twentieth century. The state feared the power of the new medium to influence public opinion, but state protection and regulation had the result of enabling the Corporation to develop its ethos of *public service broadcasting*, which gave rise to the pursuit of excellence and a distinctive mixture of education, information and entertainment. When commercial television was introduced in the mid-1950s, it would have been unthinkable for the government of the day to allow the new stations to be driven entirely by market forces, so strict quality requirements were put in place.

The requirement for political impartiality was a natural corollary of this framework, although the broadcasters have always understood that the state (especially at times of crisis) is likely to understand this as meaning impartiality within the limits of broad support for the status quo. Thus the Home Secretary still has the right to prevent the transmission of any programme or to require the transmission of material supplied by the government.[4] The former power was used from 1988 to 1994 to prevent broadcasters from transmitting the voices of members of paramilitary groups in Northern Ireland (and the political parties associated with them) in order to deprive terrorism of 'the oxygen of publicity'. Television and radio journalists were strongly opposed to this, and exploited a loophole in the government's ban by using actors' voices to speak the words of those covered by the restriction. In addition, broadcasters and the press are covered by the infamous D-notice system, a voluntary mechanism by which the government advises against the publication of material which it believes could damage Britain's national security, but this has become less effective as journalistic deference to authority has, particularly in newspapers, declined.[5]

In recent years there have been signs that the approach to the two media may be converging somewhat, with the adoption of a 'lighter touch' to television regulation and calls for the introduction of a law of privacy to constrain the actions of the press. Nevertheless the press and the broadcast media are still fundamentally different animals. This is reflected in the fact that the watchdog dealing with complaints about the broadcast media is a statutory body while the organisation dealing with complaints about the press, despite its similar remit, is only voluntary (and is regarded, by some observers at least, as ineffectual) (see box, pp. 164–5).

Press bias

An overwhelming bias towards the Conservative Party in the national press seemed, until very recently, to have become one of the permanent features of British political life. The *Sun*, Britain's best-selling tabloid, carried a famous anti-Labour headline on the day of the 1992 general election: 'If Kinnock Wins Today Will the Last Person to Leave Britain Please Turn Out the Lights'.[6] The ownership of the press by private capital has been identified as an important cause of this state of affairs: the businessmen and corporations who own newspapers have generally felt that their interests coincided with Conservative policies and their editors have reflected this view. There is undoubtedly much truth in this, but it does not tell the whole story. Additional factors which appear to influence the political stand taken by newspapers include editorial tradition, the state of the political parties and the public mood.

It is not difficult to detect the operation of these three factors in recent years. First, proprietors may prefer to adopt a 'hands-off' approach to editorial direction in order to avoid alienating existing readers, an example being the promise to do this made by the Labour peer, Lord Hollick, on acquiring the traditionally Conservative-supporting *Daily Express* in 1996. But many would question the ability of proprietors who are interested in politics (or who have interests which are likely to be affected by the political process) to practise such self-restraint indefinitely, as the appointment to the *Express* of a more left-leaning editor in 1998 seemed to confirm.

Second, the period from late 1992 to the election in May 1997 saw a dramatic loss of confidence in the Conservative government by the newspapers, triggered by the growing Euroscepticism of the press, poor economic performance and the perception of a general lack of leadership from John Major. The contrast with Labour, especially after Tony Blair's election as leader in 1994, could not have been more pronounced, and many newspapers traditionally hostile to the party approved of Labour's new policies and internal reforms. Labour, guided by Tony Blair's press secretary Alastair Campbell, spent a great deal of energy courting the tabloid press, the *Sun* in particular, and in July 1995 Tony Blair flew to Australia to address a conference held by News International, Rupert Murdoch's multinational media corporation. This was seen as a pivotal moment in Labour's relationship with the press.

Media watchdogs

The Broadcasting Standards Commission

The Broadcasting Standards Commission was established by the Broadcasting Act 1996 as a watchdog covering traditional television and radio services and the newer cable, satellite, digital and teletext media. It replaced two bodies which dealt with standards and fairness separately. Its three main tasks are:

- to produce codes of practice relating to standards and fairness which broadcasters must reflect
- to consider and adjudicate on complaints about standards and fairness
- to monitor, research and report on standards and fairness in broadcasting.

The commission cannot preview or censor broadcasts but it can report the results of its research to the Culture Secretary. Its only sanction if a complaint is upheld is to require the broadcaster to broadcast or publish details of the complaint and the commission's findings.

The Press Complaints Commission

The PCC, unlike the Broadcasting Standards Commission, is a voluntary body established by the press itself in 1991. It replaced the Press Council, which had the twin roles of defending the freedom of the press and considering complaints about the conduct of the press.

The PCC's functions are:

- to produce a code of practice relating to inaccuracy, harassment, intrusion and discrimination
- to consider and adjudicate on alleged breaches of the code.

Unlike the Broadcasting Standards Commission, it cannot deal with complaints about taste and decency: these are left to editors to deal with. A new version of the code of practice came into effect in January 1998 in response to the public mood following the death of Princess Diana.

The code includes the following requirements:

- The press should take care not to publish inaccurate, misleading or distorted material. When such material has been published, a correction and where appropriate an apology should be printed. Although newspapers are free to be partisan, they should distinguish clearly between comment, conjecture and fact.
- The right to reply should be given 'where reasonably called for'.
- Publications 'will be expected to justify' intrusions into an individual's private life. Activities such as harassment and the use of telephoto lenses to photograph people in private places are unacceptable.

continued

- Certain parts of the code (for example, the parts relating to privacy and harassment) may be overridden where this is in the public interest. This includes detecting or exposing crime or a serious misdemeanour; protecting public health and safety; or preventing the public from being misled by some statement or action of an individual or organisation (such as, for example, the government).

Like the Broadcasting Standards Commission, the PCC's only sanction if a complaint is upheld is to require the editor concerned to publish the commission's adjudication. Nevertheless, the PCC claims that the incorporation of the code into editors' and journalists' contracts of employment gives it additional force.

Third, no newspaper can afford to ignore its readers, and every newspaper wants to back a winner. The public seemed to have been attracted by New Labour and alienated from the Conservatives well before the 1997 election and this is likely to have reinforced the press in its drift away from the Conservatives during this period.

In addition, the business interests of the modern media mogul are likely to be more complex than of old, and may not be confined to a single country. Long-term loyalty to a single political party may not be the best way of promoting those interests. Some commentators suggested that before and after coming to power, New Labour adapted a number of its policies as part of its strategy to win and maintain Rupert Murdoch's support, citing its failure to outlaw the 'predatory pricing' practised by one of Murdoch's papers, *The Times*, the softening of Labour's position on cross-media ownership (that is, the extent to which ownership of different forms of media should be controlled by a single interest) and the adoption at times of a more sceptical tone on the single currency.

Of the ten national dailies in publication at the time of the 1997 election, six urged readers to vote Labour, three Conservative and *The Times* suggested they vote for Eurosceptics of whatever party (see box, p. 166). This contrasted with the situation in 1992: three Labour, five Conservative and two papers which gave no explicit preference.[7] As the authors who compiled these figures observed, it is tempting to imagine that Labour's best-ever coverage in the press and its biggest ever majority in the House of Commons 'must be linked somehow'. The *Sun*'s support undoubtedly provided a great psychological boost for Labour, but the consensus seems to be that in 1997 the press were following popular opinion rather than shaping it. The sustained criticism in the press of John Major's leadership from 1992 onwards, including that in Conservative papers such as the *Mail* and the *Telegraph* which could not bring themselves to endorse Labour, is likely to have had an even greater impact.

It will be interesting to see whether the 1997 election marks the beginning of a period in which the press deserts its traditional party loyalties and becomes more like a floating voter. This would be a natural enough response to the political parties moving closer together on many issues and voters becoming more

Circulation, readership and preferred 1997 election result of the national dailies

Ownership and title	Preferred election result	Circulation[a] (000s)	Readership[b] (000s)
News Corp Ltd			
Sun	Labour victory	3,820	10,074
The Times	Vote for Euro-sceptics	757	1,954
Mirror Group plc			
Mirror	Labour victory	2,361	6,153
United News & Media plc			
Express	Conservative victory	1,220	2,671
Daily Star	Labour victory	655	2,079
Daily Mail & General Trust plc			
Daily Mail	Conservative victory	2,154	5,309
Hollinger inc			
Daily Telegraph	Conservative victory	1,133	2,736
Scott Trust			
Guardian	Labour victory	429	1,270
Newspaper Publishing plc			
Independent	Labour victory	264	840
Pearson plc			
Financial Times	Labour victory	319	660

Sources: Butler, D. and D. Kavanagh, *The British General Election of 1997*, table 9.1; Audit Bureau of Circulations; National Readership Survey.

Notes
[a] Average May 1997
[b] Average adult readership in year ending June 1997

'de-aligned'. Nevertheless many observers believe that the right-wing press is waiting to revert to type. Roy Greenslade suggested in the *Guardian* before the election that the *Sun*'s real message to the Conservatives was: 'Get a new leader, find some new frontbenchers, adopt a rigid policy against the single European currency and we'll be back on your side in time for the millennium' (19 March 1997). It is certainly the case that for the press, the post-election 'honeymoon' with the Blair government ended sooner than it did for the electorate, but this was probably inevitable for a variety of reasons not necessarily linked to old party loyalties.

Privacy and the press

For a number of years now there have been calls for the creation of a statutory right to privacy in Britain. This would affect all of the media but the intended target is clearly the press, since existing controls make gratuitous invasion of privacy by television and radio less likely. The Thatcher government appointed a committee led by the prominent lawyer, David Calcutt, to examine the issue of privacy. The Calcutt Report recommended that 'the press should be given one final chance to prove that voluntary self-regulation can be made to work',[8] and in 1991 the newspaper industry created the Press Complaints Commission (see box, p. 164). Calcutt was later asked to review the PCC's first eighteen months. He concluded that the Commission had not been an effective regulator and recommended that 'the government should now introduce a statutory regime.'[9] Nevertheless the Major government remained opposed to the introduction of a privacy law and Labour shares this view.

The Human Rights Act 1998 fulfilled Labour's commitment to bring the European Convention on Human Rights into UK law. Many journalists were worried that the government's proposals would restrict press freedom and the government made some changes to the bill in response, but the way the Act balances the right to private life with the right to freedom of expression has led some observers to suggest that it is unlikely to act as a significant curb on the press. The Data Protection Act 1998 has been less hotly debated but may have a greater impact. It will gradually replace the existing controls on the collection and use of information on individuals. Although the media are exempt where they act in the public interest, the Act is likely to give the public a powerful means of redress where newspapers break the PCC's code of practice, including a right to have inaccurate information held on journalists' computers corrected and a right to compensation where unfair reporting has caused distress to the person concerned.

TV and radio: Due impartiality?

Television and radio stations have a duty to be politically impartial. Under the terms of the agreement between the government and the BBC of January 1996, the Corporation must 'treat controversial subjects with due accuracy and impartiality' and must issue guidance on impartiality to programme makers. This is contained in a document called the *Producers' Guidelines* (see box, p. 168). Although the BBC is not allowed to broadcast its own opinions on news and current affairs (except broadcasting issues), the agreement states that 'due impartiality does not require absolute neutrality on every issue or detachment from fundamental democratic principles.' This is obviously a very delicate line to tread.

The independent terrestrial television companies (except S4C in Wales) are regulated and licensed by the Independent Television Commission (ITC), which replaced the IBA. The ITC, like the BBC, also has to draw up guidance for the conduct of broadcasting and must do all it can to ensure that any news given (in whatever form) is 'presented with due accuracy and impartiality'. Independent radio stations are licensed and regulated by the Radio Authority.

This framework of regulation means that broadcasters must take special account of the impartiality due to 'major matters', including issues of national significance such as a serious public sector strike or highly contentious new

---

Impartiality and accuracy: The BBC's rules

Due impartiality lies at the heart of the BBC. It is a core value and no area of programming is exempt from it. It requires programme makers to show open-mindedness, fairness and a respect for truth.

There are generally more than two sides to any issue and impartiality in factual programmes may not be achieved simply by mathematical balance in which each view is complemented by an equal and opposing one.

A programme may choose to explore any subject, at any point on the spectrum of debate, as long as there are good editorial reasons for doing so. It may choose to test or report one side of a particular argument. However, it must do so with fairness and integrity. It should ensure that contentious views are signalled as such, and opposing views are not misrepresented.

Sometimes it will be necessary to ensure that all main viewpoints are reflected in a programme or in linked programmes, for example, when the issues involved are highly controversial and a defining or decisive moment in the controversy is imminent.

News programmes should offer viewers and listeners an intelligent and informed account of issues that enables them to form their own views. A reporter may express a professional, journalistic judgement but not a personal opinion. Judgement must be recognised as perceptive and fair. Audiences should not be able to gauge from BBC programmes the personal views of presenters and reporters.

(extract from the *Producers' Guidelines*, 3rd edn, 1996)

---

legislation on the eve of a crucial Commons vote. They are also regarded as having a special responsibility to avoid bias during elections. Normally, balance may be achieved over a period of time, but during an election campaign and when covering major matters television and radio stations attempt to achieve balance within individual programmes or within their overall output each day. The political parties monitor news and current affairs programmes avidly during elections and complain vociferously if they believe that they have been under-represented. Potentially controversial programmes, including those which explore a single issue from a particular viewpoint, are postponed during elections. In addition, section 93 of the Representation of the People Act 1983 gives candidates the right of veto over coverage of their constituency at election time. This rule has been criticised on the grounds that it stifles debate. It was suspended during the 1996 Northern Ireland Forum elections, but it significantly restricted coverage of the contest in the Tatton constituency during the 1997 election, where the former BBC reporter Martin Bell challenged the Conservative Neil Hamilton following allegations of 'sleaze' against the sitting MP.

The broadcasters' quest for impartiality in news programmes, as described in the BBC's *Producers' Guidelines*, depends heavily on the idea of objective *news values* which determine what is news. The newsworthiness of a particular story is assessed by journalists using their impartial, professional judgment. Whether or not a story is favourable to the government of the day, or to any of the political parties, is irrelevant to this process. The factors which make a story newsworthy are listed by a former editor of the *Guardian*: social, political, economic and human significance; drama; surprise; personalities; sex; and numbers affected.[10] Clearly the order of priority varies according to the intended audience: critics who have pointed to increasing 'tabloidisation' of the broadsheets and current affairs programmes would maintain that the trend is relentlessly downmarket.

The objectivity of news values has been subject to intense scrutiny from academics, particularly those writing from a radical perspective. The Glasgow University Media Group and others have argued that news is manufactured rather than simply discovered.[11] On this view, the 'production' of news is influenced by various organisational features of the mass media as well as by journalists' own unwitting prejudice towards consensus and the status quo. The *Producers' Guidelines* certainly give ammunition to this line of argument as they make it clear that 'contentious views' should be signalled as such. The Liverpool dockers' strike of 1995–8 is an example of an event which did not fit journalists' news values: it was a *cause célèbre* of the far left, but a lack of media interest ensured that comparatively few people were aware it was taking place. Many of the stronger claims concerning 'agenda setting' by the media have been disputed, but this is an area which will continue to generate critical interest.

PARTY POLITICAL BROADCASTS

ITV and the independent national radio stations are required by the Broadcasting Act 1990 to transmit party political broadcasts. There is no parallel duty for the BBC but the Corporation has a long-standing commitment to making airtime available on a similar basis. The general arrangements are devised together by the ITC, BBC and also S4C and the Radio Authority.

Party political broadcasts (PPBs) were first broadcast by the BBC in 1924. They were first shown on television in 1951. For most of the subsequent period the broadcasts were transmitted simultaneously on BBC and ITV, but in recent years the broadcasts have been staggered. Channel 4 adopted alternative arrangements, showing a regular party political comment slot. The allocation of party political broadcasts was determined mainly on the basis of the parties' performance in votes at the previous general election and was agreed by the Committee on Party Political Broadcasting, a rather shadowy body representing the main political parties and the broadcasters. In addition there were party election broadcasts (PEBs) on each of the five terrestrial television stations, and the main political parties also made a broadcast at the time of the Budget.

The allocation of party election broadcasts was related both to the level of support in previous elections and to the number of candidates nominated. During general elections, a maximum of five PEBs was allowed for any single party, and the party in government and the Official Opposition were given the same number of broadcasts. The rules were flexible enough to take account of strong support for new parties (such as the SDP in the 1980s) where this had been demonstrated in by-election results and opinion polls. Any party contesting at least fifty seats in a general election was entitled to at least one election broadcast (in May 1996 the additional hurdle that such parties also had to demonstrate 'proven electoral support' was dropped). PEBs were also broadcast in advance of local and European elections.

There has always been a certain amount of criticism of the system for allocating party broadcasts, particularly from the third and minor parties which have tended to feel squeezed by the traditional government/Official Opposition dominance of the arrangements. In general, the Committee on Party Political Broadcasting only met when there was failure to reach agreement over the broadcasters' proposals for allocating PPBs or PEBs. This occurred before the 1983 general election when the Liberal/SDP Alliance would not agree any allocation that did not give them parity in broadcasts with the Labour Party. The response of the broadcasters was to impose the allocation they believed fair, with the result that the Alliance received four broadcasts, and five each were offered to the Conservative and Labour parties. In June 1997 the BBC and ITV decided, on legal advice, that they would in future receive representations from the political parties directly rather than relying on the Committee on Party Political Broadcasting to convey the views of the parties.

The ITC and BBC, together with S4C and the Radio Authority, produced a consultation paper in January 1998 proposing reforms of the whole party political broadcasting system. Adopting a somewhat lofty stance, the consultation paper suggested that PPBs rely more on the techniques of the advertising world than those of public service broadcasting. The broadcasts were introduced 'for a different era' before the televising of Parliament and the current multitude of news and current affairs programmes. It seems hard to believe now, but general election campaigns were not covered at all by the television news until 1959. Viewers and listeners, the consultation paper argued, now have ample opportunity to see, hear and judge politicians on a wide range of subjects; and party political broadcasts simply give the parties free political advertising. The consultation paper did not mention viewing figures during PPBs but briefings given to the press indicated that this was an important consideration for the broadcasters: research by the BBC quoted in the *Guardian* found that recent PPBs by Labour and the Conservatives had led to switch-off rates of 36 per cent and 27 per cent respectively.

Nevertheless, the broadcasters are not keen to introduce paid political advertising on television and radio. Nor are the political parties: in the 1996 presidential campaign in the United States, where there is no system of free broadcasts, each candidate spent at least $50 million on advertising alone. The broadcasters therefore proposed that regular PPBs and the post-Budget broadcasts should be abandoned altogether and replaced with more broadcasts at election times (see box, p. 171). This system would more closely resemble arrangements in other countries. There would be PEBs for elections to the European Parliament and the Scottish Parliament and assemblies for Wales and Northern Ireland. There would also be additional PEBs for local elections, but the BBC and ITC did not propose to offer broadcasts during referendum campaigns due to the difficulty of achieving balance when parties are split on the issue in question (the possible future referendum on European Monetary Union is a case in point). Ministerial broadcasts (accompanied by a right to reply for the opposition parties) would be made only in exceptional circumstances.

Arrangements for Northern Ireland would be made more consistent with the situation on the mainland. Previously the Northern Ireland parties received 'campaign broadcasts' incorporated in programmes rather than separate PEBs. Under the new system the national political parties would not receive PEBs in Northern Ireland unless they contested one-sixth of the seats there.

These proposals received a mixed response from the political parties. The Liberal Democrats' spokesperson said that his party valued PPBs because they did not have strong support in the press or access to the 'massive advertising budgets' available to Labour and the Conservatives. Labour's Peter Mandelson wrote in *The Times* that the broadcasts were 'the only opportunity for political parties to communicate with the public without editorialising by journalists' (24 January 1998). The Conservatives' initial reaction to the proposals was more favourable. Following negotiations between the parties and the broadcasters, a compromise was reached (see box below). The majority of party broadcasts will be at election time, but there will be a small number of additional broadcasts to coincide with other key events in the political calendar, such as the Budget, the Queen's Speech and party conferences.

In the 1997 election, eight parties not currently represented in the Commons qualified for a PEB under the 'fifty seat' rule. These included the Green Party, the

---

Party political broadcasts in the year 2000: Who gets what

England, Scotland and Wales

1 Budget broadcast	March
4 PEBs (local/London mayor elections)	April/May
1 party conference	September/October
1 Queen's Speech	November

Similar arrangements will take place in subsequent years. Applies to Labour, Conservatives and Liberal Democrats, plus SNP in Scotland and Plaid Cymru in Wales. Other parties will qualify for PEBs if they contest one sixth or more of the seats fought in an election. Scheduled broadcasts will fall if they coincide with a general election.

(ITC/BBC joint News Release, 28 June 1999)

Referendum Party (Sir James Goldsmith's anti-EU party), the Natural Law Party (practitioners of Transcendental Meditation), the British National Party, and the Pro-Life Alliance (an anti-abortion party). Of these, the Referendum Party got 2.6 per cent of the total vote while the other seven polled less than 0.3 per cent each. The January 1998 consultation paper raised the possibility of single-issue campaigners or extremist parties fielding candidates purely in order to gain access to national television. The broadcasters pointed out that the real value of the election deposit has fallen greatly since it was first introduced in 1918; in the 1997 election fifty deposits cost £25,000 and secured a five-minute broadcast on five television channels. At current advertising rates on the three commercial channels alone that would cost several million pounds. The consultation paper admitted that previous attempts to distinguish 'serious political parties' from those trying to exploit the rules on PEBs had failed, and the broadcasters concluded that the best course would be to raise the threshold for broadcasts to one-sixth of all seats contested. This would mean a threshold of 110 seats for a national broadcast; parties contesting one-sixth of the seats in Scotland and Wales would qualify for a PEB in those countries only. If a party not currently represented in Parliament stood in substantially more than 110 seats, the allocation of additional broadcasts would be based on a range of factors including the percentage of votes obtained in previous elections and/or any other reliable evidence of the level of the party's electoral support.

Although editorial control over PEBs resides with the parties making the broadcasts, the television and radio companies are responsible for ensuring that the relevant laws and codes are complied with. During the 1997 campaign, broadcasters were unable to reach a consensus on the British National Party (BNP) broadcast, and two different versions were shown. ITV and Channel 4 demanded that the BNP remove some of the most offensive images from its broadcast, including footage of identifiable members of ethnic communities used without their permission. The party was unable to edit its broadcast in time for Channel 4's deadline so it was not shown on that channel. The Pro-Life Alliance was required to obscure images of abortions on taste and decency grounds (it took unsuccessful court action over this). Members of the public complained that both broadcasts breached the ITC code, but the commission rejected these complaints, finding that the BNP's policy on immigration, for example, had been 'communicated briefly and without strident language'.

The BBC/ITC consultation paper gave details of new editorial guidelines for party political broadcasts. These demand compliance with the law on areas such as libel, obscenity, incitement to racial hatred, and so on, and with broadcasting codes on such matters as taste and decency, privacy and fairness. In addition the guidelines state:

- The use of actors in a broadcast must be made clear to the audience if there is any possibility that the audience could be confused or misled by their appearance.
- No revenue-generating telephone numbers are to be used in a broadcast.

The new guidelines are somewhat less exacting than the ITC code on television advertising, which requires adverts to be legal, decent, honest and truthful. Party election broadcasts will be bound by the first two, but not the last two requirements!

PARLIAMENT AND THE MEDIA

Broadcasting Parliament

John Reith, the first director general of the BBC, campaigned over a number of years for daily radio coverage of the proceedings of Parliament, but the Prime Minister of the day, Stanley Baldwin, resisted this and in 1926 stated that there was a 'greatly preponderating body of opinion against broadcasting the proceedings of the House'.[12] In 1944, moreover, under the 'fourteen days' rule, the BBC agreed not to broadcast discussions or statements on any issue which was due to be debated in Parliament during the next fortnight. In 1955, Winston Churchill defended this practice, saying:

> I will never reconsider it. I believe it would be a shocking thing to have debates in this House forestalled time after time by the expression of opinion of persons who have not the status and responsibilities of Members.[13]

In fact, the fourteen days rule broke down after the government was humiliated by the Suez affair in 1956.

There was renewed pressure to allow sound broadcasting from Parliament in the 1960s, but regular broadcasts did not begin until April 1978. The BBC's charter requires it to broadcast a daily impartial account of the proceedings of both Houses of Parliament and since 1945 this requirement has been met by the *Today in Parliament* programme, although recorded extracts were not introduced until 1978. A re-edited version, *Yesterday in Parliament*, was introduced later. In 1998 the BBC decided, despite protests from MPs and the Speaker, Betty Boothroyd, to broadcast *Yesterday in Parliament* on long-wave only, its companion programme having already been removed from the FM waveband.[14]

During the 1980s the debate moved on to the televising of Parliament. Some MPs believed that televising the Commons would alter its character, with the risk that members would use parliamentary debates as a soapbox to address the public at large. There were fears that the broadcasts would be unrepresentative, concentrating on moments of high drama to the exclusion of more serious debate, giving the public the impression that their elected representatives were in a perpetual state of rowdy excitement. However, other MPs argued that the public might gain a better understanding of Parliament and politics if proceedings were televised, since this was now for many people the principal medium of information. Many felt that being able to watch the work of Parliament, whether in the public gallery or on TV, was a basic democratic right. More self-interested motives may also have been at work in both camps. Some on the Labour benches hoped that the activities of the opposition in Parliament would receive better coverage on television than in the press due to the broadcasters' duty to achieve balance, while some Conservatives believed that the television cameras would show the Prime Minister, Margaret Thatcher, to be a better parliamentary performer than the Labour leader, Neil Kinnock.[15]

In 1988 the Commons voted to allow television coverage on an experimental basis and this began the following year. Coverage was effectively made permanent in July 1990, while proceedings in the House of Lords had already been televised since 1985. Since 1992 continuous live coverage of the Commons has been available on cable TV. In addition, some public meetings of select committees (committees of backbench MPs which scrutinise the work of government departments) are televised. This has resulted in television news programmes giving greater prominence to their work, not least because committee members' right to cross-examine public figures who appear as witnesses often leads to dramatic encounters.

The broadcasters must respect 'the dignity of the House and its function as a working body rather than a place of entertainment'. During periods of 'grave disorder' the camera is instructed to focus on the Speaker. Unidirectional microphones ensure that the viewers hear the MP who is supposed to be speaking rather than 'sedentary' interventions (MPs are not allowed to contribute to debates while seated). Some barracking of frontbenchers can be extremely personal and on occasion even obscene; this can succeed in making speakers lose the thread of their argument and while observers in the public gallery are left in no doubt as to the cause, the television audience can be unaware of the reason for a poor performance. Channel 4 views the remaining restrictions on coverage of proceedings as censorship and refuses to transmit live broadcasts from Parliament.[16]

Michael Portillo, the former Conservative cabinet minister, voted in favour of the televising of the Commons, but later claimed to regret the decision and argued in a speech to a Conservative fringe group in January 1994 that TV coverage encouraged the public to sneer at politicians. Nevertheless most MPs now accept that, for good or ill, the cameras are a permanent fixture in Parliament. Most commentators conclude that, apart from paying increased attention to their appearance, MPs have not changed their behaviour significantly as a result of the presence of TV. In fact, it would seem that the widespread availability since the mid-1990s of a live closed-circuit television feed in MPs' offices (in combination with changes to the hours when Parliament sits as part of the so-called 'Jopling reforms' of this period) has had a greater impact on the character of the Commons than public broadcasting, as attendance during debates has fallen while many members 'remain in their rooms, from time to time watching television coverage of the Floor of the House while working on constituency matters'.[17]

Press coverage of Parliament

A number of MPs have lamented the decline in newspaper coverage of Parliament. In 1993 Labour's Jack Straw published research demonstrating a steep decline in the amount of press reporting of Parliament since the late 1980s.[18] Between 1933 and 1988, coverage of parliamentary debates on designated 'politics' pages took between 400 and 800 lines in *The Times*, and between 300 and 700 lines in the *Guardian* and its predecessor the *Manchester Guardian*. By 1992 coverage had fallen to fewer than 100 lines in both papers. Coverage in the *Daily Telegraph* had also fallen, but the decline was less marked. Straw claimed that this made it even harder for backbenchers to get press coverage. His overall conclusion was that 'this serious decline in the coverage of Parliamentary debate is bound to have an adverse effect on the public's understanding of their system of democratic government.'

The reasons identified by Straw included:

* the televising of Parliament (although the press now tend to focus on the same narrow range of events that TV and radio concentrate on, such as Prime Minister's Questions);
* the apparent invincibility of the Thatcher government, which made the outcome of Commons debates a foregone conclusion;
* a generation change among political editors, with the new guard feeling that straightforward reporting of parliamentary proceedings was 'boring';
* a consequential change in the tactics of MPs, who resort to press releases rather than speeches in Parliament to attract the media's attention.

It is certainly true that the focus of activity of ministers and politicians in general has moved away from Parliament to a large extent, but Straw's analysis does not prove that this was caused by the decline in the reporting of Parliament. It seems more likely that coverage has fallen as parliamentary proceedings have lost their newsworthiness. Most new government policies which are announced in the Commons have been trailed extensively in the media beforehand; and despite the protests from whichever party is in opposition, there is no sign of this trend being reversed. In the past newspapers reported speeches in Parliament for their information content, but the presentation of information in today's press is highly sophisticated, relying on a variety of visual techniques. As priorities have changed, political advancement may now depend less on parliamentary debating skills than on confidence on television and in the *Today* studio. It is ironic that Parliament overcame its reluctance to allow access to the television cameras at around the same time as commentators began to conclude that the Commons chamber was no longer the centre of Britain's political life. Some even remarked that outside-broadcast interviews from College Green, the patch of grass just over the road from Parliament which became at times a marketplace for MPs wanting to give their opinions and broadcasters wanting to hear them, had come to rival the Commons as a focus for political debate.

LICENCE TO SPIN: THE GOVERNMENT'S INFORMATION MACHINE

The Government Information and Communication Service (GICS)

GICS is the name given to the 1,000 communications specialists within the civil service who are responsible for the presentation of government policy and information through relations with the media, publicity and advertising. Each department employs its own press officers (many of whom also have journalistic experience) and there are currently around 370 working in the main Whitehall departments and in arm's-length government agencies such as the Child Support Agency. Other GICS staff include marketing and publications specialists.

GICS is unusual within the civil service in that its organisation and career structures operate cross-departmentally. The Cabinet Office publishes a manual known as the *Red Book* containing guidance on the work of the service (see box, p. 177).

Government press officers must attempt to separate ministers' party political role from their governmental duties. In practice, this may be difficult to achieve. According to the *Red Book*, where a minister's speech includes material of a party political nature or an attack on political opponents, either the passages in question should be omitted from the official press release, or the text of the speech should be put out through the party political machine, which is normal practice with party conference speeches. An example of the tensions which can arise appeared in press reports in October 1997 describing a dispute between an education minister and the chief press officer at the Department for Education and Employment over the minister's desire to issue a press release criticising the policies of the previous government. The official, who left his post shortly after the incident occurred, was said to have insisted that this was a party political matter which civil servants should not become involved with.

The Prime Minister's press secretary

The most visible post in the government's media team is that of press secretary to the Prime Minister, who is, in effect, the government's spin-doctor-in-chief. This crucial position has been identified as having four main roles[19]:

- spokesman or woman
- adviser on media relations
- intermediary or agent dealing with the news media, and
- manager or co-ordinator of government information services.

The power of the position can be seen from the fact that ministers must obtain permission from the Prime Minister's press office before giving interviews and making policy statements. The approach to the job has varied greatly with the

---

Government press and publicity work: The main conventions

The activities of the Government Information and Communication Service:

i   should be relevant to government responsibilities
ii   should be objective and explanatory, not tendentious or polemical
iii should not be, or be liable to misrepresentation as being, party political
iv   should be conducted in an economic and appropriate way, having regard to the need to be able to justify the costs as expenditure of public funds

The *Red Book* states: 'it is proper and necessary that the Government should explain and justify its policies and decisions.' While government publicity will acknowledge the part played by individual ministers, 'personalisation of issues or personal image-making should be avoided,' as should publicity which justifies or defends ministers' policies in party political terms or directly attacks policies and opinions of opposition parties. The manual warns that 'it would be counter-productive if the level of spending on a publicity campaign impeded the communication of the message it is intended to convey, by itself becoming a controversial issue.'

In addition, government press officers must, like all civil servants, 'conduct themselves with integrity, impartiality and honesty . . . They should not deceive or knowingly mislead Ministers, Parliament or the public' (Civil Service Code, para 5). Ministers should not ask civil servants to do things which would break their ethical code, such as taking part in 'activities likely to call into question their political impartiality' (Ministerial Code, para 56).

(extracts from the *Red Book* (Guidance on the Work of the Government Information Service) reproduced in the *Report of the Working Group on the Government Information Service*, Cabinet Office, November 1997 (the Mountfield Report))

---

personality of successive press secretaries, but it is inevitably controversial. As Colin Seymour-Ure has pointed out, if the press secretary gets too close to the Prime Minister, he risks being embroiled in Cabinet disputes and accused of partisanship; but on the other hand, if he steers determinedly clear of partisan issues, his usefulness to the Prime Minister declines.[20] The media may want the PM's press secretary to fulfil both qualities: closeness to the Prime Minister bestows *authority* and gives a reliable guide to what the PM is thinking, but the traditional civil servant's detachment provides a degree of *objectivity*. Related to this is the question of whether the Prime Minister's press secretary should come from a civil service or a party background. Sir Bernard Ingham, who served as the Number 10 press secretary from 1979 to 1990, was closely associated with the policies of Margaret Thatcher, largely because of the robust way in which he promoted her interests in his dealings with the media. Nevertheless he was a civil servant and has insisted that he did not cross the traditional barriers between government and party political interests. After the 1997 election Tony Blair appointed the former journalist Alastair Campbell as his press secretary. Mr Campbell was Mr Blair's press secretary before the election and became a crucial part of New Labour's expert presentation of policy in opposition. Since the Blair administration places so much importance on presentation, his role in government has proved both pivotal and controversial. Being a special adviser (a ministerial appointment) rather than a civil servant, he is freer to become involved in party political controversy in certain circumstances (see box, p. 179).

Communication or politicisation?

The priority given to presentation by the Blair government, and in particular the pivotal role of the Prime Minister's official spokesman, Alastair Campbell, has given rise to charges that the Government Information and Communication Service has been 'politicised'. Allegations that the traditional neutrality of the civil service is under assault are a perennial theme for opposition parties and the press, and the nature of its work makes the GICS particularly vulnerable to accusations of this kind. A number of chief press officers from government departments left their posts in the first few months of the new Labour administration and this attracted much comment in the media and a degree of concern within the civil service. Some journalists complained about the undermining of the impartial and trusted role of government press officers – although others felt they offered a less reliable reflection of current government thinking than the special advisers appointed by ministers.

A high-level working group on the government information machine was established not long after the election. Its aims were to establish best practice in the face of these allegations and to improve central co-ordination of policy presentation within the civil service, following Labour practice in opposition. There had been instances of breakdown in effective co-ordination between government press officers and special advisers in briefing the media and accusations of pre-emptive briefing by one department against another.

The working party's report (the Mountfield report) was issued in November 1997.[21] The Government Information Service became the Government Information and Communication Service, to emphasise its role in communicating government policies, but the new name is not particularly catchy and many journalists continue to use the old title. The following substantive changes were made following the report:

- A new Strategic Communications Unit based in Number 10 Downing Street was established early in 1998 to serve the whole government, with the aim of improving co-ordination of government policy presentation by keeping departments informed of activity in other parts of Whitehall. The new unit, which is answerable to the Prime Minister's press secretary, contains a mixture of civil servants and special advisers.

A Source Very Close to the Prime Minister

Alastair Campbell: Where I think I am freer than my predecessors, and I think this is a good thing, is that if the Prime Minister is the subject of a political attack I am in a position to rebut it. How I draw the distinction is this: if a Conservative politician makes a speech or puts out a press release saying, 'Here's ten reasons why Tony Blair is unfit to be Prime Minister' and I am asked by any of these gentlemen [journalists] at a briefing about my response to that, I can respond to that in a way that my predecessor who worked for John Major could not. My predecessor would have had to say, 'That is a party matter, you have to refer it to the party.' [. . .] What I cannot do and what I do not do is go into briefings and say, 'Here's ten reasons why you should not vote Tory. Here's ten reasons why William Hague is not fit to be Prime Minister.'

Andrew Tyrie (Conservative): You are clearly involved in party-political activities and, in that respect, for example, when you go down to the Labour Party Conference, you are acting, are you not, as a Labour Party spokesman?

Alastair Campbell: Well, I am acting wherever I am as the Prime Minister's spokesman and doing a number of different jobs for the Prime Minister as he wants them done.

Andrew Tyrie: But when he is at the party conference, he is there as the party leader, is he not, and, therefore, are you not also, therefore, a Labour Party spokesman?

Alastair Campbell: Well, I would certainly concede that it is a party event, but he is the Prime Minister and I am there helping him to prepare a speech and brief upon a speech that relates to his work as Prime Minister. Now, as I say, that does not mean that there will not be a party-political element to what he does. If you go back to the last party conference, to be honest, there was not at that time much interest in your party at all, and I cannot even remember whether the Prime Minister referred to your party in his speech, but what he did do was make a number of announcements in relation to policy, in relation to strategic themes that he was planning to set and I think that he would think that it was right that I was there for that.

Andrew Tyrie: And that that would constitute being a Labour Party spokesman?

Alastair Campbell: I think in doing that I can be seen as the Prime Minister's spokesman.

Andrew Tyrie: And not as a party spokesman? I am sorry to labour this point, but this does seem to me a pretty crucial distinction because what we did have was a system where we had a man who was the Prime Minister's spokesman but very clearly not a party spokesman. But your contract reads differently. The question I am asking you is whether part of your role consists of being a party spokesman?

Alastair Campbell: What my contract makes clear is that I can set things in a party political context and I have gone through some of the areas where I think I try to draw the line and stay out of the grey areas if I possibly can.

(Alastair Campbell answering questions on his role as the Prime Minister's press secretary from the Select Committee on Public Administration, 23 June 1998[22])

- The twice-daily briefings given by the Prime Minister's press secretary are now held 'on the record'.
- A round-the-clock news monitoring service was set up in the Central Office of Information (COI).
- An electronic information system for ministers and press officers, known as Agenda, was developed. It provides a diary of government events with email and briefing facilities, including 'appropriate lines to take', the Number 10 daily media briefing, the text of the Prime Minister's speeches, and the output of the media monitoring unit. Agenda is intended to enable 'instant rebuttal' of negative stories, which was a strong element of Labour's effectiveness in opposition.

In addition the government resolved to improve co-ordination between departmental press officers, policy civil servants and ministers and their special advisers. Despite the Mountfield report's promise to maintain a politically impartial service, the key role for Alastair Campbell confirmed by the report and the emphasis on special advisers working together with civil servants to co-ordinate government policy led to further charges of the 'Blairisation' of Whitehall. Nevertheless, the consensus among political commentators on this concerted effort to improve presentation was that New Labour still found it harder to control the media impact of its activities in power than it did in opposition: hardly surprising, given the immense complexity of modern government.

THE LOBBY

'The Lobby' (not to be confused with 'lobbying') refers to the two hundred or so political correspondents from the press, TV and radio who have special access to politicians at Westminster. The name comes from the Members' Lobby in the House of Commons: lobby journalists have access to this and other parts of the House of Commons which are closed to the public while the House is sitting. Some accounts of the secretive rules and rituals which used to characterise the lobby made it sound like a masonic lodge, but with a new generation of political correspondents a much more informal body has emerged, whose governing ethos is that confidences should be respected.

The lobby traditionally received non-attributable semi-official briefings ('on lobby terms') from the Prime Minister's press secretary and other 'sources close to the government' such as special advisers appointed by cabinet ministers. What the press secretary said at the twice-daily briefings for the lobby was what the Prime Minister wanted the media to report – yet the journalists did not identify their source. The rules on attribution changed recently following a long process of erosion of the principle of anonymity. The old arrangement gave the government of the day tremendous opportunities for news management, which were famously exploited by Margaret Thatcher's press secretary, Bernard Ingham. The PM's press secretary could anonymously flag up a potentially unpopular policy before the assembled ranks of the lobby so that the government could see what kind of reaction it received in the media and with the public at large (sometimes called 'flying a kite'). If the policy proved unpopular ministers could move to distance themselves from it; it could then be quietly dropped or modified. If the government decided to press on regardless, some of the sting might at least have been taken out of the official announcement when it did come.

Many lobby journalists approved of non-attributable briefings because they were told things which they would not otherwise have been told: in the words of Michael Jones of the *Sunday Times*, the only people who stood to gain from an end to anonymity were 'those who seek to control the supply of information' (*Guardian*, 25 October 1997). Others were strongly opposed to the lobby system, and the *Guardian*, the *Independent* and the *Sun* withdrew from it for a time. Critics of the system, such as Kevin Maguire of the *Daily Mirror*, maintained that while there would always be 'private chats in corridors, over lunch, on the phone or even in the back of aeroplanes with the PM', the 'institutionalised secrecy of regular mass briefing' (which amounted on occasion to 'spoon feeding' gullible journalists) was indefensible (*Guardian*, 25 October 1997). Some journalists felt that it would be harder for the government to plant deliberately misleading stories if the source could be named.

The Mountfield report noted that anonymous sources had increasingly dominated political journalism, both news and comment. This has its disadvantages: where there are conflicting anonymous sources, with briefing and leaking coming from assorted points in the system, it is difficult to say which is genuine (or, as Kevin Maguire put it, 'There are so many spin doctors now that if you don't like the spin you just change your doctor'). Following the Mountfield report, new rules on attribution were issued in order to ensure that authentic government statements, especially from Number 10, carry 'due authority' (see box, p. 182).

The twice-daily briefings given by the Prime Minister's press secretary are now held 'on the record'. They continue to be off-camera, however, and are supposed to be attributed to 'the Prime Minister's official spokesman' rather than to Alastair Campbell by name. This is to avoid, as Mountfield put it, building up an official 'too much into a figure in his own right'. Nevertheless newspapers occasionally name Mr Campbell as a source. Briefings from other ministers' special advisers and departmental press officers are now supposed to be on the record 'unless agreed otherwise'. Peter Riddell of *The Times* described the new rules as sensible and long overdue: 'There has been a gradual shift to greater openness and more direct attribution over the past decade as part of a greater transparency in government and a more open, and less clubby, style among a new generation of political journalists' (*The Times*, 28 November 1997). To many commentators, the main purpose of the new rules was to curb the activities of ministers' special advisers. There had been controversy in the summer of 1997 as a result of conflicting signals about the government's policy towards European Monetary Union. Mountfield was insistent that special advisers working outside Number 10 should not be described as 'official spokesmen'. In theory, if those people actually authorised to speak for the government did so on the record, it should

---

Can I Quote You on That?

The Mountfield Report suggested that 'a Lobby system which relies on non-attribution tends to give an unwarranted credibility to those unnamed sources who are always "senior" and invariably "close" to whichever Minister is the prime subject of the story.' It contained new draft guidance on attribution:

- *On-the-record*: all that is said can be quoted and attributed
- *Unattributable or Lobby Terms or guidance*: what is said can be published but not attributed
- *Off-the-record*: the information is provided to inform a decision or provide a confidential explanation. It is not for publication in any way.

'For maximum authority, press officers should speak *on-the-record* whenever possible . . . *Off-the-record* is for real emergencies' (if a journalist has sensitive information which he or she is determined to publish, an off-the-record briefing on the harm this could cause, such as endangering life and limb, may be the only way to prevent this).

---

be easier to spot the musings of the special advisers and take them with a pinch of salt.

In practice, political considerations will always enter the picture too. In January 1998 a biography of the Chancellor of the Exchequer, Gordon Brown, alleged a deep political rivalry between Brown and Tony Blair.[23] The recriminations which followed suggested that the thrust of the Mountfield Report had yet to be put into practice fully. When an anonymous source, apparently from Number 10, described the Chancellor as 'psychologically flawed' a leader in the *Guardian* of 20 January 1998 commented that either Mr Blair's spin doctors were acting on his orders or 'the spin machine is now out of control.' This very personal comment on the Chancellor seemed to have uncomfortable echoes of Bernard Ingham's infamous description of John Biffen, the then cabinet minister, as a 'semi-detached' member of the Thatcher government.[24] Rules about how communication should be conducted in government will always be vulnerable to political eruptions.

POLITICAL CAMPAIGNING

The sophistication of political campaigning in Britain has increased enormously during the latter half of the twentieth century. This has often been described as the Americanisation of politics because professional campaigning techniques started in the United States, but also because such methods tend to focus on the personality and image of the party leaders rather than party policy. Many see this as a move towards the presidential politics of the United States.

In a study of 'the new marketing of politics', Dennis Kavanagh identified the important differences between Britain and the United States in this respect:

> In Britain, the stronger party system means that the pollsters and experts on public relations and communications still have an insecure relationship with the politicians. In this respect British elections are still far from being Americanized.[25]

He pointed to the 5,000-plus political consultants in the United States, which far exceeds the number who earn a living as professional campaigners in Britain. Other differences include the strength of single-issue campaigns and the vast sums which must be found to back political campaigning in the United States, where there are no free party political broadcasts, and television advertising must be purchased at the going rate.

However, in the few short years since Kavanagh's study was published, Tony Blair's leadership of the Labour Party has introduced a sea change in British political campaigning. Blair's style is arguably more presidential than any previous party leader or Prime Minister, while Labour's extensive policy reviews went hand-in-hand with the development of the most professional campaigning machine which has yet been seen in Britain. One of the most notable coups was the successful *rebranding* of the party as New Labour, a corny but successful technique direct from the world of marketing. Kavanagh's description of the main features of a professional approach to campaigning seems highly apt[26]:

- the subordination of all goals to that of election victory
- the reliance on survey and focus-group research to guide the party's appeal to voters
- the pre-eminence of the mass media as the means for reaching voters
- the importance of communications specialists in campaign terms.

Another important aspect of the modernisation of political campaigning embraced whole-heartedly by New Labour was the eclipse of the locally organised campaign by central planning and co-ordination, a role fulfilled with gusto by Labour's campaign HQ in Millbank, Westminster (see box, p. 184, top).

None of the principal elements of New Labour's approach were entirely new developments: New Labour simply took the modernisation process several steps further. The main changes in the mechanics of campaigning are summarised in the box (p. 184, bottom).

Why should politicians resort to professional campaigning techniques? Because they want power. This is not necessarily a cynical position: without power their ability to make an impact on society is limited. A modern democracy represents a highly competitive market for politicians, and slickly effective presentation may give a party the edge it needs to achieve power. This is likely to mean concentrating on image and identity, and the broad sweep of policy rather than minutiae,

Labour's 1997 election campaign

Labour's campaign was [. . .] set out in detail. Blair wanted to structure our message around three anchors: Remind (about [the Conservatives'] record); Reassure (that Labour is new; that we have safe, common-sense policies); Reward (through the pledges). By November the War Book had our final dividing-lines in: leadership not drift; for the many not the few; the future not the past. These became a mantra. For the first time in perhaps thirty years Labour was getting a genuine message that would be used repeatedly by politicians. Eventually these were augmented by the culminating message of our campaign: 'Enough is Enough: Britain deserves better'. These messages appear very simple but they are the result of months of work, taking New Labour's big themes and making them completely accessible to the public.

(Philip Gould (a key Labour Party adviser from 1985 to 1997),
The Unfinished Revolution: How the Modernisers saved the Labour Party
(London, Little, Brown and Company, 1998), p. 312)

The modernisation of political campaigning

	Pre-modern campaign	*Modern campaign*
Campaign organisation	Local and decentralised	Nationally co-ordinated
Preparations	Short-term and *ad hoc*	Long campaign
Central co-ordination	Party leaders	Central HQ, specialist consultants
Feedback	Local canvassing	Opinion polls, focus groups
Media	National and local press, local leaflets, posters, etc., radio leadership speeches	TV, national poster campaign in prime commercial sites, PEBs
Campaign events	Local public meetings, whistle-stop leadership tours	Media management, daily press conferences, themed photo-opportunities, etc.
Costs	Low-budget, met locally	Higher costs, met nationally

(based on Pippa Norris, *Electoral Change Since 1945* (Oxford, Blackwell, 1997), p. 196)

but with good reason. Consider Labour in the 1980s and early 1990s. Poll after poll suggested a comfortable lead for the party in policy areas considered important by the voters, such as unemployment and the health service. But the party was not trusted, especially on crucial issues such as taxation and defence. The party leadership concluded that without trust it would not be given power, and its strategy was therefore aimed at building that trust. It was an exercise in rebranding, of a remarkably successful kind.

The elements of a professional campaign

The professional campaigners from America have given us three buzzwords which between them sum up the modern approach: photo-opportunities, sound-bites and spin doctors. These and other features of modern campaigning are described below. Opinion polls and focus groups, two tools from market research which form an integral part of the professional political campaign, were discussed in the previous chapter.

Photo-opportunities

It is important for politicians to be seen regularly – and in a flattering light – on television and in the press, because visual images have been shown to make a stronger impression on voters than mere words. From the point of view of the press and, especially, television, a story is more likely to be seen as 'newsworthy' if it has a strong visual element.

'Walkabouts' and other events staged specially for the television cameras have played an important part in campaigning in Britain since the 1970s. Party campaign managers soon realised that by planning the availability of visual images they could have a greater influence over the content of television news, so events were timed to coincide with particular news broadcasts. If a party wants to stress its sound economic policies, its leader might be despatched to a factory, accompanied by TV cameras and the whole media circus. A quick visit to a hospital might help to convince viewers of the caring, compassionate nature of the party's policies and, more importantly perhaps, of a politician's personal warmth and empathy (see box, p. 186).

Photo-opportunities of this kind have now replaced public meetings as the mainstay of election campaigns. Campaign managers generally want to exercise absolute control over such events, as a photo-opportunity which goes wrong – a politician (literally) tripping up, or appearing unsettled by an angry voter – can create precisely the opposite of the intended impression, in front of millions of viewers.

Today the parties use advisers who pay meticulous attention to politicians' appearance. Facial expression, body language, hairstyle, clothes, tone of voice and turn of phrase all come under the spotlight. Care is also taken to avoid unflattering or embarrassing backdrops. Margaret Thatcher famously underwent voice coaching and emerged with a softer, lower speaking voice. Labour received advice

---

How to create a photo opportunity

New Cash for the NHS
Photo: MP pictured outside hospital with a large hand-drawn picture of a syringe with the words 'Labour's £2 billion cash injection for the NHS' written on it.
To make the syringe you will need: a large piece of white card and a black marker. Draw a large syringe on the card, write the lettering in the tube (make it large and bold so it can be easily read). Cut around the drawing to get the syringe shape.

(recent campaigning material produced by the Labour Party's Policy and Elections Units, undated)

---

on such matters from Barbara Follett (now an MP herself) and the process of making candidates presentable became known as 'Folletting'. Men were requested to shave off their beards and women not to wear dangly earrings. In today's politics, as in the world of advertising, appearance is taken very seriously indeed.

Soundbites

For many years politicians have striven to encapsulate their appeal to voters in a short and memorable catch-phrase. The promise at the end of the First World War by the Liberal Prime Minister, David Lloyd George, to 'make Britain a fit country for heroes to live in' is a good example. As shadow Home Secretary after the 1992 election, Tony Blair made regular use of the phrase 'tough on crime, tough on the causes of crime'. This was designed to steal the Conservatives' clothes as the party of law and order, but at the same time to emphasise Labour's determination to deal with social problems like youth unemployment which, he argued, were part of the reason levels of crime had risen under the Conservatives.

Over the years journalists have become less willing to reproduce large chunks of politicians' speeches, so it has become increasingly important to capture the essence of a speech in a good soundbite. The disadvantage of this approach is that the slick slogan or pithy one-liner is hardly an adequate vehicle for developing subtle or complex arguments. Verbs are increasingly being banished from politics. Professional campaigners would argue that such subtleties are lost on the majority of voters anyway and are therefore superfluous to the parties' precious moments of prime-time television or column inches in the tabloids. As in advertising again, slogans are believed to sell.

Spin doctors

This term is used somewhat loosely as it is currently in fashion, but in the British context it generally covers party officials, special advisers appointed by cabinet ministers and government press officers. The role of the spin doctor is to ensure, by any means necessary, that the desired interpretation or 'spin' is conveyed when journalists report an issue. This is news management at its most manipulative. The way a spin doctor works is described by the BBC political correspondent, Nicholas Jones, in his entertaining book *Soundbites and Spin Doctors*[27]:

> Their natural habitat is around Westminster and at party conferences. They give advice on the content of speeches and the likely implication of votes and decisions. Their busiest times are immediately after major political developments, when journalists are often desperate to speak to authoritative sources capable of giving them an instant interpretation of what has happened and also background guidance on the likely consequences. . . . The most manipulative conversations tend to take place in private.

If a tricky political development is in the offing, a spin doctor will often start by 'guiding and tweaking the focus of the news coverage by slipping out some well-placed leaks'. When initial reports of the leaks are not denied by the party, the rest of the media assumes they are accurate and follows suit, so the desired impression is created 'without the spin doctor having to do anything as explicit as issuing an official statement'.[28] A line which has never been officially adopted can be changed much more easily if the need arises later.

One of the darker tactics employed is intimidation: bawling out a journalist who has dared to file an unfavourable story; threatening to deny him or her stories in future; or complaining to figures higher up in the news organisation. Well-placed complaints against television and radio journalists may be effective because the broadcasters are ever-sensitive to accusations of bias, given their duty to cover politics objectively.

During the 1980s two figures, Peter Mandelson (Labour's campaigns and communications director from 1985–90 and subsequently an MP and minister) and Bernard Ingham (Margaret Thatcher's press secretary), earned an almost mythical reputation in political circles for their spinning techniques. In Mandelson's case, these skills continued to be put to regular use after his election as an MP in 1990. In recent years Alastair Campbell, Tony Blair's press secretary in opposition and in government, has earned a similar reputation. Some regard spin doctors as increasingly the key figures in the political process: 'As communication flows are deliberately centralised, their authority as the source of information and opinion is further enhanced.'[29]

One of the consequences of the growing importance of spin doctors is that spin has become big news in its own right. The unravelling of who said what to whom, and on whose authority, can develop into a gripping detective story for journalists. On these occasions, spin can be counter-productive. Noted examples include the conflicting messages over Labour's policy on the single European currency which emerged in the summer of 1997, and the saga of Labour's 'Jennifer's Ear' party election broadcast in 1992. In the latter incident, Labour's broadcast highlighted shortcomings in a little girl's NHS treatment, allegedly due to under-funding. A row broke out when spin doctors from both parties went to work on the story, the identity of the patient was revealed, and political disagreements within the girl's family emerged. This seemingly trivial incident developed into a major news story about spin and the ethics of using real-life cases in political campaigns. It remained in the headlines for several days, disrupting Labour's attempts to manage the news agenda, but the Labour campaign adviser Philip Gould maintains the incident was not so harmful to the party as many people believed at the time.[30]

Spin doctors might not be necessary if politicians did not find it necessary to speak in code for much of the time. For the major parties, politics is likely to involve a succession of difficult compromises: between ideals and political realities, between party and electorate, between different factions of the party, and so on. The hints and coded messages which litter politicians' speeches result from their attempts to balance these conflicting demands. Even a speech containing unpleasant home truths for one group may have the ulterior motive of sending some sort of message to another (such as, 'It's OK, you can trust us after all'). Spin doctors occupy the space between politicians' words and their meaning. They give journalists unattributable but (usually) authoritative assistance in decoding the subtle language of political rhetoric.

Managing the news

During election campaigns, and increasingly at other times too, each party focuses on one or two issues each day in an attempt to 'set the agenda' for the day's news. Announcements will often be timed to deflect attention away from embarrassing issues or to spoil stories likely to be favourable to the other parties. Campaign managers try to restrict all of the party's media output – press conferences, speeches, photo-opportunities and even interviews – to the chosen theme. Unfortunately the parties' desire for favourable coverage verging on propaganda conflicts with the journalists' hunger for controversy and their civic role in testing the politicians' assertions on behalf of the electorate. This results, particularly during elections, in 'something of a game in which many journalists try to trap politicians and the latter try to use the former'.[31] The rules of the game, at least in respect of interviews, are spelled out by the BBC (see box below):

Cutting through the soundbites

[BBC interviewers] should appear searching, sharp, sceptical, informed – but not partial, discourteous or emotionally attached to one side of an argument. Interruption may be justified but it needs to be well timed and not too frequent [. . .] Evasion should be exposed. This should be done coolly and politely [. . .] In a well-conducted interview, listeners and viewers regard the interviewer as working on their behalf.

(extract from the BBC's *Producers' Guidelines*, 3rd edn, 1996)

In order to 'control the agenda' for television and radio interviews, party officials may conduct detailed negotiations with production teams in an effort to restrict questioning to 'safe' areas, ensure that someone is interviewed separately from opponents or critics, guaranteed the final word, or interviewed by a specific person. This is a good example of the symbiotic relationship between politicians and the media which many commentators point to. If a journalist strays into areas which have been ruled out of bounds, the politician is unlikely to walk out in the middle of the interview as this would probably make him or her look foolish, but the party may extract its revenge later by various means such as withdrawing co-operation for a time, making it harder for that programme to get prime interviewees. A good interviewer may find a way to move on to more contentious ground while staying within the letter of the agreement. Party managers go to considerable lengths to keep politicians who cannot be trusted to keep 'on message' (or who simply do not come across well on television or radio) away from the broadcasters' studios.

Negative campaigning

There has traditionally been a reluctance in British politics to resort to the direct character assassination which has featured heavily in US campaigns for many years. The main reason for this reluctance has been a feeling that voters do not like this, and it is notable that the most effective examples of negative campaigning in Britain in recent memory have been based on policy rather than personality. Examples include the Conservatives' sustained attack on 'loony left' Labour councils in the late 1980s and early 1990s and their successful attempt during the 1992 election to play on voters' fears that Labour would increase taxes. Nevertheless, the natural response to one party's attempt to build up the image of its leader is for the other to try to dent that image. During the 1997 campaign the Conservatives used their infamous 'demon eyes' posters in an attempt to undermine voters' trust in Tony Blair. There was much debate during the campaign as to whether the Conservatives' tactic was sensible: there was certainly a high public awareness of the adverts, but judging by Blair's record personal popularity ratings before and after the election they were not effective. Labour, on the other hand, was in the fortunate position of being able to benefit from widespread allegations of 'sleaze' against the Conservatives featuring prominently in the media, thereby avoiding the charge of negative campaigning itself.

Another American technique which Labour perfected during the run-up to the 1997 election was the use of 'rapid rebuttal' to counter negative campaigning and negative stories in the media before they came to dominate the day's news. A powerful database of quotations and policies, known as Excalibur, was developed to assist campaigners in this task.

Keeping politicians 'on message'

An account of modern campaigning techniques would not be complete without mention of the pager, which has assumed a hallowed place in the mythology of New Labour as an important tool by which spin doctors keep politicians 'on message'. The truth is more mundane, as most messages simply contain information from the whips about Commons business, but it does mean that anything from news of a breaking story, to a united response to an awkward development, can be broadcast swiftly and silently wherever a politician happens to be at the time. The Speaker, Betty Boothroyd, has ordered that pagers be switched to 'vibrate' mode in the Commons chamber to prevent proceedings being disrupted by manic beeping. In a neat postmodern tableau, the Prime Minister's press secretary, Alastair Campbell, interrupted his evidence to a select committee which was investigating government press and publicity work to say that his 'trusty Millbank pager' had informed him that his appearance before the committee had displaced the government's intended top story on the early evening news.

Many observers of the political scene are uneasy about the campaigning methods described here. A common charge made against New Labour is that it is preoccupied with image and presentation, supported by a 'control culture' that stifles open debate and communication. However, this judgment may simply reflect Labour's success at developing a highly effective and modern communications strategy. The Conservative Party has yet to emulate Labour's approach, but this is more likely to be the result of its difficulties in doing so than outright opposition to modern methods. Some Conservatives are suspicious of adopting such a slick presentational style (a feeling also shared in some quarters within the Labour Party), but others admire Labour's media professionalism, and the need to rebuild the Conservatives' image in a modern context is likely to dictate the party's campaigning strategy in the years to come. Professional campaigning in Britain has developed by each of the main parties leapfrogging over the other to try out some new technique, which was scorned initially but later copied by its rival. The internal reforms started by the Conservative leader, William Hague, should enhance the party's ability to campaign as a national organisation rather than a collection of semi-autonomous local units. Professional campaigning is here to stay, with the parties competing to keep ahead of the game.

WHAT EFFECT DO THE MEDIA HAVE?

The importance of the media in modern politics is universally acknowledged, but is it possible to isolate and measure the media's effect in any precise way? To do so has proved notoriously difficult, despite the widely held 'commonsense' view that the public's deep exposure to the media must have some effect on attitudes and behaviour. Pluralist accounts attribute only a relatively weak effect to the mass media. The *reinforcement* theory, for example, suggests that people tend to select sources of information which reinforce their own view of the world, filtering out dissonant voices. According to Marxist or determinist models, on the other hand, the media is, in effect, a dangerous propaganda machine which reinforces the dominant interests in society. The work of the Frankfurt School, notably Adorno and Marcuse, is the classic exposition of this approach.[32] Earlier we looked briefly at a more refined (and highly influential) version put forward by the Glasgow University Media Group, with its emphasis on the role of the media in setting the political agenda.

Hard evidence of the effect of the media on the political process in Britain – at least in relation to attitudes and behaviour – is thin on the ground, however. It may be that politics and the media are now so deeply intertwined that establishing a simple causal relationship between them is impossible. Empirical studies in Britain have been hampered by focusing almost exclusively on whether the media influences the way people vote. Pippa Norris points to research in the United States which suggests much broader (but limited) effects[33]:

> The media influences public opinion through four main avenues: enabling people to keep up with what is happening in the world (learning), defining the major political issues of the day (agenda-setting), influencing who gets blamed or rewarded for events in the news (framing responsibility), and finally shaping people's political choices (persuasion).

Adopting a similar approach, Norris offers a tentative analysis of media effects in Britain, based on recent British election surveys. All of the possible spheres of media influence described above are considered, but the evidence is found to be, by and large, inconclusive. Even where a link is established (between newspaper readership and voting patterns, for example), it is not clear what is cause and what is effect. Is voting influenced by the newspapers people read, or do people simply choose a paper that reflects their own political preferences? The study finds a significant link between watching television news and levels of political knowledge, participation and efficacy (the belief that people can influence the political process), but it may be that those who do not feel alienated by the political process, and are knowledgeable about it, watch more news programmes. The most interesting aspect of the study is that it failed to find evidence to support the agenda-setting hypothesis in Britain. For example, awareness of defence as an issue declined significantly between the 1987 and 1992 elections, but no more so among regular television viewers. 'The agendas of the media, the parties, and the public, shifted between elections, but it is not clear . . . who led (if anybody), and who followed.'[34] The media structures the political process in a whole variety of ways, but their 'effects' on attitudes and behaviour are more complex than might be supposed.

THE FUTURE OF POLITICAL COMMUNICATIONS

It is possible to detect a gradual move towards 'postmodern' campaigning in Britain, characterised by permanent campaigning, targeting different groups of voters and the full-time involvement of professional spin doctors and market researchers.[35] In the United States and some European countries, campaigners have also had to modify their approach to cope with the fragmentation of the TV audience. This has resulted from the transition from broadcasting to 'narrowcasting', the growth of stations seeking to capture a fraction of the total audience by providing specialised programmes or, more commonly, bland fare indistinguishable from that offered by dozens of other channels.

In Britain, however, the national media still predominate, creating a strong national forum for political discourse, from the *Today* programme and *Newsnight* to the *Sun* and the *Daily Mail* (although the importance of the local media should not be overlooked). Political campaigning in England is overwhelmingly governed by this central fact, and fears about the erosion of this basic feature of political life lay behind politicians' protests against ITV's decision in 1998 to scrap its *News at Ten* bulletin. In Scotland the strength of the Scottish media provides a separate national forum, and this would appear to have been an important factor in the result of the devolution referendum. The recent controversy about whether the BBC in Scotland should be allowed to replace the United Kingdom-wide 6 p.m. television news with its own version is an example of the effect of devolution on media patterns.

Satellite and cable broadcasting still occupy a relatively marginal position in Britain, but the launch of digital television could yet lead to the fragmentation of the large audiences the main channels still enjoy. Nevertheless, it is likely that television will continue to be highly regulated in Britain in comparison with many other countries, so high-quality news and analysis will continue to be available for those who want it (perhaps a dwindling band?). If the vogue for 'rolling news' stations develops, the spin doctors' activities may assume an even greater significance, as journalists chase frantically after new leads on tired stories. On the positive side, television advertising by political parties, which inevitably increases the campaigners' concentration on image and personality over policies, does not appear to be a realistic prospect in Britain.

The potential political impact of another recent development, the internet, is starting to be realised in Britain. It is now possible to visit websites created by government departments, universities, the political parties and a vast range of interest groups (see Appendix 4). When the government issues a consultation paper now it is generally available on the internet, giving a much wider cross-section of the public the ability to get hold of it easily and even to respond to it, should they feel so inclined. Access is still confined to a minority of the population, though, and there have been widespread predictions of a growing divide between information 'haves' and 'have-nots' in the twenty-first century, with potentially damaging consequences for democracy. However, it is just possible that the internet will prove a sufficiently exciting medium for political communications to capture the interest of future generations of voters while they are still at school, especially as the interactive possibilities of the net are realised. The chance even exists for a small shift in the emphasis of our democratic institutions, away from the representative towards the participatory. One American commentator predicts that 'in the electronic republic, it will no longer be the press but the public that functions as the nation's powerful Fourth Estate, alongside the executive, the legislative and the judiciary.'[36] As ever, the media offer both challenges and opportunities for the democratic process.

NOTES

1 *The Political Impact of Mass Media*, London, Constable, 1974, quoted in Ralph Negrine, *Politics and the Mass Media in Britain*, 2nd edn, London, Routledge, 1994, p. 5.
2 Bob Franklin, *Packaging Politics*, London, Edward Arnold, 1994.
3 27 April 1965. Quoted in Dennis Kavanagh, *Election Campaigning*, Oxford, Blackwell, 1995, pp. 12–13.
4 *BBC Agreement of 25.1.96*, Cm. 3152, part 8; Broadcasting Act 1990, section 10. Under paragraph 8.3 of the Agreement the government even has the right to take over the BBC's facilities at times of national emergency.
5 In August 1997 the *Observer* was issued with a D-Notice when the government became aware that it intended to publish the name of MI5's new deputy director, but it ignored this request.
6 The next day the same paper boasted 'IT'S THE SUN WOT WON IT'.
7 Margaret Scammell and Martin Harrop, in David Butler and Dennis Kavanagh (eds), *The British General Election of 1992* and *The British General Election of 1997*, London, Macmillan, 1992 and 1997.
8 *Report of the Committee on Privacy and Related Matters*, Cm. 1102, June 1990, para 14.38.
9 *Review of Press Self-Regulation*, Cm. 2135, January 1993, p. 63.
10 Alastair Hetherington, *News, Newspapers and Television*, London, Macmillan, 1985, p. 8, cited in Duncan Watts, *Political Communication Today*, Manchester, Manchester University Press, 1997, p. 55.
11 Glasgow University Media Group, *Bad News*, London, Routledge and Kegan Paul, 1976.
12 *House of Commons Official Report* (Hansard), 22 March 1926, col. 866.
13 Quoted in Geoffrey Marshall and G. C. Moodie, *Some Problems of the Constitution*, London, Hutchinson, 1959, p. 144.
14 In July 1999 the BBC announced a partial climbdown following a dramatic fall in the audience for the programme.
15 Duncan Watts, *Political Communication Today*, op. cit., p. 160.
16 The rules for television coverage of the Scottish Parliament are far more liberal, enabling anything which could be seen by a member of the public sitting in the public gallery to be captured by the cameras.
17 House of Commons Liaison Committee, *The Work of Select Committees*, HC 323 of 1996–97, 18 February 1997, para 24.
18 *The Decline in Press Reporting of Parliament*. See also, David McKie, *Media Coverage of Parliament* (Hansard Society, 1999). A similar trend in television coverage was indicated by a recent study published in Stephen Coleman, *Electronic Media, Parliament and the People* (Hansard Society, 1999).
19 Memorandum by Colin Seymour-Ure, Reproduced in Select Committee on Public

Administration, *Government Information and Communication Service*, HC 770 of 1997–98, 29 July 1998, p. 96.

20   Colin Seymour-Ure, 'Prime Minister's press secretary: the office since 1945', *Contemporary Record*, Autumn 1989.

21   *Report of the Working Group on the Government Information Service*, Cabinet Office, November 1997. The group included the Prime Minister's press secretary.

22   HC 770 of 1997–98, op. cit., questions 311–312, 378–381.

23   Paul Routledge, *Gordon Brown: The Biography*, London, Simon and Schuster, 1998.

24   J. M. Lee, G. W. Jones and J. Burnham, *At the Centre of Whitehall*, London, Macmillan, 1998, p. 75.

25   *Election Campaigning*, Oxford, Blackwell, 1995, p. 7.

26   Ibid, p. 21.

27   Nicholas Jones, *Soundbites and Spin Doctors*, London, Indigo, 1996 edition, p. 123.

28   Ibid.

29   Tony Wright, 'Inside the whale: the media from Parliament' in Jean Seaton (ed.), *Politics and the Media: Harlots and Prerogatives at the Turn of the Millennium*, Oxford, Political Quarterly/Blackwell, 1998.

30   Philip Gould, *The Unfinished Revolution: How the Modernisers Saved the Labour Party*, London, Little, Brown and Company, 1998, pp. 130–41.

31   Dennis Kavanagh, op. cit., p. 190.

32   Curran and Seaton, *Power without Responsibility*, London, Routledge, 5th edn, 1997, ch. 17, contains a more detailed account of the main theories of 'the sociology of the mass media'.

33   Pippa Norris, *Electoral Change Since 1945*, Oxford, Blackwell, 1997, p. 216.

34   Ibid., p. 222.

35   Ibid., p. 210.

36   Lawrence K. Grossman, 'The electronic republic', in E. E. Dennis and R. W. Snyder (eds), *Media & Democracy*, New Brunswick, Transaction Publishers, 1998, p. 160. Coleman (op. cit.) gives a thorough assessment of the possibilities of the new media in the context of the British political process.

FURTHER READING

There is a wide range of books on this subject. *Political Communication Today* by Duncan Watts (Manchester University Press, 1997) is a good, up-to-date introduction to all of the topics covered in this chapter. Other useful texts covering politics and the media include James Curran and Jean Seaton, *Power Without Responsibility*, 5th edn (London, Routledge, 1997); Ralph Negrine, *Politics and the Mass Media in Britain*, 2nd edn (London, Routledge, 1994); and Colin Seymour-Ure, *The British Press and Broadcasting since 1945*, 2nd edn (Oxford, Blackwell, 1996). There are also a number of books on modern political campaigning, including Dennis Kavanagh, *Election Campaigning* (Oxford, Blackwell, 1995) and Pippa Norris *et al.*, *On Message: Communicating the Campaign* (Sage, 1999). For lively accounts of the relationship between journalists and those involved in the political process, from each side of the fence, see Bernard Ingham, *Kill the Messenger* (London, HarperCollins, 1991) and Nicholas Jones, *Soundbites and Spin Doctors* (London, Indigo, 1996 edition).

7 Parliament and politicians

If Parliament is not visibly influencing events, the descent into partisan rhetoric may in part be a response to frustration. We are in danger of being turned into fans in a stadium, corralled in our team seats, shouting insultingly framed advice to those on the pitch, and organising the equivalent of the Mexican wave to provide the appropriate response to whatever is being said.

(Alan Beith MP[1])

WHAT IS PARLIAMENT FOR?

Parliament is at the heart of British government, but it does not govern. The government is mostly composed of members of parliament, and its survival depends on the continued support of a majority of them. Parliament itself, though, has no executive functions; and although a majority of its members are supporters of the government, it is also the means by which government is held to account, through scrutiny and criticism from opposition and backbench members. Besides this, Parliament makes the law, authorises taxation, represents opinions and interests, and acts as a forum for debate on the issues of the day. Altogether, its existence and activities are supposed to confer legitimacy on the government between general elections, to reassure people that governments, once elected, stay within the boundaries of their mandate and do not govern in an arbitrary way.

Can Parliament do all this properly? Unlike most other institutions of its kind elsewhere, it has an almost continuous history of hundreds of years. This has given it an enormous international prestige – England, it was famously said by the radical, John Bright, in 1865, is the 'Mother of Parliaments' – but it can also make it seem antiquated and ineffective. One recent commentator has condemned it for becoming 'incompetent and irrelevant across many of its central functions'.[2] It is often said that Parliament now occupies a smaller position in the politics of the country than it once did; that significant political debates take place in the media, not in Parliament; that Parliament's attempts to scrutinise the work of a sophisticated and professional government are amateurish; that its legislative role amounts to rubber-stamping the government's proposals; and that its power to make law is in any case drastically limited by European agreements, rulings of the courts and activities of financial institutions. Yet Parliament is still central to the political process and to the business of governing. When Parliament is not sitting, for instance, politics often appears to be dormant. But though it may seem to be busy, is it effective? (See box below.)

Busy – but how effective?

Number 10 during a Parliamentary recess is unreal. There are three levels of unreality about it. While the House is sitting a quarter of a mile away, Number 10 has about it an air of tension and uncertainty which evaporates when the House rises. Don't anyone tell me that Parliament exercises no control over the executive. When the Prime Minister leaves Number 10 for a trip abroad, or for Chequers, a great deal of dynamism and electricity drains out of the building even when the House is sitting. But when the Prime Minister departs from Number 10 during a recess the building becomes a haven of peace and tranquillity – unless, of course, a major crisis blows up.

(Bernard Ingham, *Kill the Messenger*, 1991, p. 168)

The Commons is alive with frantic activity every day of the session . . . Most MPs are creased and harassed individuals moving at a perpetual fast walk and straining the voice-box, memory and writing-hand during long working days (twelve or fourteen hours are not uncommon, day after day). They live . . . in a gossipy and self-obsessed world where sudden crises blow up, and there is always another tale ricocheting around the walls. But once the day is ended, it is often hard, standing back, to determine any good that has been done by the collective parliamentary class . . . What seems at first sight to be important is often revealed, at a second glance, to be merely self-important. . . . Letters from constituents have been answered, tens of thousands of words exchanged, deals done. Ministers have been told a thing or two, and have replied on the late-evening news. Obscure parliamentary manoeuvres have been successfully brought off, privileges upheld, procedures sprung, whips confounded. But who else is listening? And why should they?

(Andrew Marr, *Ruling Britannia*, 1995, pp. 115–16)

In a joint report on constitutional reform published just before the 1997 general election, Labour and the Liberal Democrats said that 'renewing Parliament is key to the wider modernisation of our country's system of government.'[3] Soon after the election, the new government initiated a process of reviewing the procedures and practices of the House of Commons through a new Select Committee on the Modernisation of the House of Commons. It also plans a major reform of the

House of Lords. These reforms will abolish some of the most anomalous features of Parliament. But will they make it any more effective? This chapter examines the functions of Parliament and how well it performs them. First, though, how does Parliament actually work? And who are its members – and what do they do?

HOW PARLIAMENT WORKS

Parliament and government

The relationship between Parliament and the government is central to how Parliament works. As described in Chapter 2, the 'Westminster model' of parliamentary government represents almost the antithesis of the concept of the 'separation of powers'. Rather than being separated, the executive and the legislature are intimately linked: the government is formed out of the party which has secured the most seats in the House of Commons at a general election. The Prime Minister is the leader of the winning party, and chooses most of his ministers from among the members of his party who have been elected to the House of Commons. There is a statutory limitation on the number of paid ministers who are allowed to sit in the Commons. In June 1998 there were eighty-nine ministers, supplemented by forty-five unpaid parliamentary private secretaries to ministers. These 134 MPs, about a fifth of the House and (at present) a third of the governing party's MPs, form the core of the government's support in the House of Commons and are sometimes referred to as 'the payroll vote'. The support of the remaining 'backbench' members of the party normally provides a government with the backing of a secure majority whenever its proposals are put to a vote.

This close connection between Parliament and government means that conflict between them is by definition almost impossible. Parliament is not, and cannot be, independent of government in the way that the US Congress is. Some argue that this means that Parliament's ability to act as an effective check on the executive is negligible; others that it makes it a more realistic and responsible body (see box, p. 198).

Parliament and party

Making sure that it always has the backing of its party in Parliament is therefore one of a government's major preoccupations, but all parties need to ensure that they maintain a coherent and reasonably united front in order to convey a clear message to the electorate. In Britain the constitutional link between executive and legislature is cemented by party.

Almost all of the 659 people elected to Parliament in 1997 stood as candidates selected by one of the main political parties. (Even in the exceptional case, Martin Bell's election at Tatton, his election as an independent was assisted by the withdrawal of the Labour and Liberal Democrat candidates.) Eleven parties are currently represented in the House of Commons (Table 7.1).

Parliament and government: two views

The whole structure of the Constitution, the way in which Parliament works, is that it is a party machine, and that means that the majority party and the government have a common interest and they are interdependent. The government majority backbenchers have an interest in making sure the government does its job, but also that it manages to put into effect the policies of a government. Therefore it must support the policies of the government; and equally, of course, the government depends on its majority in order to get things through. So there's a relationship and it's very close. Now, unless you can crack that detailed connection between the two, then you're not going to get anywhere in the end. It's very difficult to see how you can break this connection without changing fundamentally the whole system so that you brought it into line, if you like, with the way the Americans do it. You'd have to have it quite clear that the government and the executive were directly elected, so you'd have to go back to something like a presidential system. I think you'd also probably have to take ministers out of the House of Commons and put them, as in the American constitution, in a separate body – a genuine separation of powers.

(J. A. G. Griffith, quoted in Peter Hennessy, *Muddling Through: Power, Politics and the Quality of Government in Postwar Britain*, 1996, p. 67)

[One of the functions of Parliament] is to sustain the executive and help it make decisions in the national interest . . . I would suspect that my constituents, if asked, would greatly prefer a Parliament which helped the Government to make better decisions than a Parliament which concentrated on checking Government, delaying its decisions, introducing interminable political argy-bargy into matters which to the average citizen require a quick and energetic application of common sense.

(Douglas Hurd, 'Is there still a role for MPs?', *RSA Journal*, June 1997, pp. 35–6)

Just as the government is formed out of the largest party, the second largest party is regarded as the Official Opposition, with its leader referred to as the Leader of the Opposition. The Official Opposition has a formal status and certain parliamentary rights. Some of its members act as a 'shadow cabinet' and speak for the party in Parliament, covering the various departments. Other parties also appoint spokesmen to cover particular issues or departments. Because ministers and their opposition 'shadows' occupy the seats closest to the middle of the chamber, facing one another, they are generally referred to as the government or Opposition front bench. All other MPs are referred to as backbenchers. MPs who are not part of the government are also sometimes referred to as 'private members', although this may suggest a freedom from party control that does not exist.

Table 7.1 Parties in the House of Commons, December 1998

Labour Party	417
Conservative Party	162
Liberal Democrats	46
Ulster Unionist Party	10
Scottish National Party	6
Plaid Cymru	4
Social Democratic and Labour Party	3
Ulster Democratic Unionist Party	2
Sinn Fein	2
UK Unionist Party	1
Independent	1
Scottish Labour	1
The Speaker and her deputies	4
Total	659

Members usually vote as they are instructed by their party leadership. Each party has a group of members, known as whips, whose duty it is to ensure that members attend and vote as required: they issue instructions in a document circulated each week which is also known, confusingly, as the 'whip' (see box, p. 200). Whips have other important roles too. They are the eyes and ears of the party's leadership in the House, spotting talent, detecting discontent, enforcing discipline and sorting out problems.

Commentators frequently point out how party discipline severely limits the ability of members to perform their scrutiny roles properly, and accuse them of either slavish loyalty or knee-jerk opposition. However, from time to time MPs do defy their party leadership, voting against its policy or abstaining on key issues. Relatively uncommon between 1945 and 1970, since then instances of 'dissent' or 'rebellions' have been more frequent.[4] For example, some Labour backbenchers defied their whips in December 1997 to vote against the policy of removing benefit from single mothers. Frequent rebels are unlikely to be promoted; and in extreme cases they may even suffer the 'withdrawal of the whip' – in other words, suspension from the parliamentary party. The Conservative government withdrew the whip from nine of its backbenchers in 1994, placing its majority in jeopardy, after they had defied the whip to vote against a motion on European Union finance. Nevertheless, such dissidence is unusual, not because of the threat of sanctions but because most members' loyalty to their party is very strong. They accept the direction of their whips because it increases the effectiveness of their party in Parliament. Party and party discipline are deeply ingrained in the British parliamentary system.

A Labour Party whip

PROVISIONAL BUSINESS FOR THE WEEK COMMENCING MONDAY 22ND FEBRUARY 1999

MONDAY, 22ND FEBRUARY

1. Second Reading of the Immigration and Asylum Bill.

    THERE WILL BE A THREE LINE WHIP AT 9.00 PM FOR 10.00 PM.

2. Motion on the Northern Ireland Arms Decommissioning Act 1997 (Amnesty Period) Order.

    THERE WILL BE A TWO LINE WHIP AT 10.30 PM FOR 11.30 PM.

TUESDAY, 23RD FEBRUARY

1. Second Reading of the Welfare Reform and Pensions Bill.

    THERE WILL BE A THREE LINE WHIP AT 9.00 PM FOR 10.00 PM.

WEDNESDAY, 24TH FEBRUARY

1. Until 12.30pm, debate on the Third Report from the Northern Ireland Affairs Committee on Composition, Recruitment and Training of the RUC. Followed by a debate on the Sixth Report from the Agriculture Committee on Flood and Coastal Defence. Followed by debates on the Motion for the Adjournment of the House.

2. Remaining Stages of the Social Security Contributions (Transfer of Functions, Etc) Bill [Lords].

3. Remaining Stages of the Rating (Valuation) Bill.

    THERE WILL BE A RUNNING THREE LINE WHIP FROM 3.30 PM, WHICH WILL BE RESUMED AFTER THE CONCLUSION OF PRIVATE BUSINESS UNTIL GOVERNMENT BUSINESS HAS BEEN SECURED.

4. The Chairman of Ways and Means is expected to name Opposed Private Business for consideration at 7.00 pm.

THURSDAY, 25TH FEBRUARY

1. Debate on Welsh Affairs on a Motion for the Adjournment of the House.

    THERE WILL BE A ONE LINE WHIP.

FRIDAY, 26TH FEBRUARY

1. Private Members' Bills.

Two Houses: Commons and Lords

Parliament has two Houses, or Chambers. The consent of each is required in order to make law. (Strictly speaking, the Queen is part of Parliament, too, as her consent is also required to any law; but this is always given, and the part she plays in Parliament is purely formal.) The existence of two separate Houses is largely a matter of historical accident. A second chamber is not essential, and a number of continental legislatures do without one. Both Houses of Parliament work in basically the same way: they consider legislation, debate the issues of the day, and scrutinise the work of the government. But they are very different in character and importance.

Of the two Houses, the Commons is by far the most important. It possesses the legitimacy that comes from democratic election and is where the Prime Minister and most ministers sit. The House of Lords is neither a representative nor a democratic body. Its origins lie in the principal nobles who would advise the King in the Middle Ages. Even now, about half its members are there because they have inherited their titles; most of the remainder have been appointed by successive governments, under the Life Peerages Act 1958 (Table 7.2). Life peerages are traditionally given to (among others) former cabinet ministers who have retired from the House of Commons, prominent businessmen, lawyers and academics, some trade union leaders or party officials, and a few retired civil servants.

As in the Commons, the parties play a crucial role. The government appoints a number of peers to be ministers so that they can speak in the Lords on the government's behalf; and the Opposition makes similar appointments. Each party has its own whips, although the party system in the Lords is much weaker than in the Commons. As they cannot be voted out of their seats in an election, peers have no need of party backing to retain them. Many peers (known as 'crossbenchers') belong to no party. The Conservatives have a strong advantage, as Table 7.2 shows, with far more hereditary peers than other parties.

What is the House of Lords for? In constitutional doctrine, it is seen as a forum for revising government legislation, a sort of 'legislative long-stop', giving a further

Table 7.2 Membership of the House of Lords, December 1998

Party	Life peers	Hereditary peers	Lords spiritual (bishops and archbishops)	Total
Conservative	173	302		475
Labour	158	18		176
Liberal Democrat	45	24		69
Cross bench	120	202		322
Other	9	89	26	124
Total	505	635	26	1,166

Note: A further 134 Lords who do not have writs of summons (generally those too young to attend the House) or who are on leave of absence are excluded from all of the figures.

chance to amend bills before they are passed; and as a mechanism for delaying legislation to allow for second thoughts – particularly if the legislation concerned affects fundamental or constitutional rights. The Lords can only delay legislation, not block it entirely. Under the Parliament Acts of 1911 and 1949, a bill which the Commons passes in two successive sessions, but which is both times rejected by the Lords, may pass despite the opposition of the upper House. This procedure has only been used in full twice since the 1949 Act, including, very recently, to pass the European Parliamentary Elections Act 1999; but its existence has tended to dissuade the House of Lords in other cases from persisting with opposition to a bill strongly supported in the Commons. The Lords' powers in financial legislation have for a long time been minimal. Conscious of their lack of democratic legitimacy, the Lords are wary about using even the powers they do possess. Since 1945 (under the 'Salisbury convention') the Lords have avoided the rejection at second reading of a bill which was a manifesto commitment of the government. Reforming the House of Lords is a major preoccupation of the Blair government; but while there is wide agreement on its necessity, finding a way of achieving it is far from easy. This is discussed further later.

Setting the agenda

The government decides much of what is debated in both Houses of Parliament, although there are continuous negotiations with the whips of the Opposition and other parties in a process referred to as the 'usual channels', largely organised by a civil servant, who is private secretary to the chief whip. The private secretary's role is highly unusual in that it involves contact with both the government and the Opposition parties, and is both influential and very shadowy.

In the Commons, the amount of time that is allotted to different types of business is mainly set out in standing orders, the basic rules of the House which also determine many other aspects of how it operates, such as the powers of the Speaker to control debate, what committees are appointed, and so on. The Speaker, elected by MPs at the beginning of each Parliament, enforces the House's rules (with the assistance of a number of deputies). The Lords have their own set of standing orders, although their chairman, the Lord Chancellor, has far less power than the Speaker to enforce them. 'Erskine May', often mentioned as Parliament's rule book, is in fact simply a guide to the standing orders and the precedents and practices which govern how Parliament works.

In the Commons, standing orders set aside a number of days in each session to debate subjects chosen by the Opposition, private members or select committees, and an hour or two each day to allow members to question ministers and (through brief adjournment debates and 'ten-minute rule bills') to raise issues of their choice. The rest of the time, however, is at the disposal of the government. The pie chart (Figure 7.1) shows the amount of time spent on government business, Opposition business and private members' business in an average session. A good deal of this time is used up in routine matters. Each year, for example, the government must ensure the passage of the Finance Bill, which implements the

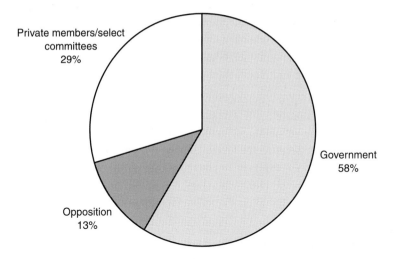

Figure 7.1 Shares of time on the floor of the House of Commons, session 1995–6

Note: Time spent on prayers each day, and time when there is no question before the House (which includes ministerial question time and statements) is excluded.

Budget. By convention, some of the time available to the government is allotted to a number of set debates: for example, the annual debates on the Queen's speech and on the Budget.

Arrangements in the Lords for setting the House's agenda are less clear cut. The standing orders do not formally give priority to government business, nor do they determine the time in each session which must be devoted to any particular item. In practice, however, the priority of the government's business is generally accepted, with arrangements made by the government chief whip in consultation with the Opposition. Most business, as in the Commons, is the government's, although most Wednesdays are reserved for debates initiated by non-government peers.

The parliamentary calendar

Parliament has an annual cycle, known as a session. It begins with the state opening of Parliament, usually in November, when the Queen reads out a speech detailing the government's plans for that session. It normally continues until about the following October, although it takes a long break during the summer, and shorter breaks at other times (the 'recesses'). Parliament sits for a total of between about 140 and 175 days in each session. The session is built around the process of approval of the government's expenditure and taxation plans, the timetable for which is governed by statute and standing order. Much planning goes into managing the timetable for the rest of the government's legislative programme, because once a bill is introduced it has to be enacted by the end of the session – or start all over again in the following one. At the end of each week the Leader of the

House, a cabinet minister who is in charge of planning the House's agenda, gives the 'business statement', indicating the government's agenda for the following week.

On each day the House sits, the 'order paper', a sort of agenda of the day's proposed business, is published and circulated. An example is shown in the box on p. 205. A normal day in the Commons begins at 2.30 p.m. with an hour's 'question time': ministers for each department answer questions put by opposition spokesmen and backbenchers on a regular rota. The period includes, every Wednesday, half-an-hour of questions to the Prime Minister. After questions, ministers may make statements to the House, perhaps to announce a new policy, or to give the government's response to some major event. On Tuesdays and Wednesdays, a backbench MP may then make a ten-minute speech proposing legislation on some subject, known as a 'ten-minute rule' Bill. After all this, the House begins the main business of the day – perhaps the second reading or report stage of a bill, or a debate on an Opposition motion – which usually continues until 10 p.m. (although the government – and only the government – may propose that for some types of business the House should extend its sitting beyond this, sometimes into the early hours of the morning). The House normally concludes its sitting with an 'adjournment' debate of half an hour, in which an MP raises a matter, typically something of constituency interest, and a minister responds. Late sittings, into the early hours, were relatively common until a set of procedural changes in the early 1990s reduced the amount of business dealt with on the floor of the House. The House has recently agreed that, for an experimental period, it will hold separate sittings – at the same time as business is being conducted in the chamber – for debates on which there are unlikely to be votes. This will allow for more discussion of (for example) Select Committee reports, or for debates on issues raised by individual MPs. On Thursdays, the House meets earlier, in order to conclude earlier, and on Fridays it meets in the morning only, with most MPs preferring to spend the day in their constituencies, dealing with business there; so it is rare for important government business requiring their presence to be set down for that day, which is often taken up with private members' bills.

The Lords usually sit from Monday to Thursday in the afternoons, and on Friday mornings. Business begins with a short period of questions, usually lasting half-an-hour; then there may be ministerial statements, as in the Commons. At the beginning of the day's main proceedings, there might be a short motion which settles how business is to be dealt with. The main business of the day itself is then entered upon. It may be followed by a short period of 'unstarred questions', an exchange between a peer and a minister something like the adjournment debate in the Commons.

MPs AND WHAT THEY DO

What sort of person becomes an MP?[5] In the present House of Commons there are 659 MPs of whom 121 are women. This is a considerably higher proportion

House of Commons

Monday 22nd February 1999

Order of Business

At 3.30 p.m.   **Private Notice Questions (if any)**

Ministerial Statements (if any)

Main Business

† 1   IMMIGRATION AND ASYLUM BILL: Second Reading.   *[Until 10.00 p.m.]*

Mr Paddy Ashdown
Mr A. J. Beith
Mr Richard Allan
Mr James Wallace
Mr Richard Livsey
Mr Paul Tyler

That this House recognises the urgent need for reform of the asylum and immigration system with the priority of reducing delays within a fair system; further supports the recognition by the Government of the contribution made to life in the United Kingdom by immigrants; but declines to give the Immigration and Asylum Bill a Second Reading as it does not provide support of asylum seekers through the benefits system as the most cost-effective and best way, as it does not provide sufficient safeguards in relation to the use of detention, as it does not repeal previous discriminatory legislation and as it builds on the previous Government's strategy of deterrence which is contrary to international agreements on the treatment of refugees.

Mr William Hague
Mr Peter Lilley
Sir Norman Fowler
Mr James Clappison
Mr John Greenway
Mr James Arbuthnot

That this House, whilst underlining Britain's commitment to genuine refugees but recognising the need to prevent fraudulent claims for political asylum and the widespread public concern on this issue, declines to give the Immigration and Asylum Bill a Second Reading because, before introducing it, the Government failed to establish an independent inquiry to consider what measures should be taken to combat such illegal immigration and because the Bill fails to create a situation whereby only genuine asylum applicants will be given permission to settle in this country.

Debate may continue until 10.00 p.m.

---

†*indicates Government Business.*
Timings are indicative only.

(18 per cent of the total) than in previous Parliaments (only 11 per cent were women at the end of the last Parliament). Most of the increase comes from the large number of Labour women, 101 now, compared with sixty-three before the election. There are nine black or Asian MPs. In terms of previous occupation (Table 7.3), most MPs have attended university and come from professional back-grounds: a large number on the Labour side were previously school or further and higher education teachers, or worked in local government or the civil service, while a high proportion of the MPs of all parties were lawyers. Conservative MPs have often been in business, as company directors or executives. Thirteen per cent of Labour MPs were manual workers (including twelve miners) in their previous existence – a much lower figure than in previous Parliaments. In all three of the main parties, a growing number of MPs are what might be called political profes-sionals – they have previously worked for their party, for a union, or as special advisers to ministers. Some have seen dangers in this, including Douglas Hurd, the former Conservative Foreign Secretary:

> the highly professional politician is particularly vulnerable to the single issue and the pressure group. They have not learned in practical work-a-day car-eers how to balance conflicting interests before they reach a decision. It is easier for them to be intoxicated by the lure of the media and the soundbite.[6]

Whether or not they have been political professionals, most MPs have been active in politics at least at local level for many years.

What do MPs do? Apart from the demands of their whips, members largely organise their own time. They receive little guidance on how they should do their job, and have no formal job description. A firm of management consultants (employed to advise on setting their pay) recently tried to produce a job description for MPs (see box, p. 208).

The last three headings should really be reversed, for it is the party political role which is dominant. A checklist of the activities of MPs might include:

- *Party:* MPs are intensely party political, and a great deal of their time is spent on party matters. Both of the larger parties have organisations at Westminster designed to represent backbenchers: Labour has the Parliamentary Labour Party (PLP); the Conservatives have the 1922 Committee. These hold weekly meetings, with other committees covering the major policy areas. There are also less formal groupings within each party bringing together like-minded Members – such as the Campaign Group in the Labour Party or Conserva-tive Way Forward in the Conservative Party – and these can be sources of pressure and influence. MPs are (as will be seen) constantly waging the party battle, through their contributions to debate, contacts with the media and other activities.
- *Constituency:* MPs maintain close links with their constituencies, spending much time dealing with constituents and their problems. Many MPs, particu-larly recently elected Members, regard this as their main role: a survey of

Table 7.3 The backgrounds of MPs in the 1997 Parliament

	Labour	*Conservative*	*Liberal Democrat*
Professions			
Barrister	12	20	4
Solictor	17	9	2
Doctor/dentist/optician	3	2	4
Architect/surveyor	–	2	–
Civil/chartered engineer	3	–	1
Accountant	2	3	1
Civil service/local govt.	30	5	2
Armed services	–	9	1
Teachers			
University	22	1	2
Polytech/coll:	35	–	1
School	54	7	4
Other consultancies	3	2	1
Scientific/research	7	1	–
Total	188	61	23
	(45%)	(37%)	(50%)
Business			
Company director	7	17	2
Company executive	9	36	7
Commerce/insurance	2	7	1
Management/clerical	15	1	1
General business	4	4	–
Total	37	65	11
	(9%)	(39%)	(24%)
Miscellaneous			
Miscellaneous white collar	69	2	1
Politician/political organiser	40	15	5
Publisher/journalist	29	14	4
Farmer	1	5	1
Housewife	–	2	–
Student	–	–	–
Total	139	38	11
	(33%)	(23%)	(24%)
Manual workers			
Miner	12	1	–
Skilled worker	40	–	1
Semi/unskilled	2	–	–
Total	54	1	1
	(13%)	(1%)	(2%)
Grand total	418	165	46

Source: D. Butler and D. Kavanagh, *The British General Election of 1997* (Macmillan, 1997), p. 205.

A job description for MPs

Job purpose
Represent, defend and promote national interests and further the interests of constituents wherever possible.

Principal accountabilities
1 Help furnish and maintain Government and Opposition so that the business of Parliamentary democracy may proceed.
2 Monitor, stimulate and challenge the Executive in order to influence and where possible change government action in ways which are considered desirable.
3 Initiate, seek to amend and review legislation so as to help maintain a continually relevant and appropriate body of law.
4 Establish and maintain a range of contacts throughout the constituency, and proper knowledge of its characteristics, so as to identify and understand issues affecting it and, wherever possible, further the interests of the constituency generally.
5 Provide appropriate assistance to individual constituents, through using knowledge of local and national government agencies and institutions, to progress and where possible help resolve their problems.
6 Contribute to the formulation of party policy to ensure that it reflects views and national needs which are seen to be relevant and important.
7 Promote public understanding of party policies in the constituency, media and elsewhere to facilitate the achievement of party objectives.

Nature and scope
An MP's work may be seen under three broad headings. The first is his or her participation in activities designed to assist in the passage of legislation and hold the Executive to account. This is traditionally seen as the 'core' role of the parliamentarian. The second area is work in and for the constituency. This is part representational: in part promoting or defending the interests of the constituency as a whole; and in part it is designed to help individual constituents in difficulty. The third part of the job is work in support of the party to which the Member belongs, and for which he/she was elected.

(Review Body on Senior Salaries, *Review of Parliamentary Pay and Allowances*, Report no. 38, 1996, Cm. 3330-II, p. 22)

MPs first elected in 1997, carried out soon after the election, found that 86 per cent of those who responded thought that 'being a good constituency member' was their most important activity. Only 13 per cent ranked 'checking the executive' higher in their list of priorities.[7] Some argue that this is the wrong way round, and that MPs should spend less time on their constituencies and more time holding government to account. Yet it is the work for which members are most directly valued by their constituents; and many MPs see it as a way in which they can really assist people, as opposed to the sometimes frustrating business of trying to influence government policy.

- *Policy:* MPs use Parliament to pursue particular policy interests, scrutinising the actions of government, and seeking opportunities to advance the causes they support. Some MPs have considerable expertise on a topic, and have a significant contribution to make in policy discussions and debates. Many devote time to work on a select committee, where they can explore issues and policies in some depth.

- *Career:* By the standards of some professions, MPs' career prospects are limited. Most of them hope to become ministers. They are constantly being assessed – by their party leadership, by their colleagues, and by the media – for their suitability for ministerial office, and the most ambitious are keen to attract this sort of attention. Yet there are many more aspirants than jobs. For the rest, there are some jobs within the House of Commons which more senior members take up, such as chairing select committees: these confer a certain amount of prestige and public attention (but no extra salary). Membership of the House of Commons is a precarious occupation: there is always the possibility of defeat at the next general election (126 Conservative members lost their seats in the 1997 election). Partly because of this, many MPs maintain other professional interests, in areas such as journalism, the law, consultancy, business or farming. However, the number who continue to keep up a significant amount of outside professional activity has been declining. There is now a greater expectation that being an MP should be a full-time job, especially as they now receive a professional salary (currently about £45,000 a year).

The possession of alternative sources of income raises the possibility that these may influence the actions of members in Parliament. Concern about what became known as 'sleaze' before the 1997 election grew with the increasingly sophisticated activities of professional political lobbyists (including their employment of MPs as consultants). The Committee on Standards in Public Life calculated that in 1995 almost 30 per cent of eligible members of parliament (that is, those who were not ministers) were consultants to public relations or lobbying firms, companies or trade associations.[8] MPs have been required to register their 'pecuniary interests' since 1975. The *Register of Members' Interests* is published annually, and gives information about directorships, paid employment, financial sponsorship, gifts, substantial investments, and so on (see box, p. 210). But a group of cases in the early 1990s in which some members accepted fees in return for asking parliamentary questions or arranging access to ministers suggested that registration, on its own, could not prevent the abuse by a few MPs of their position.[9]

The main reason for the establishment in 1994 of the Committee on Standards in Public Life was to consider whether the system of self-declaration and the rules covering the conduct of MPs needed reform. Its proposals, adopted by the

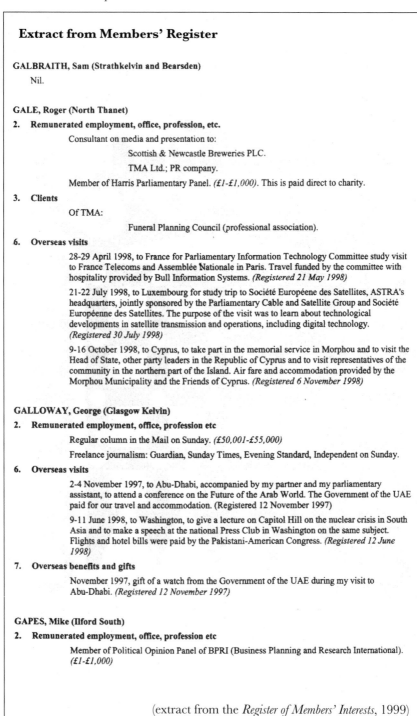

Extract from Members' Register

GALBRAITH, Sam (Strathkelvin and Bearsden)

    Nil.

GALE, Roger (North Thanet)

2.   Remunerated employment, office, profession, etc.

    Consultant on media and presentation to:

        Scottish & Newcastle Breweries PLC.

        TMA Ltd.; PR company.

    Member of Harris Parliamentary Panel. *(£1-£1,000)*. This is paid direct to charity.

3.   Clients

    Of TMA:

        Funeral Planning Council (professional association).

6.   Overseas visits

    28-29 April 1998, to France for Parliamentary Information Technology Committee study visit to France Telecoms and Assemblée Nationale in Paris. Travel funded by the committee with hospitality provided by Bull Information Systems. *(Registered 21 May 1998)*

    21-22 July 1998, to Luxembourg for study trip to Société Européene des Satellites, ASTRA's headquarters, jointly sponsored by the Parliamentary Cable and Satellite Group and Société Européenne des Satellites. The purpose of the visit was to learn about technological developments in satellite transmission and operations, including digital technology. *(Registered 30 July 1998)*

    9-16 October 1998, to Cyprus, to take part in the memorial service in Morphou and to visit the Head of State, other party leaders in the Republic of Cyprus and to visit representatives of the community in the northern part of the Island. Air fare and accommodation provided by the Morphou Municipality and the Friends of Cyprus. *(Registered 6 November 1998)*

GALLOWAY, George (Glasgow Kelvin)

2.   Remunerated employment, office, profession etc

    Regular column in the Mail on Sunday. *(£50,001-£55,000)*

    Freelance journalism: Guardian, Sunday Times, Evening Standard, Independent on Sunday.

6.   Overseas visits

    2-4 November 1997, to Abu-Dhabi, accompanied by my partner and my parliamentary assistant, to attend a conference on the Future of the Arab World. The Government of the UAE paid for our travel and accommodation. (Registered 12 November 1997)

    9-11 June 1998, to Washington, to give a lecture on Capitol Hill on the nuclear crisis in South Asia and to make a speech at the national Press Club in Washington on the same subject. Flights and hotel bills were paid by the Pakistani-American Congress. *(Registered 12 June 1998)*

7.   Overseas benefits and gifts

    November 1997, gift of a watch from the Government of the UAE during my visit to Abu-Dhabi. *(Registered 12 November 1997)*

GAPES, Mike (Ilford South)

2.   Remunerated employment, office, profession etc

    Member of Political Opinion Panel of BPRI (Business Planning and Research International). *(£1-£1,000)*

            (extract from the *Register of Members' Interests*, 1999)

House in 1995, included tighter rules and the appointment of a Parliamentary Commissioner for Standards to oversee them. The commissioner is now responsible for investigating allegations that a member has broken the rules. Her findings are reviewed by a select committee, which decides whether or not any action is necessary (for example, suspension from the House for a period). One of the commissioner's most complex investigations has been into the claims that some MPs had been paid by Mr Mohammed al-Fayed, the owner of Harrods, for various lobbying services, an investigation which contributed to the defeat at the 1997 election of Neil Hamilton, one of the members concerned, by the independent 'anti-corruption' candidate, Martin Bell. There is continuing debate about whether the Commons can regulate itself effectively or whether aspects of conduct should be regulated by statute.

WHAT PARLIAMENT DOES

Different people describe what Parliament does in different ways. Walter Bagehot, the Victorian political journalist, provided the classic description in 1867. Its principal function was to provide a means of selecting and supporting the government, to maintain 'what wisely or unwisely it deemed the best executive of the English nation'. But it also existed 'to express the mind of the English people on all matters which come before it'; to educate the country through its debates; to convey the views and grievances of the people; and, lastly, to legislate.[10] Bagehot's classification forms the basis for many more recent attempts to summarise what Parliament does. In a far more democratic constitution, though, the balance has changed. Providing the executive continues to be a crucial function; but education is no longer important now that informed discussion about the issues of the day is more easily accessible elsewhere. Nowadays, the general functions of Parliament could be described as:

- forming and sustaining government and opposition: the party basis of Parliament forms the government, provides the Opposition, and defines the activities of MPs;
- mobilising consent for the actions of government: the fact that they are approved and scrutinised by Parliament gives them a legitimacy, even if they are disliked;
- representing people: providing a channel by which the concerns of individuals and groups can be heard by government.

These are general functions. More specifically, Parliament:

- holds debates on a wide range of issues, providing an opportunity for opinions to be aired;
- scrutinises the activities of government to ensure that they are carried out properly and effectively;

- turns legislative proposals (usually from the government) into laws binding on people in the country;
- authorises the taxation of the people and the expenditure of government.

These specific functions, and the activities associated with them, are now considered in turn.

Debate – and the party battle

The time when Parliament was the pre-eminent forum for the discussion of current political issues is long gone. Radio, television and the press provide extensive coverage of political arguments – and coverage of parliamentary debates has declined considerably in recent years. Yet Parliament continues to be a place where issues and grievances, important and trivial, are aired, and where government policies are endlessly argued over. In the Commons, MPs can use debates, ten-minute rule bills, oral and written parliamentary questions, and early day motions (EDMs, proposals for debate which are published but hardly ever actually debated) to raise almost any issue they wish. A vast range of topics are discussed, such as (in one typical week) the government's review of its defence priorities; the protection of the green belt; the nuclear weapons tests by India and Pakistan; concessionary television licences; and a disused railway line in Sussex.

It is rare, though, for a debate in Parliament to have a very significant impact on policy. It is the government that makes policy, not Parliament, and most of the significant stages in the policy-making process take place outside Parliament, in think-tanks, party groups, discussions between civil servants and ministers and through consultation exercises, in which pressure groups and experts are invited to comment on government plans. Some MPs may become closely involved in the development of particular policies through discussions with ministers, work with lobby groups and through backbench policy committees of their party. Once the government has taken a policy decision, Parliament may be invited to comment; and eventually it may need to pass legislation to bring the new policy into effect. Parliament's role, though, is often restricted to making comments on a policy that has already been determined.

Partly as a result, most debates are criticised as being sterile and routine: one commentator has complained that:

> the word *debate* is something of a misnomer: little by way of challenging or responding to arguments actually takes place in a Commons 'debate'; rather, a succession of speeches are read into Hansard, with serious cut-and-thrust only during the frontbench speeches at the beginning and end, and then rarely with the intent of developing or probing the point at issue.[11]

But the effect of debates in Parliament cannot be written off entirely. When a government has a small majority, it is particularly vulnerable to pressure in a major debate, and sometimes ministers may make concessions or offer further consultation in the course of a debate. There are some issues – particularly those in which party positions are not yet fixed, or where views cross party-political lines – in which a debate may be genuinely influential.

Much of the debate that goes on in the House of Commons is intensely party political. Above everything else, Parliament is the place in and around which the party battle which underlies British politics is daily conducted. It has been called the permanent election campaign. 'Opposition days' when the subject for debate is chosen by one of the opposition parties, usually as a way of highlighting criticisms of government policy, have been called 'little more than ritual party-political point-scoring across the chamber with a higher premium on the trading of insults than the analysis of problems'.[12] 'Question time' is also routinely used to score political points. The greatest party occasion is each Wednesday's session of questions to the Prime Minister, partly because the exchanges, particularly the duel of words between the Prime Minister and the Leader of the Opposition, will be seen by many on television and commented on in the press (see box, p. 214–15). Prime Minister's question time contributes perhaps more than anything else to the lack of esteem in which some people hold Parliament, for it appears to be an unedifying and noisy spectacle. The Blair government changed it to a once-weekly period of half-an-hour, rather than the previous twice-weekly encounters of fifteen minutes each, in order to make it less confrontational and partisan, but there has been little sign of this happening.

The party battle also continues outside the chamber and the committee rooms. MPs, especially opposition frontbenchers, are constantly briefing the media about the activities of the government. There is a constant round of interviews, often in the offices very close to the Palace of Westminster where most of the political units of the major broadcasters are based, and conversations with 'lobby' journalists and others. This is 'debate' with a fiercely partisan edge.

Holding government to account

As ministers sit in Parliament themselves, they are readily accessible to members. They (not the permanent civil servants who work for them) have to explain and justify to Parliament the policies of their department. Taken to its logical conclusion, it means that Parliament may hold them, and not their civil servants responsible for any errors that their department might make. This is why MPs regularly call for ministers to resign when their department is discovered to have made a blunder – even when ministers were not personally responsible. Government, though, generally argues that ministers cannot be responsible for what they cannot control. In such circumstances, although ministers are obliged to explain what happened, even to offer redress, they cannot be expected to resign. At least in theory, Parliament has a clear system – known as 'ministerial responsibility' – by which it can hold government to account. (See Chapter 8 for discussion of this.)

They are unlikely, in any case, to have to. Occasions on which ministerial resignations are demanded quickly become party political matters, with MPs on

Prime Minister's question time (*extract*)

Mr William Hague (Richmond, Yorks): Will the Prime Minister now answer the question that he failed to answer yesterday every time that it was asked? Will he make the pound shadow the euro before the next election?

The Prime Minister: I certainly did answer that question yesterday: I said no.

Mr Hague: The Prime Minister did not say no yesterday. *[Interruption.]* No, he did not.

Madam Speaker: Order. This noise is very time consuming.

Mr Hague: In any case, the Prime Minister is not being straight with the people of this country on this subject. That is because article 121 of the Amsterdam treaty says that to join the euro requires

> 'the observance of the . . . margins provided . . . for at least two years, without devaluing against the currency of any other Member State'.

The Chancellor's advisers say it; the responsible European Commissioner says it; so why does not the Prime Minister come clean and admit to people that that is what he would have to do to join the euro?

The Prime Minister: Because it is not, and I do not accept it. I have been asked this many, many times – is it our intention to go back into the exchange rate mechanism and to shadow the euro? The answer is no, but what we will do is conduct economic policy in this country's national interest. That is precisely what we are doing, and that is the right thing to do. This is the latest of the euro scares, and it will fail like the other ones.

Mr Hague: It is the Prime Minister's friend Gavyn Davies who says that

> 'at some point the Bank of England will have to be told to "shadow" the euro (instead of inflation) for a two-year period.'

Is that a euro scare from Gavyn Davies? It is the responsible European Commissioner who says:

> 'If and when the UK decides to join the euro it will have to comply with the same conditions as . . . the first wave countries. There were five criteria for membership.'

Is the European Commission spreading a euro scare? Is Gavyn Davies spreading a euro scare? Is not the truth that the Prime Minister does not want to admit that he will have to run the economic policy of this country in the interests of joining the euro and not in the interests of Britain?

The Prime Minister: With great respect to the right hon. Gentleman, he is trying to catch up on what he lost yesterday. *[Interruption.]* After all, after

continued

yesterday we have got two Tory parties. One says, "No never," the other agrees with us, and he is the leader of neither of them. The answer is that, as other countries have not been members for two years of the exchange rate mechanism, there is no obligation upon us to do it and we do not accept it.

Mr Hague: The Prime Minister tries to refer to who lost yesterday. Is he aware that in the last six hours, 100,000 people have called *The Sun* to say that they want to keep the euro? *[Interruption.]* What is more, they regard him as a love rat. He has produced a national handover plan that does not come clean on the costs of joining the euro, that does not explain how the business cycles would converge, and that does not come clean about the fact that with convergence nowhere in sight, his plan means running the British economy in the interests of his campaign to join the euro and not in the interests of this country.

The Prime Minister: A more interesting poll may be how many of the right hon. Gentleman's Back Benchers will wish to keep him. I do not want to start another debate in the Conservative party. The national changeover plan has been produced with the consent, and at the request, of the vast bulk of British business so that we can make sensible preparations for entry into the euro, provided that the economic conditions that we have set out are met. It is supported by the overwhelming majority of people who understand that irrespective of one's view of the euro, it is surely important to make preparations. What is utterly absurd is the position that he has landed himself in, which is to say that the euro will be a disaster next Parliament but may be entirely acceptable the Parliament after. The truth is that our position sets out a clear direction and the economic conditions. It is balanced, sensible and right, and it is what this country, I believe, will accept.

24 February 1999

the government side expected to rally to the defence of the threatened Minister. For example, when the Scott report on the sales of military and other equipment to Iraq was debated in the House of Commons in February 1996, the report's conclusion that Conservative ministers had acted (albeit not intentionally) to mis-lead the House was rejected in a vote held on party lines. Ministers are sometimes forced to resign because, for one reason or another, they have lost the confidence of their own party, but these resignations cannot usually be regarded as examples of the House of Commons successfully enforcing the principle of ministerial responsibility. Various cases over the years have shown the limitations of the doctrine (see box, p. 216).

It can be argued that exposing government failure is anyway more important than attaching blame for it. To expose government failures, Parliament needs access to records; yet it cannot force ministers to surrender their official papers to

---

Ministerial responsibility: two classic cases

Crichel Down, 1954
The Minister for Agriculture, Sir Thomas Dugdale, resigned after an official inquiry criticised the ministry for administrative failures in dealing with a landowner's request to buy back land compulsorily purchased before the Second World War. Dugdale told the House of Commons that 'I, as minister, must accept full responsibility to Parliament for any mistakes and inefficiency of officials in my Department, just as, when my officials bring off any successes on my behalf, I take credit for them.' However, it is commonly argued that Dugdale's resignation was in large part due to the resentment of backbench members of his own party at the policy involved, rather than the administrative errors which Dugdale referred to as the reason.

Maze Prison escape, 1983
An inquiry following the escape of Irish Republican prisoners from the Maze Prison in Northern Ireland blamed a major failure in prison security. The prison governor resigned, but the ministers involved refused to, arguing that the faults had been in administrative actions, not in the policy for which they were responsible. The Unionist MP, Enoch Powell, called this 'a wholly fallacious view of the nature of ministerial responsibility . . . the responsibility for the administration of a Department remains irrevocably with the Minister in charge.' The ministers nevertheless did not resign.

Note: The Maze Prison case is discussed further on p. 249.

---

it. So unless ministers can be relied on to be reasonably open, and completely honest, in their dealings with Parliament, the system is ineffective. Sir Richard Scott made this point in his 1996 report on the sale of military and other equipment to Iraq:

> Without the provision of full information it is not possible for Parliament, or for that matter the public, to assess what consequences, in the form of attribution of responsibility or blame, ought to follow. A denial of information to the public denies the public the ability to make an informed judgment on the Government's record. A failure by Ministers to meet the obligations of Ministerial accountability by providing information about the activities of their departments undermines, in my opinion, the democratic process.[13]

The charge that a minister has misled the House is a serious one, because it calls into question whether there can be effective accountability at all. The Scott report showed how easily governments could avoid exposing awkward facts to Parliament if they wished to. In its aftermath, both Houses passed a resolution which

---

Ministerial accountability to Parliament: The resolution on the conduct of ministers

The following principles should govern the conduct of Ministers of the Crown in relation to Parliament:

1 Ministers have a duty to Parliament to account, and be held to account, for the policies, decisions and actions of their departments and Next Steps Agencies;

2 It is of paramount importance that Ministers give accurate and truthful information to Parliament, correcting any inadvertent error at the earliest opportunity. Ministers who knowingly mislead Parliament will be expected to offer their resignation to the Prime Minister;

3 Ministers should be as open as possible with Parliament, refusing to provide information only when disclosure would not be in the public interest, which should be decided in accordance with relevant statute and the Government's Code of Practice on Access to Government Information;

4 Similarly, Ministers should require civil servants who give evidence before Parliamentary Committees on their behalf and under their directions to be as helpful as possible in providing accurate, truthful and full information in accordance with the duties and responsibilities of civil servants as set out in the Civil Service Code.

(agreed to by both Houses, 12 and 13 March 1997)

Note: The issue of ministerial accountability is discussed further in Chapter 8.

---

underlines the obligation on ministers to be open and candid with Parliament (see box, above). The present government's commitment to legislate to provide a right of access to government papers, in a Freedom of Information Act, should make it far more difficult for governments to conceal information in the future, either from MPs or from the public. But even with unprecedented access to information, MPs are still faced with the tasks of asking the right questions and of making sense of the answers, something which requires considerable persistence, expertise and political will.

Parliamentary questions

The most basic of the tools by which MPs seek to hold the government to account is the parliamentary question. Oral questions to ministers have already been discussed; although these oblige ministers to defend and explain their policies and the actions of their departments they are an occasion more for party-political points to be made than for serious scrutiny. Written questions are a much more effective device for obtaining information from a department. The publication of the answers in Parliament's official record, Hansard, gives them wide currency. MPs constantly use written questions (they asked over 18,000 in the short session of 1996–7, with each question costing an estimated £112 to answer[14]) to obtain information in support of a campaign, to find out details about government policy or to throw light on constituency issues – for example by asking about class sizes in schools, or waiting lists in hospitals. The government is not obliged to answer parliamentary questions, although it is obliged to be as helpful as possible in response. But ministers do regularly refuse to answer questions that would take too long to research, or if they regard it as necessary to withhold the information requested on grounds such as national security or commercial confidentiality. Departments may present information in such a way as to emphasise aspects of it that are most convenient, or appear to cast a better light on the department, and they can be creative in finding ways of not revealing information while not actually concealing it or misleading Parliament. The exercise has been compared to an elaborate game (see box, p. 219).

Select committees

It is the select committees that are often seen as Parliament's most effective device for holding government to account. Select committees are normally composed of eleven members drawn from the different parties, roughly in the same proportions as they are represented in the House as a whole. Each committee is supported by a small staff (rarely more than five). Their role is to review the work of government. They gather written evidence and interview 'witnesses', normally in public. Often they travel abroad in the course of their major inquiries, to compare experience with that of other countries, or to obtain fresh ideas to feed into the policy process at home. They regularly publish reports on the topics they have investigated, which generally include recommendations addressed to government departments, to which the government is obliged to respond.

Two Commons select committees have the specific task of examining the reports of independent statutory officers. The Public Accounts Committee is the oldest of the select committees. It reviews the reports made by the National Audit Office, the government auditor, on the government's accounts and on the value for money of government expenditure. Its work provides the exception to the principle that it is a minister who is accountable to Parliament for the work of a department, for the civil servant at the head of the department (its Permanent Secretary) is formally accountable to Parliament for the propriety and efficiency of the department's expenditure, and Permanent Secretaries regularly appear before the committee to defend their departments against the findings of the National Audit Office. The Select Committee on Public Administration reviews the reports of the Parliamentary and Health Service Ombudsmen concerning complaints about maladministration by government departments and by the National Health Service. The new Environmental Audit Committee, like these two committees, is not linked to any particular department. It reviews the effects on the environment of all government policy.

The best known of the Commons select committees are the sixteen linked to the work of individual government departments (known as 'departmental' select committees). The current system of departmentally related select committees was established in 1979, and was designed to ensure that each of the main

Parliamentary questions

Sir Michael Quinlan (Permanent Secretary at the Ministry of Defence from 1988 to 1992) submitted a paper to the Scott Inquiry on the practice of civil servants in drafting answers to Parliamentary Questions. The activity of seeking and giving information in Parliament was 'in a certain sense analogous to a game . . . in the sense that it is a competitive activity conducted, within rules, largely for a purpose different from that of its apparent form.' The form was to bring information into the public domain; but its prime purpose, he believed, was, from the point of view of the questioner, 'to give the Government a hard time', and from the point of view of the Government, 'to avoid having a hard time'. 'The Opposition will seek to extract information which they can use to portray the Government in a bad light; and they will . . . feel free thereafter to exploit the information, if necessary selectively and tendentiously, to that end. The Government for its part will be reluctant to disclose information of a kind, or in a form, that will help the Opposition to do so.'

> (Report of the Inquiry into the Export of Defence Equipment and
> Dual-Use Goods to Iraq (the Scott Inquiry), HC (1995–96) 115, D4.61)

Sir Robin Butler (Cabinet Secretary and Head of the Home Civil Service, 1988–98) also gave evidence to the Inquiry on the way the Government deals with Parliamentary Questions: 'When, before Christmas [1992], the Government was being asked about contacts with the IRA, the answer that was given, which Parliament accepted was a reasonable answer, was that there had been no negotiations with the IRA. [It was subsequently revealed that the Government had exchanged messages with the IRA earlier in the year.] . . . It was not a complete picture, as subsequent events showed, but most people, I think, including the majority of Parliament, thought that, in the circumstances, it was a reasonable answer.' He denied that its purpose was to mislead: 'the purpose of it was to give an answer which, in itself, was true, was not the full situation, it was a half answer, if you like, but it was an accurate answer, and went to the point of what people were concerned about.'

> (Evidence to the Inquiry into the Export of Defence Equipment and
> Dual-Use Goods to Iraq, 9 February 1994, p. 50)

A story attributed to Lloyd George [Prime Minister 1916–22] . . . relates how . . . while motoring in the mountains of North Wales, he lost his way and inquired of a passer-by where he was. The passer-by replied: 'you are in a motor car.' Lloyd George subsequently commented that this was the perfect answer to a parliamentary question, since it was true, it was brief, and it told him absolutely nothing he did not know before.

> (Philip Laundy, *Parliaments in the Modern World*, 1989, p. 95, note 6)

government departments would be scrutinised by a select committee. The system replaced the unsystematic set of committees charged with reviewing the government's estimates (see below), and while this function lives on in the committees' formal terms of reference – 'to consider the policy, administration and expenditure' of their related department and bodies which come under it – they are now much more concerned with the main policy issues affecting their department. Something of the range of their inquiries can be seen in a list of committees meeting on a single day in 1998 (see box, p. 221).

The departmental select committees are composed entirely of backbenchers; they include neither whips nor ministers. To that extent they are independent of party and government, and although there is always a majority from the government party on each committee, select committees regularly make critical comments on government policy or administration. Some observers see the committees as a refreshing antidote to the party control and partisan rhetoric that dominate so much that the Commons does (see box, p. 222).

Yet the independence and vitality of select committees should not be exaggerated. In practice, there are tight limits to their independence, powers and effectiveness, for the following reasons:

- Though there are no whips or ministers on select committees, recommendations for select committee membership come from the whips (names have to be approved by a Selection Committee and the House, but this is usually a formality). Chairmanships similarly are usually arranged by the whips. Members of select committees may come under pressure from party whips, although this is regarded as improper.

- In order to maintain a cross-party consensus (which adds weight to their recommendations), select committees sometimes have to shy away from the most controversial issues or fudge their reports. The cost of tackling a contentious party political issue (as with the inquiry by the Select Committee on Public Administration in 1998 which covered the work of the Prime Minister's press secretary) is that the committee will split on party lines and no agreed report will be possible.

- Select committee reports do not have to be debated in the House, and in fact very few of them are. There is therefore no mechanism for ensuring that their recommendations are carried forward. A committee cannot force the government to agree with its report and recommendations. When the Trade and Industry Select Committee recommended alternative options to his programme of closing coal pits in 1992, Mr Michael Heseltine, the President of the Board of Trade, told the Commons that 'nobody believes that a Select Committee is a substitute for government. We have to study the Select Committee's proposals and we have to take the decisions.'[15]

- The committees have the 'power to send for persons, papers and records' – to insist that any British citizen appears before them, or surrenders documents to them. However, the government is able to resist a committee's request for sensitive documents (in 1998, for example, the Foreign Office resisted

---

Select committees meeting in public on Tuesday 21 April 1998

Environmental Audit
Subject: Greening Government
Witnesses: Fiona Reynolds, Director, and Mr Paul Hamblin, Environment
            Assessment Officer, Council for the Protection of Rural Eng-
            land; Mr Charles Secrett, Executive Director, and Mr Duncan
            MacLaren, Friends of the Earth

Home Affairs
Subject: Alternatives to Prison Sentences
Witnesses: Mr Graham W. Smith CBE, Chief Inspector of Probation;
            National Association of Probation Officers

Welsh Affairs
Subject: Present crisis in the Welsh Livestock Industry
Witnesses: St Merryn Meat Producers Club; Hazlewood plc; British Meat
            Manufacturers' Association

Social Security
Subject: Welfare Reform Green Paper and the Department of Social
            Security Departmental Report
Witnesses: Rt Hon Frank Field MP, Minister for Welfare Reform,
            Department of Social Security, and Department of Social
            Security officials

Foreign Affairs
Subject: Foreign Policy and Human Rights
Witnesses: Cooperative Bank plc; New Economics Foundation

Trade and Industry
Subject: Regional Policy: Reform of the Structural Funds
Witnesses: Local Government Association and COSLA

---

the Foreign Affairs Committee's request to see Foreign Office telegrams
concerning its role in the reinstatement of the elected government of Sierra
Leone). Members of Parliament and peers are not obliged to attend if sum-
moned, and governments have argued that civil servants should not be asked
to give evidence to select committees except on behalf of ministers and under
their instructions, on the grounds that the convention of ministerial responsibility requires that only the minister is accountable to Parliament for the
actions of his or her department. Although civil servants do regularly give

Life on the committee corridor

Committees *feel* important: the chamber does not. The pulse of this Administration is often better taken, now, where it throbs exposed in committee, than in set-piece clashes across the dispatch box. . . . Just take the last few days' political headlines. Few have come from the chamber. Jeff Rooker, a struggling junior Agriculture Minister, has been slammed by MPs on the Agriculture Select Committee over his efforts to ban Vitamin B6 . . . The Public Accounts Committee has denounced the tendering process for the construction of the Skye Bridge, causing a huge row in Scotland. The Foreign Secretary is locked in a serious struggle with the Foreign Affairs Select Committee, which is demanding government documents he is refusing to hand over . . . Clare Short has been attacked by the International Development Select Committee for her department's performance over Sudan . . . The Prime Minister's press secretary, Alastair Campbell, has faced inquisition, in public, by the Public Administration Committee . . . Committee work is helping to dictate the news agenda in politics. One of the reasons for this is that Government backbenchers feel emboldened by the non-party nature of Select Committee investigation, into tougher questioning or criticism of ministers than they dare venture in the chamber . . . Whips do attempt to rig and bully committees: but gingerly and behind-the-scenes. Because whips are so obviously offside when they do so, government backbenchers feel braver, and whips less able to insist.

(Matthew Parris, 'The corridor of power', *The Times*, 26 June 1998)

A perceptible shift in the balance of power is taking place at Westminster, one with potentially profound constitutional implications. Dissent and enlightenment will not be found in the obsequious tedium of the Commons Chamber. Those who seek it must turn to the long Select Committee corridor on the first floor. As one new intake Labour MP said this week: 'with such a massive majority and the Shadow Cabinet still in such a mess, Select Committees have become the one place this executive can be kept in check. You can put away your pager, the line to take or the Whips' message of the day and think for yourself.'

(Patrick Wintour, 'Labour's dissidents seize the corridor of power',
Observer, 28 June 1998)

evidence to committees, it is strictly on the understanding (made plain in the so-called 'Osmotherly rules', guidance for civil servants giving evidence) that they may only speak as authorised by ministers.

- In the face of well-prepared ministers and civil servants, select committees can seem amateurish. In the words of a management consultant closely involved in public sector management reform, 'it is relatively easy now for a highly trained executive, within the public sector, to deal with the questions of a Select Committee . . . it is, as it were, a modern organisation dealing with a rather old-fashioned form of accountability . . . instead of getting informed debate, you tend to get very formal and quite protected and carefully thought-through answers.'[16]

- Committees are unlikely to make more impact without more (and more professional) staff. The output of the departmental select committees can be compared unfavourably to the large amount of work done by the Public Accounts Committee, with all the resources of the National Audit Office (NAO) behind it, and there are calls for the NAO's resources to be shared more equally among the other committees.

Some of these criticisms give rise to proposals for improvements: for less control by the whips over nominations; for greater powers; for more staff. Yet the main constraints on select committees are the time and commitment of MPs. Most MPs have too many other commitments – in standing committees, or dealing with constituents or party matters – to devote enough time and energy to select committees to make them really effective. Furthermore, MPs are unlikely to lay aside their party allegiance to a sufficient extent to make select committees truly independent 'watchdogs'. It has been argued that service on a select committee needs to be made more attractive – for example by paying their chairmen as much as ministers. This, though, raises wider issues about the role of MPs. Nevertheless, despite the limits of the current system, over the past twenty years select committees have contributed substantially to making British government more open and accountable.

Making the law

Government bills

Most legislation that is passed is legislation proposed by the government. Because the government has such strong control over the agenda, it is able to give priority to its own legislation. There is always much pressure from government departments to find time for bills. The main government bills are announced in the legislative programme in the Queen's speech. For example, the speech at the beginning of the 1997–8 session included eighteen separate proposals; but other bills are brought forward during the course of a session (even in the short session of 1996–7, thirty government bills were passed). Government bills are drafted by a group of government lawyers called Parliamentary Counsel, on the instructions of the department concerned. An example of part of the text of a recent bill, the House of Lords Bill 1999, appears in the box on p. 224. Bills can begin their passage through Parliament in either House; but they must be approved by both. The most significant and controversial bills tend to begin life in the Commons.

Page 1 of the House of Lords Bill 1999

A

B I L L

TO

End membership of the House of Lords by virtue of a hereditary   A.D. 1999.
peerage; to make related provision about disqualifications for
voting at elections to, and for membership of, the House of
Commons; and for connected purposes.

BE IT ENACTED by the Queen's most Excellent Majesty, by and with
the advice and consent of the Lords Spiritual and Temporal, and
Commons, in this present Parliament assembled, and by the authority
of the same, as follows:—

5   **1.** No-one shall be a member of the House of Lords by virtue of a   Exclusion of
hereditary peerage.   hereditary peers.

 2. The holder of a hereditary peerage shall not be disqualified by virtue of   Removal of
that peerage for—   disqualifications in
                                                                         relation to the
 (a) voting at elections to the House of Commons, or   House of
10 (b) being, or being elected as, a member of that House.   Commons.

 3. The enactments mentioned in the Schedule are repealed to the extent   Repeals.
specified there.

 4.—(1) This Act (apart from subsections (3) and (4) below) shall come   Commencement
into force at the end of the Session of Parliament in which it is passed.   and transitional
                                                                         provision.
15 (2) Accordingly, any writ of summons issued for the present Parliament in
right of a hereditary peerage shall not have effect after that Session.

 (3) The Secretary of State may by order make such transitional provision
about the entitlement of holders of hereditary peerages to vote at elections to
the House of Commons or the European Parliament as he considers
20 appropriate.

 (4) An order under this section—
 (a) may modify the effect of any enactment or any provision made under
 an enactment, and

[Bill 34]   52/2

Procedure on bills

Procedure on bills is essentially the same in both Houses, although there are important differences of detail. The box on p. 226 shows the progress of a recent bill, the School Standards and Framework Bill. The first reading is purely formal. No debate takes place; the bill is 'presented', and is usually published immediately afterwards. The second reading will normally follow within a week or two. This is the major, set-piece debate on the principle of the bill. In the Commons, after the motion for second reading is agreed to, the bill is normally sent to a standing committee. Standing committees are composed of between sixteen and fifty members, and reflect the party balance in the House. Some bills (mainly those which are regarded as of major constitutional importance, such as the Scotland Bill and the Human Rights Bill in 1998, or those which need to be passed very quickly, such as the Landmines Bill giving effect to an international treaty in July 1998 or the anti-terrorist legislation passed following the Omagh bombing in Northern Ireland in August 1998) are not sent to a standing committee but are dealt with on the floor of the House itself in what is called a 'committee of the whole House'. In the Lords, the committee stage of most bills is done in this way, although there have been experiments with separate committees.

The committee discusses the individual clauses and schedules of the bill. MPs may propose amendments, which are debated and voted on. If a bill has been amended, there has to be a further stage in the House itself, known as the 'consideration' or 'report' stage, when MPs have another opportunity to propose and debate amendments. The final stage, called third reading, then usually follows immediately.

After a bill receives its third reading in the House in which it was introduced, it is sent to the other House, where it goes through the same procedure again. If the second House makes amendments to the bill, these have to be individually accepted by the first, which may agree with the amendments, amend them, or decide to disagree with them. If they are amended or rejected, the second House will need to accept these changes, and if agreement is not reached, deadlock may ensue. This could prevent the bill from being passed and proceeding to royal assent; but this happens very rarely, certainly with government bills.

The process of considering a bill in the Commons offers those opposed to it considerable opportunities for obstruction. In committee, clauses and schedules have to be considered individually, and there may be very many of them (both at committee and at report stage, MPs can propose as many amendments as they like). Although some will be ruled out of order as irrelevant or defective, a determined Opposition will nevertheless normally be able to propose quantities of admissible amendments. By doing so, and by deliberately prolonging debate on any of the clauses, schedules or amendments to a bill, its opponents may try to prevent it from passing altogether – to 'talk it out'. In the Commons, the Government (and only the government) can prevent this happening by using the 'guillotine' (or, more properly, the Allocation of Time Order). This is a motion which limits the amount of time available for debate at any of the stages of a bill, and

The progress of a government bill: The School Standards and Framework Act

The Act was a large government bill, with 153 clauses and 32 schedules.

House of Commons

4 December 1997	Bill introduced and given First Reading (all proceedings purely formal, without debate). The bill is printed.
22 December	Second Reading: Debate on the principle of the bill.
20 January–3 March	Detail of the bill debated in Standing Committee.
11 and 24 March	Report stage: detail of the bill debated on the floor of the House.
24 March	Third Reading immediately follows Report stage: the bill is sent up to the Lords.

House of Lords

26 March	First Reading (proceedings purely formal, without debate). The bill is printed.
7 April	Second Reading: Debate on the principle of the bill.
5, 19 May, 1, 4, 8, 10 and 16 June	Detail of the bill debated in Committee of the whole House.
30 June, 2 and 7 July	Report stage: Detail of the bill debated on the floor of the House.
13 July	Third Reading: the bill is returned to the Commons for consideration of the Lords amendments.

House of Commons

15 July	Commons consider Lords amendments, and make amendments to some of them.

House of Lords

21 July	Lords accept the Commons amendments to their amendments.
24 July	The bill receives royal assent, and so becomes an Act.

sets a time by which all of the proceedings on the bill have to be completed. There is no power to impose a guillotine in the Lords, but it is rare for peers to try to wreck a bill by prolonging debate. In the Commons guillotine procedures are resorted to when informal agreements between whips on the progress of legislation break down. In the 1987–92 Parliament, guillotines were used for twenty-eight bills; in the 1992–7 Parliament, they were used for nine.

Private members' bills

Thirteen Fridays in each session are earmarked in the Commons for private members' bills – legislation initiated by backbench members. At the beginning of the session, MPs who wish to promote legislation enter their names in a ballot for the time available. The first six drawn out win the right to have a debate on the second reading of their bills on one of the days available. It can be difficult for a private member's bill to progress any further. Backbench members have no power to propose a guillotine on their bills, and therefore it is relatively easy for their opponents to 'talk them out'. Those who put forward uncontroversial or minor measures, and have support from the government, are usually successful in getting their bills passed. Those who put forward more controversial proposals, perhaps with backing from a pressure group, have much less chance of success. A recent example is the attempt to ban foxhunting in the Wild Mammals (Hunting with Dogs) Bill (see box, p. 228). In the Lords, backbench peers can also put forward their own bills. Twenty private members' bills became law in the short session of 1996–7, with four of them originating in the Lords.

Delegated and European legislation

Many Acts of Parliament give ministers the authority to change details of the law without having to go through the process of passing another Act of Parliament. This is done by means of 'delegated' or 'secondary' legislation. Most delegated legislation takes the form of 'statutory instruments'. In 1996, 3,291 of these were issued. Recent examples include regulations about the system for the clamping or removal of illegally parked vehicles, regulations concerning the welfare of farm animals, and an order prohibiting (for reasons of public health) fishing for particular kinds of shellfish in certain sea areas. In the more important cases, the parent Act will reserve to Parliament the power either to annul, or explicitly to approve, the minister's decision. A select committee of both Houses – the Joint Committee on Statutory Instruments – reviews most statutory instruments to ensure that they are within the power given by the parent Act. Instruments which have to be explicitly approved by Parliament are subject to what is known as the 'affirmative' procedure. In the Commons, these are routinely referred to a standing committee for debate, although the House itself has formally to vote on whether or not to approve them. Instruments which may be annulled are only debated if a member (usually the Opposition frontbench spokesperson) has tabled a motion to annul it (the 'negative procedure'). In the Lords, statutory instruments are debated in the House itself.

Concern is often expressed about the amount of delegated legislation that is made, the adequacy of parliamentary consideration of it, and the power it can give to ministers. The greatest anxiety comes over the powers to repeal or amend other Acts of Parliament by delegated legislation, in particular under the European Communities Act 1972 and the Deregulation Act 1994. Special committees

---

The fate of a private member's bill: The Wild Mammals (Hunting with Dogs) Bill

22 May 1997	Ballot for private members' bills: Michael Foster MP drawn first in the ballot
18 June	Michael Foster presents his bill. Formal first reading.
28 November	Second reading: the bill is approved in a division by a majority of 411 to 151. The bill is committed to a standing committee.
17 Dec.– 25 Feb. 1998	Standing committee stage: ten sittings for the bill's seven clauses. A total of almost twenty-two hours.
6 March	Report stage. 28 new clauses and 149 amendments are tabled to the bill. At 2.30 pm, when time for consideration of the bill runs out, only one new clause has been dealt with.
13 March	There is a further opportunity to continue with the debate on report stage, because promoters of other bills allow it to take precedence over theirs. But time runs out after only five further new clauses have been dealt with. One of the supporters of the bill says 'The bill was carried on Second Reading by a very substantial majority, which in our view reflects the feeling in the country. Given that overwhelming majority, is there any protection against the parliamentary vandalism that we have seen throughout the bill's consideration that could enable it to go through Parliament?' (Official Report, vol. 307, col. 914) As there are no further opportunities in the session to debate the bill, it is abandoned.

– the Deregulation Committee in the Commons and the Delegated Powers and Deregulation Committee in the Lords – have been set up to consider orders made by ministers under the latter Act.

Much of the legislation which Parliament deals with now originates in proposals for harmonising European Union rules and regulations which have been made by one or other of the institutions of the Union, usually the Council or the Commission. Although the UK Parliament, and the Parliaments of other EU member states, have no formal rights of involvement in this process (if the proposals are accepted by the governments of the countries of the Union, they have then to be separately adopted by national Parliaments), Parliament does have a process which enables it to comment on such proposals before ministers discuss them at European level. In the Commons, the Select Committee on European Legislation reviews them, and recommends some for debate, usually in a special form of standing committee, which allows ministers to be questioned in some detail on the proposals. The Lords have a similar select committee, which likewise may recommend some documents for debate to the House.

How well does Parliament legislate?

It is often claimed that parliamentary scrutiny of government legislation is superficial and badly organised. In 1993 a weighty study of the subject concluded that 'both Houses fail to fulfil their legislative functions as effectively as they could do.'[17] The most frequently heard complaints are that:

- Bills are drafted too hurriedly and with insufficient care, in order to meet political deadlines;
- Governments are more keen to ensure that a bill is efficiently and quickly processed through Parliament than that it is subjected to searching scrutiny: whips discourage MPs on the government side from participating in debate, and ministers are reluctant to accept any amendment to their text;
- Legislation is often considered by committees composed of MPs who have no specialist knowledge of the subject concerned. The real experts – the civil servants who have drafted the bill and the pressure groups most directly interested in it – are not allowed to give evidence.

The result can be poorly thought-out and occasionally unworkable legislation. An analysis of the making of the poll tax – widely recognised as a political disaster for the government of Mrs Thatcher – pointed out that it had been exhaustively discussed in Parliament (over 200 hours of debate over forty parliamentary days between December 1987 and July 1988); that there was little enthusiastic support for it among government backbenchers, and that some of them vigorously opposed it. Yet no significant changes were made to the bill. The process, the study concluded, was a 'futile marathon'.[18] The results of parliamentary scrutiny of government legislation are sometimes so meagre – in terms of changes to bills prompted by the concerns of MPs and peers – that some have questioned whether Parliament really does more than rubber-stamp government legislation.

These problems have long been recognised, and various solutions have been suggested. One is to allow bills to be scrutinised in a less formal and less partisan way, through select committee-style hearings. It is already possible to send bills to 'special standing committees', which can invite ministers, civil servants and pressure groups to give evidence about the bill and its effect before they go on to consider it in the normal way. But this procedure has been used only rarely, usually on technical and uncontroversial bills (only seven bills were dealt with in this way between 1980 and 1998). Another method is for the government to publish its bills in draft form, to allow a period of consultation – which may include consideration by one of the departmental select committees – before they are formally introduced. The present government published a number of bills in draft in the 1997–8 session, following a proposal of the Modernisation Committee.

Governments can be reluctant to submit legislation to these additional types of scrutiny because it will mean that a bill will take longer to complete its passage through Parliament, and increase the possibility that the Opposition might delay it until the end of a session, thereby forcing the government to start all over again. The Modernisation Committee has proposed that it should be possible to pick up proceedings on a bill from the stage they had reached in the previous session – to 'carry over' bills from one session to the next. This might make governments more willing to allow longer for full consideration of legislation. But the fact that the Opposition can threaten the loss of a bill by delaying it places some pressure on the government not to try to force it through by sheer weight of numbers. Therefore the Modernisation Committee have said that it should only be used in exceptional circumstances.[19]

One proposal that is now seen as a means of reconciling the government's need to pass its legislation with the requirement for proper scrutiny is that there should be formal timetables set down for the consideration of major bills. Informal timetables for government bills are often agreed through the 'usual channels', but these agreements are easily broken. If the Opposition has refused to co-operate on setting an informal timetable the government can set down a formal timetable by means of the guillotine, described earlier. The Modernisation Committee has tried to find a middle path by encouraging moves to set down formal 'programmes' for bills by agreement between the parties, giving the government the reassurance that the bill will complete its passage through the Commons in a certain time, while allowing the Opposition a degree of control over the timing of debates. A number of the most important bills in the 1997–8 session were programmed in this way.

Taxing and spending

The power to authorise the taxation of the people, and control over how governments spend the money obtained from taxation, were central to Parliament's early growth and significance. The annual process of deciding how tax should be *raised* still takes up a good deal of time in the House of Commons. But Parliament barely considers how it should be *spent*, even though the question of how money should be allocated across Whitehall is bitterly fought between government departments and the Treasury.

Every year the Chancellor of the Exchequer announces in his Budget statement in March how much tax the government wants to raise, and how it intends to raise it. The Budget is one of the major events in the parliamentary calendar; its impact on people's own finances means that it is scrutinised by the media more closely than any other government statement. After a debate lasting several days, the House votes on a series of resolutions which approve the proposals in principle, and the Finance Bill is brought in to give them effect. In the Commons, the bill is debated in much the same way as any other. The Lords have no power to amend it, and their consideration of it is essentially limited to a general debate on its second reading.

The Finance Bill deals with the collection of taxes. All taxes are paid into the Consolidated Fund, a sort of government current account. But it requires further statutory authority for the government to draw money out from the fund, to pay for its normal expenses; and the purpose for which the expenditure is made must also be authorised by an Act of Parliament. Each year, the government goes through a process, known as the Public Expenditure Survey, of deciding what resources are needed to pay for its activities over the next three years. When completed, the overall results are presented to Parliament – in recent years in November. In March, individual departments publish their annual reports, which set out their expenditure plans for the next three years, and detail their activities over the previous year. At the same time, the government publishes the main 'supply estimates', which show the sum that each department thinks it needs to obtain from the Consolidated Fund in order to finance its work. If significant extra expenditure has become necessary during the year, the government may seek parliamentary approval for expenditure at other times, generally in 'supplementary estimates', normally presented three times a year.

The House of Commons has now all but abandoned detailed consideration of these figures. In theory the task is delegated to the departmental select committees (whose remit includes consideration of the expenditure of the department concerned), but more particularly to the Public Accounts Committee and to the National Audit Office. The time allowed in the House itself under its standing orders for discussion of the estimates is mainly used as an opportunity for debates on select committee reports. After these debates the House almost always approves the estimates without a division. Once they have been approved, a Consolidated Fund Bill is brought in, which authorises the Treasury to issue the required amount of money out of the Consolidated Fund. These bills are not debated at all, and are almost always accepted without a vote. Proceedings on them in the Lords are purely formal. This process usually happens three times a year, for the various estimates that are presented during the course of the year. The last Consolidated Fund Bill of the session has an additional purpose: it 'appropriates' the money whose expenditure has been authorised by Parliament to the purpose for which it was granted: in other words, it makes it illegal to use the money for anything other than the specific purposes which have been mentioned in the Consolidated Fund Bills. After it has received the royal assent it becomes known as the Appropriation Act. The fact that these procedures relating to government spending have now become largely formal reveal a good deal about Parliament's modern role.

MODERNISATION AND REFORM

Modernising the Commons

Much of the dissatisfaction about the way Parliament works expressed in the press and among MPs themselves, has been about its old-fashioned procedures and practices. Two of Labour's policy-makers, in an influential book published before the 1997 election, declared that 'Parliament . . . needs to be dragged (probably kicking and screaming) into modern times.'[20] The establishment of the Modernisation Committee has provided a chance for the House of Commons to review critically its procedures, conventions and habits, and to address the problems in the way it operates (see box, pp. 233–4).

However, it is clear that the 'modernisation' process will not fundamentally change the nature of Parliament. The committee's reforms have generally been seen by some commentators as useful, but modest. Deeper reform runs up against the vested interests of both government and Opposition, as Peter Riddell points out:

> Reform of the Commons always proceeds slowly because of the opposition of two opposite, but influential, vested interests. First, Opposition parties are always suspicious of changes that might be seen to threaten their theoretical, in practice largely illusory, power to hold up government business. Second, government whips dislike any changes that might strengthen the role of the Commons and make their control of business less predictable.[21]

The executive's control of Parliament, along with the dominance of party, will always mean that political considerations are likely to overrule the wish to subject the government to more vigorous scrutiny, especially when the issues involved are politically sensitive. There is also the fundamental fact that Parliament is a legislature in which the ambition of most of its members is to join the executive. Any further strengthening of the House of Commons' ability to undertake its scrutiny functions more effectively reduces the freedom of manoeuvre of the government; and no government is likely to surrender such freedom easily.

Reforming the Lords

The biggest challenge is the reform of the House of Lords. The House of Lords as presently constituted looks anomalous in a modern democracy. Its reform was a manifesto pledge of the Labour government elected in May 1997, and the government has now put the case for the removal of the rights of hereditary peers to sit and vote in the House in its January 1999 white paper (see box, p. 234).

The statistics on government defeats in divisions in the Lords bear out the government's claim that there is an 'in-built majority' for the Conservative Party: from 1970–71 to 1997–8, the average number of government defeats per session under Labour governments is 63, compared with 8 for Conservative governments (Figure 7.2).

There is wide agreement that hereditary peers can no longer claim a place as of right in the legislature. The government in January 1999 published the House of Lords Bill to 'end membership of the House of Lords by virtue of a hereditary

Reforming the Commons: The work of the Modernisation Committee

29 July 1997	*The legislative process*	Demand for more frequent publication of bills in draft form: six bills have now been published in draft
29 July 1997	*Work of the committee: first progress report*	Minor changes to the way in which divisions are conducted: implemented Simplification of form and content of order paper: implemented
3 December 1997	*Explanatory material for bills*	Changes to the information published with bills, to make them more informative and comprehensible: implemented
2 March 1998	*Carry-over of public bills*	Acceptance in principle that public bills may be carried over to the next session in limited circumstances: agreed
2 March 1998	*Conduct in the chamber*	Changes to some of the conventions used in debates and divisions and to the power of the Speaker to limit the length of speeches; greater sanctions for misconduct during debate: implemented
3 June 1998	*Voting methods*	No changes to the method of recording votes proposed, following a consultation exercise: but issue to be discussed further

continued

9 June 1998	*The scrutiny of European business*	Changes to the system for scrutinising European legislation, including more committees, and greater informal links with the European institutions
2 December 1998	*The parliamentary calendar: initial proposals*	Experiment with earlier sittings on Thursdays; greater freedom for standing committees to meet irrespective of when the House is sitting
13 April 1999	*Sittings of the House in Westminster Hall*	Experiment with debates taking place in a separate chamber at the same time as the House is sitting
19 July 1999	*Thursday sittings*	Recommends that the experiment with earlier sittings on Thursdays be continued for another session

---

The House of Lords: the case for reform

The hereditary peerage numbers well over half the membership of the House of Lords. The presence in the House of this large number of hereditary peers constitutes an element of the Lords which is unresponsive to political and social change. No matter what the outcome of a general election, political control of the second chamber of Parliament never alters. It ensures that the Conservative Party has a 3 to 1 built-in majority over the Labour Party. Taken as a whole, the hereditary peerage is not representative of the country politically, socially, economically or above all by gender or ethnic origin. While the hereditary peers retain their dominant position, the House as a whole can never hope to be representative.

(Modernising Parliament: Reforming the House of Lords,
Cm. 4183, January 1999, para. 16)

peerage', which it hopes to enact by the end of the 1999–2000 session, if possible with a measure of cross-party agreement. For the short term, the government also intends to change the way life peers are nominated to ensure that cross-bench peers are truly independent.

Reform will not stop there: the government is committed to longer-term

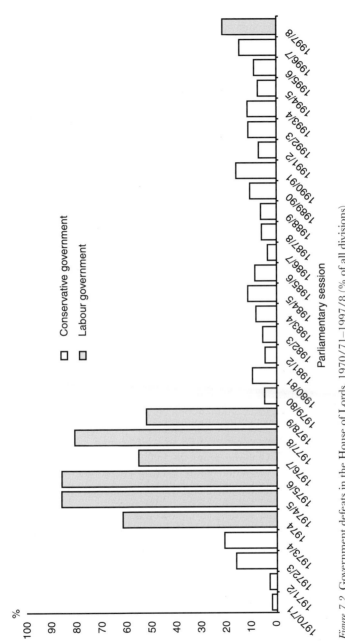

Figure 7.2 Government defeats in the House of Lords, 1970/71–1997/8 (% of all divisions)

Reform of the House of Lords, 1909–1999

On summer evenings and winter afternoons, when they have nothing else to do, people discuss how to reform the House of Lords. Schemes are taken out of cupboards and drawers and dusted off, speeches are composed, pamphlets written, letters sent to newspapers. From time to time, the whole country becomes excited. Occasionally legislation is introduced; it generally fails.

(Janet Morgan, 'The House of Lords in the 1980s', *The Parliamentarian*, October 1982)

1909–11   After the House of Lords' rejection of the Finance Bill containing Lloyd-George's 'People's Budget' the Liberal government, having forced the Lords to back down, introduces the Parliament Act, limiting the Lords' powers to veto legislation, and containing a commitment to 'substitute for the House of Lords ... a second chamber constituted on a popular instead of a hereditary basis'.

1917–18   The all-party Bryce commission makes proposals for an indirectly elected second chamber; but these are never acted upon.

1948   Following the introduction by the post-war Labour government of a bill to place further limits on the Lords' veto, an all-party conference reconsiders the composition of the House of Lords, but breaks up without agreement.

1958   Conservative government seeks to revitalise the House of Lords through the introduction of life peerages.

1968   Labour government proposes a bill to limit the number of hereditary peers allowed to vote: despite agreement with the Official Opposition on the bill, it was abandoned after determined opposition from Labour backbenchers (who wanted more radical reform) and Conservative backbenchers (who were opposed to reform).

1999   Government announces proposals to remove the rights of hereditary peers to sit and vote in the House of Lords, and to establish a Royal Commission to consider proposals for the future of the House.

reforms to the way in which the House is constituted and operates. But achieving this will require a delicate balance. The past century has been punctuated by attempts to reform the Lords, and its survival up to now in its present form is largely because there has been little agreement on how to do it (see box, above). The main difficulty is that any change may radically affect its status, and consequently, the balance of power in Parliament. At present, the House of Lords is indisputably the less significant House. Though it performs a useful function in examining legislation, and in providing a degree of safeguard against the abuse by a government of a Commons majority, its lack of real legitimacy derived from popular election means that it cannot seriously challenge the Commons. The primacy of the Commons is acknowledged, and there is a machinery – the two Parliament Acts – for ensuring that its will, based on democratic election, takes precedence in any dispute. If the hereditary peers were to be replaced by elected members, then the Lords might begin to challenge the primacy of the Commons. If a dispute arose between the two Houses, which one could be said to represent more nearly the wishes of the people? However, if the existing hereditary peers were simply to be replaced by more appointed peers, the Lords would present less of a threat to the Commons, but it would also be condemned as a huge extension of the government's powers of patronage, the biggest 'quango' in the country. As Vernon Bogdanor has pointed out:

> Unless an upper house is directly elected, it will lack the authority to challenge a majority government. But where it is directly elected, any challenge will be as much a party battle of opposition against the government as it is a fulfilment of the functions of revision and constitutional protection.[22]

The government hopes (as previous governments have done) to achieve a cross-party agreement on the question by means of a Royal Commission, which is to report by the end of 1999. It has strongly indicated, however, that the Commons should remain the principal of the two Houses, and its own preference seems to be for a House which is partly nominated and partly elected – directly, indirectly or both. Furthermore, it suggests a role for the new House of Lords in giving representation to the regions and devolved governments of the country (a similar role is played by second chambers in France and Germany), arguing that 'the second chamber could provide a forum where diversity could find expression and dialogue, and where such an expression could work towards strengthening the Union'.[23]

WHAT FUTURE FOR PARLIAMENT?

The government's wider political reforms may begin to alter the fundamental realities of the British constitution. Exactly what their impact will be remains unpredictable. The proposals to reform the House of Lords may change the balance of power between the two Houses, perhaps reinvigorating part of the parliamentary system. Devolution to Scotland, Wales and Northern Ireland means that new relationships will need to be established between the legislatures within the United Kingdom, and could lead to pressure for a more comprehensive system of devolved regional government, covering English regions as well. A Freedom of Information Act will have implications for the way members of parliament seek to hold government to account. If it was decided to introduce a system of proportional representation for parliamentary elections, although there would be little direct effect on the procedures of the Commons, there could be a vast influence on the way it conducts its business.   One close observer has warned that the result of all this is 'an unstable half-way stage. Important innovations are being grafted on to the traditional doctrine of parliamentary sovereignty. But it can no longer bear the weight.'[24] Only the years ahead will show whether or not this analysis is right.

NOTES

1 21 July 1998, House of Commons Debates, vol. 316, col. 940.
2 Andrew Marr, *Ruling Britannia*, Michael Joseph, 1995, pp. 106–7.
3 *The Report of the Joint Consultation Committee on Constitutional Reform*, 1997, p. 15.
4 Philip Norton, *Dissension in the House of Commons, 1974–1979*, Clarendon Press, 1980.
5 On the background and motivation of MPs see also Peter Riddell, *Honest Opportunism*, Hamish Hamilton, 1993.
6 Douglas Hurd, 'Is there still a role for MPs?', *RSA Journal*, June 1997, p. 36.
7 Philip Norton and Austin Mitchell, 'Meet the New Breed', *The House Magazine*, 13 October 1997, p. 13.
8 *First Report of the Committee on Standards in Public Life*, Cm. 2850-I, p. 22.
9 The case that precipitated the appointment of the Committee (among a number of other allegations, and the resignation of two ministers) was that reported on by the Committee of Privileges in April 1995. First Report of the Committee of Privileges, *Complaint concerning an Article in the 'Sunday Times' of 10 July 1994 relating to the Conduct of Members*, HC (1994–95), 351.
10 Walter Bagehot, *The English Constitution*, Fontana edn, 1963, pp. 150–4.
11 Andrew Adonis, *Parliament Today*, 2nd edn, Manchester University Press, 1993, pp. 142–3.
12 Ibid., p. 143.
13 *Report of the Inquiry into the Export of Defence Equipment and Dual-Use Goods to Iraq and Related Prosecutions*, HC (1995–96) 115, section K 8.3.
14 House of Commons Debates, vol. 302, col. 641W (written answer, 11 December 1997).
15 House of Commons Debates, vol. 221, col. 1246 (25 March 1993).
16 Kate Jenkins, evidence to the Public Service Committee, HC (1995–96) 313-iii, QQ.692, 700.
17 *Making the Law: The Report of the Hansard Society Commission on the Legislative Process*, 1992, p. 79.
18 David Butler, Andrew Adonis and Tony Travers, *Failure in British Government: The Politics of the Poll Tax*, Oxford University Press, 1994, pp. 233–45.
19 See Third Report of the Select Committee on the Modernisation of the House of Commons, *Carry-over of Public Bills*, HC (1997–98) 543.
20 Roger Liddle and Peter Mandelson, *The Blair Revolution*, Faber, 1996, p. 203.
21 Peter Riddell, 'MPs should consider move to a smaller House', *The Times*, 31 March 1998.
22 Vernon Bogdanor, 'The problem of the Upper House', in *Politics and the Constitution: Essays on British Government*, 1996, p. 258.
23 *Modernising Parliament: Reforming the House of Lords*, Cmnd. 4183, January 1999, para. 9.
24 Peter Riddell, *Parliament under Pressure*, Victor Gollancz, 1998, p. 223.

FURTHER READING

The best short introductions to Parliament are by Paul Silk and Rhodri Walters, *How Parliament Works*, 4th edn (Longman, 1998), and by Andrew Adonis, *Parliament Today*, 2nd edn (Manchester University Press, 1993). A longer and more detailed study is by John Griffith and Michael Ryle, *Parliament* (Butterworths, 1989: a new edition is in preparation). The most recent detailed discussion of parliamentary reform is by Peter Riddell, *Parliament under Pressure* (Victor Gollancz, 1998). Still useful, though now a little out of date, is John Garrett, *Westminster: Does Parliament Work?* (Victor Gollancz, 1992). For a more theoretical approach, there is David Judge, *The Parliamentary State* (Sage, 1993). The history of proposals to reform the House of Lords and details of some of the possible schemes are presented in Vernon Bogdanor, *Power and the People: A Guide to Constitutional Reform* (Victor Gollancz, 1997). The most authoritative recent studies of the House of Lords are Donald Shell, *The House of Lords*, 2nd edn (Harvester Wheatsheaf, 1992) and Donald Shell and David Beamish, *The House of Lords at Work* (Clarendon Press, 1993). There are many more detailed studies of various aspects of Parliament's work: among the most influential of the recent ones is Philip Giddings (ed.), *Parliamentary Accountability: A Study of Parliament and Executive Agencies* (Macmillan, 1995).

8 Governing at the centre

The first thing to be noted about the central government of this country is that it is a federation of departments.

(Sir William Armstrong, former head of the civil service, in 'The Civil Service Department and its tasks', *O & M Bulletin*, May 1970)

It must be a conviction government. As Prime Minister I could not waste time having any internal arguments.

(Margaret Thatcher, *Observer*, 25 February 1979)

THE CENTRAL EXECUTIVE

At the heart of the British political process are the Prime Minister, Cabinet and senior civil servants. These form the engine which drives forward policy and they can be described collectively as the central executive. In addition to government departments, agencies and quangos also carry out executive functions, raising questions of accountability, at least in terms of traditional models of ministerial responsibility to Parliament. This chapter maps out the territory of the executive and examines the mechanisms which attempt to bring some coherence to the varied terrain of central government in Britain.

Issues about co-ordination and accountability tend to dominate discussion of the central executive: how can the Prime Minister ensure that the party programme is implemented? Does the Cabinet still operate as a body which takes the major decisions? Is the departmental nature of British government a barrier to effective policy-making? Can the civil service remain in any sense unified if key decisions have been delegated to agencies? Do ministers really control their departments? What real accountability remains when ministers refuse to resign over policy errors? These are the kind of questions that lie behind an examination of how central government works – and need to be kept in mind in what follows.

The map of Whitehall

Whitehall, the collective name for the central administration, is organised through a series of separate departments. The most important departments are grouped in the box (below), in terms of the main areas of government activity. All departments also have executive agencies (for example the Benefits Agency and the Driving Standards Agency) which carry out major administrative functions, such as the payment of benefit or the administration of driving licences.

The most important government departments

- *External relations*: Foreign and Commonwealth Office, Ministry of Defence, Department for International Development
- *Social issues*: Departments of Health, Social Security, Education and Employment, Culture, Media and Sport, Home Office
- *Economic, financial and industrial responsibilities*: The Treasury, Department of Trade and Industry, Customs and Excise, Inland Revenue, Ministry of Agriculture, Fisheries and Food, Department of the Environment, Transport and the Regions
- *Policy and administration*: Cabinet Office, Prime Minister's Office, Privy Council Office
- *Legal affairs*: Lord Chancellor's Department, Crown Prosecution Service
- *Secret intelligence*: Security Service (MI5), Security Intelligence Service (MI6), Government Communications Headquarters

---

Central government is responsible directly or indirectly for public spending of about £330 billion, equivalent at present to about 40 per cent of gross domestic product. Some of the spending is actually carried out by other bodies, for example the National Health Service or local authorities. The current distribution of public spending is shown in Figure 8.1.

The individual subject departments, into which central government is organised, are responsible for developing policies in their areas. In practice this means the ministers who provide political leadership and the civil servants who provide administrative leadership within departments. It is necessary, therefore, to examine the role of ministers and civil servants – and the relationship between them.

CIVIL SERVANTS

On 1 January 1998 there were 468,183 permanent civil servants representing about 2 per cent of the working population in employment. However, they are not the only people who work for government in Britain: they do not include, for example, those working in the National Health Service, local authorities, centrally funded schools, the armed forces and the police. In fact, civil servants represent only about 10 per cent of all public sector employees.

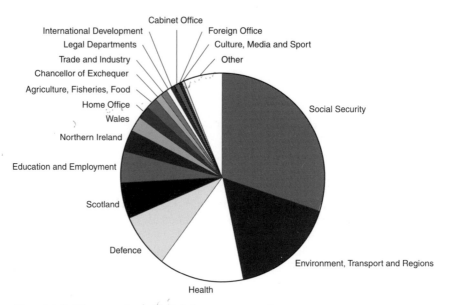

Figure 8.1 Public expenditure 1998–9, by government department

---

What is a civil servant?

It may safely be asserted that, as matters now stand, the Government of the country could not be carried on without the aid of an efficient body of permanent officers, occupying a position duly subordinate to that of the Ministers who are directly responsible to the Crown and to Parliament, yet possessing sufficient independence, character, ability, and experience to be able to advise, assist, and to some extent, influence, those who are from time to time set over them.

(Northcote-Trevelyan Report (1853): the report which set out the principles of the modern British civil service)

A civil servant is a servant of the Crown working in a civil capacity who is not: the holder of a political (or judicial) office; the holder of certain other offices in respect of whose tenure of office special provision has been made; a servant of the Crown in a personal capacity paid from the civil list.

(*Civil Service Statistics 1997*, Government Statistical Service, 1998, p. 20)

Yet they have a wide variety of roles (see the above box). The civil service has been said to have a 'greater diversity of function than any other organisation in the country, performing tasks from weather forecasting to economic forecasting, from the management of conference facilities to the administration of social security benefits'.[1] Only about 5 per cent of civil servants are in the central departments in London that work directly to ministers, that is, in 'Whitehall' proper. Altogether, around one in five work in London; but there are large numbers in every region of the country.

Departments

Each of the main departments is headed by a cabinet minister, usually (though not always) known as the Secretary of State. There may be a number of junior ministers as well, who are given defined policy areas to deal with. Each cabinet minister has a civil servant as a private secretary, who co-ordinates the minister's relationship with the rest of the department. The department also has a civil service head, its permanent secretary, who is formally responsible for its administration, but in practice has a pivotal role in assisting ministers to co-ordinate and direct the policies of the department. Departments are usually organised into a number of policy 'directorates'; most will have responsibility for a number of Executive Agencies and some of the bigger departments will have their own outposts within the government's regional offices. Many oversee the work of various other bodies including non-departmental public bodies or 'quangos' (such as the Arts Council) which are fully independent of the department, even if closely linked; or advisory bodies which bring outside experts to advise on particular technical issues.

Departments are large bureaucracies, carrying out many different functions: for example, the Department for Education and Employment is the body responsible for developing policies on schools, further and higher education, and provision for unemployed people. It also, through the Employment Service, pays the Jobseeker's Allowance to unemployed people and, through programmes such as the New Deal for 18–24 year olds, provides help and support to people trying to find jobs. In 1998–9 the Department (including the Office for Standards in Education, a non-ministerial department for which it also has responsibility) had a total expenditure of £13.1 billion, with £2.7 billion of this going on grants or other support to local authorities. The organisational chart for the department, one of Whitehall's largest, is shown in Figure 8.2.

Key features of the civil service

There are three features of the British civil service which determine its essential character. These are:

* accountability through ministers to Parliament
* selection and promotion on merit, and
* political neutrality.

These features of the civil service in Britain set it apart from other models in Europe and the United States, where senior public officials are closely linked with

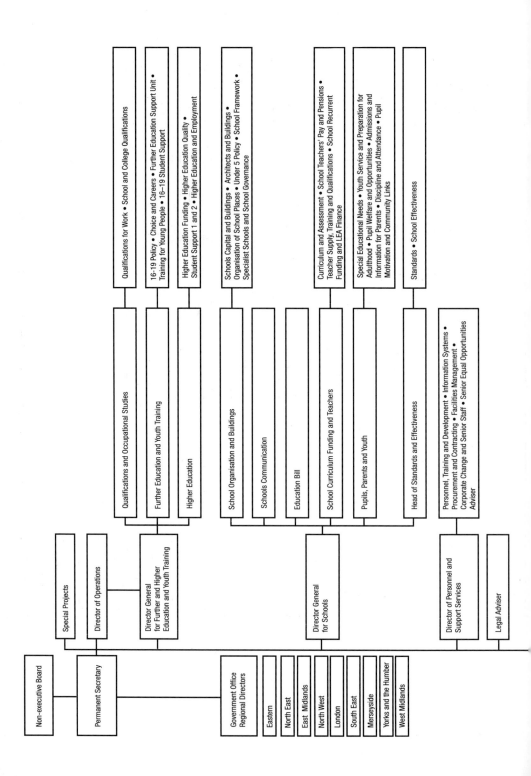

Non-executive Board

Permanent Secretary

Special Projects

Director of Operations

Director General for Further and Higher Education and Youth Training

Qualifications and Occupational Studies — Qualifications for Work • School and College Qualifications

Further Education and Youth Training — 16-19 Policy • Choice and Careers • Further Education Support Unit • Training for Young People • 16–19 Student Support

Higher Education — Higher Education Funding • Higher Education Quality • Student Support 1 and 2 • Higher Education and Employment

School Organisation and Buildings — Schools Capital and Buildings • Architects and Buildings • Organisation of School Places • Under 5 Policy • School Framework • Specialist Schools and School Governance

Schools Communication

Education Bill

Director General for Schools

School Curriculum Funding and Teachers — Curriculum and Assessment • School Teachers' Pay and Pensions • Teacher Supply, Training and Qualifications • School Recurrent Funding and LEA Finance

Pupils, Parents and Youth — Special Educational Needs • Youth Service and Preparation for Adulthood • Pupil Welfare and Opportunities • Admissions and Information for Parents • Discipline and Attendance • Pupil Motivation and Community Links

Head of Standards and Effectiveness — Standards • School Effectiveness

Government Office Regional Directors

Eastern

North East

East Midlands

North West

London

South East

Merseyside

Yorks and the Humber

West Midlands

Director of Personnel and Support Services — Personnel, Training and Development • Information Systems • Procurement and Contracting • Facilities Management • Corporate Change and Senior Staff • Senior Equal Opportunities Adviser

Legal Adviser

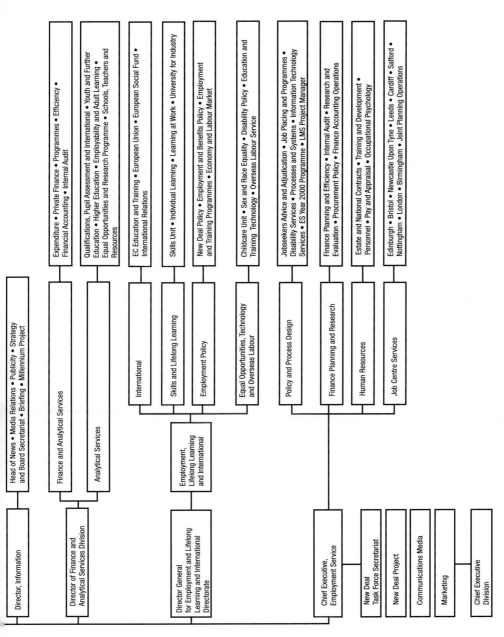

Figure 8.2 The organisation chart of the Department for Education and Employment

the party in power. Each feature is now examined in turn, beginning with the most fundamental – the position of civil servants under the doctrine of ministerial accountability.

Ministerial accountability

Under the British system, civil servants are not directly accountable to Parliament: they are servants of the Crown, and hence owe their loyalty to the government of the day. It is through ministers that the government is accountable to Parliament for its actions. This doctrine is of central importance to British constitutional arrangements – and to the position of civil servants (see box below).

Ministerial accountability: The classical doctrine

It is upon Ministers, and not upon civil servants, that the powers of Government have been conferred: and it is Ministers – who are Members of one or other House of Parliament, whose dismissal from office Parliament can bring about if it so chooses – who are answerable to Parliament for the exercise of those powers. Save in special cases, . . . civil servants have no powers of their own. They can take no decisions or do anything, except insofar as they act on behalf of Ministers, and subject to the directions and control of Ministers.

It may be noted that no other system would be workable so long as Ministers are served by permanent officials who serve all governments alike and are debarred from overt party affiliation, and from party controversy: and that any change in the system would have far-reaching effects on basic features of our constitution.

It follows that a civil servant, having no power conferred on him by Parliament, has no direct responsibility to Parliament and cannot be called to account by Parliament. His acts, indeed, are not his own. All that he does is done on behalf of the Minister, with the Minister's authority express or implied: the civil servant's responsibility is solely to the Minister for what he may do as the Minister's servant.

(memorandum by Sir Edward Bridges, Permanent Secretary to the
Treasury, 1954)

The doctrine of ministerial accountability makes a neutral and permanent civil service possible. Civil servants are protected by it from being the target for political attack. It provides them with a cloak of anonymity. But the doctrine has its origins in a time when ministers could be expected to be closely concerned with everything that went on in their departments. Nowadays, when some departments have thousands of staff, this is clearly no longer possible. Yet the doctrine is still seen as vital, if the principle of a non-political civil service is to be maintained.

Successive governments have tried to square the circle, by preserving the principle while arguing that ministers cannot be held responsible for everything that goes on: they have a duty to account to Parliament, if required, for all the department's activities, but they are not to be held 'responsible' for all this activity nor expected to take personal blame for administrative failures. This is known as the 'Butler' doctrine, after the former head of the civil service, Sir Robin Butler, who developed it during the 1990s in evidence to the Scott inquiry and to the Treasury and Civil Service Select Committee. It has become the officially revised doctrine. (see box below).

Ministerial accountability: The revised doctrine

In the Government's view, a Minister is 'accountable' to Parliament for everything which goes on within his department, in the sense that Parliament can call the Minister to account for it. The Minister is responsible for the policies of the department, for the framework through which those policies are delivered, for the resources allocated, for such implementation decisions as the Framework Document may require to be referred or agreed with him, and for his response to major failures or expressions of Parliamentary or public concern. But a Minister cannot sensibly be held responsible for everything which goes on in his department in the sense of having personal knowledge and control of every action taken and being personally blameworthy when delegated tasks are carried out incompetently, or when mistakes or errors of judgement are made at operational level. It is not possible for Ministers to handle everything personally, and if Ministers were to be held personally responsible for every action of the department, delegation and efficiency would be much inhibited.

(*Taking forward Continuity and Change*, January 1995, Cm. 2748, pp. 27–8)

Yet this position is hardly satisfactory. The distinction between 'accountability' and 'responsibility' means that there may be occasions when Parliament will find it difficult to identify whom it can blame when something goes wrong. Ministers may deny personal responsibility, while civil servants are shielded by the convention that ministers are responsible. In fact, the convention has not always protected civil servants from being identified if they are clearly to blame: public inquiries have regularly named civil servants in these circumstances (for example, a number of civil servants were criticised in the 1996 report of Sir Richard Scott's inquiry into the export of weapons and related equipment to Iraq).

Recent developments in the civil service, especially the creation of devolved agencies to perform various executive tasks, have also revealed the limitations of the doctrine of ministerial responsibility. Because responsibility for policy-setting (which remains the task of ministers) has been divided from responsibility for the implementation of policy (which is devolved to the civil servant, usually a chief executive, in charge of the agency), it has become more possible to identify who is to blame for the agency's failures of performance – as resignations of chief executives in the Crown Prosecution Service and the Child Support Agency have illustrated. It has become harder to fit the new shape of the civil service into the old doctrine of ministerial responsibility.

The convention of ministerial responsibility includes:

- *Informing and explaining.* Ministers explain their actions to Parliament through parliamentary answers, statements, consultation documents and other means.
- *Apologising.* Ministers who admit an error, either by themselves or by their officials, are expected to apologise to Parliament, as part of a full explanation.
- *Taking action.* A minister who is responsible for an unsatisfactory state of affairs will be expected to take appropriate remedial steps, whether or not this is accompanied by a resignation.
- *Resigning.* This is the ultimate accountability sanction, but resignation issues can become party-political battles.

Over the years there have been many cases which show the difficulties in pinning down what responsibility really means in practice (see box, p. 249).

In practice, ministers are likely to resign only when caught up in personal scandals, or where they have lost the support of their own party and when staying would cause more political embarrassment than going. This political reality is far removed from the nice distinctions between responsibility and accountability, policy and administration, ministers and civil servants, that the constitutional doctrines wrestle with.

Following the Scott Report, a new parliamentary resolution was passed in March 1997 setting out the responsibilities of ministers to Parliament which included being held to account for 'the policies, decisions and actions of their Departments and Next Steps Agencies' (see box, p. 217). Jack Straw told Parliament that as Home Secretary he would be fully accountable for the actions of the Prisons Agency. But it appeared to be business as usual when the Foreign Secretary, Robin Cook, came under pressure to resign in 1997 in the Sandline affair concerning arms embargoes to Sierra Leone: he set up an official inquiry which exonerated ministers but recommended management changes in the Foreign Office.

However, the Scott Report considered that resignation was not the most important duty involved in ministerial responsibility, arguing that the key issue was accounting to Parliament through the provision of full information. If MPs took up the challenge of pursuing ministers for detailed evaluations, rather than ritually calling for resignations, more light might be thrown on the reasons for policy failures and mistakes. Yet this might in turn throw more light on the role of civil servants, which the traditional doctrine of ministerial accountability sought to avoid.

Ministerial responsibility: A case study

The Maze Prison escape, 1983

In September 1983 there was a mass escape from the Maze Prison in Northern Ireland during which a prison officer was killed; an inquiry by the Chief Inspector of Prisons, James Hennessy, found that there had been 'a major failure in security for which the governor must be held accountable'.[2] In response to questions on the Hennessy Report, the Secretary of State for Northern Ireland, James Prior, said: 'the report shows that no policy decisions contributed to the escape. For that reason, I believe that there are no grounds for ministerial resignation.'[3] This was disputed by Enoch Powell, in a later debate on the report,[4] arguing that Prior 'drew a distinction, which I believe to be invalid, between responsibility for policy and responsibility for administration. I believe this is a wholly fallacious view of the nature of ministerial responsibility. . . . But even if all considerations of policy could be eliminated the responsibility for the administration of a Department remains irrevocably with the Minister in charge. It is impossible for him to say to the House or the country "The policy was excellent and that was mine, but the execution was defective or disastrous and that has nothing to do with me." If that were to be the accepted position, there would be no political source to whom the public could complain about administration or from whom it could seek redress for failings of administration.'

However the Official Opposition did not seek Prior's resignation, with Peter Archer, the Labour spokesman, stating 'we must consider whether Northern Ireland would benefit if a particular Minister resigned.'

In response to Powell, the junior Northern Ireland minister, Nicholas Scott, said that Powell had 'outlined a constitutional convention which he might wish existed, which perhaps once did exist, but frankly, has not existed in politics for many years.'

Similar issues arose in the 1991 Brixton Prison escape when Kenneth Baker was Home Secretary; and in 1995 with the escape from Parkhurst Prison, when the Home Secretary, Michael Howard, drew a distinction between policy and operation and sacked the head of the Prison Service Agency, Derek Lewis.[5]

Selection on merit

The modern civil service has its origins in the Northcote-Trevelyan Report of 1853, which recommended the creation of an elite cadre of civil servants 'to provide, by a proper system of examination, for the supply of the public service with a thoroughly efficient class of men', who would be transferable between departments. Their role would be distinguished from that of support staff who could undertake the purely executive tasks. The Civil Service Commission was established to oversee the appointment of such people. The result, eventually, was a group of top-level administrators who became a national caricature: the clever, usually Oxbridge-educated, male, good at drafting elegant minutes, but useless at managing money or staff, without technological expertise or entrepreneurial flair. This picture was exaggerated, but not wholly unjust. Over recent years political and practical pressure has forced the higher civil service to try to break its elitist, generalist character. It still takes most of its staff through an extremely demanding recruitment process, but has increasingly sought to recruit more women, people from a broader range of universities, science graduates and those with specialist skills. In 1997 Oxbridge graduates accounted for 34 per cent of successful candidates in the fast-stream recruitment competition; 39 per cent of successful candidates were women; and of the 277 successful candidates only seven were from ethnic minorities.

At the most senior grades, change has been slow. Still only 16.8 per cent of senior civil servants are women and only 1.5 per cent come from ethnic minorities. An increasing number of senior posts have been recruited from outside the civil service (sixty-four were appointed from outside in 1996). The continuing challenge is to combine selection from merit with wider recruitment to meet the needs of a changing civil service.

Political neutrality

The civil service is expected to serve governments of different parties with equal loyalty and efficiency. Civil servants, while they may have their private political views, must not to allow these to interfere with their work in carrying out the policy of the elected government. This principle is firmly defended (with senior civil servants not permitted to undertake any political activity) but it is often under strain. Ministers are sometimes suspicious of the political views of civil servants; 'leaks' to the press are frequently blamed on civil servants unhappy about ministerial policies. Individual civil servants may become closely identified with a particular policy, and seemingly more committed to a particular government than would be required simply to carry out its policies. This is most likely when the same government has been in power for a long time; and during the extended period of Conservative rule in the 1980s and 1990s Labour raised questions about the neutrality of some prominent civil servants. However Tony Blair as Prime Minister made a point of congratulating the civil service on its management of the transition from one government to another. The previous government had agreed to enshrine the principle of political neutrality in a new code of conduct for the civil service, with a system of appeal to the Civil Service Commission in cases where a complaint that a civil servant had been asked to act in a way contrary to the code could not be resolved internally (see box, p. 251).

The role of the special adviser to ministers helps to insulate civil servants from the more political aspects of their work. Cabinet ministers are allowed to appoint up to two special advisers paid for by the department. They formally become civil

---

Neutrality: Codifying the principle

The constitutional and practical role of the civil service is, with integrity, honesty, impartiality and objectivity to assist the duly constituted Government of the United Kingdom, the Scottish Executive or the National Assembly of Wales, constituted in accordance with the Scotland and Government of Wales Act 1998, whatever their political complexion, in formulating their policies, carrying out decisions and in administering public services for which they are responsible.

(Civil Service Code 1999, paragraph 1)

---

servants, but some of the conventions about political activity and neutrality are held not to apply in their case. They are the only 'political' civil servants that the British system of government allows. As well as providing policy advice, special advisers perform tasks that civil servants would not be able to be involved with, such as drafting the more party-political passages in speeches or giving a highly political 'spin' to the minister's activities when talking to the press (with the role of Gordon Brown's special adviser, Charlie Whelan, attracting particular comment in the early days of the Blair government).

The creation of devolved assemblies in Scotland and Wales is likely to put the principle of neutrality under particular strain. The civil service will remain a British institution and this may raise questions about ultimate loyalty – say to the Welsh Assembly or to Whitehall – particularly as promotion prospects for the senior civil service will still be assessed by the latter. This will be an issue to watch. Northern Ireland has a separate civil service of its own, resulting from its earlier experiment with devolution.

MINISTERS

Ministers are the politicians in the central executive. The relationship between ministers and civil servants can be much more complex than constitutional theory suggests. In particular the idea that ministers decide policy and civil servants implement it is far too simple to be true.

British legislation is framed on the assumption that it is individual ministers who have duties or powers in relation to the government. References to the Prime Minister or to the Cabinet are only incidental, and even the existence of the office of Prime Minister was not recognised in statute until the Chequers Estate Act 1917. A few ministerial offices, such as President of the Council and Chancellor of the Duchy of Lancaster, are traceable back to the medieval state; and the office of Secretary of State developed from a secretarial office in the royal household in the late seventeenth century. Modern departments such as Environment or Social Security reflect the changed role of government. There is a maximum number of ministers who can sit in Parliament, set at ninety-five, with twenty-one paid cabinet ministers, under the Ministerial and Other Salaries Act 1975 – a piece of legislation rooted in eighteenth-century concerns about the dominance of Parliament by the executive through patronage.

There is a ministerial promotion ladder which often begins with an MP becoming an unpaid parliamentary private secretary (PPS) to a minister or serving a spell in the whips' office. The first real rung on the ladder is a parliamentary under secretary of state (PUSS), then a minister of state, then a full cabinet minister. The work of junior ministers will often revolve around Parliament, answering questions, speaking in debate and shouldering much of the business of taking a bill through its various stages. It also means being a representative of the department, attending meetings, going on visits and offering an ear to pressure groups. It is the senior minister in the department who will allocate duties to junior ministers and, under the doctrine of ministerial responsibility, will be accountable to Parliament for their actions. Every minister will have a private office staffed with civil servants, who will control both access to the minister and ministerial access to the rest of the department.

The life of a minister

Ministers find themselves surrounded and protected by the Whitehall machine. They can feel lonely and isolated, as the former Labour cabinet minister Barbara Castle has described: 'The pattern of the minister's day is fixed by the private office and the gulf with the outside world begins. The minister is alone; the loneliness of the short-distance runner. We will not be there very long and Heaven knows what new minister will very shortly be greeted in the same charming, efficient and no doubt very genuine way. But the minister is the one person who cannot afford to be cut off from the political lifeline which got her there in the first place and which is going to sustain her in the next job'.[6] Ministerial memoirs are full of vivid accounts of the demands and excitements of the job (see box, p. 253).

Ministers are essentially amateurs who have to pick up the main policy issues of their department and try to make some impact on them, while maintaining a punishing schedule of meetings and other activities. A minister has a number of key roles:

- *Parliamentarian.* This will involve answering questions, steering bills and appearing before select committees.
- *Departmental advocate.* The minister has to act as advocate for the department in bilateral meetings, to secure finance, promote policy and get a slot in the legislative timetable.
- *Manager.* As its political head, a minister must ensure that the department is managed efficiently, not least because ministerial responsibility will be invoked if things go wrong.
- *Ambassador.* The minister must represent the public face of the department at

meetings and visits to places and projects as well as defending and promoting departmental policies in the media.

- *Decision-maker.* There is a constant stream of decisions for a minister to make, in answering letters, issuing regulations and considering policy options. Much of the administrative spadework is done by civil servants, but each night a minister takes home departmental red boxes stuffed with official documents requiring ministerial action of some kind.

Ministerial life

Throughout my six years as Secretary of State for Defence, I worked harder than I had ever imagined. I toiled ten to twelve hours a day for five or six days a week, in my own office or in Cabinet committees; then I spent several hours every night across the road in Admiralty House on my despatch boxes. This routine was broken by regular visits to our forces at home and abroad and occasional meetings with my colleagues in NATO or the Commonwealth. It was not easy to squeeze in my monthly weekends at Leeds and more difficult still to find time with my family.

Yet I loved every minute of it. It was the most exhilarating period of my life. The work itself was challenging in the extreme, and it stretched me to the limit . . . After nineteen years' apprenticeship at Transport House and in Opposition, I felt like a man who, after driving his Jaguar for hours behind a tractor on narrow country lanes finally reaches the motorway.

(former Chancellor Dennis Healey on taking office in 1964 in the first Labour government since 1951, remembered in *The Time of My Life* (1989))

Some ministers will give more attention to (and be more adept at) certain of these roles rather than others, but it is a formidable list. Not every minister wants or expects to reach a senior position; some are appointed as a reward for faithful service and serving a couple of years before bowing out. On average, senior ministers tend to be moved every two years or so, while junior ministers have even less time in one post. The most successful minister is a generalist who moves around several departments before entering the Cabinet (for example, Kenneth Clarke had no experience at all of the Treasury before he was appointed Chancellor in 1993).

Prime ministers have less leeway than it might seem in making ministerial appointments, as a sizeable chunk of the parliamentary party is likely to be unsuitable by reason of age, ability, outlook or temperament. Age is a critical factor in promotion, as MPs who are ministers by their early forties are well placed to make the leap to Cabinet by their fifties. Promotion prospects increase substantially at every rung of the ladder. Few ministers are appointed from outside Parliament since experience in the Commons or Lords is usually seen as a vital part of the ministerial job specification. The job is insecure, with regular

---

Getting the sack

I always saw first those who were being asked to leave the Cabinet. I began with Ian Gilmour and told him of my decision. He was – I can find no other word for it – huffy. He left Downing Street and denounced government policy to the television cameras as 'steering full speed ahead for the rocks' . . . Christopher Soames was equally angry, but in a grander way. I got the distinct impression that he was . . . in effect being sacked by his housemaid.

(Margaret Thatcher, *The Downing Street Years* (1993), p. 151)

'reshuffles' turning ministers into ex-ministers overnight. This can be a painful experience (see box above).

However, it can sometimes be dangerous for those who do the sacking. Prime Minister Harold Macmillan was gravely weakened by his 'night of the long knives' in 1962 when he sacked a third of his Cabinet, and although Margaret Thatcher sacked twelve senior ministers between 1979 and 1990 she was in the end sacked by her own Cabinet as an electoral liability when she attempted to retain her position as leader of the party.

Ministers and civil servants

The creative friction generated by putting amateur ministers in charge of professional civil servants is what governs Britain. Incoming ministers often have little idea of what to expect from their private office or permanent secretary but may be thrown straight into major decisions. The former Conservative minister James Prior found that the minute he reached his office as the new Minister for Agriculture the permanent secretary came to him for urgent decisions on measures to tackle a brucellosis outbreak and a rabies scare. Civil servants need ministerial decisions, while ministers need civil service support.

However, the relationship between civil servants and ministers can be an awkward one. The professional neutrality of the civil servant may sometimes appear to the minister to be obstruction or at least lack of commitment to the minister's policies; and some ministers have suspected that their policies are being undermined by civil servants who preferred the bureaucratically convenient solution to a problem. On the other hand, experienced civil servants can feel superior to transient politicians (especially those who are weak or incompetent) and seek to subject policy enthusiasms to the test of practicability. Ministers will find their civil servants poised to implement their policy proposals – as long as they are seen to be workable (see box, p. 255).

Ministers on civil servants

Harriet Harman on becoming Secretary of State for Social Security after Labour was elected in 1997:

We've all watched *Yes Minister*, so you expect everyone to be lurking, looking through the slits of the bunkers, waiting to frustrate your every move. So then, when I arrived, and opened my day one brief in its red folder, and saw 'New Deal for Lone Parents; Help to the Poorest Pensioners' I thought 'It's amazing! These people think just like I do!' They'd read all my speeches, all my parliamentary questions – it wasn't just the manifesto they'd gone through line by line – and there they were in our first meeting with their pens literally poised to write down and implement what I wanted to do. Sometimes it felt almost spooky!

(interview with Lynn Barber, *Observer Life*, 21 May 1998)

The question that civil servants ask themselves when required to advise in implementing polemical proposals is not, 'Do I agree with it?' but, 'Can it be made to work?' If they think it can, they will help to make it work. If they think it cannot, they will do their best to stop it. This is not a very heroic posture, and it can be very irritating, even maddening. Politicians who want to excite the country with imaginative proposals find them watered down in the interests of practicality. And when you become involved with the Whitehall machine, you will find that to satisfy it you have to answer as many questions as you ask. It is suspicious of innovations . . . Be sure of this: when you become a Minister, the system will be there waiting for you and watching you. Antagonize it, and you can do little. Win its co-operation, and you can do quite a lot. But nobody has yet worked out a method of harnessing it to achieve the fulfilment of a complete and cohesive political programme.

(former cabinet minister Gerald Kaufman, *How to be a Minister* (2nd edn, 1997, p. 35))

Ministerial conduct: The code

From shadowy beginnings in 1945 as a note of general procedure for Cabinet members to follow, the *Ministerial Code* has become an essential aspect of cabinet government – its 'highway code'. Peter Hennessy has called it the 'only official working definition we have of what the Cabinet is for.'[7] Formerly known as *Questions of Procedure for Ministers* (and first published with this title in 1992) the Ministerial Code sets out the terms of individual ministerial responsibility and collective responsibility. It stresses the need for co-ordination of policy by departments, upholds the distinction between party and government by warning against inappropriate use of civil servants for party briefings and exhorts ministers to behave with propriety in their personal affairs. The code is promulgated by the Prime Minister on the advice of the Cabinet Secretary and is seen as binding on ministers, although it has no legal force. Its constitutional status has undergone rapid development since its publication in 1992, prompted by the Committee on Standards in Public Life and by the Scott inquiry. The first paragraph of the current code encapsulates ministerial responsibilities in the uncodified constitution (see box, p. 257).

The Committee on Standards in Public Life had recommended that the terms of the code should give the Prime Minister explicit responsibility for its enforcement; but this particular recommendation was rejected by the Major government and remains unimplemented.

Cabinet collective responsibility

Only about twenty senior ministers, selected by the Prime Minister, form the Cabinet. In classic constitutional theory the Cabinet is the 'central directing instrument of government'[8] whose executive power emanates from its control of the legislature. In Walter Bagehot's famous description: 'A Cabinet is a combining committee – a hyphen which joins, a buckle which fastens, the legislative part of the State to the executive part of the State.'[9] Its origins lie in the late eighteenth century, as a body which gradually developed as a collective administration separate from the Crown. The Cabinet model found its purest expression in the nineteenth century, when it operated as the informal forum where a committee of senior ministers took major policy decisions. This was the period when the concept of collective responsibility took shape (see box, p. 258).

Ministerial responsibility is central to British government; and as *collective* responsibility it serves to bind a government together so that it faces the Monarch, Parliament and the public united. Yet the operation of this concept depends as much, if not more, on political reality and convenience as on constitutional doctrine.

Historically, the development of collective responsibility was a means of achieving one of the defining shifts in the constitutional and political landscape. By becoming a collegiate body with common ideas and aims rather than a grouping of individual ministers, each of whom was in practice as well as in theory responsible to the Sovereign, ministers wrested political control from the Monarch in the course of the eighteenth and nineteenth centuries. This enabled the Cabinet to become, in Bagehot's language, the 'efficient' executive, relegating the Monarch to the role of the 'dignified' executive.

Collective responsibility has also become a vital tool of party and governmental cohesion (nowadays even applied to 'shadow cabinets' too) and acts as a sanction against dissent. It bolsters the power of the Prime Minister in that (unlike the doctrine of *individual* ministerial responsibility) it emphasises the collegiate nature of the government rather than the responsibilities of an individual minister of the Crown. It is for the Prime Minister alone to decide how and when collective responsibility applies (including 'agreements to differ', free votes and the like) rather than any constitutional rulebook on the convention.

Code for ministers

1 Ministers of the Crown are expected to behave according to the highest standards of constitutional and personal conduct in the performance of their duties. In particular, they must observe the following principles of Ministerial conduct:
   i)   Ministers must uphold the principle of collective responsibility;
   ii)   Ministers have a duty to Parliament to account, and be held to account, for the policies, decisions and actions of their Departments and Next Steps Agencies;
   iii) It is of paramount importance that Ministers give accurate and truthful information to Parliament, correcting any inadvertent error at the earliest opportunity. Ministers who knowingly mislead Parliament will be expected to offer their resignation to the Prime Minister;
   iv)   Ministers should be as open as possible with Parliament and the public, refusing to provide information only when disclosure would not be in the public interest, which should be decided in accordance with relevant statute and the government's Code of Practice on Access to Government Information;
   v)   Similarly, Ministers should require civil servants who give evidence before Parliamentary Committees on their behalf and under their directions to be as helpful as possible in providing accurate, truthful and full information in accordance with the duties and responsibilities of civil servants as set out in the Civil Service Code.
   vi)   Ministers must ensure that no conflict arises, or appears to arise, between their public duties and their private interests;
   vii) Ministers should avoid accepting any gift or hospitality which might, or which might reasonably appear to, compromise their judgement or place them under an improper obligation.
   viii) Ministers in the House of Commons must keep separate their role as Minister and constituency Member;
   ix)   Ministers must not use resources for party political purposes. They must uphold the political impartiality of the Civil Service, and not ask civil servants to act in any way which would conflict with the Civil Service Code.

These notes detail the arrangements for the conduct of affairs by Ministers. They are intended to give guidance by listing the principles and precedents which may apply. They apply to all members of the Government (the position of Parliamentary Private Secretaries is described separately in Section 4). The notes should be read against the background of the duty of Ministers to comply with the law, including international law and treaty obligations, and to uphold the administration of justice, the general obligations listed above; and in the context of protecting the integrity of public life. Ministers must also, of course, adhere at all times to the requirements that Parliament itself has laid down. For Ministers in the Commons, these are set by the Resolution carried on 19 March 1997 . . . It will be for individual Ministers to judge how best to act in order to uphold the highest standards. They are responsible for justifying their conduct to Parliament. And they can only remain in office for as long as they retain the Prime Minister's confidence.

(extract from *Ministerial Code*, Cabinet Office, 1997)

Collective responsibility: Telling the same story

Bye the bye, there is one thing we haven't agreed upon, which is, what are
we to say? Is it better to make our corn dearer, or cheaper, or to make the
price steady? I don't care which: but we had better all tell the same story.

(Lord Melbourne, Prime Minister, to his Cabinet on the Corn Laws,
1841, quoted in Spencer Walpole, *The Life of Lord John Russell,*
1889, vol. 1, p. 369)

What the convention says

There are three main strands to the doctrine of collective responsibility:

1 *Unanimity.* All members of the government speak and vote together in
   Parliament, except when the Prime Minister and Cabinet make an explicit
   exception such as a free vote or an 'agreement to differ'.
2 *Confidence.* A government can only remain in office while it retains the confidence of the House of Commons, which can be assumed unless and until
   proven otherwise by a vote of no confidence.
3 *Confidentiality.* Unanimity is a constitutional fiction, but it requires confidentiality so that there can be frank discussion within Cabinet and government.

The consequences of the doctrine are that:

*   *A minister must not vote against government policy.* To do so would require resigna-
    tion or produce dismissal.
*   *A minister must not speak against or fail obviously to support government policy.* How-
    ever, ministers find ways, when they wish, of maintaining formal support
    while sending out contrary signals. Nigel Lawson's failure to append his
    name to the Local Government Finance Bill in 1988 (the 'poll tax' legislation)
    is a notable example of this:

    > It is virtually unheard of for the Chancellor not to be a backer of a major
    > financial Bill presented by a colleague. . . . I was of course asked to be
    > one but declined. Nor could I bring myself to make a speech in support
    > of the Poll Tax; although collective Cabinet responsibility obviously
    > prevented me from speaking in public against it.[10]

*   *All decisions are decisions of the whole government.* This means that all ministers
    have to accept responsibility for everything.
*   *A former minister must not reveal cabinet secrets.* However, this has proved difficult to
    enforce, with Richard Crossman's *Diaries of a Cabinet Minister* in the late 1970s
    leading the breach.

What collective responsibility means is spelled out in the text of the *Ministerial Code*. Its first paragraph (p. 257) declares that 'Ministers must uphold the principle of collective responsibility,' but a later section explains exactly what this passage means in practice (see box below).

Collective responsibility: The code

16 The internal process through which a decision has been made, or the level of Committee by which it was taken, should not be disclosed. Decisions reached by the Cabinet or Ministerial Committees are binding on all members of the Government. They are, however, normally announced and explained as the decision of the Minister concerned. On occasions it may be desirable to emphasise the importance of a decision by stating specially that it is the decision of Her Majesty's Government. This, however, is the exception rather than the rule.

17 Collective responsibility requires that Ministers should be able to express their views frankly in the expectation that they can argue freely in private while maintaining a united front when decisions have been reached. This in turn requires that the privacy of opinions expressed in Cabinet and Ministerial Committees should be maintained. Moreover Cabinet and Committee documents will often contain information which needs to be protected in the public interest. It is therefore essential that, subject to the guidelines on the disclosure of information set out in the Code of Practice on Access to Government Information, Ministers take the necessary steps to ensure that they and their staff preserve the privacy of Cabinet business and protect the security of Government documents.

(*Ministerial Code*, Cabinet Office, 1997)

Departures from collective responsibility: 'Agreements to differ'

Perhaps nothing demonstrates more clearly the conventional basis of Britain's unwritten constitution, and the pivotal role of the Prime Minister, than the few examples of authorised waiver, for strictly limited periods, of the doctrine of collective responsibility. As Prime Minister James Callaghan put it in 1977: 'I certainly think that the doctrine should apply, except in cases where I announce that it does not.'[11] It has been argued that an agreement to differ is itself a collective cabinet decision, and that any division between fellow ministers is therefore not a breach of collective responsibility, but this approach attempts to square a tricky constitutional circle. The two main examples of the doctrine's suspension are to be found in 1932 and 1975 (a further possible example in 1977, over legislation on direct elections to the European Assembly, is much less clear cut).

1932: Tariffs policy

The first official 'agreement to differ' occurred in 1932 because of disagreements between Conservatives and their coalition partners over tariff reform. After the 1931 election, four cabinet members disagreed with the decision to impose a general tariff and proposed to resign. The Prime Minister, Ramsay MacDonald, offered to allow them to express their disagreement publicly, and the official terms of this 'agreement to differ' were published in *The Times* (see box below).

The 'Special Provision' (1932)

The Cabinet has had before it the report of the Committee on the Balance of Trade, and after prolonged discussion it has been found impossible to reach unanimous conclusion on the Committee's recommendations.

The Cabinet, however, is deeply impressed with the paramount importance of maintaining national unity in presence of the grave problems that now confront this country and the whole world. It has accordingly determined that some modification of usual Ministerial practice is required and has decided that Ministers who find themselves unable to support the conclusions arrived at by the majority of their colleagues on the subject of import duties and cognate matters are to be at liberty to express their views by speech and vote.

The Cabinet, being essentially united on all other matters of policy, believes that by this special provision it is best interpreting the will of the nation and the needs of the time.

(*The Times*, 23 January 1932)

Stanley Baldwin defended the 'special provision' for the government on the grounds that the British constitution was a 'living organism' with a flexibility that was beneficial to the country. Also the fact that the government was a 'National' rather than a party one, with a huge majority (493), meant that the usual constitutional conventions need not apply: 'The fate of no party is at stake in making a fresh precedent for a National Government. Had the precedent been made for a party government, it would have been quite new, and it would have been absolutely dangerous for that party.' But was it constitutional? This was Baldwin's answer[12]:

> Who can say what is constitutional in the conduct of a national Government? It is a precedent, an experiment, a new practice, to meet a new emergency, a new condition of things, and we have collective responsibility for the departure from collective action. Whatever some ardent politicians may think, it is approved by the broad common sense of the man-in-the-street. The success or failure of this experiment will depend on one thing only, and that is the spirit in which it is conducted.

1975: EEC referendum

The June 1975 referendum on EEC membership was a quite different – and more significant – case. Three senior cabinet ministers wrote to the Prime Minister, Harold Wilson, in these terms: 'Ministers will have very deep convictions that cannot be shelved or set aside by the normal process of Cabinet decision-making. . . . The only solution might be to reach some understanding on the basis of "agreement to differ" on this single issue and for a limited period.'[13] With government and party divided, only the suspension of collective responsibility seemed to offer a way out.

In a parliamentary statement the Prime Minister said:

> The circumstances of this referendum are unique, and the issue to be decided is one on which strong views have long been held which cross party lines. The Cabinet has, therefore, decided that, if when the time comes there are members of the Government, including members of the Cabinet, who do not feel able to accept and support the Government's recommendation, whatever it may be, they will, once the recommendation has been announced, be free to support and speak in favour of a different conclusion in the referendum campaign.[14]

Under questioning, the Prime Minister again emphasised the unique nature of the arrangement:

> I recognise . . . that this is a matter on which my right hon. and hon. Friends feel very deeply even to the point – some of them, on one side or the other – of feeling that they would rather leave politics than accept something unacceptable. I respect that position. . . . This is a matter of fundamental importance. I believe that it is right to give this freedom to differ on this matter because we are so united on everything else.[15]

That April, Mr Wilson set out the guidelines for the agreement to differ, as approved by the Cabinet (see box, p. 262).

This position was tested almost immediately by a Commons speech two days later by a junior minister, Eric Heffer, during which he said that 'the guidelines of the Common Market are as unacceptable as the guidelines on the question of ministerial discussion in the House.' Although there was a free vote and Mr Heffer said he was speaking 'as the member for Liverpool, Walton', he was immediately dismissed. The Prime Minister informed him that:

> Your deliberate decision to speak against the Government's motion in today's debate, although you had been informed of the Cabinet's decision that ministers who dissented from the Government's recommendation should not speak in the debate, makes it impossible for me to retain you in the Government.

The 'unique circumstances' (1975)

In accordance with my statement in the House on 23rd January last, those Ministers who do not agree with the Government's recommendation in favour of continued membership of the European Community are, in the unique circumstances of the referendum, now free to advocate a different view during the referendum campaign in the country.

This freedom does not extend to parliamentary proceedings and official business. Government business in Parliament will continue to be handled by all Ministers in accordance with Government policy. Ministers responsible for European aspects of Government business who themselves differ from the Government's recommendation on membership of the European Community will state the Government's position and will not be drawn into making points against the Government recommendation. Wherever necessary Questions will be transferred to other Ministers. At meetings of the Council of Ministers of the European Community and at other Community meetings, the United Kingdom position in all fields will continue to reflect Government policy.

I have asked all Ministers to make their contributions to the public campaign in terms of issues, to avoid personalising or trivialising the argument, and not to allow themselves to appear in direct confrontation, on the same platform or programme, with another Minister who takes a different view on the Government recommendation.

(Harold Wilson, Prime Minister, House of Commons written answer,
7 April 1975)

The 'agreement to differ' in this case caused difficulties for normal government and parliamentary business. One minister, Peter Shore, explained that 'when I am speaking from the Dispatch Box I am reflecting Government policy as a whole, except when I am clearly reflecting my own policy as the Secretary of State for Trade.' Another minister, Tony Benn, resorted to an equally ingenious formulation when he stated, in reply to a question, 'I have nothing to add to the speeches made by my right hon. Friend the Member for Bristol South-East [that is, himself] in other parts of the country.' Although the 'unique circumstances' were stressed in 1975 (as in 1932), the fact was that collective responsibility had been suspended when an issue could not be contained by it because of party divisions. There was speculation in 1998 that the issue of electoral reform might also have to be handled in this way – no doubt also as a 'unique' case.

THE KEY PLAYERS: PRIME MINISTER, CHANCELLOR AND CABINET

We now look at the role of the Prime Minister and the Cabinet and examine the administrative structures which support these key politicians in the exercise of power. This includes the debate as to whether real power is exercised by the Prime Minister or the group of ministers forming the Cabinet. Wherever power lies, co-ordination is the key problem for central government and the latest initiatives on this are also discussed below.

Prime Minister

The Prime Minister is the most powerful minister in the government, the 'first among equals' in theory but often much more than this in practice. Yet the Prime Minister lacks a separate department with its own large staff to implement policy. This means that it is necessary to work through other ministers to carry out the government's programme. It also means that the power of the Prime Minister (which Prime Minister? When?) can be difficult to pin down with any precision.

The office of Prime Minister emerged in the eighteenth century but it was not really until the early twentieth century that it took its modern form: held by the leader of a mass political party, elected on a manifesto, and commanding a majority in the House of Commons. Only in 1870 was it finally established that the Prime Minister alone could call a meeting of the Cabinet. A secretariat to service the Cabinet and Prime Minister emerged in the First World War, while later developments such as policy units and advisers have enhanced the capacity of the Prime Minister's Office. Prime ministerial power lies in the appointment of colleagues and the general direction of the Cabinet, particularly in economic and foreign affairs, although the integration of the British central executive into EU policies and structures has diminished the premier's room for manoeuvre in these policy areas. It is a formidable array of power (see box, p. 264).

There has been a long debate in British political science about whether the Prime Minister has now replaced the Cabinet as the overall source of political power in Britain. Media attention is increasingly focused on the Prime Minister, aided by his role in international and European summitry. Modern election campaigns place party leaders at the centre of attention. The complexities of modern government impose an intolerable workload on the Cabinet. On the other hand, prime ministers do not possess formal executive power and have a tiny number of civil servants working directly for them. They must maintain the confidence of their colleagues to survive in office, and executive overload – compounded by the sheer exhaustion of constant international travel – means that the energy and capacity to achieve effective coordination may be lost. Much turns on person-alities and political developments – John Major was a 'weak' Prime Minister and Tony Blair a 'presidential' one largely because of different political circumstances. Mrs Thatcher dominated her Cabinet but was eventually brought down by it.

The Prime Minister

has:

- substantial powers of appointment and dismissal over ministers
- powers to make appointments to the senior civil service, public bodies and committees of inquiry, as well as the established church
- overall direction of Cabinet and central executive, including chairing Cabinet and several cabinet committees
- power to ask for dissolution of Parliament (that is, set the date of a general election)
- a major role in direction of foreign and defence policy, including international summitry, treaties, security services and weaponry
- important input into economic policy, EU policy, defence policy, or specialist policy areas.

The death of the Cabinet is regularly announced – but it is resurrected equally regularly. The underlying trends are what matters.

One such trend derives from the development of the EU, which has led to an important extension of the Prime Minister's policy-making arena. He will represent Britain at a host of international summits and play a key role in policy decisions, as with John Major's negotiation of an 'opt out' from the Social Chapter at Maastricht. Foreign, defence and economic policy are the other major areas of prime ministerial activity. Attlee's decision to authorise the development of a British atomic bomb after the Second World War was not communicated to the full Cabinet at all. Yet the influence of the Prime Minister over these issues is severely limited by external pressures and events, world economic cycles, international tensions and much else. Integration into EU structures and policies has led to a 'hollowing out' of the British state and the Prime Minister can often exert only limited influence over events. It is not enough just to assess Prime Ministerial power in relation to the Cabinet alone.

Chancellor and Treasury

After the Prime Minister (who also carries the title of First Lord of the Treasury) the Chancellor of the Exchequer is considered the most important single minister – more important than someone who may have the title of Deputy Prime Minister – due to the wide range of responsibilities over monetary policy, taxation and public expenditure. The Treasury has a crucial role within the cabinet structure as its approval must be secured before a cabinet committee recommends a new spending policy. The Treasury develops the annual budget in conditions of secrecy and this is the only major government policy that is not formally developed in the cabinet system. However, the Prime Minister is kept closely informed and the relationship between these two key players is central to the success of a particular government. As Lord Lawson, Chancellor under Mrs Thatcher, has said of their relationship: 'they do not have to be cronies or soul mates but they do have to be on the same wavelength.'[16] The Chancellor has a key role in several cabinet committees. In the early 1960s a Chief Secretary to the Treasury was appointed as the second Treasury minister of cabinet rank, in order to relieve the Chancellor of the minutiae of expenditure control. The Chief Secretary will argue the spending case with individual ministers and departments and support the Chancellor in Cabinet. The Treasury is central to the work of every department and keeps an eagle eye on spending (see box below).

Treasury: here, there and everywhere

. . . if somebody had managed to penetrate security and called on me at a random hour of the working day, he would probably have found me, not considering interest rates or exchange rates or government borrowing, but playing a substantial role on a Cabinet Committee on a vast range of subjects, from defence procurement to social security reform, from broadcasting to education reform, from the National Health Service to reform of the legal system. It is not for nothing that the Treasury is known in Whitehall as the Central Department.

(Lord Lawson, *The View from No 11: Memoirs of a Tory Radical*, 1992, p. 273)

Naturally we are not enthusiasts for spending schemes. It is not our role in life to be enthusiastic about expenditure.

(senior civil servant, Leo Pliatzky, then Treasury under-secretary, giving evidence to the Commons Trade and Industry Sub-committee on Expenditure 1970–71, p. 64)

The Treasury has to possess the technical capacity to monitor expenditure and to analyse economic developments but it is also 'the most political of departments', as its former permanent secretary, Lord Bridges, once observed in 1971. It must establish effective relations with the spending departments to have any chance of success and this means that it has some hand in the shaping of nearly all departmental policies. Public policy analysis in British government has always been founded on financial considerations, and the Treasury's sometime rival, the Cabinet Office, does not have the same battalions of officials to scrutinise the work of departments. Attempts to set up an 'economic policy' department to counter the Treasury – notably with the short-lived Department of Economic Affairs in the 1960s – have also ended in failure. During the twentieth century the Treasury has struggled to establish control over public expenditure, through regular economic crises. It is now at the apex of its success. Treasury control has never been more complete.

As Chancellor, Gordon Brown introduced a comprehensive spending review which has drawn up public expenditure plans on a new three-yearly basis and which rewards departments for innovation and cross-departmental initiatives. One example is that services for asylum seekers will now be managed by one department instead of five. Each department agrees a public service contract with the Treasury. In each service area the contract requires reform in return for investment, with departmental targets, including efficiency targets, that have to be met. The Treasury is further extending its co-ordinating and control function across Whitehall.

Cabinet committees

Cabinet committees are perhaps the main mechanism for co-ordinating policy and processing business. The demands of total war in 1914–18 had prompted the creation of cabinet committees to handle complex issues, with subsequent reports to the cabinet itself. The Second World War intensified the use of cabinet committees on domestic issues, and, after the war, Clement Attlee formalised these committees in an attempt to give strategic direction to his government and to cope with the sheer pressure of work caused by the expansion of the welfare state. Committees had also begun to include civil servants and ministers. In six-and-a-half years Attlee's government created 466 cabinet committees.[17] Today there are permanent standing committees, *ad hoc* committees set up to tackle a particular issue (such as drugs policy) and committees consisting only of officials.[18] A snapshot of the committees in existence in 1998 shows their vast range (see box, p. 267).

It can be argued that part of the power of the Cabinet has gone upwards to the Prime Minister and Cabinet Office and part down to committees and even individual departments. Churchill attempted to rein in the use of committees and restore to the Cabinet effective power over decision-making, but his successors continued to develop the cabinet committee system as a response to the increasing complexity of government. Wilson reduced cabinet meetings to once a week, discouraged appeals to Cabinet by ministers and formalised a substructure of four standing committees (overseas and defence, home, economic and on legislation). Peter Riddell has noted that in the 1940s the Cabinet ceased to be the decision-making body considering most issues, but that it retained until the 1980s its role as court of appeal or forum for discussing big issues. Even that role has now been superseded by bilateral discussions; Mrs Thatcher liked to conduct these, and they have become a feature of the Blair administration. Full cabinets now often last less than an hour and have no formal agenda. The number of cabinet committees has also been reduced, in favour of *ad hoc* task forces and bilateral negotiations.

Government by committee? Cabinet committees in October 1998

Economic and domestic

Ministerial Committee on Economic Affairs (EA) chair Chancellor of the Exchequer

Ministerial Sub-Committee on Welfare to Work (EA(WW)) chair Chancellor of the Exchequer

Ministerial Sub-Committee on Energy Policy (EA(N)) chair Chancellor of the Exchequer

Ministerial Committee on Public Expenditure (PX) chair Chancellor of the Exchequer

Ministerial Committee on the Environment (ENV) chair Deputy Prime Minister

Ministerial Committee on Local Government (GL) chair Deputy Prime Minister

Ministerial Sub-Committee on London (GL(L)) chair Deputy Prime Minister

Ministerial Group on Utility Regulation (MISC 3) chair Secretary of State for Trade and Industry

Ministerial Group on Biotechnology and Genetic Modification (MISC 6) chair Minister for the Cabinet Office

Ministerial Group on Better Government (MISC 7) chair Minister for the Cabinet Office

Ministerial Committee on Home and Social Affairs (HS) chair Deputy Prime Minister

Ministerial Sub-Committee on Health Strategy (HS(H)) chair Leader of the House

Ministerial Sub-Committee on Drug Misuse (HS(D)) chair Minister for the Cabinet Office

Ministerial Sub-Committee on Women's Issues (HS(W)) chair Leader of the House of Lords

Ministerial Committee on The Queen's Speeches and Future Legislation (QFL) chair Leader of the House

Ministerial Committee on Legislation (LEG) chair Leader of the House

Ministerial Group on Food Safety (MISC 1) chair Leader of the House

Ministerial Group on Youth Justice (MISC 2) chair Home Secretary

Ministerial Group on Millennium Date Change (MISC 4) chair Leader of the House

Constitution

Ministerial Committee on Constitutional Reform Policy (CRP) chair Prime Minister

Ministerial Sub-Committee on Incorporation of the European Convention of Human Rights (CRP(EC)) chair Lord Chancellor

continued

Ministerial Sub-Committee on Freedom of Information (CRP(FOI)) chair Lord Chancellor

Ministerial Sub-Committee on House of Lords Reform (CRP(HL)) chair Lord Chancellor

Ministerial Committee on Devolution Policy (DP) chair Lord Chancellor

Joint Consultative Committee with the Liberal Democratic Party (JCC) chair Prime Minister

Overseas and defence

Ministerial Committee on Defence and Overseas Policy (DOP) chair Prime Minister

Ministerial Committee on Northern Ireland (IN) chair Prime Minister

Ministerial Committee on the Intelligence Services (CSI) chair Prime Minister

Ministerial Group on the Restructuring of the European Aerospace and Defence Industry (MISC 5) chair Trade and Industry Secretary

European

Ministerial Sub-Committee on European Issues ((E)DOP) chair Foreign Secretary

(Cabinet Office website, 1998)

Decline and fall of Cabinet government?

Although many of these developments derive from the sheer weight of business in modern government, there are other pressures that work against the Cabinet acting as a collective body. It has little time at its disposal (see box below).

Cabinet meetings

Lord Lawson:

A normal Cabinet meeting has no chance of becoming a grave forum of statesmanlike debate. Twenty-two people attending a two and a half hour meeting can speak for just over six and a half minutes on average. If there are three items of business – and there are usually far more – the ration of time just exceeds two minutes, if everyone is determined to have his say. Small wonder then that most Ministers keep silent on most issues or confine themselves to brief but pointed questions or observations.

(Lord Lawson, *The View from No. 11: Memoirs of a Tory Radical*, 1992)

Cabinet ministers tend to promote the interests of their departments first and foremost and so have almost no time or energy to involve themselves in issues beyond their departmental briefs. As a senior civil servant, Sir Douglas Wass, noted in 1983: 'No minister I know of has won political distinction by his performance in Cabinet or by his contribution to collective decision-making.'[19] Senior ministers make their name through departmental successes. Ministers tend to be generalists who can easily be submerged in learning about their own ministerial brief, while frequent reshuffles prevent more experienced ministers from making a collective contribution as they are moved to new portfolios. Private offices are not in a position to provide a policy brief about another department's initiative, and there is rarely any time for a member of the Cabinet to put together an informal case about a matter concerning another department. The issue that provoked the first parliamentary rebellion of the Blair government – on behalf of benefits for lone parents – had not even been discussed by the Cabinet.

Departmentalism can augment prime ministerial power by locking ministers into policy specialisms, while also impeding prime ministerial objectives through bureaucratic obstruction. As James Callaghan observed: 'departmental ministers and officials . . .believe that Prime Ministers should not trespass on their policy cabbage patches.'[20] Some commentators have concluded that cabinet government has therefore been replaced by departmental government.

Yet the importance of collegiality, as Simon James has noted,[21] is fundamental to the existence of the Cabinet, and underpins collective responsibility. Collegiality represents the exercise of authority by a group of people acting jointly who have some kind of common ethos, rather than one person acting alone. It forms part of the basic culture of British politics and its preservation is the real issue surrounding the rise of prime ministerial government. Thatcher fell because she was felt to have flouted the principle in a fundamental way over Europe: first Chancellor Nigel Lawson, then Foreign Secretary Geoffrey Howe, resigned over her abandonment of the cabinet line; as Howe put it: 'Cabinet government is all about trying to persuade one another from within . . . [but] every step forward risked being subverted by some casual comment or impulsive answer.'[22] Major attempted to restore a collegiate feel to his cabinet, but its cleavage over Europe eventually forced him to seek re-election as party leader. Even this manoeuvre failed to quell dissent and he admitted to the Group of Seven seminar in Nova Scotia in November 1995 that: 'I am a coalition government on my own.'[23] The Blair government restored collegiality, but not by restoring cabinet government.

The Cabinet Office

The Cabinet Office is the body that provides the secretariat for the Cabinet and cabinet committees, but its role is much more far reaching. Its head, the Cabinet Secretary, is in charge of the Home Civil Service and is responsible for the formal co-ordination of government business, revising and monitoring rules of cabinet conduct, oversight of security and intelligence operations and supervision of a wide range of public appointments. In recent years the Cabinet Secretary has acquired a higher public profile and is now expected to undertake the role of a commissioner for standards in government, indicating to select committees, civil servants and inquiries the 'range of legitimate actions by prime minister, ministers and civil servants within the constitutional tradition.'[24]

The Cabinet Secretary, Sir Richard Wilson, was asked by Tony Blair in 1998 to carry out a review with the aim of enhancing the strategic role of the Cabinet Office so that it could tackle policy questions which cross departmental boundaries. This review rejected the idea of a prime minister's department in favour of a strengthened Cabinet Office. Sir Peter Kemp, architect of the executive agencies, has warned that 'unless this is achieved the Treasury will step into the vacuum.'[25] For the first time an annual report was produced by the Cabinet Office in 1998 listing the achievements of the first year of the Blair government, with an inevitably partisan note in its presentation of policy developments.

The Cabinet Office organises the flow of government business, and can offer a cross-departmental view on policies, particularly through its influential European secretariat. Other units within the Cabinet Office have broad civil service responsibilities, such as deregulation or the development of the 'Next Steps' programme of executive agencies. The Office of Public Service has had responsibility for a range of public service matters such as freedom of information and conditions of service, but as a result of the Wilson review it has been merged into the rest of the Cabinet Office and a new Performance and Innovation Unit[26] focuses on issues crossing departmental boundaries and acts as a source for policy analysis across Whitehall, complementing the Treasury role without the financial imperative. As part of these reforms a new Centre for Management and Policy Studies acts as a conduit for new management training for the senior civil service, and a Management Board for the Civil Service, consisting of senior civil servants, has strengthened the Cabinet Office's corporate management role.

The Blair team made careful preparations before their election for a more proactive Cabinet Office, acting as a 'Whitehall whip' to drive the machine forward to implement the key election pledges. The new *Ministerial Code* reflects a determination to strengthen central control by requiring departmental ministers to clear all major statements in good time with the Number 10 press office. This represents an unprecedented degree of control over the birth of new policy initiatives (and may not be sustainable in practice). A new 'enforcer' minister was appointed to oversee the Wilson reforms and to give government a more strategic dimension. However, some commentators observed that Whitehall was littered with the bleached bones of former ministers given the job of co-ordinating government without sufficient authority over senior colleagues.

Development of the Prime Minister's Office

Along with the debate on prime ministerial versus cabinet government there has been long-standing discussion about whether a prime minister's department is needed to give the premier more levers of power. Opponents argue that the strength of British government lies in its collegiality, which means that the aim should be to beef up the Cabinet Office rather than Number 10. Yet these aims need not be mutually exclusive: as one permanent secretary remarked in 1979, 'of course it is perfectly obvious that we need a Prime Minister's Department, so long as it is still called the Cabinet Office.'[27]

Lloyd George created a 'garden suburb' of prime ministerial advisers in 1916 to assist in policy formulation and what would now be called 'spin'. Much of this machinery was considered too ambitious for post-war use and was dismantled, but inter-war prime ministers did have special advisers. Chamberlain relied greatly on the civil servant Horace Wilson for foreign policy advice while Churchill had a number of special advisers to assist in the conduct of the Second World War. Edward Heath created the Central Policy Review Staff (the 'Think Tank') in 1971 to be a vehicle for strategic policy advice by the Cabinet, but no formal policy unit for the Prime Minister alone was established until 1974 when Harold Wilson set up a Policy Unit, headed by the non-civil servant Bernard Donoghue. Its main focus was economic policy, reflecting the dominant concerns of the 1970s.

When Mrs Thatcher came to power in 1979, she appointed her own economic policy adviser, Sir Alan Walters. Value-for-money scrutinies were established by Lord Rayner and became institutionalised in the Efficiency Unit in the Cabinet Office. The Central Policy Review Staff was abolished in 1983, but the Policy Unit retained an important role in briefing the Prime Minister on departmental policies and suggesting alternatives. David Willetts, who worked in the Policy Unit under Mrs Thatcher, has described its function at its grandest as support to the Prime Minister in implementing the strategic policy goals of the government; whereas the Cabinet Office's role was to ensure that the machinery of government ran smoothly, without any policy emphasis. John Major maintained the Policy Unit, with Sarah Hogg at its head, and it played an important economic role during the 1992 Exchange Rate Mechanism crisis. Although one of the main objectives of the Policy Unit is to pull in ideas from outside the civil service machine, it is essential for it to have effective contacts with Whitehall to infiltrate the policy networks. Sarah Hogg describes the role of the Policy Unit in this way:

> The Prime Minister can use his Unit as storm troops, invading the complacent hinterland of Whitehall, or as a peacemaker, building bridges between warring departments and Ministers. In practice the Unit tries to do a bit of both and to be both grit and oil in the government machine.[28]

The Policy Unit is just one part of the Downing Street machinery that makes up the Prime Minister's Office, which is composed of a:

- Private Office run by civil servants who manage official relations with the government and Parliament;
- Policy Unit staffed by twenty non-civil servants on short-term appointments, offering policy advice;
- Political Office staffed by party workers who help write speeches and maintain links with the party, paid for out of party funds;
- Strategic Communications Unit run largely by civil servants, although the press secretaries are often outsiders, such as Alastair Campbell, handling relations with the media and the outside world.

There have been several developments in these arrangements under the Blair premiership. Jonathan Powell, a non-civil servant, was appointed as a special adviser but acts as a chief of staff, a role which is just as political as that carried out in the 1980s by his brother, a civil servant, Sir Charles Powell, when he was Mrs Thatcher's foreign policy adviser. Until the Blair government there was a mixture of seconded civil servants and political advisers in the Policy Unit. The 1997 intake of advisers are known more for their political closeness to Blair than for independent expertise. The focus has been on the development of links between the Policy Unit and the Cabinet Office to enable concerted initiatives from the centre. In August 1998 there were twenty members of the Policy Unit while the creation of a Strategic Communications Unit to provide an enhanced public relations service for government has meant the installation of another eight officials in Number 10. These numbers, although expanded, remain small, and are a long way from being a fully-fledged prime minister's department.

Another characteristic of the Blair administration has been the use of 'task forces' of outside experts to develop new initiatives. The Social Exclusion Unit, based in the Cabinet Office, may well be the precursor of a whole range of units established to cut across departmental boundaries and tackle the 'wicked issues' which need to be addressed horizontally across government. As yet it is not clear how the work of these task forces will be linked through cabinet committees.

Both Thatcher and Major experimented with a chief of staff to assist the Prime Minister in strategy and co-ordination; and, following his re-election as Prime Minister in 1995, John Major institutionalised this experiment with the appointment of Michael Heseltine as Deputy Prime Minister with a brief to co-ordinate the presentation of policy. A new cabinet committee was set up under the chairmanship of Heseltine with this same purpose. Blair continued this initiative with the appointment of Peter Mandelson as minister without portfolio within the Cabinet Office, then with Jack Cunningham as Cabinet Office minister to support the Prime Minister and Cabinet in the strategic co-ordination and presentation of government policy. All these initiatives are part of a continuing attempt to reconcile government by department with strategic direction and central co-ordination.

Has the Prime Minister become a President?

From the early 1960s there has been concern that the Prime Minister has amassed power far beyond other cabinet members and approaching those held by a president on the American model. The term 'presidential' is somewhat misleading since the British Prime Minister remains a member of the legislature whereas the US President cannot be a member of Congress. Nevertheless, it is a useful shorthand for a model which emphasises the extent of power held by the premier. The main arguments for and against the validity of the model can be summarised like this:

For

- There are no formal constitutional limits on the Prime Minister's power and formidable premiers can virtually take over the government, as with Churchill in the Second World War.
- The Prime Minister appoints and dismisses Cabinet colleagues and decides the date of the general election. The office-holder has far more power than simply being 'first amongst equals'.
- The Cabinet is no longer the forum for decision-making, with policy developed instead in a mixture of cross-departmental committees. The Prime Minister controls this network by strategic appointments to cabinet committees and task forces.
- The modern media focus is on the Prime Minister, rather than the Cabinet, and in an era of international summitry it is the premier who is seen as representing Britain.
- Departmental ministers are overworked and lack time and expertise to challenge policy decisions outside their area. This is why Margaret Thatcher was able to push through the poll tax against the opposition of senior ministers and civil servants.
- Key financial and economic decisions are not communicated to the Cabinet, but developed by the Chancellor in consultation directly with the Prime Minister.
- The Cabinet Office and the Number 10 Policy Unit co-ordinate cross-departmental initiatives and increasingly act as the Prime Minister's eyes and ears in Whitehall.

Against

- The Prime Minister has few clearly delineated powers in an unwritten constitution and has to have regard to conventions laid down by predecessors if criticism is to be avoided.
- The Prime Minister only has a small staff of less than a hundred (compared to 4,000 for the US President) and has to rely on departments to develop policies. It was Gordon Brown who engineered the Comprehensive Spending Review and who is widely believed to have scuppered the welfare reform plans of the former minister Frank Field, Tony Blair's appointee.
- The Cabinet has the power to revolt against the Prime Minister and electoral circumstances may provoke this. Margaret Thatcher had to resign when she realised that most of the Cabinet wanted her to go. A Prime Minister has no separate electoral mandate from that of the party. There is danger in surrounding oneself with uncritical supporters.
- The Prime Minister is constrained in the appointment and dismissal of ministers by party considerations. Appointments need to reflect the balance of power and opinion within a party. John Major found it necessary to have both Europhiles and Europhobes in his Cabinet.
- The central executive has become so complex that no single person can hope

to be in charge of it. Even Margaret Thatcher had to accept policies that she instinctively disliked, such as the Single European Act in 1985, and her government was unable to cut public expenditure by anything more than a marginal amount.

- The media can be a powerful enemy when they turn against a Prime Minister, as with John Major and sleaze in the 1990s, and Jim Callaghan after the 'winter of discontent' in 1978–9.

It is only necessary to run through these contrary arguments to realise that it is unsafe to make sweeping conclusions on the basis of what may be particular circumstances. A prime minister who looks indomitable when conditions are favourable (for example, electoral popularity and a united party) can soon look vulnerable when conditions change. It is more useful to try to identify the underlying trends.

Prime Minister and Cabinet: The trends

A Stronger Centre?

The service which the Cabinet Office provides to any Prime Minister is always to the Prime Minister in his corporate collective capacity . . .

I think you are right to identify a wish in this Government . . . to have a stronger, more strategic role carried out by the centre. This is not about taking over the role of departments as I have described it. It is about making sure that the Government is pulled together in a way which conveys the themes and messages of the Government and gets across its overriding philosophy.

(Sir Richard Wilson, Cabinet Secretary, giving evidence to the Public Administration Committee, 1998, *The Government Information and Communication Service* HC 770 1997–8)

Commentators such as Peter Riddell and Peter Hennessy have warned of the dangers that a 'Blair presidency' could bring. Riddell believes that 'the Blairites are confused about the role of the Cabinet, focusing on its shortcomings as a decision-taking body, rather than on its broader political role.'[29] As well as the machinery of government changes, Blair has adopted an 'above politics' stance expressed to impressive effect in his words and actions after the sudden death of Princess Diana and this conditions his approach to the policy process. His team of policy advisers sets a rapid and focused pace, intervening and co-ordinating on all fronts, but senior ministers need to be fully involved if there is not to be a collapse of collegiality. Blair's 'can-do' approach to government (see box above) makes him seem impatient with committee-type structures, seen also in his desire to promote strong executives in local government, and a return to decision-making through a formal cabinet committee structure looks unlikely.

A rather different approach would be to develop an 'inner' cabinet of the key ministers, as advocated among others by Lord Lawson. Both world wars saw an inner 'War Cabinet', but this style of government has not flourished in peacetime. Churchill attempted a system of 'overlord' ministers, freed from individual departmental responsibilities, in order to co-ordinate policy across related ministries; and Harold Wilson played with the idea of an inner cabinet in the face of accusations that the real influence lay with an unelected 'kitchen cabinet' of advisers and personal staff. Major had an 'A' team of ministers to deal with the 1992 election, the exchange rate crisis and the long struggle to secure parliamentary approval for the extensions to EU power in the Maastricht Treaty. However, formal inner cabinets have problems of their own, as they cause anguish to excluded ministers without offering sufficient expertise to an overloaded premier. Conflict with the Cabinet Office might also result unless a full restructuring of the machinery of government took place.

The inclusion of another party in office would involve fundamental reappraisals of the operation of the cabinet system in Britain, for any kind of peacetime coalition has only occurred in the early 1930s at a time of economic crisis, and recently in post-devolution Scotland. For example, New Zealand moved to coalition government in the 1990s, with painful consequences for politicians, who now have to negotiate policies and ministerial portfolios, without any certainty of being able to implement manifesto commitments. The possibility that the Prime Minister might come from a minority coalition partner, as with Ramsay MacDonald in 1931 or Lloyd George in 1916, cannot be discounted, which would prompt a re-assessment of the balance of power within the Cabinet. It is unlikely, for example, that the party which held the premiership would also hold all the other key positions, such as Chancellor of the Exchequer and Foreign Secretary. Judging by European experience, larger and more unwieldy cabinets would be likely with less frequent cabinet reshuffles. Collective responsibility is a central doctrine of cabinet government, but multi-party government might place the convention under strain. One innovation on this front has already occurred under Blair, in the form of a joint consultative cabinet committee with the Liberal Democrats to discuss 'policy issues of joint interest', mainly constitutional reform.

The creation of a prime minister's department, on the model of the Taoiseach's office in Ireland, might well result if a more proportional electoral system ushers in a coalition government. In single-party government the prime minister's interests are supposed to reflect those of the whole cabinet; but where two or more parties are in a ruling coalition the Prime Minister might feel under pressure to develop more distinctive policies to sustain political support and to compensate for diminished influence over cabinet committees and departmental initiatives. For the moment though, what can be said about the Blair government is that it is engaged in the most concerted attempt in peacetime to give central control, direction and co-ordination to British government. Whether this will leave a lasting impact on the central executive, and on the relationship between its various parts, remains to be seen.

THE WIDER EXECUTIVE TERRITORY

It remains to look at the wider territory of the central executive and to examine recent developments such as quangos and the civil service executive agencies. Under pressure from new management techniques largely borrowed from the private sector, government in Britain has become more fragmented – and this has raised questions about both accountability and efficiency.

Policy networks

It was noted earlier that the term 'central executive' is frequently used as a short-hand way to describe government by and through ministers, including the Prime Minister, Cabinet and civil service. However the central executive really extends further and wider than this suggests. It is traditionally seen as having its natural boundary at the edge of the civil service, but this can be misleading. Some public bodies are subject to a high level of central control or have functions that cross departments (for example, the Countryside Commission or the British Council) but are not staffed by civil servants. The central executive is a more complex territory than some traditional descriptions acknowledge.

For example, Rod Rhodes[30] has identified the existence of what he calls 'policy networks', where a relevant central government department and public body linked to it routinely decide on policy, only occasionally involving Parliament or the Cabinet. These are alliances of bureaucrats and professionals, across types and tiers of government, including the EU. On this view of the central executive, local government is an essential element, since the centre relies on its local professional expertise to implement government policy; and these professional groups, such as planners, social workers and environmental health officers, provide opportunities for experiment and policy innovation which may later be extended nationally.

Although one of the fundamental principles behind the central executive has been the concept of a unitary state, in which power is concentrated at the centre, the policy initiatives of recent years have led to a growing fragmentation in its structure. Departments have 'hived off' major executive functions to agencies, while pay and personnel issues have been delegated to departments and agencies throughout the civil service. Public bodies, or quangos, with varying degrees of autonomy, have also been given responsibility for developing and implementing policy initiatives (for example, the Housing Corporation developed the Tenant's Charter for housing association tenants). Privatisation of major utilities once owned by the state has become commonplace and there now exists a plethora of stand-alone bodies in the fields of education, training and health. One result has been confusion, especially for the consumer: for example no fewer than seven different channels offer assistance to single parents. It is unlikely that the electronic government initiative 'Better Government' will be effective until the activities of the central executive can be simplified and made comprehensible to citizens. Finally, devolution for Scotland, Wales and London further undermines the old centralised state.

Mechanisms are clearly required to co-ordinate this great mass of policy initiatives and to achieve effective implementation. Rhodes has identified this as the role of the *core executive* which he describes as the 'complex web of institutions, networks and practices surrounding the Prime Minister, Cabinet, cabinet committees and official counterparts, less formalised ministerial clubs or meetings, bilateral negotiations and interdepartmental committees.'[31] He includes the co-ordinating departments such as the Treasury, Cabinet Office, Foreign Office, law officers, security and intelligence services within this definition. It can be argued that this is a fuller and more accurate description of what makes government work in practice than the term cabinet government, especially since almost all major decisions are taken outside the weekly cabinet meeting. Some of the features of the new public administration are examined below.

Quangos

Quangos are appointed bodies which carry out public functions, ranging from major executive bodies such as the Arts Council to small advisory groups such as the Expert Advisory Group on AIDS. Their members are often appointed by ministers, but they are always at 'arm's length' from the government. They are normally not part of the civil service and have a degree of autonomy in the way they operate, although it is generally ministers who determine the extent of their powers.

The term *quango*, which emerged in the 1970s, is an acronym, standing originally for *quasi autonomous non-governmental organisation*. The lack of precision surrounding the term causes great difficulty in deciding which organisations are quangos and which are not. This has led to the adoption of alternative names with a more specific focus. The Conservative government introduced the term *non-departmental public bodies* (NDPBs) and also used the general term public bodies, with an NDPB defined as 'a body which has a role in the processes of national government, but is not a government department or part of one, and accordingly operates to a greater or lesser extent at arm's length from Ministers.'[32] Stuart Weir and Wendy Hall coined the alternative name *extra-governmental organisations* (or EGOs) defined as 'executive bodies of a semi-autonomous nature which effectively act as agencies for central government and carry out government policies.'[33] On the face of it this may seem remarkably similar to the official description of an NDPB, although one important difference is that an EGO must have an executive role (that is, administer a policy area) whereas NDPBs include advisory and quasi-judicial bodies. The crucial difference, however, is that Weir and Hall's term is a deliberately broad definition covering spending bodies at local and national levels outside the traditional structures of central and local government, thereby highlighting alleged lack of accountability inherent in the growth of the 'quango state'. By contrast, NDPB is a much more restrictive term, limiting the number of quangos the government has to own up to (and 'public bodies' sounds nicer too).

Concern about the increasing numbers of quangos was raised by the Conservative Party when in opposition during the1970s, with a particular focus on issues of patronage (the power of ministers to make appointments) and accountability to Parliament. An early review of quangos carried out by the Thatcher government (the Pliatzky review) produced relatively modest results (such as the merger of the Herring Industry Board with the White Fish Authority).[34] A further review, announced in November 1984, led to savings of around £33 million a year.

Interest in quangos was rekindled in the early 1990s, but this time as a charge against the Conservative government. John Stewart popularised the term 'new magistracy' to describe the rise of an unelected elite which he believed was taking over the role of local government:

> There is no sense in which those appointed can be regarded as locally accountable, indeed the membership of these bodies is largely unknown locally. Nor are they necessarily subject to the same requirements for open meetings, access to information and external scrutiny that local authorities are subject to.[35]

The growth of the 'quango state' and the 'new magistracy' was hotly debated during the Major years. Labour successfully linked these issues to its wider assault on Conservative 'sleaze'. A number of surveys indicated a high level of appointments from business, but the Conservatives' view was that business people had skills which could make public services more efficient and responsive to consumers. There were charges that a disproportionate number of Conservative supporters had been appointed to quangos.[36]

However, other voices warned that it would be unwise to dismiss altogether the value of appointed bodies. One pamphlet argued that it was too easy simply to identify elective government with accountable government, since elections 'do not by themselves entail a continuing practice of accountability.'[37] The author concluded that the undemocratic aspects of appointed bodies might be tackled by finding ways of appointing people who were more representative of the community. A document produced by the Blair government sought to take stock of the various arguments about quangos (see box, p. 279).

Nolan and after

The Committee on Standards in Public Life (the Nolan Committee) was appointed in October 1994 by the former Prime Minister, John Major, in response to allegations of 'sleaze' in government. Its terms of reference included quangos of all descriptions. The committee's first report, published in May 1995, recommended that appointments to the boards of executive NDPBs and NHS bodies should be made on the basis of merit, with the aim of obtaining a balance of relevant skills and backgrounds. Research commissioned by the committee did not clearly demonstrate political bias in the making of appointments. Nolan recommended that responsibility for appointments should remain with ministers, but advised by committees with independent members. A totally independent body for making appointments to quangos was rejected as impractical.

Quangos, pros and cons

The trouble with quangos . . .

- *Quangos are 'unelected and unaccountable'.* Since the boards of quangos are unelected and independent from ministers, there is no obvious mechanism by which quangos can be held to account for their activity.
- *Quangos are secretive.* For example, it is difficult to find details of quango members. Meetings of quango boards are not generally open to the public and there is no access to the minutes of these meetings.
- *The number and power of quangos keep growing.* Over the years, quangos have continued to grow and their functions and powers have increased, with the public having little realistic chance of forming and keeping a clear picture of what exactly these bodies are doing.
- *Many quangos appear remote and unresponsive to the communities they serve.*
- *Appointments are unfair and secret.* There has been concern that Ministers have used their powers of patronage (appointment) to fill the boards of quangos with people of the same political persuasion.

. . . But quangos can be really useful

- *There are some government functions which are, perhaps, best carried out at arm's length from ministers.* These include regulation (for example, by the Health and Safety Commission and Executive, and the Environment Agency) and decisions on funding – for the sciences, for example, where expertise is essential and where it has long been agreed that political considerations should play no part in decisions on the allocation of scarce resources between competing, worthy claimants.
- Many quangos provide *expert advice to ministers* on technical or other very specialised issues, bringing national experts in a particular field together in advisory bodies without compromising their independence.
- Quangos offer the opportunity of *bringing a large number of ordinary people into public life.*
- Quangos – particularly advisory bodies – can provide a *quick and flexible response to matters of particular concern.* For instance, the last government set up the Nolan Committee to address concerns about sleaze in many areas of public life.
- Quangos can provide a valuable mechanism for bringing together a *partnership between government and other interests.* This is done, in some instances, by enabling other bodies to nominate members. For example, the boards of Housing Action Trusts include nominees from local authorities, and nominees elected by residents of the trusts' areas.
- Quangos can carry out a range of *commercial activities*; this requires a degree of independence from government.

(based on *Opening Up Quangos*, Cabinet Office, November 1997)

Nolan found the main weakness in the Conservatives' approach to quango appointments to be a lack of external scrutiny. He recommended that a Public Appointments Commissioner should be appointed, to regulate, monitor and report on the public appointments process. It should be mandatory for each executive NDPB and NHS body to have a code of conduct for board members, and a similar code for staff. Arrangements for 'whistleblowing' should be developed, to enable quango staff who have concerns to be able to express them without fear of recrimination. The Conservative government implemented most of Nolan's recommendations on quangos. The first Commissioner for Public Appointments, Sir Leonard Peach, was appointed in November 1995; and in April 1996 he published a code of practice for public appointment procedures.

The second Nolan Report in 1996 concentrated on local quangos, which it termed local public spending bodies. Nolan felt that the thorny question of whether local or central government should be responsible for local services was beyond its terms of reference, although observing that central government's desire to keep a tight rein on local spending bodies in order to ensure that public money was being spent wisely was tending to weaken local responsibility and accountability. He recommended that ways of taking account of the views of local councils and other interested bodies should be found in order to improve the accountability of local quangos.

Labour's anti-quango rhetoric while in opposition has become a more measured approach in government. The Welsh Assembly and the Scottish Parliament have wide-ranging powers to reform and scrutinise many of the quangos for which they have become responsible. The elected authority for London and the regional chambers envisaged in other parts of England will also be able to scrutinise local quangos, and local authorities may be able to develop a similar (though less formal) role. Other government proposals on quangos were set out in two papers published by the Cabinet Office in June 1998.[38] These included:

- a bigger role for House of Commons select committees in scrutinising quangos;
- quangos to hold annual open meetings, publish annual reports and summary reports of meetings, and take various other steps to consult and inform their users and the public at large;
- the long-awaited Freedom of Information Bill to cover quangos;
- more information on quangos to be published by the government;
- action to increase representation of women and ethnic minorities, with the long-term aim of achieving equal numbers of men and women on quangos, and representative numbers of people from ethnic minorities.

As if to prove that everything comes round again sooner or later in politics, early in 1998 the Conservative health spokesman accused the Labour Health Secretary Frank Dobson of making politically partisan appointments to NHS bodies. Mr Dobson countered that a number of elected councillors had been appointed, and that Labour's success in local elections in recent years meant that it was much more likely that suitable Labour councillors would be found than Conservative ones. The charge was dismissed by the Public Appointments Commissioner.

A similar sense of *déjà vu* surrounded the green paper *Opening Up Quangos* (November 1997) which promised that the number of quangos currently in existence would be reviewed and that the government would set up a new NDPB 'only when it can demonstrate that this is the most appropriate and cost-effective means of carrying out the given function.' This repeated almost word for word a promise made by Margaret Thatcher in 1984.[39]

Change in the civil service

Over the last twenty years the civil service has been subject to a range of initiatives, although much of the overall architecture of the central civil service remains in place. It has been increasingly argued that the traditional structure of the civil service needs to be re-modelled in line with the changing demands on it (see box below).

Dinosaur or service deliverer?

The structure of Whitehall is well out of date. It would be familiar to Winston Churchill and Clement Attlee if they were with us today. Substantial re-fashioning, to reflect changes over the last century – globalisation, Europe, the way people live, information technology, the environment and crucially, devolution, and so on, are needed. . . . Departments and agencies however structured will almost always be vertically oriented, while many of the things which most affect us as citizens or otherwise involve horizontal co-operation and interworking between different departments and agencies, as well as entities outside government such as local authorities or the health service.

(Sir Peter Kemp, former civil servant and architect of the
Next Steps Executive Agencies programme in evidence to the
Lords Select Committee on the Public Service, HL 55-I 1997–8)

In recent years, the civil service has been abandoning the unified systems of pay and personnel management which had been in place since the late 1960s. In April 1996 responsibility for pay and grading of staff below the most senior levels was delegated to individual departments and existing national pay arrangements were abandoned. Growing delegation, the spread of private sector methods and attitudes, and the recruitment of senior staff from outside the civil service have prompted fears that the central values of the civil service might be lost. *The Civil Service Code*, introduced in 1996 on the basis of a recommendation from the Treasury and Civil Service Select Committee of the House of Commons, was partly intended to ensure that those values continued to be recognised throughout a more diverse organisation. The government also hoped to maintain the sense of unity by retaining a single structure at the most senior levels with a single pay, grading and appraisal system for the Senior Civil Service, a body of about 3,000 people spread across all departments and agencies. Economic necessity – the financial crises of the mid-1970s – encouraged a trend to cut costs in the organisation and to make it more efficient and effective. This has mirrored changes in the public sectors of many countries, a movement often referred to as the 'new public management'. It involves focusing on the results of work done, rather than the way in which it is done (processes); the needs of the individual customer; a trend towards delegation and empowerment of local managers; and the effective management of resources. In Britain the Financial Management Initiative of 1982 was one of the first steps in this process, intended to give managers a clear view of their objectives, well-defined responsibility for making the best use of resources, and proper managerial and financial responsibility.

The *Next Steps* Report of 1988 took these initiatives further by proposing the separation of many of the executive functions of government from the policy departments into distinct 'Executive Agencies', which would undertake specific tasks on the basis of semi-contractual agreements with the department, contained in a series of documents (the 'framework document', business plan and corporate plan). The introduction of agencies was linked to another project, 'Competing for Quality', which involved subjecting each government activity to regular reviews of whether the activity was necessary, whether it should be carried out by the department, privatised or turned over to an agency. Agencies proliferated in the 1990s, strongly encouraged by the government, and with general cross-party support. By the end of 1997 there were 138 executive agencies, as well as four government departments operating on 'Next Steps' lines.

Agencies have been widely regarded as a success: the increased information they have generated about the costs of various operations, and questioning of the reasons for undertaking any particular activity and the way in which it is undertaken, have led to efficiency gains and more professional management within the civil service. Yet there have also been difficulties. One of the most awkward has been that of political accountability. Agencies are a means of devolving managerial responsibility, but the political responsibility is retained by the minister. Therefore, where an agency is politically sensitive, the minister may well be reluctant not to intervene in its management. The most obvious case has been the prison service, where the degree of ministerial involvement in day-to-day decisions was notorious both before and after the service became an agency in 1993. Derek Lewis, its former director-general, has described the extent of involvement by ministers in the prison service (see box, p. 283).

It is clear that politically controversial activities cannot easily be made into successful agencies. The new government has been less keen than its predecessors to press further on with the Next Steps initiative, not least because it has become increasingly difficult to find more activities that are suitable for the agency approach. Instead it has sought to improve the performance of existing agencies since some of the claims for their success have been based on performance targets that were relatively unchallenging. The Conservative government had begun to

---

At arm's length from the minister?

The sacking of one Director General, the near sacking of a second over the early release of prisoners, regular rows, accusations of deception and a deterioration in the relations between the service and ministers provide incontrovertible evidence that the constitutional arrangements for the service are not working properly. Agency status has been a step in the right direction, but too often, under Michael Howard, it has left Prison Service staff unsure of who is calling the shots. The fuzzy relationship between ministers and the Director General makes it all the easier for prisons to be used as a political pawn, whereby changes in policy are made to meet short-term needs, rather than provide a better long-term service to the public. And the current constitutional arrangements are too dependent on the personal chemistry between the Home Secretary and the Director General of the day.

(Derek Lewis, former Director General of the Prison Service, in
Hidden Agendas: Politics, Law and Disorder, 1997, pp. 230–1)

---

experiment before the election with the use of information technology to provide a better service for those who had dealings with bodies such as the Benefits Agency or the Inland Revenue. The Labour government has placed this project at the centre of its policy for the public service. The 'Better Government' programme is intended to cut bureaucracy and improve service delivery. The project reviews government services from the user's perspective, with the aim that people should be able to deal with all central government agencies through a single contact. But much of the wider criticism of the way in which government services operate – reflected in the quotation from Peter Kemp on p. 281 – remains as a challenge.

The task force future?

The Blair government has brought no sign of a move away from the aims of the 'new public management'. Budgetary pressures still drive an interest in getting the most out of the resources available, while improvements in technology allow considerable advances in creating useful management information. The Conservative government initiated a radical (though little noticed) change in financial management in the form of resource accounting and budgeting, an accounting system which brings government departments closer in line with the accounting conventions of the private sector. The Labour government has continued this; and its Comprehensive Spending Review develops earlier exercises done by previous governments.

The Labour government has also placed a strong emphasis on bringing departments together to share more information, overcome boundary problems and co-operate on policy, in particular through task forces – which bring together civil servants from many departments and outside experts and practitioners – to get to grips with knotty problems that involve a number of different agencies. The Conservative government established a deregulation task force in the mid-1990s to identify laws which were unnecessarily restricting the freedom of businesses, and Labour has seen the task force model as a means of overcoming departmental obstruction and getting a co-ordinated focus on issues. The Social Exclusion Unit is a leading example of the task force approach (see box below).

Tackling social exclusion

Social exclusion is a shorthand label for what can happen when individuals or areas suffer from a combination of linked problems such as unemployment, poor skills, low incomes, poor housing, high crime environments, bad health and family breakdown. The Government has policies that are targeted at reducing all of these individually, but Government programmes have been less good at tackling the interaction between these problems or preventing them arising in the first place. The purpose of the unit is to help break this vicious circle and co-ordinate and improve government action to reduce social exclusion by first improving understanding of the key characteristics of social exclusion, and the impact on it of Government policies; and, secondly, by promoting solutions, encouraging co-operation, disseminating best practice and, where necessary, making recommendations for changes in policies and machinery or delivery mechanisms . . . in its first phase, the unit will also focus on improving mechanisms for integrating the work of departments, local authorities and other agencies at national level and on the ground, so money spent on excluded groups is used more effectively and has more chance of meeting its objectives. . . . The unit is part of the Economic and Domestic Affairs Secretariat in the Cabinet Office. It will report to me and work closely with the No. 10 Policy unit. It will be staffed by civil servants from other Whitehall departments and secondees from local authorities, voluntary bodies and other main agencies . . . The unit will draw extensively on outside expertise and research, and lock into relevant external networks to hear views from local authorities, business, voluntary organisations and other organisations/ individuals with experience of dealing with exclusion.

(The Prime Minister, announcing the establishment of the
Social Exclusion Unit, 8 December 1997)

The task force approach is one illustration of how recent governments have become willing to seek advice on policy and its implementation from outside the civil service as well as within it. A total of 30 task forces were set up in the period from the election in May 1997 to July 1998 on subjects as diverse as disability rights and football. The emphasis now is on an integrated means of understanding, preventing and tackling problems, which involves changing how government works. There is much talk of 'joined up' and 'holistic' government.

CONCLUSION

Prime Ministers have often been frustrated by the lack of power at the centre of government. The Prime Minister has a relatively small staff and the office has very limited capacity to undertake effective co-ordination of policy. Although connected at cabinet level, and with many formal and informal links at various levels, departments have a good deal of autonomy and even a strengthened Cabinet Office may have difficulty in altering this fundamental picture. It seems unlikely that the combination of more task forces and greater central control will lead quickly to an end to the traditional department. Too much of the system – not least both cabinet and ministerial responsibility – depends on it.

NOTES

1 Fifth Report from the Treasury and Civil Service Committee, *The Role of the Civil Service*, HC 27-I 1993–94, p. xiv.
2 HC 203 1983–4 para. 10, 12 January 1983.
3 House of Commons Debates, vol. 52, 26 January 1984, col. 1065.
4 House of Commons Debates, vol. 53, 9 February 1984, col. 1059–60.
5 Anthony Barker, *Public Administration*, vol. 76, no. 1, Spring 1998, 'Political responsibility for UK prison security: ministers escape again'.
6 Quoted in Peter Barberis (ed.), *The Whitehall Reader: The UK's Administrative Machine in Action* (Open University Press, 1996).
7 Peter Hennessy, *The Hidden Wiring: Unearthing the British Constitution* (Victor Gollancz, 1995), p. 103.
8 Leo Amery, 1947, quoted in Peter Hennessy, *The Hidden Wiring* (Victor Gollancz, 1995), p. 94.
9 Walter Bagehot, *The English Constitution*, with an introduction from Richard Crossman (Fontana, 1963).
10 Nigel Lawson, *The View from No. 11: Memoirs of a Tory Radical* (Bantam Press, 1992), p. 584.
11 House of Commons Debates, vol. 933, 16 June 1977, col. 552.
12 House of Commons Debates, vol. 261, 8 February 1932, col. 535.
13 See Roy Jenkins, *Tony Benn: A Political Biography* (Writers and Readers, 1980) p. 219; Tony Benn, *Against the Tide: Diaries 1973–76* (Hutchinson, 1989), pp. 274, 283.
14 House of Commons Debates, vol. 884, 23 January 1975, col. 1746.
15 Ibid., col. 1758.
16 Nigel Lawson, *The View from No. 11: Memoirs of a Tory Radical* (Bantam Press, 1992), p. 273.
17 Peter Hennessy and Andrew Arends, *Mr Attlee's Engine Room: Cabinet Committee Structure and the Labour Government 1945–51* (Strathclyde Papers on Government and Politics no. 26, 1983).
18 Further detail is given in *Cabinet Committee Business: A Guide for Departments*. Cabinet Office, 1997.
19 Sir Douglas Wass in Reith Lectures series 'Cabinet: directorate or directory?' *Listener*, 24 November 1983.

20 Quoted in Bernard Donoghue, *Prime Minister: The Conduct of Policy Under Harold Wilson and James Callaghan* (Cape, 1987).
21 Simon James, *British Cabinet Government*, 2nd edn (Routledge, 1999).
22 House of Commons Debates, vol. 180, 13 November 1990, cols. 461–5.
23 Independent, 17 June 1995, 'I'm a coalition government on my own, declares Major', cited in Peter Hennessy, *The Hidden Wiring: Unearthing the British Constitution* (Victor Gollancz, 1995).
24 J. M. Lee, G. W. Jones and June Burnham, *At the Centre of Whitehall: Advising the Prime Minister and Cabinet* (Macmillan, 1998), p. 250.
25 Peter Kemp and David Walker, *New Statesman*, 3 December 1997, 'The Prime Minister needs a machine to match the Treasury; your job is to build it'.
26 See Simon James, *British Cabinet Government*, 2nd edn (Routledge, 1999).
27 Quoted in Peter Riddell, *The Times*, 20 April 1998, 'Taking over the enterprise'.
28 Sarah Hogg and Jonathan Hill, *Too Close to Call* (Little Brown, 1995).
29 *The Times*, 5 January 1998, 'RIP Cabinet government'.
30 Rod Rhodes and Patrick Dunleavy (eds), *Prime Minister, Cabinet and Core Executive* (St Martin's Press, 1995).
31 Ibid.
32 Cabinet Office, *Public Bodies 1997*. This is the government's annual statistical digest of NDPBs. The term NDPB derives from the Pliatzky review of quangos ordered by Margaret Thatcher, which reported in 1980.
33 *EGO Trip: Extra Governmental Organisations in the UK and their Accountability* (Democratic Audit, 1994).
34 Anthony Barker (ed.), *Quangos in Britain: Government and the Networks of Public Policy Making* (Macmillan, 1982).
35 John Stewart, 'The rebuilding of public accountability' in *Accountability to the Public* (European Policy Forum, 1992).
36 George Howarth MP, 'Quangos and Political Donations to the Tory Party' (press release, 1993).
37 Tony Wright, *Beyond the Patronage State* (Fabian Society, 1995).
38 Cabinet Office, *Quangos: Opening the Doors* and *Quangos: Opening up Public Appointments*, 1998.
39 House of Commons Debates, vol. 68, 19 November 1984, cols. 57–8w.

FURTHER READING

Cabinet (Blackwell, 1986) by Peter Hennessy remains a readable introduction to the subject and is updated by *British Cabinet Government*, 2nd edn (Routledge, 1999) by Simon James. *The British Cabinet System* (Wheatsheaf, 1996) by Martin Burch and Ian Holliday has useful case studies of the Cabinet at work. Donald Shell and Richard Hodder Williams (eds), *Churchill to Major: The British Prime Ministership since 1945* (Hurst, 1995) looks at the interaction between Prime Minister and Cabinet and Sarah Hogg and Jonathan Hill's *Too Close to Call: Power and Politics – John Major in No 10* (Little Brown, 1995) is a lively account of the most recent premiership. *British Government: The Central Executive Territory* by Peter Madgwick (Philip Allen, 1991) summarises much of contemporary debate, but is now supplemented by Martin J. Smith's *The Core Executive in Britain* (Macmillan, 1999). *Ministers of the Crown* (Clarendon, 1997) by Rodney Brazier sets out the legal and constitutional duties of ministers. *The British Civil Service* (Prentice Hall/Harvester Wheatsheaf, 1995) by Robert Pyper gives a good recent history of developments in the civil service. *Whitehall* (Secker and Warburg, 1989) by Peter Hennessy remains an excellent guide to the culture of the civil service.

9 Governing beyond the centre

In the ideally-sized [administrative] unit a dissatisfied farmer anywhere within its boundaries ought to be able to travel by public transport to the administrative capital, horse-whip the responsible official, and get home again by public transport, all in the same day.

(unidentified respondent to the Kilbrandon Commission on the Constitution, Cmnd 5460, 1973, quoted in *Scotland's Parliament: Fundamentals for a New Scotland Act*, Constitution Unit, London, 1996, p. 11)

This chapter covers the following key aspects of the British political process beyond the centre:

- *The European Union.* The development of the EU and its constituent parts; the history of Britain's troubled relationship with Europe; and law-making in Europe and the ability of national parliaments to influence that process.
- *Devolution.* A brief history of devolution in Britain; arguments for and against devolution; and details of the Blair government's programme of devolution, including the powers of the new Scottish Parliament and National Assembly for Wales ('Welsh Assembly').
- *Northern Ireland.* The separate status of Northern Ireland; key dates in Ireland's history; and details of the Good Friday Belfast agreement and the Northern Ireland Assembly which was created in its wake.
- *Local Government.* The theory and frequently adversarial practice of central–local relations in Britain; the basic structure and organisation of local government; how it is financed; and the use of private contractors to carry out many of local government's key activities.

INTRODUCTION

Westminster remains the centre of the British political process, but not all activity is confined to the Westminster/Whitehall village. Important elements of the political process take place at international and sub-national levels. The diffusion of power upwards to the European and international levels, and downwards to the regional and local levels, has had a significant impact on the national political system.

Some international organisations of which Britain is a member

- United Nations (UN) (including various agencies such as UNICEF, UNESCO)
- European Union (EU)
- North Atlantic Treaty Organisation (NATO)
- Organisation for Economic Co-operation and Development (OECD)
- Organisation for Security and Co-operation in Europe (OSCE)
- World Trade Organisation (WTO)
- Commonwealth
- Council of Europe
- Western European Union (WEU)

Since the Second World War, one major characteristic of political development has been the growth in the number of multinational international organisations, covering a wide range of areas, in which national governments co-operate and act together. These include such bodies as the United Nations (UN), the World Trade Organisation (WTO), the North Atlantic Treaty Organisation (NATO), and the Organisation for Economic Co-operation and Development (OECD). All these have established binding commitments and obligations for national governments under international law, and operate principally on the basis of intergovernmental co-operation. Britain is a member of a range of international organisations (see box above), but the one which is most significant with regard to the domestic political process is the European Union.

At the sub-national level, the development of the welfare state and government regulation of a wide range of commercial and other activities has led to the development of increasingly complex local mechanisms for delivering government policy. Local government continues to be a major partner in the performance of many of the key activities of the state, such as education and community care. The profusion in recent years of quangos, an alternative method of providing public services at a local or national level, was considered in the previous chapter.

All of this has prompted attention to what is now generally known as the principle of subsidiarity, meaning (broadly speaking) that decisions should be taken at the most 'appropriate' level. The traditional view of Britain as a unitary state, with Parliament maintaining sovereignty over all things, is compatible with Parliament *lending* powers to other bodies in order to improve accountability or efficiency, but the question of what is the right balance between international, national and sub-national powers has proved controversial. Furthermore, membership of the EU requires member states to 'pool' their sovereignty in some areas, leading to complaints of a major and irrevocable diminution of parliamentary sovereignty. More recently, the devolution of political power to sub-national parliaments or assemblies, a major component of the Labour government's programme of constitutional reform, has come to the fore. Devolution has been widely accepted by politicians and observers of the political process where public support for it seems strong (particularly in Scotland and Northern Ireland), but some have argued that it will lead to a permanent loss of power from the centre.

It is important to look at the ways in which the British political system has adapted at both the international and domestic levels in order to meet these challenges, and at the development of new procedures and institutions, to get a fuller understanding of how the system works as a whole (although the full impact of the profound changes described in this chapter is only likely to become apparent after some years). An important task has been – and continues to be – ensuring that these new procedures and institutions meet the twin tests of efficiency and accountability.

THE EUROPEAN UNION

When the legislation to give effect to membership of the then European Community was laid before Parliament in 1972, the effects of membership on the British political process were described as being 'a situation for which there is no precedent in this country'.[1] Although regional and international co-operation is increasingly common, the specific nature of that co-operation in Europe and its impact on the political systems of the member states is unique.

Most international organisations operate primarily on the basis of inter-governmental co-operation, meaning that states have agreed to co-operate in a specific area or areas, usually through a common institution which operates on the basis of unanimity. This means that all participating states possess the right of veto. NATO provides a good example of such an organisation. The EU is unique in the extent to which it is *supranational* in nature. This means that the participating member states have agreed to create an institution capable of independent and coercive action, and to 'pool' their sovereignty in limited areas, establishing a new political and legal environment. Many international organisations have some supranational elements, but the EU has a much wider and deeper authority than any of the other international bodies of which Britain is a member.

The existing European Union has both supranational and intergovernmental elements. Historically, there has been tension between those member states who would like a more supranational EU, and those who would prefer to keep as much as possible on an intergovernmental basis. Britain has generally supported inter-governmental co-operation, and been resistant to increasing the supranational elements of the EU. The extent to which the European Union should be supranational has been amongst the major issues of debate throughout the Community's history. Linked to this is the debate regarding the future 'final destination' of the European Union. Advocates of a federal, or politically united Europe, have argued for a greater degree of supranationality. Others have rejected the concept of a 'United States of Europe' in favour of a looser association of sovereign states, and advocated maintaining co-operation on an inter-governmental basis as much as possible.

By 1994, the British government considered that up to one-third of all British law came from 'Brussels'. The term 'Brussels' has been used as shorthand to refer to the EU's complex institutions and procedures. This obscures the reality of the functioning of the EU, the way in which European law is made, and the role played by the British government and Parliament in the European political process.

Community of six to Union of fifteen

What is now known as the European Union (see box below) began life in 1951, with the Treaty of Paris. This established a European Coal and Steel Community (ECSC) between six European countries – West Germany, France, Italy, the Netherlands, Belgium and Luxembourg. Britain refused to take part. The ECSC placed the coal, steel and iron production of the participating countries under a common authority, and established a set of supranational institutions to administer the Community. A further step was taken towards integration when, in 1957, the same six countries signed the Treaty of Rome establishing the European Atomic Energy Community (Euratom) and the European Economic Community (EEC). Britain again refused to join.

The most significant of the three communities was the EEC, which was created to establish a huge 'common market' amongst the participating countries. In 1965 a merger treaty was agreed, which from 1967 (when it came into effect) unified the legislative and executive functions of Euratom, the EEC and the ECSC. The three communities became referred to as the European Community (EC). The Community had four major institutions: the Commission, the Council of Ministers, the European Parliament (EP), and the European Court of Justice (ECJ). In 1993, the Treaty on European Union (commonly known as the Maastricht Treaty), established the European Union (EU).

Europe: A note on terms

EU   Refers to the European Union established at Maastricht.

EC   Refers either to before Maastricht, or specifically to the first pillar of the EU.

EC/EU Used where the statement refers to both before and after Maastricht.

Exact terminology is often confused even at an official level.

The European Union created at Maastricht was based on three so-called 'pillars'. This term was used to demonstrate that there were three separate parts of the EU. The existing European Community, which was mostly supranational, became the first 'pillar'. The EC continues to exist as a distinct body, but now shares its institutions with the rest of the European Union. The second 'pillar' consisted of a new Common Foreign and Security Policy, which provided for co-operation in foreign policy matters. The third 'pillar' provided for co-operation in justice and home affairs. Examples of the areas covered by this 'pillar' include police and judicial co-operation across national borders on subjects such as organised crime, drug smuggling and terrorism. Both the second and the third pillar were based on intergovernmental co-operation, without the supranational elements of the EC first pillar.

From the original Community of six member states, successive rounds of enlargement increased the number of members of the EC/EU to fifteen by 1995 (see box below). Britain, Denmark and Ireland became members on 1 January 1973. Greece became a member on 1 January 1981, and Spain and Portugal joined on 1 January 1986. The most recent members, Austria, Finland and Sweden, became members of the European Union on 1 January 1995. Further enlargement to include countries of Central and Eastern Europe has been agreed in principle.

Member states of the European Union (1999)

- Germany, France, Italy, the Netherlands, Belgium, Luxembourg (1957)
- United Kingdom, Denmark, Ireland (1973) (Norway rejected membership)
- Greece (1981)
- Spain, Portugal (1986)
- Austria, Sweden, Finland (1995) (Norway rejected membership a second time)

The treaties establishing the EC created supranational institutions, empowered to act independently of national governments within their areas of competence as specified by the treaties, and a new legal order, establishing rights and obligations upon individuals and organisations. European law has *direct effect* on the individuals and organisations which it regulates, and the rights and obligations so created must be upheld by the domestic courts of the member states. It also has *primacy*, which means that it is superior to domestic (British) law. European law now affects a wide range of activities, from agriculture to employment legislation and the environment. The European Court of Justice (ECJ), which is independent of the member states, is charged with upholding the treaties and the body of Community law. Its judgements are binding upon the member states. The second and third pillars of the European Union are outside the Community's supranational institutions, and operate on an intergovernmental basis.

Each time the member states want to make changes to the powers and institutions of the EC/EU, it is necessary for them to agree a new treaty. Treaties are negotiated by the member states at an Intergovernmental Conference (IGC) and must be agreed unanimously. A new treaty must then be ratified in each member state according to their own constitutional arrangements. In some European countries, this often requires a referendum. In Britain, ratification is undertaken by the government after the 1972 European Communities Act has been appropriately amended by Parliament.

Since Britain joined the EC in 1973, there have been three major treaties which have developed the powers and institutions of the Community. The first was the Single European Act of 1986 (SEA). This created a legal base for the development of the single European market. It also included a number of policy areas not included in the existing EEC treaty, including environment, health and safety, and economic and social cohesion. This represented a significant extension of the involvement of EC institutions in issues previously dealt with in a national context. It also introduced the principle of qualified majority voting (QMV) in a wide range of areas connected with the single market. Member states now no longer had a veto over decisions in many areas of Community competence. In QMV, each country has a number of votes allocated to it on the basis of size. Large countries have more votes than small countries, and to block a proposal, a coalition of at least three states must be collected together. Qualified majority voting is only allowed where the treaties have explicitly specified it.

The second major treaty affecting the powers and institutions of the Community was the Treaty on European Union 1992. This established the two new 'pillars', as well as providing a legal base and timetable for achieving economic and monetary union within the first, EC pillar. It also included the principle of 'subsidiarity', stating that in areas outside its exclusive competence, the Community 'shall take action . . . only if and in so far as the objectives of the proposed action cannot be sufficiently achieved by the Member States and can therefore . . . be better achieved by the Community'.[2] Subsidiarity was a very popular concept at the time of the Maastricht Treaty, and means that decisions should be taken at the most 'appropriate' level. In the UK, this was interpreted to mean that decisions should be taken at the national rather than European level wherever possible. Some other European countries have interpreted 'appropriate' to mean the lowest possible level, and therefore include regional and local government levels within their understanding of the subsidiarity principle. However, the Maastricht Treaty contained no clear definition of subsidiarity, and therefore no clear division of responsibilities between different levels of government – whether national, regional, local or European.

Lastly, the Amsterdam Treaty signed on 2 October 1997 transferred a range of 'third pillar' (justice and home affairs) matters out of intergovernmental co-operation into the first, EC pillar. This means that these matters will now be dealt with according to the far more supranational EC procedures and institutions. A limited number of new competencies for the EU as a whole were also introduced. This most recent treaty included a new protocol on subsidiarity, which provides a clearer definition of the concept and makes it subject to the ECJ.

Britain and Europe: A troubled relationship

When Britain became a member of the European Community on 1 January 1973, it was more than ten years after its original application to join. Britain had declined to participate in both the Treaty of Paris of 1951, and in the Treaties of Rome of 1957, but by the 1960s political thinking in Britain had changed. In 1961 Britain submitted an application to join. Both this and a second application in 1967 failed due to disagreement over the terms of accession and opposition to British membership from the President of France, Charles de Gaulle. After de Gaulle's replacement by Georges Pompidou in 1969, formal agreement to open negotiations was finally reached. The Treaty of Accession was signed early in 1972, the legal basis for membership was provided by the European Communities Act 1972 (see box below), and Britain became a member of the EC at the beginning of 1973.

Britain's relationship with Europe: The legal basis

General
implementation
of Treaties

2(1) All such rights, powers, liabilities, obligations and restrictions from time to time created by or arising under the Treaties, and all such remedies and procedures from time to time provided for by or under the Treaties, as in accordance with the Treaties are without further enactment to be given legal effect or used in the United Kingdom shall be recognised and available in law, and be enforced, allowed and followed accordingly [. . .]

(European Communities Act 1972, section 2(1))

The question of EC membership has always been controversial in Britain. Both the Labour and Conservative parties have been divided on the issue, and public support for membership of the EC/EU has varied considerably over time (Figure 9.1).

The Conservative Party supported British membership from 1961, and Mrs Thatcher was elected in 1979 on a pro-membership platform, although her government, and that of her successor John Major, became increasingly sceptical about further moves towards political and economic integration. More recently, and in opposition, the Conservative Party voted against the legislation implementing the Amsterdam treaty, the first time the party has formally opposed major European legislation. Visible divisions within the party have become more apparent than ever, in particular on the subject of Economic and Monetary Union (EMU, the single currency).

Labour's policy towards EC membership has changed a number of times. It was the Labour Prime Minister Harold Wilson who submitted Britain's application for membership in 1967, but only five years later he led his party in opposition to the membership terms negotiated by the Conservative government. Labour won the election of 1974 on a pledge to renegotiate the terms, and they were submitted to a referendum in 1975. Divisions in the party were such that the Cabinet was split almost down the middle. Wilson could not afford to have nearly half his cabinet resigning at once over the matter, so decided to take the

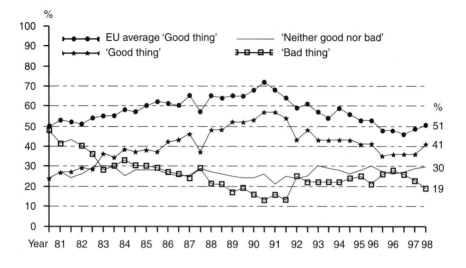

Figure 9.1 Support for European Union membership (United Kingdom), 1981–98

Source: *Standard Eurobarometer 49*, figure 2.5a, European Commission, September 1998.

unusual step of waiving collective cabinet responsibility to allow ministers to campaign on opposing sides. Although the results of the referendum supported continuing British membership of the EC, the divisions within the Labour Party did not disappear. In opposition from 1979 Labour adopted a policy of withdrawal from the EC. During the 1980s, the party moved back towards support for membership, and since the Labour victory at the general election of May 1997 the British government has adopted a more positive tone towards the European Union, in particular in its policy towards Economic and Monetary Union (EMU).

Opposition to (and support for) British membership of the EC/EU has always cut across party lines. The 1972 European Communities Act was fought bitterly by opponents of membership on both the left and the right, as was the 1978 European Assembly Elections Bill, which provided for direct elections to the European Parliament. The 1992 European Communities (Amendment) Bill, which was necessary to implement the Maastricht Treaty, took up 163 hours in committee on the floor of the House of Commons. It was passed only with great difficulty, and with the government making a number of issues votes of confidence (so putting the survival of the government itself at stake) to ensure passage. This was another episode in Britain's long-troubled relationship with Europe (see box, p. 295).

It has been argued that European law, as having primacy and direct effect in member states, conflicts in principle with the doctrine of parliamentary sovereignty. According to this doctrine, no court in Britain can question the validity of an Act of Parliament, and no law-making body, whether in Britain or outside, can be superior to Parliament. Yet membership of the EC passed policy-making

---

Britain's history in Europe

1951   Treaty of Paris (European Coal and Steel Community). Britain does not join

1957   Treaties of Rome (European Economic Community and Euratom). Britain does not join

1963   first British application to join vetoed

1967   second British application vetoed

1970   British application renewed under Heath's Conservative government

1973   Britain becomes a member of the European Community (with Ireland and Denmark)

1975   referendum on renegotiated terms of membership results in two-thirds majority in favour of continuing British membership of the EC

1986   Single European Act, introducing the single market programme and majority voting in the Council of Ministers

1992   Treaty on European Union (Maastricht Treaty). Britain secures opt-outs on EMU and the Social Chapter

1992   (September) Black Wednesday – sterling forced out of the Exchange Rate Mechanism (ERM)

1997   Treaty of Amsterdam

1997   (October) Chancellor Gordon Brown announces that Britain will not join the single currency in the first 'wave', but sees no constitutional bar on joining

1998   opening of enlargement negotiations with Poland, Czech Republic, Hungary, Slovenia, Estonia, Cyprus.

1999   (January) launch of Economic and Monetary Union (EMU) among eleven member states. Britain does not join

---

competence in various sectors to the institutions of the Community, legislation passed by those bodies would not require the assent of Parliament, and the courts were to have the power to give precedence to EC law over domestic British law. This was given legal effect by the 1972 European Communities Act. In legal terms, Parliament can take away the domestic effect of European Community law by repealing the 1972 European Communities Act, although it cannot take away Britain's international obligations. British courts have taken the view that, as long as the 1972 European Communities Act remains in force, British legislation should be interpreted in line with European law. It is unclear what would happen in the unlikely event that Parliament intentionally passed legislation which was contrary to European law. The terms of the 1972 European Communities Act give precedence to European law over domestic law, but it would amount to a constitutional revolution for a British court to strike down or refuse to apply legislation duly passed by Parliament. The constitutional significance of this issue is discussed further in Chapter 2.

Making laws in Europe

At the European level, laws are made quite differently from national legislation. In most cases, legislation must first be proposed by the European Commission. Such a proposal must be explicitly based on rights and powers given in the Treaties. The Commission cannot act in areas which are not within its competence according to the treaties and, should it try to do so, legislation may be rejected by the Council or struck down by the European Court of Justice (ECJ). Within the European Community 'pillar' of the EU, the Commission has the exclusive right of initiative, which means that only the Commission may bring forward proposals for legislation. The Commission is sometimes called the 'guardian of the treaties', because it has the power to bring a member state before the ECJ for alleged nonfulfilment of treaty obligations. For obvious political and public relations reasons, the member states and the Commission are generally reluctant to pursue cases all the way to the Court, and most disputes are resolved at an early stage. The Commission consists of full-time officials, headed by twenty commissioners, appointed by the member states, but required to renounce national allegiances. The Commission is not elected.

The main decision-making body of the EU is the Council of Ministers (see Figure 9.2). This comprises ministers from every member government, each meeting drawing together the ministers with responsibility for the sector involved. For example, an Agriculture Council would bring together the ministers for agriculture from each member state, while the Transport Council brings together the ministers responsible for transport. The Council of Ministers makes decisions in principle on legislative proposals, which are subject to different processes according to the treaties. Some proposals can be decided on the basis of qualified majority voting (this includes most legislation concerned with the single market), which means that no single member state has a veto over decisions. Other proposals must be agreed on the basis of unanimity, meaning that each member state has a veto. Areas which require unanimity are usually the most controversial or politically sensitive areas. The principle of QMV is a controversial one, but in practice the Council tends to avoid forcing a vote wherever possible. Discussion is often continued until a consensus is reached, and QMV is only used on about 20 per cent of eligible issues.[3]

The European Parliament (EP), which consists of 626 directly elected MEPs, has certain powers to approve and amend legislation, although it cannot initiate legislation. Some legislation is subject to a procedure called co-decision, which gives the EP an equal position within the legislative process, and allows it to reject or amend legislation which has been approved in principle by the Council. In other areas the powers of the EP are more restricted.

Community legislation usually takes one of two forms. *Regulations* have the immediate force of law in all member states. These are mainly highly detailed or technical measures. *Directives* are binding as to the effect to be achieved, but leave the form and method of implementation to the member states. These are usually more policy-oriented legislation, although there is no clear rule about which form

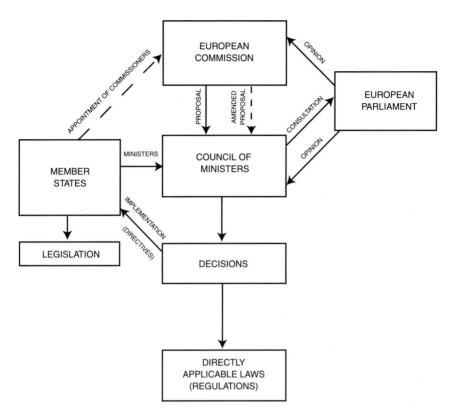

Figure 9.2 The European Union's decision-making process

of legislation should be used in each case. Directives have to be carried into UK law, either by primary or secondary legislation, often under the European Communities Act. In addition, the Commission can also issue *decisions*, which are more like administrative than legislative measures, and are binding but not of general application.

Where Britain fits in

Central to the debate on the relationship between the European and national level is the question of national governmental and parliamentary control and influence in relation to the European system. As a predominantly supranational organisation, the EU has a high level of independence from individual member states, but there are a number of points at which national governments and parliaments have some input into the European decision-making system. National governments are represented by government ministers in the Council of Ministers, and therefore represent government policy in the European legislative process. One British expert on European matters has said that, 'the only clear point of influence, real influence and real leverage, for any national parliament . . . is on ministers who represent the Government of this country.'[4] However, the ability of an individual member state to gain its desired outcome in the Council is limited in areas where qualified majority voting applies, as no single member state can veto legislation with which it does not agree.

Political input from the governments of the member states is provided by the twice-yearly meetings of the European Council. This is not formally a European institution, but in practice it has come to play an important role. The European Council consists of the top political leader in each country, often assisted by their foreign ministers, and provides overall political direction to the Community. Member states take it in turns to assume the presidency of the European Council for six months, and during that time they have some opportunity to influence the development of the EU through setting agendas and chairing meetings. The European Council usually meets once during each presidency to set the overall political agenda, and to resolve any potentially intractable problems.

The British Parliament only has a limited function within the Community legislative system. It has some role when legislation is required to implement Community directives, but has no power to negate them. Amendments to the treaties which make up the European Union usually have to be approved by Parliament through amendments to the 1972 European Communities Act. In the case of the Amsterdam Treaty of 1997, there were changes affecting the powers of the European Parliament, which meant that amendments also had to be made to the European Parliamentary Elections Act of 1978. The Maastricht Treaty included the first treaty reference to the role of national parliaments, with a declaration encouraging the 'greater involvement of national parliaments in the activities of the European Union' through the exchange of information between the EP and national parliaments, and the granting of reciprocal facilities. However, national parliaments still play little formal role in the Community decision-making process.

The major way in which Parliament can play a role in the Community process is through control of ministers' activities in the Council. As representatives of national government, ministers are responsible to Parliament for the decisions they take in the Council. The Council of Ministers takes its decisions behind closed doors, which severely limits the extent to which national parliaments can hold ministers accountable for decisions made in Council. Since the early 1990s the results of votes have generally been published, and under the Amsterdam Treaty the results of votes and any explanations or statements in the minutes will be made public. This provision will help to make ministers more accountable to Parliament, and increase democratic accountability in the European Union. However, the bulk of Council discussions will still not be made public, which limits the effectiveness of national scrutiny and control procedures.

Soon after joining the EC, the British Parliament established a system to scrutinise proposals from the Commission. Similar arrangements exist in most other national parliaments in EU countries. The House of Commons European

Scrutiny Committee concentrates on the scrutiny of documents drawn up by the Commission for submission to the Council of Ministers or European Council. The committee is charged with assessing the legal and political importance of documents, but it does not consider the merits of proposals and policies. It also does not consider documents arising from the second and third pillars (foreign and security policy, and justice and home affairs). Approximately 1,000 documents are deposited each year, and approximately 90 are recommended by the committee for further consideration (debate) by the House. Ministers and expert witnesses can also be called to give evidence to the committee.

The scrutiny procedure is intended to increase Parliament's influence and control over the position taken by British ministers in the Council of Ministers. Under the terms of a resolution passed in 1980 and modified in 1990, ministers are limited in what they can agree to in the Council prior to completion of scrutiny by the House. This is called the scrutiny reserve, and provides that a minister should not give agreement to any proposal for EC legislation which has not completed its scrutiny procedure in the House. There are a few exceptions to this, and some documents – usually less than 10 per cent – are agreed before the scrutiny stage is completed by the House.[5] A scrutiny reserve has no formal legal status in the Council's procedure, but it is recognised by all member states as a practical constraint on those ministers who are subject to it.

Parliament also has the opportunity to question ministers in departmental select committees, for example the Foreign Secretary and Home Secretary appear before the foreign affairs and home affairs committees respectively before each meeting of the European Council. Members of parliament may also raise European issues in question time and in debates. Two general debates are held in the House of Commons each year, before the twice-yearly meetings of the European Council, and there are debates on subjects such as the EC budget, agricultural price fixing, and fishing. However, despite the relatively efficient scrutiny procedures, and the scrutiny reserve system, there are constitutional limitations on the capacity of both Houses to have a continuous and substantial impact on the making of European legislation. Neither House has any power to negate Commission proposals, a position they share with other national legislatures. Parliament is also limited in the time and resources it can devote to European issues.

A new Protocol on the Role of National Parliaments was included in the Amsterdam Treaty, which attempts to meet some of the criticism from national parliaments about the inadequacy of access to European documents sufficiently quickly for them to be scrutinised before decisions are taken in the Council of Ministers.[6] The protocol will require a period of six weeks' delay between a legislative proposal being made available by the Commission in all languages to the European Parliament and the Council, and a decision being taken by the Council. This is based on a proposal submitted during the Intergovernmental Conference (IGC) by the British government, on the basis of a recommendation by the European Scrutiny Committee. This indicates how national legislatures can play a role in European negotiations, even if a very circumscribed one.

The conduct of relations with the EC/EU has primarily been a matter for the Foreign and Commonwealth Office. However, the European Union has also had a major effect on the way that policy is made in other government departments. Many government departments now have close links with their counterparts in other national ministries and in the Commission. Responsibility for negotiating and implementing Community agreements and legislation often falls to national departments and their civil servants. For example, the Ministry of Agriculture is heavily involved in the Community Common Agricultural Policy, whilst the Single Market programme was primarily overseen by the Department of Trade and Industry.

Britain in Brussels

Each member state is represented in Brussels by its Permanent Representative, who is a kind of ambassador to the EU. The British presence (known as UKREP) is headed by a career diplomat, with staff drawn mostly from the Foreign and Commonwealth Office, although officials from other government departments are sometimes seconded to Brussels as well. Permanent representatives participate in an important and powerful committee called COREPER (the French acronym for the Committee of Permanent Representatives), which prepares and vets proposals for discussion before Council meetings.

As decisions which affect Britain are taken at the European level, so lobbying has grown up at a European level too. Political parties, local authorities, businesses, financial and public institutions, have all established offices or representatives in Brussels to keep them informed of developments and to attempt to influence policy in their favour. Each of the German regional governments, the Länder, have offices in Brussels, as do other regional governments from around Europe. The Scottish Parliament established an office in Brussels in October 1999 and the Welsh Assembly is considering whether to do the same.

Looking ahead

As has been seen, the European Union already exerts a substantial effect on the British political process. Two major developments will further increase its impact. These are the launch of Economic and Monetary Union (EMU, the single currency), and the opening of enlargement negotiations with a number of countries from Central and Eastern Europe.

On 1 January 1999, all EU countries apart from Britain, Sweden, Denmark and Greece, participated in the launch of EMU. This has created a huge single currency zone across much of western Europe, with major implications for the economic and political management of member states and the EU as a whole which will continue to be felt well into the future. Britain will not join in the 'first wave', but the launch of such a project by most of the countries of the EU is almost certain to have a significant impact on the country, economically and politically, as well as on the operation of the EU itself. If Britain decides to join the single currency at a later date, this would have fundamental implications for its management of economic and financial policy.

Meanwhile, enlargement negotiations with five Central European countries (Poland, Hungary, the Czech Republic, Slovenia, Estonia), plus Cyprus, were launched in early 1998. In addition there are a further five or more countries of Central and Eastern Europe waiting to begin enlargement negotiations, and the long-standing question of Turkey's application to join remains unresolved. Enlargement on this scale will bring problems for the EU – its existing institutions, designed for a Community of six, are already strained in a Union of fifteen, and expansion to the poorer countries of Central and Eastern Europe will increase the pressures on Community policies and on the Community budget. Proposals for substantial reform of the EU's institutions were postponed at Amsterdam due to widespread lack of agreement, but they will return to the agenda once the enlargement process begins. It is clear that with substantial future enlargement of the EU imminent, the debate about the future shape and nature of the EU will continue, including the relationship between the European Union and its constituent national parts. The role of the European issue in British politics is likely to prove as controversial and significant in the period ahead as it has been in the past.

DEVOLUTION

While Britain's involvement in the EU requires the recognition of a new source of political authority outside its traditional boundaries, devolution – while no less challenging for Westminster – involves a ceding of power in the opposite direction. The term devolution, a familiar idea in British politics whose time has finally come, usually refers to *political devolution*, devolving political decision-making power from the centre to sub-national units. This is different from *administrative devolution*, which is about the creation of local divisions or departments within the administrative machinery of central government. Political devolution is also different from *federalism*, which seeks a settlement based on a constitutionally guaranteed division of powers between the national (federal) government and a number of semi-autonomous states or regions. By contrast, political devolution involves no loss of sovereignty at the centre, for powers which are devolved could, in theory at least, be taken back again by Act of Parliament at some point in the future. Devolution therefore stops well short of the calls for *independence* which have been heard for some time now in Scotland and Wales (and even Cornwall). Nevertheless, some see devolution as a stepping-stone to independence. Prior to the 1997 election, the debate between Labour and the Liberal Democrats on the one hand, and the Conservatives on the other, was focused on whether devolution would strengthen the United Kingdom by enabling it to accommodate divergent political demands in different parts of the country, or lead to its eventual disintegration.

The United Kingdom is, uniquely, composed of four countries with different histories and different political traditions. A large degree of administrative devolution already existed in Scotland, Northern Ireland and Wales before the Blair government came to power. Each has a Secretary of State who represents the interests of that country in the Cabinet. Scotland and Wales have separate civil service departments to deal with most matters within each country, as opposed to the subject-based departments in England. In addition, Scotland has a separate legal system. In Northern Ireland most day-to-day government business is carried out by a separate, subject-based Northern Ireland civil service, but certain matters including security are dealt with by the Northern Ireland Office which is part of the main UK civil service. There have also been varying degrees of administrative devolution in England at different times during the twentieth century, such as the Government Offices for the Regions created in 1994. However, prior to constitutional reforms introduced by the Blair government, the power to make decisions on the main political issues of the day rested entirely with the UK Cabinet and the Westminster Parliament.

Scotland and Wales

The demand for 'home rule' (as devolution was formerly known) for Scotland and Wales emerged in the late nineteenth century. This cause was espoused by the Liberal Prime Minister Gladstone, but with the decline of the Liberal Party during the early part of the twentieth century and the adoption of other priorities by the Labour Party, devolution faded from national politics until the growing strength of the Scottish National Party and Plaid Cymru (the Welsh nationalist party) forced it back onto the agenda in the late 1960s and early 1970s. The nationalist parties had once sought devolution but now they demanded independence. This threatened the two main parties and over the next few years they both sought to come to terms with the new politics of devolution (see box, p. 305).

In May 1968 Edward Heath, Conservative Leader of the Opposition, made a speech which became known as the Declaration of Perth. He proposed the creation of a directly elected Scottish assembly and suggested that devolution was necessary as a counterweight to the centralising tendencies of the EEC. Labour, on the other hand, did not formally adopt devolution in Scotland as a policy until just before the October 1974 election. Labour had been committed to a Welsh Assembly since 1966, but the Conservatives preferred an Advisory Council to assist the Secretary of State.

The Conservative election manifesto for 1970 promised partial devolution for Scotland (with Westminster retaining the final say over legislation), but the Heath government did not bring forward proposals for a Scottish assembly. The Royal Commission on the Constitution (known as the Kilbrandon Commission), which had been created by Harold Wilson in 1968, reported in October 1973, towards the end of Edward Heath's period in office.[7] The commission was split on the devolution issue, but the majority report and an accompanying minority report both favoured devolution in varying degrees. The Labour government of 1974–9 eventually succeeded in pushing through Bills to create devolved assemblies in Scotland and Wales, but at great political cost as the Labour Party was split on the

Devolution: For and against

The following arguments were deployed before the creation of the Scottish parliament. They are mainly taken from the Scottish Constitutional Convention's 1995 report *Scotland's Parliament, Scotland's Right* and the Conservatives' 1997 Scottish general election manifesto. Many of the same arguments, sometimes with a different emphasis and perhaps a greater or lesser degree of conviction in some cases, have been used about devolution in other parts of the UK.

For

- The Scots' strong sense of national identity leads to a demand for a large degree of self-government.
- The political arithmetic of the United Kingdom means that Scots risk having their affairs managed by a government against which they have voted not narrowly but overwhelmingly.
- There is a lack of democratic control over many aspects of Scottish life 'from Scottish water to Scottish Opera' which are run by quangos – the so-called 'democratic deficit'.
- Government from London leads to perceived and genuine practical difficulties due to its physical remoteness from Scotland.
- Scotland has particular economic needs which will not be met by policies designed for the United Kingdom as a whole.
- The Scottish people desire a higher level of welfare services than Westminster has been prepared to provide in recent years; devolution would enable them to make political choices of this kind and bear any additional costs stemming from their decisions.
- The creation of a Scottish parliament is 'the settled will of the people of Scotland' as demonstrated in opinion polls, election results (and, in September 1997, in the result of the referendum).

Against

- Scottish influence in the British Parliament and government will be weakened.
- Scotland's influence in Europe will be weakened (it will not have separate negotiating rights).
- An extra 'tartan tax' imposed uniquely on Scotland will make Scotland the highest taxed part of the United Kingdom and a less attractive place for companies to locate.
- Financial tensions will be created between a Scottish parliament and Westminster, endangering Scotland's funding, 97 per cent of which will be determined at Westminster.

continued

- The West Lothian question (named after the former constituency of the Labour MP Tam Dalyell) will 'poison democratic government'. Put simply, this is the proposition that after devolution takes place, Scottish MPs at Westminster should not be able to vote on English matters if English MPs cannot vote on Scottish matters.
- Tensions between a Scottish parliament and local government will be created: a Scottish parliament could take for itself many of the powers held by councils.
- Checks and balances on Scottish legislation will be removed – the proposed parliament will have no equivalent to the House of Lords.
- The administrative costs of the Scottish parliament will be considerable.
- By and large the existing arrangements serve Scotland well; to introduce constitutional innovations which are ill-thought out 'would corrode the strong bonds underpinning our Union'.

issue. After Margaret Thatcher became leader of the Conservative Party in 1975, the Tories took a strongly anti-devolutionist line (although there was, initially, some dissent on the issue within the party).

The Scottish Assembly proposed in 1978 would have had legislative powers while the Welsh Assembly would only have been given executive powers (that is, the powers of the Secretary of State for Wales). The Scotland Act and Wales Act of 1978 made the creation of the new assemblies subject to popular approval by referendum – this had originally been a wrecking device introduced by anti-devolutionists in earlier Bills. Although in Scotland the people voted yes in the 1979 referendum, it was not in sufficient numbers to meet the threshold which the legislation required, 40 per cent of the electorate (this was another wrecking device which the government had not been able to quash). The next referendum, nearly twenty years later, was to be a different story (see box, p. 305).

The election of Margaret Thatcher as Prime Minister in 1979 temporarily removed devolution from the forefront of British politics, but the issue gradually resurfaced, fuelled in part by the growing unpopularity of the Conservative government in Scotland and Wales. Many felt that the Conservatives had no mandate to govern there, and the use of Scotland as a testing ground for the unpopular Community Charge or 'poll tax' in 1989 contributed to feelings of alienation from government at Westminster. In Wales the 'democratic deficit', the belief that too many aspects of the government of Wales were being given to unaccountable quangos, fuelled the pressure for devolution. Demands for regional government also resurfaced in those parts of England which felt most isolated from politics at Westminster, particularly the North East. The Major government introduced limited administrative and parliamentary reforms with the intention of further cementing Scotland's place in the Union but these did not make a deep impression on the Scottish public.

A discussion group, the Scottish Constitutional Convention (SCC), was founded in March 1989 to promote 'the sovereign right of the Scottish people to

Referendums in Scotland and Wales: 1979 and 1997

Scotland			Wales		
1979 – devolution			*1979 – devolution*		
Yes	1,230,937	51.6%	Yes	243,048	20.3%
No	1,153,502	48.4%	No	956,330	79.7%
Yes as % of electorate		32.9%	Yes as % of electorate		11.9%
Turnout[a]		63.6%	Turnout[a]		58.8%
1997 – Parliament			*1997 – Assembly*		
Yes	1,775,045	74.3%	Yes	559,419	50.3%
No	614,400	25.7%	No	552,698	49.7%
Yes as % of electorate		44.7%	Yes as % of electorate		25.2%
Turnout[b]		60.2%	Turnout		50.1%
1997 – tax varying powers					
Yes	1,512,889	63.5%			
No	870,263	36.5%			
Yes as % of electorate		38.1%			
Turnout[b]		60.2%			

[a] Adjusted to take account of changes in register since qualification date.
[b] Higher of number of people voting on Parliament or tax-varying powers.

determine the form of Government best suited to their needs'. Labour and the Liberal Democrats participated, but the Conservatives and the SNP stayed away (see box, pp. 303–4). However, the SCC was very successful in attracting representatives from the whole range of Scottish 'civil society', including the churches, local government, business, the unions, women and ethnic minorities, and so on. After a long gestation the convention's blueprint for a Scottish parliament emerged in November 1995: *Scotland's Parliament, Scotland's Right*. The proposals contained in the Scotland Bill which was published just over two years later had much in common with this earlier document.

Prior to the 1997 election Labour adapted its policy on devolution in Scotland and Wales in order to pre-empt Conservative attacks, which had been a prominent theme of John Major's general election campaign in 1992. Devolution would only proceed if accepted by a majority vote in a referendum. In Scotland the referendum would also contain a separate question on whether the Scottish Parliament should be given the ability to raise its own taxes (limited to an additional 3p on the rate of income tax). In order to undermine opposition in Parliament, the poll would take place prior to the bill setting up the devolved assemblies being passed (for procedural reasons, constitutional bills take up a great deal of parliamentary time if strongly opposed and devolution therefore had the potential to crowd out much of

---

Devolution for Scotland and Wales: Key dates in the twentieth century

1925   The Welsh Nationalist Party – later known as Plaid Cymru – is founded

1934   Scottish National Party founded

1968   Ted Heath proposes devolution for Scotland in the 'Declaration of Perth'

1973   Report of the Kilbrandon Commission on the constitution

1974   Labour returns to power committed to devolution for Scotland and Wales. After the October election SNP has 11 MPs and Plaid Cymru 3

1978   Bills to devolve power to Scotland and Wales passed by Parliament, but are not implemented following referendums

1989   Scottish Constitutional Convention (SCC) founded

1995   SCC's blueprint for a Scottish parliament published

1997   Labour government elected. Referendums on devolution produce a clear 'yes' majority in Scotland, but a narrow 'yes' victory in Wales

1998   Scotland Act and Wales Act passed

1999   First elections for Scottish Parliament and Welsh Assembly held on 6 May. Power formally devolved on 1 July.

---

the rest of Labour's programme). Labour's tactics provoked criticism from both sides of the debate: pro-devolutionists thought a referendum unnecessary, since devolution was to form a key part of Labour's manifesto, while anti-devolutionists were unhappy about putting the question to the people before the fine detail of the scheme had been enacted by Parliament or even published in a bill.

After Labour's election victory the referendums on devolution for Scotland and Wales were held in September 1997. The people voted in favour – convincingly in Scotland, narrowly in Wales – and the Bills to create devolved assemblies in both countries commenced their passage through Parliament not long afterwards. The legislation set out how the new bodies would work (see box, pp. 307–9). The first elections were held in May 1999 (see box, p. 307) and powers were formally transferred on 1 July 1999.

The issue of money is likely to loom large in the new arrangements. The *Barnett formula*, which will be used to calculate the Welsh Assembly and Scottish Parliament's Treasury grant entitlement, ensures that *changes* to spending in the different countries of the United Kingdom are in line with their relative population levels. In fact, the system perpetuates a higher level of per capita public expenditure in Scotland, Wales and Northern Ireland than in England. Politicians in those countries usually maintain that a higher level of funding is necessary to provide the same level of public services outside England, but there has been no recent official attempt to establish to what extent this is true. The Treasury may view the Barnett

The first devolved elections in Scotland and Wales: 6 May 1999

Scotland		*Wales*	
Labour	56	Labour	28
SNP	35	Plaid Cymru	17
Conservative	18	Conservative	9
Liberal Democrat	17	Liberal Democrat	6
Other	3	**Total**	**60**
Total	**129**		

Labour failed to win an overall majority in either country. In Scotland, Labour and the Liberal Democrats entered a formal coalition, with Labour's Donald Dewar as First Minister and the Lib Dems' Jim Wallace as Deputy First Minister. In Wales, Labour decided to form a minority government, with Alun Michael becoming First Secretary.

The Scottish Parliament and Welsh Assembly: How they work

In July 1999 the Scottish Parliament and Welsh Assembly assumed responsibility for a wide range of matters affecting Scotland and Wales, but the nature of their powers is different. The devolved powers are those which were previously the responsibility of the Secretaries of State for Scotland and Wales, and include:

- Health and personal social services
- Education and training
- Local government
- Housing
- Aspects of economic development
- Transport
- The Environment, including the natural and built heritage
- Agriculture, forestry, fisheries and food
- Sport and the arts.

In Scotland, responsibility for criminal and civil law was also devolved to the new Parliament. Certain powers which operated on a common basis throughout the United Kingdom before devolution are retained by Westminster (in Scotland these are known as the reserved powers). They include:

- Some constitutional matters
- Foreign policy, including relations with Europe
- Defence

continued

- Macro-economic policy and taxation
- Overseas trading policy
- Employment legislation
- Social security
- Broadcasting.

Both the Scottish Parliament and the Welsh Assembly have an executive arm which operates in a similar way to the British government and will be held to account by the Parliament/Assembly. The Scottish Executive is headed by the First Minister and the Executive Committee of the Welsh Assembly (which is something of a hybrid between Whitehall-style cabinet government and the committee-based approach traditional in local government) is headed by the First Secretary. The main difference between the powers of the Scottish and Welsh devolved bodies is that the Scottish Parliament has full law-making powers over the areas for which it is responsible, but the Welsh Assembly cannot alter the basic framework of the law contained in Acts of Parliament, known as *primary legislation*. Within this basic framework, however, it shares with the Scottish Parliament the power to make rules and regulations in what is known as *secondary legislation*. For example, in Wales the detail of the school curriculum and the designation of environmentally sensitive areas are set out in secondary legislation.

Both countries remain integral parts of the United Kingdom, and the Queen is still Head of State. The Parliament at Westminster is and will remain sovereign. Scottish and Welsh MPs will continue to play a 'full and constructive part' there, but the number of Scottish seats will be reviewed due to Westminster's loss of law-making powers over the powers devolved to the Scottish Parliament. There are still Secretaries of State for Scotland and Wales, Westminster politicians who will represent Scottish and Welsh interests within the British government.

The main source of finance for both devolved bodies is a grant from the Treasury calculated according to what is known as the *Barnett formula*, equivalent to the budgets previously assigned to the Scottish Office and Welsh Office. This is worth around £7 billion to the Welsh Assembly and £14.5 billion to the Scottish Parliament (which will also have the power to increase or decrease the basic rate of income tax set by the UK Parliament by up to 3p). They will use this income principally to allocate resources to public services such as local authorities and the NHS. Given the budgetary constraints which have become a way of life for public services in Britain, this is likely to be a sensitive task.

Both bodies will supervise local government and quangos, and will have the power to limit local authority expenditure by means of *council tax capping*. The Scottish Parliament will also be able to alter the primary legislation within which councils and quangos operate.

The Scottish Parliament and the Welsh Assembly are elected using

continued

an *additional member system* (a form of proportional representation or PR) designed to combine the benefits of a constituency link for members with a closer relationship between votes cast and seats won than under the traditional *first-past-the-post* system. In Scotland there are, for the time being, 129 members of the Scottish Parliament (MSPs), seventy-three directly elected on a constituency basis plus fifty-six additional members chosen from party lists allocated to ensure the overall result more directly reflects the share of votes cast for each party. Each Scottish Parliament will have a four-year fixed term. The number of MSPs will be reduced when, prior to the election after next the number of Scottish MPs at Westminster is reduced. The Welsh Assembly has sixty members (AMs), also elected every four years, with forty members representing constituencies and the remaining twenty selected from party lists.

formula less favourably after devolution takes place, especially if the Scottish Parliament levies extra income tax and allows local government to set higher levels of council tax. On the other hand, any attempt to claw back money from Scotland might endanger Labour's electoral support there.

And England?

Devolution in England, also known as *regionalism*, has been famously described as 'the dog that never barked' because of its failure to make a stronger impact on English politics.[8] The 1992 Labour manifesto promised that elected regional governments would eventually be created in England, but policy developments in the party since then have seen a watering down of Labour's commitment. The Blair government has created a network of quangos known as Regional Development Agencies (RDAs) to stimulate economic growth at a regional level. Regional 'chambers' are being set up alongside these to represent local authorities and other regional stakeholders and improve the RDAs' local accountability, but the agencies will still be mainly accountable to central government. The regional chambers may develop into directly elected regional assemblies where the demand exists, but not in the immediate future. Some have suggested that devolution in all other constituent parts of the United Kingdom and the creation of a new Greater London Authority in the year 2000 (consisting of a directly elected mayor and an assembly) will stimulate interest in devolution for England. Nevertheless, the fact remains that most of England's regions do not have a coherent identity in the same way that Wales and Scotland do, which means that any attempt to impose 'devolution all round' without clear local demand would risk doing so on the basis of artificial territorial constructs which have no link with people's political and cultural identity. However, the English dimension of devolution is likely to be much debated in the years ahead.

NORTHERN IRELAND

Northern Ireland forms part of the territory of the United Kingdom by virtue of the Act of Union 1800. However, the province remains constitutionally and politically separate. Until the Good Friday Agreement of April 1998 its status was frozen and unresolved – for over twenty-five years Westminster had imposed supposedly temporary direct rule on the first part of the United Kingdom to be given devolved government. The future remains uncertain, but the politics of Northern Ireland are likely to retain a distinctive character, with parties unknown and irrelevant outside the province taking control of the new devolved Assembly.

Historical upheavals aside, Northern Ireland is the only part of the United Kingdom in modern times where major legislation enacted by Parliament simply could not be enforced, in 1914, 1920 and in 1974. Mass revolt on this scale cannot be envisaged elsewhere in the British state. The reasons lie, as always in Ireland, in a cultural and political experience separate from the rest of the United Kingdom (see box, pp. 311–12). Ireland was conquered by the English monarchy, but until the Act of Union was left largely unabsorbed; cultural differences intensified after the Reformation; the disastrous Great Famine altered its demography permanently; and religious and land questions came to the fore, fuelling the demand for home rule which was resisted by the Protestant minority. By 1914 Ireland was in crisis and the outbreak of the First World War simply postponed the reckoning.

The Government of Ireland Act 1920 partitioned Ireland but was unworkable in its original form; the North refused to accept any all-Ireland institutions and the South refused the constitutional status of a devolved legislature. Therefore only the Stormont Parliament came into force, and Britain effectively ceded sovereignty over the rest of Ireland to its people, conducting a treaty with them, against the terms of the Act of Union. It was the first time that the 'people' had successfully claimed sovereignty over the territory of the British Isles.

Yet Ireland as an independent state retains a peculiar status, summed up in the Ireland Act 1949: 'it is hereby declared that, notwithstanding that the Republic of Ireland is not part of His Majesty's dominions, the Republic of Ireland is not a foreign country for the purposes of law in any part of the United Kingdom'. Irish people came to Britain without any investigation of their immigration status and voted in British elections long before the concept of the European citizen had emerged, the major reason being that it would not have been practicable to have checked the status of each Irish person in Britain. Following the Good Friday Agreement new legislation has explicitly established that if a majority of those voting in Northern Ireland wish to join with the Republic that desire will be granted immediately. There is union only with consent. This means that Northern Ireland is the only part of the Union where the people are sovereign. Neither the Scotland Act nor the Government of Wales Act have any provisions allowing secession.

The Good Friday Agreement was endorsed by a dual referendum held simultaneously north and south of the border on 22 May 1998. In Northern Ireland, 71 per cent of those voting, on an 81 per cent turnout, backed the agreement. In

Ireland: Key dates

1171	Native princes acknowledge Henry II as lord of Ireland
1558 onwards	Elizabeth I makes Anglican Church of Ireland state church and anglicises Irish institutions; soldier-farmers begin settlements
1649–55	Oliver Cromwell lays waste and institutes systematic plantation of settlers
1690	William of Orange defeats deposed James II at the Battle of the Boyne. Penal laws restrict rights of Catholics
1798	Rebellion led by Protestant Wolfe Tone defeated
1800	Union with Great Britain
1829	Catholic emancipation granted following the first modern political campaign in British history, led by Daniel O'Connell. Catholics could take seats at Westminster
1848–9	The Great Famine – over one million people died. Large-scale emigration began
1886–93	Two home rule bills founder at Westminster, partly on the question of Ulster, and put the Liberals out of power for over a decade
1914	Asquith's new Home Rule Act provokes Protestant resistance and is immediately suspended on the outbreak of the First World War. Ulster Volunteers import arms illegally
1916	Easter Rising; Sinn Fein proclaim an Irish Republic which is put down by the British and its leaders executed
1920	Government of Ireland Act introduces partition: separate parliaments North and South and a Council of Ireland for common concerns. There is sporadic violence throughout Ireland
1921–2	Lloyd George conducts negotiations with Republican rebels culminating in the Anglo-Irish Treaty; Treaty is narrowly approved by Irish Dail and Irish Free State is given the same status as the dominions of Canada, Australia etc.; there is civil war between pro and anti Treaty supporters, but in the North Unionist politicians establish devolved government at Stormont. Westminster effectively stops intervening in Ireland
1949	Ireland leaves the Commonwealth; Britain passes Ireland Act which entrenches the constitutional position of Northern Ireland, as not subject to change without the consent of its Parliament
1968	The Troubles begin, as northern Catholics claim their civil rights; Stormont is overruled by Westminster and the troops are sent in to restore order

continued

1972	Direct rule imposed on the six counties
1973–4	Northern Ireland Constitution Act establishes new Assembly with a power-sharing Executive, but a new Council of Ireland proposed by the British and Irish governments at Sunningdale provokes Unionist resistance; direct rule is reimposed after the Ulster power workers' strike wrecks the constitutional settlement. The UK and the Republic of Ireland both join the EEC
1985	Anglo Irish Agreement allows the Republic an input into Northern Ireland affairs, causing Unionist outrage, but recognises that there can be no change in the status of Northern Ireland without the consent of its people
1993	In the Downing Street Declaration issued by the British and Irish governments the British government declares that it has no 'selfish strategic or economic interest in Northern Ireland', and the Irish government promises changes to the claims on the North made in the 1937 Irish constitution
1994	The IRA announce a ceasefire, followed by Loyalist para-militaries; protracted discussions begin about formal talks to which Sinn Fein could be admitted, but founder on the question of decommissioning of terrorist arms
1996	IRA ceasefire ends, but there are elections to the Northern Ireland talks; Sinn Fein is not admitted
1997	Second IRA ceasefire; Sinn Fein is admitted without any decommissioning
1998	Good Friday Agreement signed. Following a referendum, a new Assembly is set up. Power is not transferred to the Assembly due to continuing disagreement on decommissioning of terrorist weapons

the Republic, 94 per cent, on a 56 percent turnout, did the same. The Reverend Ian Paisley's Democratic Unionist Party campaigned against the agreement, but it was supported by the main Unionist and republican parties.

The complex arrangements for governing Northern Ireland set out in the Good Friday Agreement simultaneously devolve power to a sub-national unit and establish supra-national forums for dealing with issues of mutual interest to the United Kingdom and Ireland. A new devolved assembly was established under the Northern Ireland Act 1998 (see box, p. 313). Other elements of the agreement include:

- A North/South Ministerial Council brings together Ministers from Ireland and the Northern Ireland Assembly to work together on matters of mutual interest.
- A British–Irish Council (the so-called 'Council of the Isles') brings together

---

The Northern Ireland Assembly

The new Assembly would have full law-making powers over a similar range of subjects to the Scottish Parliament, including:

- Agriculture
- Education
- Health and social services
- Economic development
- The environment.

The powers retained by Westminster are similar to the reserved powers in Scotland, although in Northern Ireland the list is divided into two categories: excepted and reserved matters. Reserved matters such as law and order could be devolved to the Assembly in the future, subject to cross-community support, but excepted matters, including foreign policy and defence, cannot be transferred.

The executive arm of the Assembly would consist of a First Minister and Deputy First Minister and up to ten ministers with departmental responsibilities. The Assembly's first First Minister and Deputy First Minister, David Trimble (UUP) and Seamus Mallon (SDLP), were elected in July 1998. There would be committees with a scrutiny, policy development and consultation role for each minister's department. They would approve relevant secondary legislation and take the committee stage of relevant primary legislation. Allocations of ministers, committee membership and chairs of committees would be made in proportion to party strength. Key decisions would be taken on a cross-community basis (the voting system aside, this is the crucial difference between devolution in Scotland and Northern Ireland). For example, the First Minister and Deputy First Minister require the votes of a majority of the designated Nationalist members and a majority of the designated Unionist members in order to secure election.

The election of the 108 members is by single transferable vote (STV) with six members from each parliamentary constituency.

---

the British and Irish governments and representatives of devolved administrations in Northern Ireland, Scotland and Wales, and from the Channel Islands and the Isle of Man.
- A programme for the accelerated release of paramilitary prisoners was established. There will also be a process for the decommissioning of weapons held by the paramilitary groups in Northern Ireland.

Elections to the Assembly took place on 25 June 1998. The Social Democratic and Labour Party (SDLP) gained the highest percentage of first preference votes (21.96 per cent) for the first time in a Northern Ireland election, with the Ulster

Unionist Party (UUP) following at 21.26 per cent. How this converted into seats in the new Assembly is shown in the box (see below).

With the main anti-agreement group in the Assembly, the Democratic Unionist Party (DUP), having only twenty seats, the pro-agreement parties seemed likely to have a workable majority for key decisions where cross-community support is required, so long as the support of all UUP members could be relied upon. The detonation by a republican splinter-group of a car bomb in Omagh in August 1998, resulting in the loss of twenty-nine lives, seemed to have the effect of strengthening the peace process rather than destabilising it. A number of deadlines set for the power-sharing executive to be established were not met, however, following continued disagreements over the decommissioning of arms. This meant that the transfer of power to the Assembly did not take place. The disagreements centred on whether the executive should be established before decommissioning commenced (Sinn Fein's position) or vice versa (the UUP position). The leadership of both parties was seen as having little room to compromise, if they were to maintain the support of hard-liners within their own camps. In the summer of 1999 the government introduced a Bill designed to overcome the impasse. Under the government's proposals, the executive would be set up but Sinn Fein would be quickly excluded from it if a clear sign that decommissioning was about to start, failed

---

First election for the Northern Ireland Assembly, June 1998: Seats won by each party

Ulster Unionist Party (UUP): the strongest Unionist party; pro-Agreement	28
Social Democratic and Labour Party (SDLP): the strongest Nationalist party, pro-Agreement	24
Democratic Unionist Party (DUP): anti-Agreement party; led by Ian Paisley	20
Sinn Fein: a Nationalist party traditionally regarded as having links with the IRA; pro-Agreement	18
UK Unionist Party (UKUP): anti-Agreement	5
Alliance Party: draws support from both sides of the community; pro-Agreement	6
Independent Unionists: anti-Agreement	3
Progressive Unionist Party (PUP): has links to loyalist paramilitary organisations; pro-Agreement	2
Women's Coalition: a non-sectarian party seeking to combat the under-representation of women in NI politics; pro-Agreement	2
Total	*108*

Note: In broad terms, Unionists support Northern Ireland remaining part of the United Kingdom while Nationalists favour a united Ireland

to start 'within days'. At the time of writing, these proposals had not yet been agreed as a way forward by all sides.

In Northern Ireland, devolution serves a completely different purpose from devolution in Wales and Scotland, despite the attempt to build common concerns in the new British–Irish council which will contain representatives from constituent parts of the United Kingdom and the Channel Islands and Isle of Man. The new Northern Ireland Assembly has more in common with developments in European states struggling with disaffected national minorities than with the product of a desire for self-government evident in the relatively homogeneous cultures of Scotland and Wales. This difference is reflected principally in the voting system and the complex power-sharing arrangements for the Assembly. Devolution in Northern Ireland is a bargained compromise between two communities with different aspirations; and ultimately its success will depend on the degree of common purpose which their representatives can establish.

LOCAL GOVERNMENT

Central–local relations

In most European countries, elected sub-national governments are protected by the constitution. Their right to exist, to represent their citizens and to intervene on their behalf, is equal to that of the national government (although their sphere of influence may be narrower). Britain has a different tradition, however. Although some see the doctrine of parliamentary sovereignty as being under threat from Europe, reports of its demise, when seen from the perspective of local government, can seem greatly exaggerated. Under Britain's unwritten constitution, the legal status of local government in Britain is that of an emanation of the centre. Parliament may insist on fundamental changes to the way local government operates and, technically at least, has the power to order its total abolition – although some authorities such as Martin Loughlin maintain that in practice local government has a greater degree of constitutional entrenchment than this rather extreme description of its status suggests.[9] What is significant, however, is that many people (including central government) have come to see local government in these terms. Given the strong centralising tendency in British politics, the stage is inevitably set for potential conflict between Westminster, which tends to think it knows best, and Britain's sub-national governments which claim democratic legitimacy and are anxious to preserve whatever rights and privileges they have acquired over the years. At no time since the birth of modern local government in the nineteenth century was this conflict greater than under the Thatcher government of 1979–91.

Margaret Thatcher, it seemed, had little time for local government. It was bureaucratic, inflexible and under the thumb of the town hall unions. Many councils resisted her attempts to control public spending and introduce radical new 'consumer' oriented policies, including the right to buy council houses. Some, like Lambeth, Liverpool and the Greater London Council under the leadership of Ken Livingstone, seemed to be challenging even her right to govern. The controversy aroused by the Community Charge or poll tax, her grand scheme to enable voters to identify the true cost of local services, was an important factor in her downfall in November 1990.

So why, then, did the Thatcher government not just get rid of local government? As we have seen, the absence of a written constitution in the United Kingdom means that Parliament can in theory vote to abolish any institution it chooses. Some claim that the Conservatives did just that in all but name, citing a familiar roll call of powers lost to local government during this period:

- Greater London Council and metropolitan county councils abolished
- Control over schools greatly reduced
- Control over further education ended
- Housing stock slashed by 'right to buy'
- Housing associations given main role in building new social housing
- Compulsory competitive tendering (CCT) forced councils to 'privatise' dustbin collection, etc. if they could not match the private sector's bid
- Rate-capping and various other financial constraints introduced.

In reality, though, local government still performs a wide range of important tasks, spending something in the region of £75 billion each year, around a quarter of all public expenditure. It is responsible for many basic public services (see box, p. 317). Central government would be loath to take these on itself, and to hand all of local authorities' responsibilities to quangos would cause political uproar. Another reason why local government is still important in the British political process is its democratic aspect: even if local elections occasionally resemble nothing more than a barometer for the state of national politics, councils and councillors provide a focus for local concerns in a way which an outpost of Whitehall never could.

Tensions between local and central government were not unique to the Thatcher years. Although her radical agenda led to conflict with local priorities on many occasions, this is likely to be true of any government which believes that it has a mandate for change. The previous Labour government, for example, forced councils who wanted to retain selective education (based on grammar schools and secondary moderns) to introduce the non-selective comprehensive system, and not long after taking power the Blair government sent a 'hit squad' to investigate the chronic failure of education services in the London borough of Hackney. This brings us to the nub of the central–local relationship. Local government performs many of the functions which are crucial for the successful operation of the modern welfare state, such as education and community care. Yet in the eyes of the public, and often of local and national politicians, accountability for local services is blurred.

For example, most people are aware that state schools are run by local councils,

What does local government do?

The services for which local government has responsibility include:

- Education
- Social services
- Entertainment, culture, recreation
- Libraries, museums and galleries
- Environmental health
- Refuse collection and street cleansing
- Consumer protection/trading standards
- Environmental protection
- Housing
- Planning
- Industrial promotion and development
- Transport.

Note: In Northern Ireland twenty-six district councils carry out a limited range of activities but many functions which are assigned to local government on the mainland are performed by Area Boards which have more in common with quangos than local government.

but government education ministers are held responsible for failings in the education system generally. This is likely to be especially true of the Blair government, which was elected on a platform of 'education, education, education'. Ideally, local and central government would work in partnership to improve standards and implement changes (and much of the time they do so), but the essence of local democracy is that different places have different priorities, or different ideas about how to do the same thing. Given the long-standing tradition of a strong centre in British politics and the fact that Parliament always has the upper hand over local authorities when push comes to shove (ie. in framing the laws within which councils must operate), it is difficult for ministers to resist the temptation to impose their will on occasions. Many ministers, in fact, would insist that it is their *duty* to protect the public from councils' worst failings. Further impetus towards central intervention (or interference) is created by the fact that around 80 per cent of councils' cash is provided by central government. As the saying goes, he who pays the piper calls the tune.

A credible argument can be mounted against the tendency towards centralisation, but central government carries what it sees as the trump card: superior democratic legitimacy. Turnout in local elections averages around 40 per cent (it fell as low as 6 per cent in one recent by-election in Liverpool); and this compares with a turnout of over 70 per cent in general elections. In addition there has been the tendency, already mentioned, for local elections to be decided on national rather than local issues. Therefore, it is implied, local government's mandate cannot compete with that of central government. Although it is true that local government cannot be complacent while this situation persists, the authority of central government's mandate needs to be treated with caution. New Labour won a landslide majority in the House of Commons in 1997 but won only 44 per cent of votes polled, amounting to just under a third of the electorate. At a local level, people may see policies pursued by councils as having a greater legitimacy than those pursued by national government. Evidence of this was given by a referendum mounted by the massive Strathclyde Regional Council (now defunct) in Scotland in 1994, which demonstrated overwhelming public opposition to the Conservative government's plans to remove water services from local authority control.

The Blair government believes that reform to increase the democratic legitimacy of local government is needed urgently. Its 'modernisation' programme for local government was set out in a white paper published in July 1998 (see box below).[10]

One of the principal reforms proposed is to alter the local electoral cycle in England and Wales, so that voters in most areas get the chance to vote for a local representative once a year. This is intended to give electors more frequent opportunity to pass judgment on the council's performance. In fact, a similar system already operates in most major urban areas outside London, and the often indifferent turnout in such areas suggests that people may not jump at the chance of more frequent elections. The government will encourage councils to experiment with innovations designed to increase turnout, such as electronic voting and having polling booths in supermarkets, and will also encourage the use of refer-

---

Modernising local government

Proposals contained in the Blair government's white paper:

- Replacement of the current committee system with new arrangements involving the separation of the executive role from the backbench role. One option will be a directly elected executive mayor with a cabinet
- A move to annual elections for most councils
- A new framework to govern the conduct of councillors and council employees
- Replacement of compulsory competitive tendering (CCT) with a duty to achieve 'best value'
- A new duty for councils to promote the economic, social and environmental well-being of their area
- Council Tax capping to be used only in extreme cases
- A new power to set a small supplementary business rate; any income raised would need to be used in ways agreed between the council and local businesses
- A scheme to select 'beacon councils' to serve as pace-setters and centres of excellence. As an incentive, beacon councils will have greater freedom from central controls.

endums to decide local issues. The government's argument is, in essence, that local government will be given greater independence when it demonstrates that it is truly accountable to local people.

In Scotland and Wales, the central–local relationship is being transformed by the establishment of devolved bodies. These have replaced central government as the principal point of contact for local authorities and are responsible for deciding the controversial issue of how money from the Treasury is to be divided up amongst the different councils (although legislation on local government in Wales will continue to be the exclusive preserve of Whitehall). The government established an independent commission early in 1998 to advise the Scottish Parliament on relations with local government and to 'consider how councils can best make themselves responsive and democratically accountable to the communities they serve'.[11] The Labour leadership would clearly like to see the Scottish Parliament adopting an agenda for local government similar to that envisaged for England and Wales and had initiated some reforms, such as the establishment of 'best value' (described on p. 324), before devolution came into effect.

How local government is organised

Everywhere in Britain has at least one layer of local government. Most areas in the English shires have two main layers of local government (counties and districts) although in some places these have recently been merged into a single layer, known as *unitary* authorities. A similar process established unitary authorities across the board in Scotland and Wales. London, however, will *gain* a second layer when the Greater London Authority comes into being in the year 2000. Many areas outside London have an additional, subsidiary, layer of local government: parish, town or community councils, which perform relatively few functions.

One writer noted recently that there have now been forty years of successive structural reviews.[12] Central government, it might seem, is forever in search of the ideal structure for local government, and this has caused considerable disruption. The main aims of these reviews have been to create:

(a) a structure which is efficient and suited to the functions which local government has been given;
(b) local units of government which correspond to community identity in order to foster a sense of belonging.

Unfortunately these goals would seem to be incompatible in many places, with the result that the current patchwork has emerged. The most recent review took place under the Major government between 1992 and 1995, with new 'unitary authorities' (councils which perform most or all local government functions) being created in the whole of Scotland and Wales in 1996 and in forty-six places in England between 1995 and 1998. Further reorganisation may be in prospect if England's regions wish to have elected assemblies: in order to avoid accusations of bureaucratic clutter, Labour's policy is that a predominantly unitary system of local government should be put in place first. Many commentators point out, however, that even a perfect structure does not guarantee good local government. The culture within each authority has more influence on whether it is efficient or responsive to local needs.

The largest local authority in mainland Britain, Kent County Council, has over 1.3 million residents. The smallest (excluding parish councils) is Teesdale in Durham, which has 24,000. Councils are made up of elected representatives – councillors – who are elected for fixed four-year terms. They employ a large staff to carry out the tasks which the council must perform – managers and administrators, teachers, social workers, environmental health officers and so on – although some services may now be provided by contractors rather than by direct employees of the council. Council staff must carry out the policies decided upon by their employers in the same impartial way that civil servants serve their elected masters.

There are more than 20,000 councillors in Britain. A recent survey found that, in England and Wales, 73 per cent are male and 97 per cent are white, their average age being nearly fifty-six years.[13] Unlike MPs, councillors have no fixed salary, but they receive allowances which are set by the council itself and are intended to reflect their responsibilities. In recent years the restrictions on councillors' allowances imposed by central government have been relaxed and there have been substantial increases in some areas. Nevertheless it remains the case that most councillors devote considerable time and energy to their duties, for comparatively meagre financial reward: a survey by the *Local Government Chronicle* found that an average councillor in England received around £3,700 in 1997–8, with a council leader's allowance averaging £7,750.

Once, many councillors stood as independents, but since the Second World War the party system has come to dominate local elections. There is now a widespread feeling that the single-party dominance of particular councils which exists in some areas is unhealthy for democracy and can lead to corruption. Some observers believe that proportional representation might help to address this issue, although the government has indicated that, for the time being, it does not intend to introduce PR for council elections in England and Wales.

The question of how local government's political leadership is organised and the way councils take decisions (known as *internal management*) is very close to the top of the Labour government's agenda. Councils have traditionally set up committees to run individual services like education, and only major decisions like the annual budget are made by the full council. The leader of the council and the committee chairs are chosen by the majority party on the council. Party discipline is now generally enforced at a local level by whips in much the same way as it is in the House of Commons, ensuring in most cases that votes taken in committees reflect the view of the council leadership. The committee system has been criticised for inefficiency, tunnel vision and a failure to encourage policy innovations (see box, p. 321).

We Can't Go on Meeting Like This . . .

Traditional committee structures, still used by almost all councils, lead to inefficient and opaque decision-making. Significant decisions are, in many councils, taken behind closed doors by political groups or even a small group of key people within the majority group. Consequently, many councillors, even those in the majority group, have little influence over council decisions.

Councillors also spend too much time in committee meetings which, because the decisions have already effectively been taken, are unproductive. Councillors attend too many council meetings. The evidence is that many wish to spend much more time in direct contact with those they represent. They may have had little say in the decisions taken, but they are required to explain the actions of the council, or their party group, to the people they represent. The emphasis ought to be on bringing the views of their community to bear on the council's decisions, and on scrutinising their performance.

Equally, there is little clear political leadership. This is not a reflection on the qualities of council leaders. It is caused by the structures in which they work.

People often do not know who is really taking the decisions. They do not know who to praise, who to blame or who to contact with their problems. People identify most readily with an individual, yet there is rarely any identifiable figure leading the local community.

This is no basis for modern, effective and responsive local government.

(extract from the white paper *Modern Local Government: In Touch with the People*, July 1998, chapter 3)

Some councils, particularly those under Liberal Democrat control, have experimented with neighbourhood committees which reflect the political balance in a particular part of the authority's area and are responsible for all services within the neighbourhood. A working party established by the Major government proposed further experiments based on experience in other countries. One proposal was elected mayors, designed to encourage a strong, presidential style of leadership which would raise the council's profile and encourage a higher turnout at elections. Another was a cabinet-style executive. Both models would lead to a formal separation of the roles of frontbench and backbench councillors, and for this reason many councillors oppose such moves (especially the ones likely to end up on the back benches). The Labour government's view is that such changes would enable backbenchers to participate in new committees for scrutinising the actions of the executive or mayor, modelled on Commons select committees.

Tony Blair is very keen on elected mayors and the government's first move in this direction was legislation to establish an elected mayor and strategic authority in London, a proposal approved in a referendum in May 1998. The mayor takes up office in July 2000, following elections in April. Further legislation will extend changes in decision-making procedures to all councils in England and Wales, which will have to choose from a range of options for reform, including the elected mayor and cabinet models. It seems that, given the choice, most authorities would prefer a cabinet system to an elected mayor, but some have called for the government to decide to prevent councils from making this decision without first holding a referendum. In the big cities in particular there may be strong pressure for elected mayors. It is a period of intense debate and fundamental reform as far as the organisation of local government is concerned.

Paying for local government

Nowhere is the tension between centre and locality more obvious than in the area of local government finance. Local government wants financial autonomy but central government – anxious about the economic effects of higher public spending and the voters' reaction to higher taxes – is reluctant to allow this. The extent to which local government is financially dependent upon the Treasury, rather than upon its own resources, is clear from the figures (see box below).

Local government: Where the money comes from

- Council Tax, a local residential property tax: 22 per cent
- Government grant (including a grant financed by the national or 'uniform' business rate, a non-residential property tax): 77 per cent

The figures are for England in 1996/97 (source: DETR), but there is a similar ratio in Scotland and Wales. Revenue from charges for services is excluded from the figures.

The current system means that it is hard to make truly local decisions on spending. The bulk of the money the Treasury makes available for local government is divided up using a complex formula known as the *Standard Spending Assessment* (SSA), which attempts to measure as objectively as possible councils' relative financial needs (the Scottish equivalent of the SSA is *Grant Aided Expenditure*). But if a council believes that the SSA underestimates the true level of need in its area, it has only limited room for manoeuvre. The high ratio of central to local funding means that every additional 1 per cent in a council's budget requires, on average, an increase in council tax of around 5 per cent (this is known as the 'gearing effect'). However committed local people may be to local services, tax increases of the order necessary to make a significant difference are generally seen as political suicide. At the same time, central government wants to keep a tight grip on public spending and for this reason *council tax capping* prevents any additional council tax rises when a council's budget reaches a level which the government considers excessive. Local authorities' spending is thus caught in a pincer movement which allows little deviation from the government's spending targets.

The arrangements described above may prompt the question: Why does central government provide such a high proportion of local finance? If local people decide on their priorities for local services in local elections, why should they not meet the cost of their choices rather than relying on the national taxpayer to fund them? Almost everybody agrees that, in theory, this is a good idea, but there is no consensus on how to go about it. One major problem is that areas wishing to spend more money on local services, to reduce the impact of social problems, tend to be poor areas which have less ability to raise their own funds. An advantage of central government bankrolling local government is that the nation as a whole is better equipped to help tackle severe local hardship than the areas in need. There are also specific problems relating to the various forms of local taxation which are available. The main considerations involved are:

- Domestic property taxes such as the council tax are always unpopular and there is a limit to how much people would be prepared to see them rise – even if income tax or VAT was reduced in return.
- Returning business rates to local control is one option (at present they are set nationally), but this too presents problems due to the uneven concentration of businesses across the country. In addition, business fears being milked by cash-hungry councils if they regain this power. The government has decided to retain the national business rate but it has said that it will legislate to allow councils to set a small local supplement (or give a local rebate).
- Some advocate a local income tax to boost local autonomy. This might prove a more robust tax base than property taxes but the two major parties are opposed to this idea, although it has long been Liberal Democrat policy.

The 1997 Labour manifesto promised that council tax capping would only be used in extreme cases. The Local Government Act 1999 is intended to introduce, in England and Wales, a more sophisticated form of capping which is consistent with the Blair government's desire to provide financial incentives for good performance. The new rules will allow ministers to take account of factors such as a council's overall performance and its financial position over a number of years before deciding whether to impose a cap. It will be up to the Scottish Parliament to decide what controls, if any, it wishes to impose upon councils' spending.

Leaders and enablers: A new role for local government?

In the 1980s the Conservative politician Nicholas Ridley set out a vision of councils as *enablers* rather than *providers* of services. This model worked on the assumption that most things done by local authorities could be done better and more cheaply in the private sector. In line with this assumption, the Local Government Act 1988 extended *compulsory competitive tendering* or CCT to most blue collar council services (legislation in 1980, based on a Labour government green paper, had already introduced CCT for highway and construction work). CCT forced local authorities which wanted their services to be performed by their own workforce to bid against private sector contractors. In the mid-1990s CCT for various white collar activities such as personnel, legal advice and IT started to be phased in.

Labour, local government and the unions were bitterly opposed to CCT, which they saw as undermining councils' autonomy and workers' job security. A study commissioned by the Conservative government found that CCT was leading to savings of around 6 per cent, but at the cost of poorer pay and conditions for the workforce. Over time, however, a change in attitudes began to take place. Local government was unimpressed by the level of bureaucracy entailed by the tendering process (which the legislation set out in excruciating detail to prevent councils exploiting loopholes), but some councillors and officials began to be impressed by the way that drawing up a detailed specification for a contract forced them to think hard about what the service was trying to achieve. In addition, Labour began to believe that if councils played an enabling or commissioning role this might allow them to develop their *leadership* and *representative* roles at the same time, the idea being that if councils no longer saw their main task as being to provide services directly ('in-house') they would be better able to represent local people's views on services rather than being forced always into defending the council's record. However, opposition to contracting out remained strong in parts of the Labour movement, especially in the trade unions and in Scotland.

Labour's 1997 manifesto promised to replace CCT with a duty to achieve *best value* and the Local Government Act 1999 fulfils that commitment in England and Wales. Pilot schemes in England, Scotland and Wales were already well underway when the bill was introduced. Best value is intended to take account of quality as well as price. Councils will have to carry out five yearly fundamental performance reviews and meet annual performance targets for efficiency, cost and quality. It will be up to the councils how they meet these targets, but if performance failures emerge the government will have powers to intervene. Ministers have stressed that although there should be no ideological assumption about whether services should be provided directly or contracted out, they should not be delivered in-house if other means are more efficient and effective (see box, p. 325).

In Scotland the government attempted to ensure that the principles of best value were well established before it handed responsibility for local government to the Scottish Parliament by granting exemption to CCT if councils made satisfactory progress in this area. As one prominent academic commented recently, it remains to be seen whether best value will allow councils to develop services in ways which are suited to local needs and priorities, or will merely end up imposing central government's idea of what is 'best'.[14]

The conduct of councils and councillors has received considerable attention in recent years. The received wisdom has long been that corruption is relatively uncommon in local government, but Labour has been embarrassed by a steady trickle of allegations against Labour councils over the past few years (Glasgow, Monklands, Doncaster, Hull, and others), and there have been examples of

---

A 'third way' for councils?

[Best Value] is a demanding process. But if local people are to receive quality services on a consistent basis, then it has to be this way. Best Value is not a short cut for getting out of compulsory competitive tendering. Nor does it mean councils going soft on competition and just going back to automatically delivering services themselves. The new local government will mean councils doing less but being involved in more spheres of activity. But the competition must be fair – fair to Council Tax payers and fair to employees. Cost counts, but so does quality. Where councils can show that they can provide best value by delivering quality services in a cost-effective and competitive manner in-house, then it will make sense for them to do so – but only if they meet those conditions. Increasingly the pattern will be for authorities to enter into more partnerships and joint ventures with businesses and voluntary agencies and other public bodies to deliver local services.

(from Tony Blair's pamphlet, *Leading the Way: A New Vision for Local Government*, IPPR, 1998)

---

misconduct by councillors in all of the main political parties. The main sanction available at present is surcharge, which involves the recovery of any cost to the public purse resulting from corruption or wilful negligence from the councillors or officials responsible. This was the power invoked against Shirley Porter and others from the Conservative-controlled Westminster Council after the infamous 'homes for votes' scandal. The Nolan Committee's third report focused on propriety in local government, and recommended the creation of a new criminal offence of misuse of public office, to replace the existing power of surcharge.[15] The government accepted this proposal, which will apply equally to national and local politicians as well as members of quangos (there is no power to surcharge ministers under existing law). There will also be an independent board to investigate all serious allegations of malpractice.

Over the past few years the idea of a new role for local government has emerged: that of community leadership. An important aspect of this role is for councils to use their democratic mandate to bring together a range of different agencies and interests, including business, community groups and public agencies such as the police, the NHS and local quangos, in order to tackle persistent, complex problems (the so-called 'wicked issues') like poverty, drug abuse, crime, poor health and run-down estates and town centres. This type of approach is envisaged for the mayor of London who, the government hopes, will have a mandate to achieve change much stronger than his or her formal legal powers. Some have claimed, however, that the mayor will be a toothless wonder. A pamphlet written by Tony Blair in 1998 warned that if local government failed to rise to the challenge in this and the other priority areas of high quality services and democratic legitimacy, the government would seek 'new partners' in carrying out its policies.[16] This will ensure that local government remains at the centre of political debate in the period ahead.

CONCLUSION

Governments do not readily give up powers. This applies especially in Britain, with its tradition of a strong centre. A good reason for this reluctance is that powers ceded now will not easily be regained in the future, whether those powers were relinquished for democratic reasons, as with the Scottish Parliament, or for more pragmatic ends, as with Britain's involvement with the European Union. In theory, Westminster could vote to abolish its Scottish sibling at any time, but that will not be politically acceptable so long as the Scottish Parliament is supported by the Scottish people (and the Scottish media). In the EU, Britain could argue for a new settlement returning competence over various matters to Westminster, but success would depend on the agreement of its partners in Europe. It could even vote to leave Europe altogether, but this is not generally regarded as a practical option because of the implications for Britain's trade. Most, if not all, of the new arrangements described in this chapter will therefore endure for many years to come.

Some have claimed that a contradiction has emerged between Labour's decentralising policies and its instinct to maintain a strong central grip on the levers of power. The party leadership, for example, seems uneasy with the idea of the Scottish Parliament pursuing distinctively Scottish policies, but these will surely emerge given the semi-proportional nature of the voting system for the Scottish Parliament and the consequent need for collaboration across the parties. Pressure for independence is likely to grow if the Scottish people believe that the strings of its political leaders are being pulled from Westminster. Some also claim to see this contradiction between words and deeds in Labour's policy towards local government.

Britain's enmeshment in the European system is symptomatic of the way in which national governments have attempted to deal with the increasing internationalisation of many political and economic issues. The European Union is the most significant of the international bodies of which Britain is a member, but it is only one of an increasing number of organisations which are intended to manage and control the complex international system. Many issues which have traditionally been dealt with by national governments are now dealt with through international institutions. One important consequence of this is the problem of combining such international solutions with democratic accountability, as the ability of elected national governments individually to control policy is challenged. This ensures that the lively debate over the powers and nature of such bodies, particularly of the European Union, will continue to be a central feature of national politics for many years to come.

For some time now, political pundits have predicted that this globalisation of the world's problems will weaken the idea of the nation state, perhaps making it altogether redundant. On this view, more flexible political institutions will arise, both at the supra-national and sub-national levels. Britain, as we have already seen, has ceded powers in both directions while retaining a powerful attachment to the idea of national sovereignty. It should, therefore, be an excellent testing ground for this theory over the decades ahead. But other members of the EU seem now to be pulling back from the idea of a United States of Europe, and Britain's strong island identity suggests that it is not ready to abandon the idea of the nation state just yet.

NOTES

1 *Legal and Constitutional Implications of UK Membership of the European Communities*, Cmnd. 3301, 1967, para. 22.
2 Article 3b, Treaty on European Union, 1992.
3 Professor Helen Wallace, Memorandum submitted to the Select Committee on Procedure, 17 July 1996, *Third Report, European Business*, HC 77 of 1996–97, p. 19.
4 Ibid., p. 22.
5 Select Committee on European Legislation, *Twenty-seventh Report, The Scrutiny of European Legislation*, HC 51 of 1995–96, p. x, para. 15.
6 Protocol 13, Treaty of Amsterdam, 1997.
7 *Report of the Royal Commission on the Constitution*, Cmnd 5460 ('The Kilbrandon Report').
8 Christopher Harvie, in B. Crick (ed.), *National Identities: The Constitution of the UK* (Political Quarterly/Blackwell, Oxford, 1991).
9 Martin Loughlin, *Legality and Locality* (Clarendon Press, Oxford, 1996).
10 *Modern Local Government: In Touch with the People*, Cmnd. 4014.
11 The McIntosh Commission reported in June 1999 (*Moving forward: Local Government and the Scottish Parliament*, Scottish Office, 1999). Its most noteworthy conclusion was that proportional representation should be introduced for council elections in Scotland, a conclusion which the Scottish Parliament seems likely to accept.
12 Robert Leach, 'Local Government Reorganisation RIP?', *Political Quarterly*, vol. 69, no. 1, Jan–March 1997.
13 *First National Census: Survey of Local Authority Councillors in England and Wales in 1997* (Local Government Management Board, 1998).
14 Michael Clarke, *Rebuilding Trust? Central-local Relationships in the New Millenium* (European Policy Forum, London, July 1998).
15 Committee on Standards in Public Life, *Standards of Conduct in Local Government in England, Scotland and Wales*, Cm. 3702, July 1997.
16 *Leading the Way* (Institute for Public Policy Research, 1998).

FURTHER READING

Derek Urwin's *The Community of Europe: A History of European Integration since 1945* (London, Longman, 1995) offers an excellent and accessible introduction to the history of the European Community. The relationship between Britain and Europe, and the impact of the European system on the British political process, is traced in Colin Pilkington's *Britain in the European Union Today* (Manchester, Manchester University Press, 1995). Stephen George provides a more detailed assessment of Britain's membership of the European Community in *An Awkward Partner: Britain in the European Community* (Oxford, Oxford University Press, 1994).

Devolution in the United Kingdom by Vernon Bogdanor is a comprehensive and authoritative analysis of this subject (Oxford University Press, Oxford, 1999). A series of publications by the Constitution Unit, based in University College, London, offer well thought-out analysis of some of the practical issues raised by devolution. See especially *Constitutional Futures: A History of the Next Ten Years*, edited by the unit's director, Robert Hazell (Oxford University Press, Oxford, 1999). A number of research papers produced by the House of Commons Library cover aspects of devolution, including the West Lothian Question, the Barnett Formula, and the recent developments in the government of Northern Ireland (January 1998 onwards, only available via the Internet, at www.parliament.uk). *The People Say Yes* by Kenyon Wright, the executive chair of the Scottish Constitutional Convention, provides an account of the making of Scotland's Parliament (Argyll, Argyll, 1997) and the excellent quarterly *Scottish Affairs* devotes extensive space to the devolution issue. *The Scottish Parliament: An Introduction* by Jean McFadden and Mark Lazarowicz (T. and T. Clark, 1999) takes the reader through the essential aspects of the new Parliament. The Institute of Welsh Affairs has produced a valuable series of pamphlets on Wales.

There is an extensive literature on the politics of Northern Ireland, including *The Ulster Question since 1945* by James Loughlin (Macmillan, London, 1998) and *Politics in Northern Ireland*, edited by Paul Mitchell and Rick Wilford (Westview Press, Oxford, 1999).

For good basic textbooks on local government see *Local Government in the United Kingdom* by David Wilson and Chris Game, 2nd edn (Macmillan, Basingstoke, 1998) and *Local Government Today* by J. A. Chandler (Manchester University Press, Manchester, 1996). *Local Government since 1945*, by Ken Young and Nirmala Rao (Blackwell, Oxford, 1997) offers a valuable historical perspective. *Failure in British Government* by David Butler *et al.* analyses the rise and fall of the poll tax, 'a public policy failure of the first magnitude' (Oxford University Press, Oxford, 1994). Those seeking an insight into New Labour thinking on local government should read Tony Blair's pamphlet *Leading the Way* (Institute for Public Policy Research, 1998) or anything by Gerry Stoker, Professor of Politics at the University of Strathclyde. Up-to-the-minute critical analysis is provided in the fortnightly column of George Jones and John Stewart in the *Local Government Chronicle*.

10 Whither British politics?

There is no precedent since 1688 for such a concentrated and deliberate rebuilding of the constitutional architecture.

(Peter Hennessy, 'Re-engineering the State in Flight',
Lloyds TSB Forum Lecture, April 1998)

As the twentieth century ends and the twenty-first century begins, the British
political process is in the middle of a period of dramatic and fundamental change.
Previous chapters have identified particular aspects of this. On all sides old institutions and traditional assumptions are being challenged and reformed. The task in
this final chapter is briefly to identify some of the larger themes, issues and
directions behind the particular changes – and to offer some speculative thoughts
on where it might all be leading. The only certain fact is that the familiar accounts
of British politics will require radical revision. Chapter 1 identified some of the
traditional characteristics of the British political system. In this last chapter, the
task is to explore how these are now changing.

BRITISH POLITICS IN FLUX

It is only necessary to map the alterations to the political system that are now
being made, then to add in those that are proposals or prospects, to see the scale
and significance of what is happening. In the first session of Parliament following
the 1997 general election, no less than twelve constitutional bills were introduced
by the new Labour government; and this is only the beginning of a larger and
longer programme of political and constitutional reform (see box pp. 330–31). Each
development comes laden with implications for the future pattern of politics in
Britain. For example, devolution to Scotland and Wales raises questions about the
management of the United Kingdom. The Northern Ireland agreement brings
with it new political arrangements throughout the British Isles. Bringing the
European Convention on Human Rights into domestic law turns the spotlight
onto the role of judges – and their relationship to politicians. Freedom of information legislation enforces a different culture in government. The establishment of

Political reform since 1997: The story so far

Referendums *Referendums (Scotland and Wales) Act* (1977)
Authorises referendums in Scotland and Wales on devolution
proposals

Scotland *Scotland Act* (1998)
Implements proposals for Scottish Parliament set out in white
paper *Scotland's Parliament* (Cm. 3658, 1997)

Wales *Government of Wales Act* (1998)
Implements proposals for Welsh Assembly set out in white
paper *A Voice for Wales* (Cm. 3718, 1997)

Europe *European Communities (Amendment) Act* (1998)
Implements provisions of the Amsterdam Treaty

European elections *European Parliamentary Elections Act* (1999)
Introduces proportional representation by regional party lists
for European Parliament elections (only passed after battle
with House of Lords)

Bank of England *Bank of England Act* (1998)
Gives operational independence on monetary policy to Bank

Human rights *Human Rights Act* (1998)
Brings European Convention on Human Rights into domestic
law (with implementation in year 2000)

London *Greater London Authority (Referendum) Act* (1998)
Authorises referendum on government of London proposals
Greater London Authority Act (1999)
Implements proposals in consultation paper *New Leadership for
London* (Cmnd. 3724, 1997) and white paper *A Mayor and
Assembly for London* (Cmnd. 3897, 1998) on mayor and
assembly for London

House of Commons New Select Committee on Modernisation of the House of
Commons established (1997); various reports published

House of Lords *House of Lords Bill* (introduced January 1999)
Removes the voting rights of hereditary peers
White paper *Modernising Parliament: Reforming the House of Lords*
(January 1999) sets out options for further reform and
transitional arrangements
Royal Commission established to consider 'stage two' reform,
with a Joint Committee of both Houses to follow

Freedom of White paper *Your Right to Know* (Cm. 3818, 1997)
information Draft bill introduced (1999)

Regions *Regional Development Agencies Act* (1998)
Implements proposals for regional development agencies in
England in white paper *Building Partnerships for Prosperity* (Cm.
3814, 1997)

continued

Northern Ireland	*Northern Ireland (Elections) Act* (1998) Sets up arrangements for election to new Assembly *Northern Ireland Act* (1998) Implements Belfast Agreement, with new Assembly and cross-border bodies
Political parties	*Registration of Political Parties Act* (1998) Provides for parties to register names and emblems
Party funding	Committee on Standards in Public Life (Neill Committee), report on *The Funding of Political Parties* (Cm. 4057, 1998) Legislation to follow on new party funding and election rules
Voting system	Commission on the Voting System (Jenkins Commission) reports (Cm. 4090, 1998), proposing new voting system for House of Commons Referendum promised, but no date set
Local government	White paper *Modern Local Government: In Touch with the People* (Cm. 4014, 1998), with proposals to change the political structure of local government Draft bill introduced (1999)

regional development bodies in England opens the way to a serious English regionalism. A mayor for London suggests a new model for urban government. More proportional systems of election for Scotland, Wales and Europe make the issue of electoral reform for Westminster harder to evade, with consequences for the British tradition of 'strong' government. The prospect of a reconstructed House of Lords raises questions about its relation to the House of Commons. Wherever we look, it seems, the system is in flux.

No institution is immune from this wind of change. For example, polls in 1998 showed that more people now thought that Britain would not have a monarchy in fifty years time than those who thought it would (see box, p. 332). In 1990 only 11 per cent of people believed the monarchy would not be around in fifty years time; but by 1998 this view was shared by 44 per cent of people. This is a remarkable change, no doubt largely brought about by the turbulent internal life of the royal family during this period, but also probably owing something to changing social attitudes. As traditional authority declines, institutions and practices are required to change and adapt if they are to sustain themselves. It was recently reported that the Queen has enlisted the device of a 'people's panel' as a sounding-board for the monarchy as it seeks to modernise itself.[1] In the nineteenth century Bagehot famously warned of the dangers of letting in 'daylight upon magic' as far as the monarchy was concerned; but now the danger comes from keeping the daylight out.

This matter of changing attitudes is a reminder of the larger context surrounding the political process. Politicians may like to give the impression that they are in charge of events, but in reality they are often responding to events and forces over which they have little or no control. Sometimes they may even make a virtue of this by explicitly transferring responsibility to somebody else, as with Chancellor Gordon Brown's transfer of responsibility for setting interest rates from the

What future for the monarchy?

Looking to the future, do you think Britain will or will not have a monarchy . . .

	Jan 1990 (%)	*Feb 1991 (%)*	*May 1992 (%)*	*Dec 1992 (%)*	*Feb 1996 (%)*	*Dec 1996 (%)*	*Aug 1997 (%)*	*Sept 1997 (%)*	*Aug 1998 (%)*
. . . in ten years?									
Will	95	90	85	76	76	77	80	73	79
Will not	2	5	8	18	17	19	15	19	16
Don't know	3	5	7	6	7	4	5	8	5
Net *will*	+93	+85	+77	+58	+59	+58	+65	+54	+63
. . . in fifty years?									
Will	69	55	46	36	33	33	35	30	32
Will not	11	21	30	42	43	48	48	45	44
Don't know	20	23	24	22	24	19	17	25	24
Net *will*	+58	+34	+16	−6	−10	−15	−13	−15	−12
. . . in one hundred years?									
Will	49	38	29	22	20	20	20	18	19
Will not	20	31	39	52	50	56	58	51	55
Don't know	31	31	32	26	30	24	22	31	26
Net *will*	+29	+7	−10	−30	−30	−36	−38	−33	−36

Source: MORI

Treasury to the Monetary Policy Committee of the Bank of England, but such an open embrace of impotence is unusual. Yet much of the defining context of British politics lies elsewhere. The most obvious example is Europe, not merely as the source of much British legislation, but with the single currency making a nonsense of traditional views about national 'sovereignty'. The proposed referendum on British entry to the currency will confront old doctrines with new realities.

However, the need to give a wider context to British politics goes far beyond the particular issue of the European Union. Similar societies are to be found grappling with similar problems. These range from trends in social behaviour (such as family breakdown, drugs and crime) to the competitive demands of a global economy transformed by new technologies. On key issues – for example, environmental sustainability or the regulation of the international economy – Britain can only hope to work with other countries to make any kind of serious progress. The electoral resistance to direct taxation that produced Labour's pledge in the 1997 election not to increase income tax levels is also not confined to Britain. Issues that are central to politics in Britain, such as welfare reform, are central elsewhere too as societies and labour markets change. None of this is intended to suggest that politics will be the same everywhere, for common problems meet local traditions (in Britain, the issue of the European Union is always the clearest example of this) and different political systems respond to demands in differing ways, but it serves as a useful reminder of the wider context within which much of British politics now has to be seen.

Where Britain is distinctive, certainly in relation to its own recent past, is in its comprehensive programme of political reform. Perhaps one of the attractions of this programme, at least for its proponents, is that institutional reform of this kind does not depend upon forces over which politicians have only limited control, but represents a concrete enterprise of domestic modernisation. In other words, if Britain wants to change its voting system or remodel its second chamber, then it can. In an uncertain world, such a programme clearly has its attractions. Not only this, what is remarkable about political reform in Britain is that it is not being undertaken as a response to constitutional crisis, social upheaval or national emergency. Radical constitutional reconstruction is usually prompted by such factors. Yet Britain is undertaking a revolution without a revolution. In Peter Hennessy's phrase, the British state is being 're-engineered in flight'. It has not crashed and (with the possible exception of Scotland, and the standing exception of Northern Ireland) re-engineering is being freely chosen and not compelled by events.

Even more remarkable is the fact that it is being undertaken by a party with a huge majority in the House of Commons. The beneficiaries of existing arrangements are not usually those who are most eager to change them. Yet that is what is happening in Britain, as the Blair government drives on with its enterprise of constitutional reform (supported by the Liberal Democrats and opposed by the Conservatives). How is this to be explained? There are a number of factors at work, but the main one is Labour's conversion to the cause of political reform as a direct response to the experience of prolonged Conservative rule from 1979 to 1997. In this sense it is Mrs Thatcher who perhaps has the best claim to be regarded as the real architect of constitutional reform in Britain. She provided an object-lesson in the nature of power in Britain's 'flexible' constitution and, at the same time, a crash course of constitutional education for the Labour Party. The Conservative years did produce constitutional innovations. The organisation and management of government saw radical changes under Mrs Thatcher, while John Major took steps (for example, on open government, and setting up the Nolan Committee on standards in public life) that he hoped might hold the line against more sweeping reforms. It was a vain hope, for the taint of sleaze that finally enveloped his government ensured that political reform would provide a beacon for his successor.

The arrival of comprehensive constitutional reform also marked the end of British 'exceptionalism' in this respect. For a long time the British political tradition had seemed uniquely untroubled by the kinds of constitutional engineering required elsewhere (and took some pride in being so untroubled). The tasks that such engineering were required to undertake – representing divided societies, protecting basic rights, preventing arbitrary government – were not ones that were required in the fortunate conditions of Britain. In Britain it was a culture of constitutionalism, not formal constitutional architecture, that ruled. Constitutions, certainly of the written kind, were the necessary devices of luckless foreigners.

As Britain now turns its own hand to radical constitutional engineering, it is difficult to sustain this claim to exceptionalism. It grapples with some of the problems, and turns to some of the remedies, that are familiar elsewhere. It begins to be interested in how other countries handle the territorial management of devolved government, operate freedom of information, construct their second chambers, or organise their electoral systems. Previously alien devices such as referendums ('a device so alien to all our traditions' in the words of Labour's leader, Clement Attlee, in 1945[2]) and elected mayors are embraced with enthusiasm. The European protection of rights is domesticated. There is a sense that, having for so long believed itself to be an exceptional case as far as such matters are concerned, Britain discovers that it also needs to become a modern pluralist democracy. The novelty of this discovery gives freshness and vigour to its approach to political reform.

But where is it all leading? Is it possible to discern the future shape of British politics from current developments? What are the big trends behind the particular measures and events? Great caution is needed in thinking about such questions. The warning in Chapter 1 about the perils of prediction, and about confusing transient circumstances with eternal truths, needs to be sounded again here. It is always salutary to remember the leading article in *The Times* at the end of 1945 which declared that it was unlikely that the Conservatives would be in office again during the rest of the century. The British political process is currently on the move, but it is far from clear where it will come to rest. Party fortunes are dramatically reversed, ideological antagonisms muted, relationships with Europe strengthened, constitutional reforms embarked upon: the landscape of British politics is being transformed, but this does not (yet) mean that a new settlement has been established. It is a moment for questions, reflections and speculations about what is happening to the political process in Britain. Some leading questions of this kind are briefly discussed below.

IS BRITAIN MOVING TOWARDS A WRITTEN CONSTITUTION?

It may be, though it does not think that it is. The idea of a written constitution forms no part of the political reform programme of the Blair government. However, as the British constitution is more properly described as uncodified rather than unwritten, there is no doubt that a process of increasing codification is underway. In other words, ever more aspects of the political system are coming under assorted kinds of regulation and control. Informal understandings are being written down. Conventions are being translated into codes. Codes are being translated into laws. The unregulated spaces in the constitution are being regulated.

Examples of this process have been identified in previous chapters. When they are put together, the trend in unmistakable. The conduct of members of parliament has come under a new code, following the recommendations of the Nolan Committee, regulated by a new commissioner. Civil servants have acquired a code of their own. Ministers have had their responsibility to Parliament defined in a parliamentary resolution. A non-statutory code on access to government information was established, then developed into legislation. Party funding is being regulated, following the report by the Neill Committee, and parties have been legally registered. The conduct of elections and referendums is being subjected to new controls, with a new regulatory commission.

It is only necessary to recite a list of this kind to see the emerging pattern of codification. When the list is added to with the codifying consequences from other directions – for example, the procedures for resolving disputes between the courts and Parliament on European Convention on Human Rights issues, or the 'concordats' between Whitehall and the devolved governments that have been devised – it is clear that traditional descriptions of Britain's informal, unwritten and flexible constitution need radical revision. In key areas the new constitutional settlement is being written down and enshrined in legislation, as with the Human Rights Act and devolution legislation, and this process will continue as reform reaches new territory (as with the House of Lords, where the role and composition of a second chamber is having to be identified). In other areas, non-legislative codification is underway. Together these trends represent a major departure from a famously 'unwritten' constitution.

This does not mean that the British constitution is about to be written down, in a comprehensive and systematic way, as a rulebook for the state and its citizens. Not only is there no present intention to do this, but the scale and speed of current changes would make such an enterprise difficult if not impossible. We know, in constitutional terms, where Britain has come from; but it is not yet possible to know with any certainty where it may be going. Too much still has to unfold and settle down. The middle of a revolution is not the best moment to proclaim a durable settlement. In the words of the judge, Sir Stephen Sedley:

> Simply to put in writing our arrangements for the distribution and exercise of state power at a point in history where no comprehensive new consensus has emerged is to risk consolidating state power wherever it happens at that moment to reside. Constitution-making is for life, not just for Christmas.[3]

All that can really be said, therefore, is that a process is in train which certainly represents a many-sided codification of constitutional arrangements in Britain and may eventually come to be seen as a transition towards a 'proper' written constitution. When codification has reached a point which includes most significant matters, that may be the time when it will seem sensible to consolidate it all (and fill in any gaps) in systematic written form. Alternatively, this task may then seem less necessary or pressing. For the moment, the process is what matters, not the ultimate destination. A flexible constitution is being variously formalised and, because it is difficult to put changes into reverse once they are made, the new arrangements are in practice (if not in constitutional theory) being entrenched. An ancient constitution is on the move.

IS THERE A COHERENT PACKAGE OF POLITICAL REFORM?

Far from it, which may cause some difficulties further down the line. There is no grand plan. Instead there is a series of separate initiatives with their own motivations and expressions. This makes it a typically British approach to reform. The Blair government rejected the idea of an initial bill (or white paper) setting out the over-arching framework of constitutional reform; and was not interested in establishing new machinery through which the constitutional programme could be developed in a co-ordinated way. No less than eight Whitehall departments have been involved in different parts of this programme. In view of this, the co-ordination has been impressive, but this may become more difficult as the process moves from legislation to implementation.

Although each measure may have its own history – for example, the pressure for devolution in Scotland, or the growing demand for freedom of information legislation – it is only when they begin to be put into effect that their cross-cutting implications become apparent. What begins as a shopping list ends up as a jigsaw, but a jigsaw without a guiding picture of the final pattern. This is not to suggest that in practice political reform could have been delivered as a tidy plan (for the reasons described below), but it is nevertheless significant that there was no real attempt to approach the enterprise of reform in a coherent or systematic way. It was very much horses for courses. The long absence of serious constitutional debate in British politics also meant that it was difficult for such a debate to take place – even when it was needed – because its terms were so unfamiliar.

Yet a programme of political reform, certainly one as far-reaching as that in Britain, has two features which will eventually ensure that it does not remain as a set of separate and self-contained measures. First, it soon becomes apparent that changing one part of a political system has direct implications for other parts. This may not be the intention, but it is the inescapable consequence. It could be described as the law of interlocking effects. For example, the strong devolution demand from Scotland pulls in its wake the weaker demand from Wales. As Scotland and Wales develop forms of self-government, other parts of the United Kingdom are stimulated to explore the effects and to frame demands of their own. Similarly, reform of the House of Lords has implications for the role of the House of Commons, just as any proposal to change the voting system for elections to the Commons raises questions about how a reformed House of Lords should have its membership chosen. In this way the separate boxes collapse in on each other – and need to be sorted out in a more orderly manner. It is likely that these interlocking issues will become ever more central to the process of political reform as it unfolds.

This will also be necessary because of the second feature of any political reform programme. This is its dynamic character, setting off forces that acquire a momentum of their own and in turn generating other forces, a process that leads in directions far removed from the more limited compass intended at the outset. We could describe this as the law of unanticipated consequences. In this sense at least those who oppose constitutional reform on the basis of fears about 'where it will lead' are right, for once the dam breaks the whole landscape is likely to be transformed – and in ways that it is not possible to foresee (let alone control) with any degree of certainty.

It is not difficult to identify some of the issues at stake here. Devolution to Scotland and Wales may end up transforming the nature of the United Kingdom as a whole. Removing the hereditary element from the House of Lords may lead to new forms of representation. Elected mayors may eventually shift the balance of power between the centre and the localities. Giving judges a more visible role through the European Convention on Human Rights may stimulate demand for a domestic Bill of Rights, as well as calling into question traditional notions of parliamentary sovereignty. This list could easily be extended much further, but the central point is clear enough. None of these consequences formed part of the particular measures that put them in train, yet such consequences (or other ones) are inherent in the process of reform itself.

Some will find this threatening, while others will find it exciting. Yet there is no going back now. The constitutional status quo is no longer available and a dynamic process of change is under way. It is genuinely a period of transition in the life of the British political tradition, as its familiar fixtures and fittings start to come down but before their replacements are securely in place. The language of constitutional argument is having to be learned. Inquiries and commissions have to be invented to carry the reform process forward. The organisation of government has to be adapted for its new tasks. The coherence (both of ideas and of machinery) that was absent at the beginning of the reform process is slowly remedied, as interconnections press in and the dynamic is released. The crises that are sure to come will make their own contribution. The British may have muddled their way into political reform; but they are now required to think their way through it.

IS BRITAIN BREAKING UP?

Some fear so, others hope so, but there is no inevitable reason why it should. The question is raised by the cluster of devolution initiatives that together imply a very different kind of United Kingdom. These initiatives were presented as a way of maintaining and strengthening the Union, but there were also warnings that a slippery slope had been embarked upon that would eventually destroy the Union (see box, p. 338). On this latter view, the forces of nationalism would be unleashed and would prove unstoppable, taking Britain down with them.

The story is likely to be more complex than either of these two alternatives suggests. Instead of the Union simply being strengthened or destroyed, what may

---

The Union: Strengthened or destroyed?

The Union will be strengthened by recognising the claims of Scotland, Wales and the regions with strong identities of their own. The Government's devolution proposals, by meeting those aspirations, will not only safeguard but also enhance the Union

(White paper, *Scotland's Parliament*, Cm. 3658, July 1997)

Go down this route, and there will no longer be a single focus for democracy. Set up rival parliaments or assemblies, and they will grow hungry for more power. Of course, there's nothing to stop people voting to undermine or destroy the Union ... if they want to embark on a voyage into the unknown, uncharted waters of tempestuous change. The choice is – rightly – theirs. Our task is to warn them of the perils of doing so.

(John Major, Prime Minister, speech on the constitution, Centre for Policy Studies, 26 June 1996)

---

develop is a different kind of United Kingdom which has to be governed in quite new ways. Issues of territorial management, either long neglected or reduced to an ancestral distinction between 'high' politics (the preserve of the centre) and 'low' politics (suitable for the localities and peripheries), will come to assume a critical importance. The politics of class that has dominated much of twentieth-century British politics may find itself replaced, at least in part, by a new politics of territory, place and identity. There will be more attention to the geography of inequality. This will bring new issues on to the political agenda, requiring formidable political skills in negotiating them. The United Kingdom will have to learn to be a union state which is not a unitary state.

This will not be easy. The recognition of a genuinely multinational kingdom involves an equivalent recognition that it cannot be governed on the old terms. As devolutionary pressures extend from Scotland and Wales to England and its regions, the centre will have to respond. If local government finds more vigorous forms of civic expression, it is unlikely to be content with its present subordinate status. None of these developments fits into a tidy scheme. The way in which devolution makes itself felt in practice is likely to be as disparate and untidy as the assorted initiatives that set the process in motion in the first place. Scotland, Wales, London, elected mayors, regional agencies in England: there is no uniformity of approach in this package of 'devolving' measures and there will be no more uniformity in how they work themselves out.

There has been a deliberate emphasis on tailoring new institutional arrangements to particular needs, circumstances and demands. The result is that Scotland, Wales and Northern Ireland have acquired assemblies with different powers and with different kinds of executives, while the nine Regional Development Agencies in England have relationships with different kinds of regional chambers and with different prospects of growth towards regional assemblies. At the same time, the development of elected mayors – first in London, with other cities likely to follow – offers a further (and perhaps rival) model of sub-national government. On one view all this represents a pragmatic diversity in response to an assortment of challenges; on another view, it looks like a mess.

It may be a mess, but it is probably a necessary mess. Just as the constituent parts of the United Kingdom became part of the Union in different ways, times and circumstances, it is hardly surprising that the remaking of the United Kingdom as an explicitly multinational state involves similar diversity. What is emerging does not fit neatly into familiar categories. No longer a unitary state, it has not become a federal state either (as it might have become a century ago if the demand for 'home rule all round' had been met). It is difficult to find a name for the new untidy arrangements, which is why terms like 'quasi-federalism' and 'asymmetrical devolution' make their unlovely appearance. Power is being spread around, but in an uneven fashion.

The effect of such unevenness, necessary though it may be, is that it will be easy to find places to trip up. The problems and issues that are likely to make their presence felt in the politics of the 'new' United Kingdom are plentiful and apparent. There will be arguments between the devolved governments and the centre about a range of matters, crucially money, requiring mechanisms to resolve them. Political leaders in the new assemblies and executives will be judged on their robustness in standing up to London, rather than their party loyalty to the centre, and this will serve to fragment central political control. Electorates in the devolved areas are likely to respond best to parties and politicians promising a vigorous representation of their devolved interests, with voting behaviour showing somewhat different patterns at assembly and general elections. The uneven settlement may produce a politics of leapfrog, with different areas engaged in a competitive scramble to catch up or stay ahead (the English regions wanting to join the game, Wales wanting to emulate Scotland, Scotland wanting to stay in front . . .) in a system in dynamic motion.

Then there is England. The effect of devolution may well be to invent the English question in British politics. England may speak last, but she may also speak loudest. As the overwhelmingly dominant partner in the multinational enterprise of the United Kingdom, England is being forced to respond to the new configuration of power. What the eventual nature of this response will be has yet to be seen. It may be the trigger for English regionalism, or for nationalism. It may produce demands for some form of English assembly at Westminster to deal with England-only issues. It will certainly involve more attention to how public spending is distributed in relation to need between the different countries of the United Kingdom (with an English focus on over-spending in Scotland) and within the English regions (where the position of the South East is likely to come under critical scrutiny). The devolution settlement largely ignored England and the wider Union dimension, just as England traditionally ignored the fact that it was part of a multinational kingdom. Such ignorance will now no longer be possible.

With so many difficulties in prospect, it would clearly be foolish to dismiss the possibility of break-up. In practice it would not be possible to prevent a refer-endum in Scotland on the independence question if political circumstances com-pelled it. Not only that, but with the secession option already offered to the people of Northern Ireland it would be difficult to deny the same option to the people of Scotland if they clearly wanted to exercise it. This does not mean that it will happen. Devolution has two faces: 'It can be a stepping stone to secession, but it can also invigorate an existing union.'[4] Ultimately the United Kingdom will sur-vive if its various peoples want it to. The old shared symbols and identities of 'Britishness' (such as the empire and the monarchy) have either disappeared or declined, and the question is whether new ones can take their place.

What is clear is that the kind of United Kingdom that is now developing, involving multiple identities and devolved governments, will require political and administrative leadership of a high order if it is to operate successfully. Territorial management will be central to British politics, with relations between London and Edinburgh as the crucial axis, and involving new mechanisms for inter-governmental co-operation. There will also be opportunities for mutual learning, as different parts of the United Kingdom organise themselves in different ways (for example, the Scottish Parliament may stimulate reform at Westminster) and engage in policy innovation. The fact that devolution in the United Kingdom is necessarily untidy need not mean that it is inevitably chaotic. Pluralism is messy. The task will be to manage the mess, at least for those who want the United Kingdom to survive.

IS STRONG GOVERNMENT GIVING WAY TO ACCOUNTABLE GOVERNMENT?

In important respects the balance is shifting in this direction, but in other respects the picture looks rather different. On this key question, the jury is still out – and may be for some time. In the first chapter, the tradition of 'strong government' was identified as a key feature of British politics, the basis for a system of concen-trated executive power with few effective checks and balances on a government with a parliamentary majority, and with a much weaker tradition of account-ability sitting alongside it. Against this background, it becomes important to ask whether the programme of political reform in Britain – and other changes in the conduct of politics and government – represents a rebalancing of these traditions.

There can be no doubt that in a number of important ways it does. The effect of what is being done will be to insert new checks and balances into the system and to strengthen the accountability of central government. Devolution will cre-ate new centres of power, unscrambling the old centralised state. Human rights legislation puts a protective barrier around what ministers can do. Freedom of information makes traditional secrecy much more difficult. A reformed second chamber with greater legitimacy will be a more effective check on the Commons. It is only necessary to assemble a list of this kind (and it could be extended further) for it to be clear that a significant rebalancing of the British political tradition is taking place. Linked to the process of regulation and codification discussed earlier, the wide open spaces available to governments under Britain's famously flexible constitution begin to look rather more constrained.

Yet the picture is complicated by other considerations, which seem to some to point in a contrary direction, and make a final assessment of underlying trends less straightforward than it might at first sight appear to be. There are two main factors involved here. The first concerns the extent to which political control is being increasingly centralised. This has been the charge levelled against Tony Blair's New Labour in particular, with its tight control of political communication, disciplined approach to party management, more centralised supervision of candidate selection, and a strengthening of central direction within government. Britain is witnessing an unprecedented centralisation both in the operation of party and in the peacetime conduct of government. The former is justified as a response to the indiscipline and unprofessionalism of the past (for which parties were punished by the electorate); the latter as necessary to ensure that New Labour's pledges to the voters are implemented through vigorous 'can do' government from the centre. Whatever the motivation, the paradoxical effect is that a period which is rightly associated with a historic dispersal of power from the centre and new mechanisms of accountability can also be presented as the triumph of dirigisme over pluralism.[5] It remains to be seen which trend will prove more significant and durable.

The second complicating factor concerns the failure to develop more effective forms of accountability in the central executive territory of government. This issue goes to the heart of the British political process. It turns on the balance between the executive and the legislature, the directing and the scrutinising functions, strong government and accountable government. The need to make Parliament a more effective instrument of accountability has long been recognised, but it has also been more recognised than acted upon. As government has expanded its functions over the last century, and in more recent times has developed new ways of organising itself (as with quangos and executive agencies), the challenge for Parliament has been to devise new forms of accountability appropriate to this changing executive territory. It has not been notably successful at doing this. This is not because it is unclear what a more effective Parliament would look like,[6] but because there has not been the political will to create one.

Here another paradox presents itself. The Blair government's political reform programme included a commitment to 'modernise' Parliament, yet the intensification of party management and the strengthening of central direction within government inevitably makes this a problematic enterprise. With party control at its zenith, Parliament is unlikely to be let off its leash. Modernisation can point in different and contrary directions. It can mean more efficiency in the way that Parliament processes executive business, or more effectiveness in the way it holds the executive to account. While a little progress has been made with the former kind of modernisation, the latter kind has so far been the absent guest at the political reform feast. Yet it should really be the item that defines and shapes the whole reform programme, for it is the place where the crucial balance between strong and accountable government is to be found.

This is why it provides an acid test of the general direction in which political change in Britain is moving. Unless the legislature is conspicuously strengthened in relation to the executive, the root of the matter in terms of the essential character of British politics will not have been attended to. There is no doubt that this is what New Labour accepted in its pre-election commitment to parliamentary modernisation, but the perspective from government can be rather different. There are fundamentals at stake here, which governments (especially ones with a commanding parliamentary majority) have an interest in leaving undisturbed. It would mean exploring why the grand doctrine of parliamentary sovereignty amounts in practice to routine parliamentary supineness in the face of the executive. Parliament is a poodle posing as a rottweiler, which makes for an absurd spectacle. The myth of parliamentary sovereignty serves as a convenient substitute for real accountability.

The question is whether this imbalance at the heart of the British political system is likely to be remedied, if only modestly, as the state is re-engineered. There are three main ways in which this might happen. The first would involve radical re-engineering, replacing the fusion of executive and legislature with a separation of powers. This would guarantee a vigorous Parliament, freed from its umbilical link with the executive, but it is also the most unlikely solution in any foreseeable future. The second way would involve changing the electoral system, so that majoritarian single-party government became less likely and Parliament became a more unpredictable animal to control. But that is precisely what those opposed to electoral reform want to avoid. This leaves the third way, which is for a government which recognises the need for at least some modest re-balancing of the executive–legislature relationship in the interests of accountability to put in hand initiatives that Parliament could build on. It is too early to assess whether this is likely to happen in any serious fashion under the Blair government, but the early omens (apart from the production of more bills in draft form for parliamentary and public scrutiny) are not very promising.

It is perfectly sensible to want to have both effective ('strong') government and accountable government. The balance can tip too far in either direction, as political systems around the world demonstrate. The British political tradition represents a particular version of strong government, the product of a long history of concentrated executive power at the centre, and this brings with it a particular weakness in relation to the mechanisms of accountability which (between elections) are designed to check and scrutinise what governments do. A recent 'audit' of government in Britain provides detailed evidence on this imbalance.[7] A re-balancing exercise would properly want to retain the directing role of the executive that is central to the British system while also seeking to strengthen its accountability, through Parliament and beyond. It is interesting to note that the report of the Jenkins Commission on the voting system, published in October 1998, made much of the fact that its recommendations were consistent with 'the British tradition'.[8] It remains to be seen whether the British tradition of strong government is going to be required to accept a stronger dose of accountability than it has been accustomed to expect.

IS A REALIGNMENT TAKING PLACE IN BRITISH POLITICS?

Something significant is clearly happening in British politics, but it is far too soon to judge whether this will come to be seen as a permanent realignment of political forces. Labour (and the Liberal Democrats) hope so, the Conservatives fear so; but neither hopes nor fears should be confused with political trends. These will become clear only much later. After the 1992 general election, the fourth in a row won by the Conservatives, it was widely asserted that the era of permanent Conservative rule had arrived and that Labour was in terminal decline. After the 1997 general election, won by Labour with more seats than any party since 1935 and with the Conservatives winning less than at any election since 1906, it was possible to believe that a political earthquake had occurred that would permanently transform the landscape of British politics. This may turn out to be so; but a more cautious assessment might suggest that the earth is still moving.

History will certainly see the years between 1992 and 1997 as an extraordinary period, as an ascendant Conservative Party disintegrated and a rejected Labour Party remade itself. The reversal of political fortunes was seismic and unprecedented. It crossed all classes and every part of Britain. The period may come to be seen as the Strange Death of Conservative Britain. It was all the more remarkable because it involved not merely a routine swing of electoral fortune but something much more fundamental: nothing less than a reversal of the way in which voters had been accustomed for so long to think about the basic characteristics of the two major parties. This was the heart of Labour's strategy, the basis of 'new' Labour, and it eventually became the fatal hole in the Conservative position. When the 1997 election came, instead of reverting to old identities the voters affirmed their new ones. This was the real difference between 1992 and 1997.

The question is whether the new identities will last. The whole of Tony Blair's approach to government is designed to ensure that they will. His oft-repeated mantra that 'we were elected as New Labour and we shall govern as New Labour' has this as its purpose. The internal realignment within the Labour Party was seen as the precondition for a larger realignment within British politics. On any test, the strategy has been audacious and successful. But will it last? Will Labour's remarkable victory in 1997 – and long honeymoon thereafter – come to be seen as the beginning of a prolonged period of New Labour ascendancy in British politics? There is no doubt that this is the scale of the ambition set for himself by Tony Blair, often expressed as a determination to replace the Conservative dominance of the twentieth century with a 'progressive' dominance of the twenty-first century (see box, p. 344), but of course ambition is not the same as achievement.

It would certainly be a remarkable achievement when set against the history of the recent past. Between 1945 and 1997 the Conservatives governed for twice as

Building a new consensus?

The ultimate objective is a new political consensus of the left-of-centre, based around the key values of democratic socialism and European social democracy, firm in its principles but capable of responding to changing times, so that those values may be put into practice and secure broad support to govern for long periods of time. To reach that consensus we must value the contribution of Lloyd George, Beveridge and Keynes and not just Attlee, Bevan or Crosland. We should start to explore our own history with fresh understanding and an absence of preconceptions . . .

Part of that rediscovery is to welcome the radical left-of-centre tradition outside of our own Party, as well as celebrate the achievements of that tradition within it . . . The task of the left-of-centre today is to put these two strengths together, led by Labour and providing the same broad consensus for change that a previous generation did in 1945.

I am not interested in governing for a term, coming to power on a wave of euphoria, a magnificent edifice of expectations, which dazzles for a while before collapse. I want to rebuild this Party from its foundations, making sure every stone is in its rightful place, every design crafted not just for effect but to a useful purpose.

(Tony Blair, *Let Us Face the Future: The 1945 Anniversary Lecture*, Fabian Society, 5 July 1995)

many years (thirty-five) as Labour (seventeen), but even these figures are over-generous to Labour as the party had no secure majority for a third of its years in government and never managed to govern for two consecutive full terms. To reverse this historical trend, rather than merely to win a general election, might seem a daunting task. Yet there are favourable factors at work. The modern Labour Party is a formidable political machine; while Tony Blair is a formidable political leader. Blairism commands the political agenda and embraces a wide swathe of the electorate. While Labour is less factionalised than at any time in its history, the Conservative Party remains deeply divided. There is also the fact that expectations of what governments can do are sharply reduced compared to the 1970s, when Labour was last in office, and this should make the business of governing easier: 'One of the striking features of British politics over the last decade has been a reduction in expectations of the state'.[9] A decent competence in the service of modest objectives, rather than immodest expectations and inevitable disillusionment, seems to be the spirit of the age.

Yet none of this guarantees that the Blairite ambition will be realised. Even the long after-glow of an electoral landslide eventually confronts the political realities that dog the life of any government: economic difficulties, policy failures, intractable problems, splits, rivalries, scandals, staleness, boredom. Even a government with epic historical ambitions remains, at bottom, only a government. Also the

Conservatives will, presumably, at some point decide that they would like to be in office again and start seriously to do something about it. Then there is the nature of the modern electorate itself, which may have delivered an electoral landslide in 1997 but which may be quite capable of future dramatic shifts too. Increasingly dealigned and without enduring anchors of allegiance, the electorate is more 'available' to political offers than was formerly the case. This makes Labour's crushing victory in 1997 rather more fragile than it might seem. One analysis of electoral behaviour puts it like this: 'The danger for new Labour is encapsulated in the phrase "easy come, easy go".'[10]

What this means is that the electorate is increasingly likely to exhibit the fickleness of political consumers. Support has to be constantly 'reinvented'; it cannot be taken for granted. The task for Labour is to sustain the cross-class coalition of support it assembled in 1997 (just as the task for the Conservatives is to prevent this happening). Performance in office, measured in terms of governing competence and the ability to deliver the practical improvements that were promised, will be the decisive factor in this. Voters may decide they still like the product they bought in 1997, or they might be tempted to shop around again. All that can really be said is that New Labour may have put together a durable electoral constituency. Whether it really has remains to be seen.

The same applies to the ideological identity of Blairism itself. This is endlessly debated. The question is whether Blairism's self-description of a 'radical centre' (or 'third way') that confounds ancestral categories of left and right provides the basis for a new consensus in British politics of a lasting kind. Even if it does, this does not necessarily mean that New Labour will preside over it. The Labour government of 1945 to 1951 was the architect of the post-war consensus, but this did not prevent the Conservatives presiding over it from 1951 to 1964. A key issue for the Conservatives now is whether, in a similar way, they want to fight Labour for the new centre ground or continue on an ideological excursion of their own. The evidence so far seems to suggest that most voters now locate Labour in the centre ground, where they also position themselves, whereas the Conservatives are seen to be out on the right (Figure 10.1). This represents a significant realignment of opinion.

Blairism is often compared with Thatcherism, in terms of both carving out a particular ideological identity and putting together a coalition of electoral support around it. Whatever their other similarities, Blairism and Thatcherism both stand for modernisation. For Thatcherism this was market modernisation; while Blairism can perhaps best be described as a doctrine of *inclusive modernisation*. It is radical, but it is also a politics without enemies. It claims to represent the new common sense. What used to be called the 'hegemonic' project of the left involved making its ideas into the common sense of the people; but Blairism's project involves making the common sense of the people into the left's ideas.

There is clearly the potential for radical political realignment in all of this. Tony Blair is quite explicit about this, in talking of a 'new politics' that breaks with old traditions and in seeking to assemble a broad 'progressive' coalition that draws upon assorted elements in Britain's past. The agreement with the Liberal

Figure 10.1 Who's left and right now
(a) How the parties look to the average voter (%)

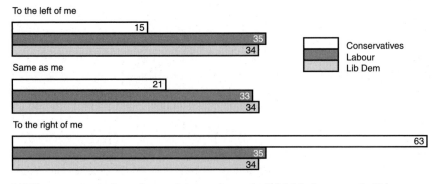

To the left of me

	15
	35
	34

◻ Conservatives
▨ Labour
▨ Lib Dem

Same as me

	21
	33
	34

To the right of me

	63
	35
	34

(b) Where voters put themselves and the parties on the left/right/centre scale (%)

	Voters	Lab	Con	Lib Dem
Left wing	7	8	5	5
Left of centre	15	21	5	18
Centre	37	23	10	34
Right of centre	13	15	25	7
Right wing	5	7	29	3

Source: ICM, October 1998

Democrats was a concrete expression of this 'big tent' approach. Proposals for electoral reform have the issue of future political realignment at their centre, with the capacity to redefine the whole shape of both the party system and the political system. Yet all this remains only as potential. After the electoral earthquake of 1997, British politics may slowly return to normal. However, Britain has a Prime Minister who seems determined that this should not happen.

CONCLUSION

For all the reasons discussed in this chapter, 'normalcy' is not really an option as far as the British political process is concerned. Even if the party battle eventually settles back into a more or less familiar shape after the effects of 1997 are fully digested, the political system itself will not. As the programme of constitutional reform begins to bite, with new institutions and arenas in place, the nature of political life in Britain will inevitably change. A particular way of doing politics – highly centralised, poorly constitutionalised – will no longer be possible in the new environment; and new ways will have to be learned. This may not have been the intention, but it will necessarily be the effect. A dynamic process of political change is underway and there is no going back. Indeed, the momentum is likely to be in the direction of going further.

What is taking place can perhaps be described as a shift from 'parlia-

Figure 10.2 Cartoon from *The Observer*, 3 October 1999. Copyright © Christopher Riddell

mentary' to 'popular' sovereignty. As such, it goes to the heart of Britain's traditional political arrangements. Parliamentary sovereignty is associated with concentrated executive power and the absence of formal constitutional constraints on majoritarian politics. Popular sovereignty is associated with constitutional protection for the rights of citizens, checks and balances on what governments can do, and greater involvement in decision-making. In so far as Britain is engaged in a process of pluralising and diffusing power, and putting a new framework of accountability around the unregulated spaces of the constitution, it can be seen to be moving from one conception of sovereignty to another (notwithstanding what was said above about the failure of reform to get to grips with the central executive territory). It is unlikely to be described in quite this way in practice, but that does not diminish the importance of what is happening.

Any mention of sovereignty in Britain inevitably raises the issue of Europe. As power is decentralised within Britain, this may produce a new way of thinking about the European Union. The nation state remains pivotal, but it has to learn to live with other centres of power both downwards and upwards. This way of thinking about power has proved more difficult in Britain, where the sovereignty argument has been mobilised against it, than in more pluralistic political traditions; but this may now be changing. The decision on whether to join the European single currency will demonstrate whether this is indeed the case. More than this, it may even be that Britain's own exercise in quasi-federal constitution-building will enable it to contribute positively to the similar task that is required in Europe. The British contribution is likely to remain a distinctive one (with the Blair government as resistant to full-blown integrationism as its predecessor), but it may well be rather more constructive and imaginative than in the past.

This is a reminder that a political system will be judged by its success in negotiating the world, and tackling the problems, that a country faces. For Britain the relationship with Europe is clearly a pivotal issue, with a long and troubled history,[11] and defines a view of Britain's place in the world (something thrown into sharp relief again at the end of 1998 when Britain alone joined the United States in bombing Iraq). It is not simply a matter of relations with Europe, but a view of the kind of Europe that is envisaged. For example, there is clearly some difference of emphasis between the Blairite 'third way' approach to social and economic issues and the approach of the other centre-left governments in the European Union. Yet all face the same pressures from a dynamic global environment – and this will condition the nature of their response. But one thing is absolutely clear. Europe, with its single currency, is a formidable bloc in the world; and Britain's destiny is inescapably attached to it.

For a long period, especially after the Second World War, Britain's political system was widely admired as a model of effective and stable government. There then followed a period when the preoccupation with British 'decline' produced a much less favourable view of the performance of the political system, coupled with a developing argument about its democratic deficiencies. What is interesting about what is happening now is not just that 'modernisation' has replaced decline as the defining theme of the age, but that it emphatically includes the political system too. Whatever else the government elected in 1997 will be remembered for, its programme of political reform will undoubtedly be seen as having historic significance.

However, what is also interesting is that political reform is allied with a determination to make government deliver on the other programmes – education, health, welfare reform, crime and the rest – which formed its contract with the electorate. Political reform by itself butters very few parsnips with the electorate, and politicians know what they will be judged on. Not only does this mean that constitutional issues must not come to be seen as a distraction from the so-called 'real' issues, but also there can be tension between an iron determination from the centre to make government deliver (which is certainly a characteristic of the Blair government) and a programme of diffusing and pluralising power. This takes us back to the earlier discussion about 'strong versus accountable government' that has been central to British politics – and the evident need for both effectiveness and accountability. The programme of political reform is being undertaken by a government that is clearly not prepared to compromise its capacity for effective action or disciplined political management. This may prove to be a source of future tension.

As Britain entered the twentieth century, its politicians presided over a great empire and a great industrial economy. Its political institutions, still largely untouched by the forces of organised democracy, carried the confidence of their unbroken history. The symbols of nation sustained an unexplored Britishness. As Britain enters the twenty-first century, it does so as a medium-sized, post-imperial power. Its politicians define their task as the modernisation of ancestral institutions and attitudes. The nature of the United Kingdom – and of Britishness – has to be renegotiated. A new relationship with Europe has to be established. Its political and constitutional tradition has to be rebalanced. On any test, it is a period of challenge and change, requiring all the resources of a rich political culture to see it through. At the beginning of a new century, the British political process is both the agency and object of fundamental change.

NOTES

1 ' "People's Panel" to advise the Queen', *Independent on Sunday*, 1 November 1998.
2 Quoted in V. Bogdanor, *The People and the Party System* (Cambridge University Press, 1981), p. 35.
3 S. Sedley, 'The constitution in the twenty-first century', in Lord Nolan and S. Sedley, *The Making and Remaking of the British Constitution* (Blackstone, 1997), p. 88.
4 R. Hazell and B. O'Leary, 'A rolling programme of devolution: slippery slope or safeguard of the Union?' in R. Hazell (ed.), *Constitutional Futures* (Oxford University Press, 1999), p. 23. Also see V. Bogdanor, 'Devolution: decentralisation or disintegration?', *Political Quarterly*, vol. 70, no. 2, 1999.
5 For example, by D. Marquand, *Must Labour Win?*, Ninth ESRC Annual Lecture, Fabian Society, December 1998.
6 P. Riddell, *Parliament under Pressure* (Gollanz, 1997) provides a convincing recent account.
7 S. Weir and D. Beetham, *Political Power and Democratic Control in Britain* (Routledge, 1999).
8 *Report of the Independent Commission on the Voting System*, Cmnd. 4090, October 1998, para. 45–49, pp. 13–17.
9 R. Jowell *et al.*, *British Social Attitudes: The 14th Report* (Social and Community Planning Research/Ashgate, 1997), p. 97.
10 D. Sanders, 'Voting and the electorate' in P. Dunleavy, A. Gamble, I. Holliday and G. Peele (eds.), *Developments in British Politics 5* (Macmillan, 1997), p. 73.
11 The relationship is traced in H. Young, *This Blessed Plot: Britain and Europe from Churchill to Blair* (Macmillan, 1998).

FURTHER READING

A good supplement to any textbook is P. Dunleavy, A. Gamble, I. Holliday and G. Peele, *New Developments in British Politics 5* (Macmillan, 1997). The analysis in P. Riddell, *Parliament under Pressure* (Gollancz, 1997) is well worth reading, while D. Kavanagh, *The Reordering of British Politics* (Oxford University Press, 1997) provides an overview of the recent past. An ambitious 'audit' of the contemporary condition of British democracy is provided by S. Weir and D. Beetham, *Political Power and Democratic Control in Britain* (Routledge, 1999). An excellent exploration of the implications of constitutional reform is to be found in R. Hazell (ed.), *Constitutional Futures: A History of the Next Ten Years* (Oxford University Press, 1999). One important strand is discussed by V. Bogdanor, *Devolution in the United Kingdom* (Oxford University Press, 1999), L. Nolan and S. Sedley, *The Making and Remaking of the British Constitution* (Blackstone, 1997) and R. Blackburn and R. Plant (eds), *Constitutional Reform: The Labour Government's Constitutional Reform Agenda* (Addison Wesley Longman, 1999). Finally, the special issue of the *Political Quarterly* on 'Democracy in Britain' (vol. 70, no. 2, 1999) contains a range of interesting articles.

Appendix 1: Key terms – A glossary of 100 key words and phrases used in British politics

Act of Parliament A law which is passed by Parliament and agreed to by the monarch.

Additional member system (AMS) A voting system in which electors have two votes; the first for an individual to represent the constituency, and the second for a candidate on a party list.

Adjournment debates Short debates introduced by backbench MPs, often on constituency issues, at the close of daily parliamentary business, and on Wednesday mornings.

Alternative vote (AV) A voting system in which the candidate with an absolute majority wins, calculated by eliminating the candidates with the least votes and distributing their second preference votes.

Backbenchers Members of Parliament without posts in the government or Official Opposition who sit either on the back benches of the Chamber or on the front benches below the first gangway.

Barnett formula A method of adjusting the public expenditure for Scotland, Wales and Northern Ireland to reflect changes in comparable programmes in England (or, in the case of Northern Ireland, Great Britain).

Bill A proposed law which has to be discussed and approved by Parliament.

Boundary Commission An independent body appointed to determine the boundaries of electoral areas and constituencies.

Budget The government's proposals for balancing the country's income and expenditure for the next year.

By-election An election to fill a vacancy in a specific electoral area occurring between main elections.

Cabinet The group of senior government ministers who are responsible for running the departments of state and deciding government policy.

Capping Council tax capping is a method by which central government may limit the budgets of individual local authorities.

Commission (EU) A group of representatives from each EU member state which proposes and carries out Community policies.

Constituency The geographical area that each member of parliament represents.

Constitution   The fundamental rules of the state, usually (though not in Britain) contained in a written document.

Conventions   Unwritten rules or descriptions of usual practice.

Council of Ministers (EU)   The EU's principal decision-making body, on which each government is represented.

Cross benchers   Peers in the House of Lords who do not represent a political party, and who sit between the two main sets of benches.

Delegated legislation   Legislation which is made by an authority, other than Parliament, whose powers to legislate are delegated by Parliament through an Act. It usually takes the form of Orders, Regulations or Rules made by a minister, or by the Queen in Council (that is, the Privy Council).

Deregulation   Orders to amend or repeal provisions in an Act of Parliament which are considered to impose a burden on business or others.

Devolution   The delegation of certain powers to lower levels or tiers of government, usually in specific geographical areas, such as Scotland, Wales or Northern Ireland.

Directive (EU)   A law passed by the EU with which national parliaments have to comply.

Dissolution   The ending of a Parliament, which is then followed by a general election.

Division   A formal method whereby Parliament decides on a matter by voting.

Early day motion (EDM)   A motion set down in the House of Commons for 'an early day', used as a device by MPs to register views and gather support on almost any subject.

Erskine May   Parliament's textbook of procedural rules and precedents, named after its original author, Sir Thomas Erskine May.

Federalism   A union composed of sub-national units (such as states, provinces) of equal competence.

First past the post (FPTP)   A voting system in which each constituency elects its own representative, and the candidate with the most votes wins the seat.

Focus group   A representative group of voters gathered to test opinions about policies and issues.

Front bencher   A senior member of either the government or the Opposition who sits on the front benches in the Chamber.

Green paper   A consultative document published by the government setting out policy proposals for discussion prior to final decision.

Guillotine   Allocation of time order, fixing a compulsory timetable for the conclusion of proceedings on a bill in the House of Commons.

Hansard   The definitive official report of what was said in Parliament, edited by removing repetitions and correcting obvious mistakes.

Holyrood   A term used as shorthand for the Scottish Parliament in Edinburgh; its new parliamentary building.

Judicial review   The ability of the courts to decide whether a minister, or other public body or official, has acted within the law.

Junior minister   A minister who is not in the Cabinet.

Law Lords   Peers who hold high legal office; collectively the final point of appeal for most purposes in the British legal system.

Lobby   A group of selected journalists from newspapers, TV and radio, who have privileged access within the House of Commons and can be given unattributable government briefings.

Lobbying   Trying to influence ministers, officials, MPs or peers to introduce or change legislation in favour of a particular group.

Mandate   The political authority to carry out the policies set out in a party's manifesto, endorsed by the electorate at a general election.

Manifesto   A document in which a political party sets out its policies, usually at an election.

Minister   A politician who is a member of the government.

Ministerial responsibility   The doctrine that ministers take responsibility for any errors or wrongdoings of their departments and, if necessary, resign as a consequence.

Next Steps executive agencies   Sections of the civil service converted into separate agencies responsible to the relevant minister through a chief executive.

Nolan (Neill) Committee   The committee on standards in public life, first chaired by Lord Nolan and then by Lord Neill.

Non-departmental public bodies (NDPBs)   Another term for quangos.

Official Opposition   The largest non-government party in the House of Commons.

Ombudsman   An independent official appointed to deal with complaints against public authorities.

Opinion poll   Survey of people's views taken by questioning a representative sample of the population.

Parliamentary private secretary (PPS)   An MP appointed by a minister to be an unpaid assistant.

Party political/election broadcast (PPB/PEB)   A short broadcast by political parties carried free on all TV channels (and BBC radio).

Patronage   The ability to use political power to give public jobs to friends or supporters.

Permanent secretary   The most senior civil servant in a government department.

Poll tax   A flat rate local tax introduced to replace the rates, now replaced by the Council Tax.

Prerogative   The power of government to take decisions without recourse to Parliament, derived from the historical rights of the Crown.

Primary legislation   Acts of Parliament, also known as statutes.

Private member's bill   A bill initiated by a backbench MP.

Privy Council   The group of senior politicians and others that advises the Queen.

Programme motion   An agreed timetable for the consideration of a bill in the House of Commons.

Prorogation　The period between the end of one session of Parliament and the beginning of the next; also the act of ending a session.

Qualified majority voting (QMV)　A system of decision-making in the EU Council of Ministers in which no veto is allowed, but more than a simple majority is required.

Quangos　Quasi-autonomous public bodies appointed and financed by government.

Queen's speech　The speech at the opening of each session of Parliament in which details of the government's legislative programme are set out.

Recess　A period when either House of Parliament is not sitting, but not dissolved.

Redistribution of seats　A realignment of constituency boundaries to reflect population movements.

Referendum　A ballot in which all voters can make a decision on a specific issue.

Regional list　A voting system in multi-member constituencies in which voters choose either a party or an independent candidate; with seats allocated to the party which would at each stage have the highest average vote per seat, and to candidates in the order in which their party has listed them.

Revenue support grant (RSG)　The grant paid by central to local government to help pay for local services and thus reduce the level of local taxation.

Royal assent　The final stage of an Act of Parliament becoming law, by the Queen formally giving her agreement.

Rule of law　The doctrine that laws should apply equally to everyone in the state.

Salisbury convention　The doctrine that the House of Lords should not reject at second reading any government legislation which carries out an electoral or manifesto commitment, especially if it has been passed by the House of Commons.

Secondary legislation　Another name for delegated legislation.

Secretary of state　Minister who heads one of the most important government departments.

Select committee　A parliamentary committee which investigates a particular topic or monitors the work of a government department.

Separation of powers　The theoretical separation of the executive, legislative and judicial branches of government.

Shadow cabinet　The group of senior members of the Official Opposition.

Single transferable vote (STV)　Electors list the candidates in order of preference in multi-member constituencies; a candidate is elected once their votes reach a specified quota, with any excess votes transferred to other candidates until all the seats in the constituency are filled.

Sleaze　A term denoting low standards or corruption, especially in a political context.

Soundbite　A short quote designed to make maximum political impact in the media.

Sovereignty   The area over which a state and its government have unfettered freedom of action.

Speaker   Presides over the House of Commons and is responsible for keeping order during debates and ensuring that the rules of the House are obeyed.

Special adviser   A political adviser who works for, and is appointed by, a minister.

Spin doctor   A publicist who presents information in the best possible light for a politician or party.

Standard spending assessment (SSA)   The formula by which the government grant is distributed amongst local councils.

Standing committee   A committee of the House of Commons that considers bills in detail.

Standing orders   Rules of either House (or of a body such as a local authority), which continue in force ('stand') from one session to another.

Statute book   A notional 'book' in which each statute, or Act of Parliament, is a separate chapter.

Statutory instrument   Delegated legislation made by a minister and approved by Parliament.

Subsidiarity   The principle that decisions should be taken at the most appropriate (or lowest) level.

Swing   A measure of the number of voters who have switched from one party to another, calculated by adding the rise in one party's percentage share of the vote to the fall of another's, and dividing by two.

Tactical voting   The practice of voting for a non-preferred candidate so as to prevent a less-preferred candidate from being elected.

Ten-minute rule bill   Introduced by backbench MPs, who can give a short speech (up to ten minutes) outlining their proposals, but with little chance of proceeding further.

Timetabling   Programme motions or allocation of time orders ('guillotines') that set out a timetable for the conclusion of proceedings on a bill.

Uniform business rate   A system of taxing business property at a uniform percentage of valuation throughout the country.

Unitary authority   A single tier of local government dealing with all or most delegated functions in a particular area.

Usual channels   Regular contacts between government and opposition whips' offices designed to smooth the passage of parliamentary business.

Westminster   A term used as shorthand for parliamentary activity in and around the Palace of Westminster.

Whips   Parliamentary party business managers who try to ensure that MPs act, speak and vote in line with party policy; and written instructions to that end.

Whitehall   A shorthand term to denote government departments or government bureaucracy.

White paper   Statement of government policy which sets out proposals for legislative change, often before a major bill is introduced.

Appendix 2: Key dates – An outline chronology of key events in British political history from the beginning of universal suffrage

1918 (Feb)	Representation of the People Act gives vote to nearly all men and women over 30
1918 (Nov)	End of First World War
1918 (Dec)	Lloyd George's coalition government re-elected in the 'coupon election'
1919 (Jun)	Treaty of Versailles establishes peace in Europe
1920 (Dec)	Government of Ireland Act establishes a Northern Ireland parliament
1922 (Oct)	Bonar Law becomes Prime Minister (PM)
1923 (May)	Baldwin becomes PM
1924 (Jan)	MacDonald becomes first Labour PM
1924 (Dec)	Baldwin becomes PM again
1926 (May)	General strike
1928 (July)	Voting age equalised at 21 for men and women
1929 (Jun)	MacDonald becomes Labour PM for the second time
1931 (Jul–Aug)	Gold crisis; MacDonald resigns, re-elected to lead national government
1935 (Jan)	Death of George V
1935 (Jun)	Baldwin wins general election
1935 (Dec)	Abdication of Edward VIII; accession of George VI
1937 (May)	Neville Chamberlain succeeds Baldwin as PM
1939 (Sep)	Britain declares war on Germany
1940 (May)	Churchill becomes PM
1941 (Dec)	Japan attacks Pearl Harbor; United States enters the war
1942 (Dec)	Beveridge report on social security published
1944 (Jun)	D-Day invasion of France
1944 (Aug)	Butler's Education Act passed
1945 (May)	End of the war in Europe
1945 (Jul)	General election: Labour landslide and Attlee becomes PM
1945 (Aug)	End of the war in the Far East
1948 (Jul)	NHS established
1950 (Feb)	General election: Labour returned with tiny majority
1951 (Oct)	General election: Conservatives win with Churchill as PM

1952 (Feb)	Death of George VI: accession of Queen Elizabeth
1955 (May)	General election: Eden becomes PM
1956 (Oct–Nov)	Suez crisis
1957 (Jan)	Eden resigns; Macmillan becomes PM
1957 (Mar)	Treaty of Rome establishes EEC
1959 (Oct)	General election: Conservatives increase majority
1962 (Feb)	Commonwealth Immigration Act – first immigration controls introduced
1963 (Jan)	France vetoes Britain's application to join EEC
1963 (Oct)	Douglas-Home succeeds Macmillan as PM
1964 (Oct)	General election returns Labour to power under Harold Wilson
1965 (Nov)	Capital punishment for murder abolished
1966 (Mar)	General election: Labour increases majority
1967 (Nov)	Devaluation of the pound
1969 (May)	Voting age reduced to 18
1970 (Jun)	General election: Conservatives return to power under Heath
1972 (Jan)	Miners' strike
1972 (Mar)	Northern Ireland parliament abolished
1973 (Jan)	Britain joins European Common Market
1974 (Feb)	Miners' strike; general elections in February and October return Labour with small majorities
1975 (Jun)	Referendum confirms British membership of the Common Market
1976 (Apr)	Callaghan succeeds Wilson as PM
1976 (Dec)	Public expenditure cuts following loan from International Monetary Fund
1977 (Mar)	Lib-Lab pact formed
1977–8	'Winter of discontent' – widespread industrial unrest
1979 (Mar)	Devolution referendums in Wales and Scotland
1979 (May)	General election: Conservatives return to office under Thatcher: first woman PM
1981 (Mar)	Social Democratic Party launched
1982 (Apr–Jun)	Falklands war
1983 (Jun)	General election: Conservatives returned with huge majority
1984–5	Miners' strike
1985 (Nov)	Anglo-Irish Agreement signed
1986 (Feb)	Government signs Single European Act
1987 (Jun)	General election: Conservatives re-elected with huge majority
1989 (Apr)	Poll tax introduced in Scotland
1989 (Nov)	Berlin Wall demolished
1990 (Apr)	Poll tax introduced in England and Wales
1990 (Nov)	Major replaces Thatcher as party leader and thus PM
1991 (Jan–Feb)	Gulf war
1992 (Apr)	General election: Major re-elected with small majority

1993 (Aug)	Britain ratifies Maastricht Treaty; Northern Ireland peace initiative
1995 (Jun–Jul)	Major resigns as Conservative Party leader but stands again and is re-elected
1997 (May)	General election: Labour returned under Blair with massive majority
1997 (Jun)	Hague replaces Major as Conservative Party leader
1998 (Apr)	Good Friday agreement on the future of Northern Ireland
1999 (May)	Elections for the Scottish Parliament and the Welsh Assembly
1999 (June)	Powers transferred to the Scottish Parliament and the Welsh Assembly

Appendix 3: Key facts – British politics and society

This appendix has two main purposes. First, it sets out some basic information about the British political process over the past century: details of governments and their leaders; general election results and how people voted; and how the volume of legislation has grown. Second, it describes some of the changing background of British society against which the political process works. Most of the tables and charts here are self-explanatory, but where this is not so a word of explanation has been added. Those in search of further detail are referred to the original sources.

The material here is necessarily only a small sample of what is available, but there are many sources of further information. The most comprehensive and accessible include two key volumes of political and electoral facts, both of which are updated from time to time. These are David and Gareth Butler's *British Political Facts* (new edition *20th Century British Political Facts*, Macmillan, 2000) and Colin Rallings and Michael Thrasher's updating of Fred Craig's *British Electoral Facts* (new edition, Ashgate, forthcoming). The Office for National Statistics (ONS) produces numerous compilations of useful statistics including three excellent annual publications of a general kind: *Social Trends*, the *Annual Abstract of Statistics* and *Britain: The Official Yearbook of the United Kingdom*. The last not only includes many useful statistics but also provides a comprehensive summary of information on almost every aspect of life in Britain.

Table A.1 Twentieth-century Prime Ministers and their governments

Dates of office	Prime Minister	Composition of govt	Govt majority (general election)	Total seats
Jun 1895–Jul 1902	Marquess of Salisbury	Con	135 (Sep 1900)	670
Jul 1902–Dec 1905	Arthur Balfour	Con		670
Dec 1905–Apr 1908	Sir Henry Campbell-Bannerman	Lib	129 (Jan 1906)	670
Apr 1908–May 1915	H. H. Asquith	Lib	none (Jan 1910)	670
			none (Dec 1910)	670
May 1915–Dec 1916	H. H. Asquith	Coalition		
Dec 1916–Oct 1922	David Lloyd George	Coalition	283 (Dec 1918)	707
Oct 1922–May 1923	Andrew Bonar Law	Con	74 (Nov 1922)	615
May 1923–Jan 1924	Stanley Baldwin	Con		
Jan–Nov 1924	James Ramsay MacDonald	Lab	none (Dec 1923)	615
Nov 1924–Jun 1929	Stanley Baldwin	Con	210 (Oct 1924)	615
Jun 1929–Aug 1931	James Ramsay MacDonald	Lab	none (May 1929)	615
Aug 1931–Jun 1935	James Ramsay MacDonald	National (coalition)	492 (Oct 1931)	615
Jun 1935–May 1937	Stanley Baldwin	(coalition)	242 (Nov 1935)	615
May 1937–May 1940	Neville Chamberlain	(coalition)		
May 1940–May 1945	Winston Churchill	Coalition		
May–Jul 1945	Winston Churchill	Caretaker		
Jul 1945–Oct 1951	Clement Attlee	Lab	147 (Jul 1945)	640
			6 (Feb 1950)	625
Oct 1951–Apr 1955	Winston Churchill	Con	16 (Oct 1951)	625
Apr 1955–Jan 1957	Anthony Eden	Con	59 (May 1955)	630
Jan 1957–Oct 1963	Harold Macmillan	Con	99 (Oct 1959)	630
Oct 1963–Oct 1964	Alec Douglas-Home	Con		
Oct 1964–Jun 1970	Harold Wilson	Lab	5 (Oct 1964)	630
			97 (Mar 1966)	630

Table A.1 continued

Dates of office	Prime Minister	Composition of govt	Govt majority (general election)	Total seats
June 1970–Mar 1974	Edward Heath	Con	31 (Jun 1970)	630
Mar 1974–Apr 1976	Harold Wilson	Lab	none (Feb 1974)	635
			4 (Oct 1974)	635
Apr 1976–May 1979	James Callaghan	Lab	44 (May 1979)	635
May 1979–Nov 1990	Margaret Thatcher	Con	144 (June 1983)	650
			102 (Jun 1987)	650
Nov 1990–May 1997	John Major	Con	21 (Apr 1992)	651
May 1997–	Tony Blair	Lab	178 (May 1997)	659

Table A.2 Votes cast at general elections since 1918

	Con[a]	Lab[b]	Lib/Dem[c]	Others	Total
1918	4,144,192	2,245,777	2,785,374	1,611,475	10,786,818
1922	5,502,298	4,237,349	4,139,460	513,223	14,392,330
1923	5,514,541	4,439,780	4,301,481	291,893	14,547,695
1924	7,854,523	5,489,087	2,928,737	367,932	16,640,279
1929	8,656,225	8,370,417	5,308,738	312,995	22,648,375
1931	13,156,790	6,649,630	1,476,123	373,830	21,656,373
1935	11,755,654	8,325,491	1,443,093	472,816	21,997,054
1945	9,972,010	11,967,746	2,252,430	903,009	25,095,195
1950	12,492,404	13,266,176	2,621,487	391,057	28,771,124
1951	13,718,199	13,948,883	730,546	198,966	28,596,594
1955	13,310,891	12,405,254	722,402	321,182	26,759,729
1959	13,750,875	12,216,172	1,640,760	254,845	27,862,652
1964	12,002,642	12,205,808	3,099,283	349,415	27,657,148
1966	11,418,455	13,096,629	2,327,457	422,206	27,264,747
1970	13,145,123	12,208,758	2,117,035	873,882	28,344,798
1974 (Feb)	11,872,180	11,645,616	6,059,519	1,762,847	31,340,162
1974 (Oct)	10,462,565	11,457,079	5,346,704	1,922,756	29,189,104
1979	13,697,923	11,532,218	4,313,804	1,677,417	31,221,362
1983	13,012,316	8,456,934	7,780,949	1,420,938	30,671,137
1987	13,760,583	10,029,807	7,341,633	1,397,555	32,529,578
1992	14,093,007	11,560,484	5,999,606	1,960,977	33,614,074
1997	9,600,943	13,518,167	5,242,947	2,141,647	30,503,704

Sources: F. W. S. Craig, *British Electoral Facts 1832–1987* (Dartmouth, 1989); C. Rallings and M. Thrasher, *Britain Votes 5* (Dartmouth, 1993); *Britain Votes 6* (Ashgate, 1998).

Notes
[a] Includes National, National Liberal and National Labour 1931–45; and Unionist candidates in Northern Ireland before 1974.
[b] 1931 figure includes votes for 25 unendorsed candidates.
[c] Includes Liberal and National Liberal 1922, Independent Liberal 1931, Liberal-SDP Alliance (1983–7) and Liberal Democrat (1992 on).

Table A.3 Shares of the vote at general elections since 1918 (%)[a]

	Con[b]	*Lab*[c]	*Lib/Dem*[d]	*Others*
1918	38.7	20.8	25.6	14.9
1922	38.5	29.7	28.8	3.0
1923	38.0	30.7	29.7	1.6
1924	46.8	33.3	17.8	2.1
1929	38.1	37.1	23.5	1.3
1931	60.7	30.9	7.0	1.4
1935	53.3	38.0	6.7	2.0
1945	39.6	48.0	9.0	3.4
1950	43.4	46.1	9.1	1.4
1951	48.0	48.8	2.6	0.7
1955	49.7	46.4	2.7	1.2
1959	49.4	43.8	5.9	0.9
1964	43.4	44.1	11.2	1.3
1966	41.9	48.0	8.5	1.5
1970	46.4	43.1	7.5	3.1
1974 (Feb)	37.9	37.2	19.3	5.6
1974 (Oct)	35.8	39.3	18.3	6.6
1979	43.9	36.9	13.8	5.4
1983	42.4	27.6	25.4	4.6
1987	42.3	30.8	22.6	4.3
1992	41.9	34.4	17.8	5.8
1997	31.5	44.3	17.2	7.0

Sources: F. W. S. Craig, *British Electoral Facts 1832–1987* (Dartmouth, 1989); C. Rallings and M. Thrasher, *Britain Votes 5* (Dartmouth, 1993): *Britain Votes 6* (Ashgate, 1998).

Notes
[a] The shares are adjusted to allow for multi-member seats which existed prior to 1950.
[b] Includes National, National Liberal and National Labour 1931–45; and Unionist candidates in Northern Ireland before 1974.
[c] 1931 figure includes votes for 25 unendorsed candidates.
[d] Includes Liberal and National Liberal 1922, Independent Liberal 1931, Liberal-SDP Alliance (1983–7) and Liberal Democrat (1992 on).

Table A.4 Seats won in general elections since 1922

	Con[a]	Lab	Lib/Dem[b]	PC/SNP	Northern Ireland	Other	Total
1922	334	142	114	–	12	13	615
1923	248	191	157	–	12	7	615
1924	400	151	39	–	12	13	615
1929	249	287	59	–	12	8	615
1931	511	52	36	–	12	4	615
1935	418	154	21	–	12	10	615
1945	201	393	12	–	12	22	640
1950	287	315	9	–	12	2	625
1951	312	295	6	–	12	–	625
1955	334	277	6	–	12	1	630
1959	353	258	6	–	12	1	630
1964	291	317	9	–	12	1	630
1966	242	363	12	–	12	1	630
1970	322	287	6	1	12	2	630
1974 (Feb)	296	301	14	9	12	3	635
1974 (Oct)	276	319	13	14	12	1	635
1979	339	268	11	4	12	1	635
1983	397	209	23	4	17	–	650
1987	375	229	22	6	17	1	650
1992	336	271	20	7	17	–	651
1997	165	418	46	10	18	2	659

Sources: F. W. S. Craig, *British Electoral Facts 1832–1987* (Dartmouth, 1989); C. Rallings and M. Thrasher, *Britain Votes 5* (Dartmouth, 1993); *Britain Votes 6* (Ashgate, 1998).

Notes
[a] Includes National, National Liberal and National Labour 1931–45; but not Northern Ireland Unionists.
[b] Includes Liberal and National Liberal 1922, Independent Liberal 1931, Liberal-SDP Alliance (1983–7) and Liberal Democrat (1992 on).
[c] Includes Speaker where standing for re-election.

Table A.5 Voting by gender (%)

	Con	Lab	Lib/Dem	Con lead
Men				
1970	43	48	7	−5
1974 (Feb)	37	42	18	−5
1974 (Oct)	35	45	16	−10
1979	43	39	13	4
1983	41	30	26	11
1987	41	33	23	8
1992	39	38	18	1
1997	31	45	17	−14
Women				
1970	48	42	8	6
1974 (Feb)	39	40	20	−1
1974 (Oct)	37	40	20	−3
1979	46	36	15	10
1983	44	28	26	16
1987	43	31	23	12
1992	43	34	18	9
1997	32	45	17	−13

Sources: 1970–74, British Election Study (I. Crewe, A. Fox and N. Day, *The British Electorate 1963-1992* (Cambridge University Press, 1995)); 1979–92, Harris/ITN exit polls; 1997, NOP/BBC exit poll.

Note
Methodological differences between the surveys used to collect these figures mean that they are not strictly comparable over time.

Table A.6 Voting by age (%)

	Con	Lab	Lib/Dem	Con lead
18–29 year-olds				
1979	35	41	17	–6
1983	39	32	25	7
1987	36	35	26	1
1992	40	38	17	2
1997	22	56	18	–34
30–44 year-olds				
1979	46	34	15	12
1983	39	28	30	11
1987	41	31	26	10
1992	37	37	20	0
1997	26	49	17	–23
45–64 year-olds				
1979	45	39	12	6
1983	44	26	27	18
1987	44	31	22	13
1992	42	34	20	8
1997	33	43	18	–10
65+ year-olds				
1979	43	35	16	8
1983	45	28	21	17
1987	47	31	19	16
1992	47	36	14	11
1997	43	33	16	10

Sources: 1970–74, British Election Study (I. Crewe, A. Fox and N. Day, *The British Electorate 1963-1992* (Cambridge University Press, 1995)); 1979–92, Harris/ITN exit polls; 1997, NOP/BBC exit poll.

Note
Methodological differences between the surveys used to collect these figures mean that they are not strictly comparable over time.

Table A.7 The volume of legislation: Numbers of
pages of Acts and Statutory Instruments, 1911–97

	Acts	*Statutory Instruments*
1911	430	330
1921	420	1,080
1931	280	1,050
1940	370	1,970
1950	720	2,970
1955	540	2,340
1960	850	3,020
1965	1,340	4,730
1970	1,110	4,880
1975	2,060	6,210
1980	2,110	5,440
1985	2,380	4,760
1990	2,390	6,550
1991	2,250	7,630
1992	2,700	8,960
1993	2,640	7,940
1994	2,340	10,140
1995	3,000	9,690
1996	3,150	10,230
1997	2,060	n/a

Note
The figures do not include Northern Ireland (Stormont)
Acts or Statutory Rules. Pre-1987 figures are adjusted to
current page sizes.

Table A.8 An ageing population (% of total)

	1971	1981	1991	1996-based projections		
				2001	*2011*	*2021*
	1971	*1981*	*1991*			
Pre–school (0–4)	8.1	6.1	6.7	6.0	5.6	5.6
School age (5–15)	17.4	16.1	13.6	14.2	12.8	12.2
Working age (16–retirement age)	58.2	59.9	61.4	61.7	62.3	63.0
Pension age	16.3	17.8	18.3	18.0	19.3	19.2
Total	100.0	100.0	100.0	100.0	100.0	100.0

Source: Office for National Statistics, *Annual Abstract of Statistics 1999*, 1999, table 5.3.

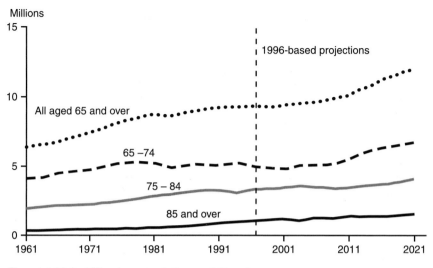

Figure A.1 United Kingdom population aged 65 and over

Source: Office for National Statistics, *Britain 1999*, © Crown copyright 1999, p. 108.

Table A.9 A multi-cultural population: Population by ethnic group in Great Britain, 1995/6

	000s	*% of total*
Black Caribbean	484	0.9
Black African	289	0.5
Black other	243	0.4
Indian	868	1.5
Pakistani	554	1.0
Bangladeshi	184	0.3
Chinese	123	0.2
Other ethnic minority	506	0.9
All ethnic minority	3,251	5.8
White	52,903	94.2
Total (incl. not stated)	56,169	100.0

Source: Office for National Statistics, *Population Trends*, Summer 1997, p. 22.

Table A.10 Households by size (Great Britain, % of total)

	1961	1971	1981	1991	1998
One person	14	18	22	27	28
Two people	30	32	32	34	35
Three people	23	19	17	16	16
Four people	18	17	18	16	14
Five people	9	8	7	5	5
Six or more people	7	6	4	2	2
Number of households (millions)	16.3	18.6	20.2	22.4	23.6
Average household size (number of people)	3.1	2.9	2.7	2.5	2.4

Source: Office for National Statistics, *Social Trends*, © Crown copyright 1999, figure 2.2.

Table A.11 A consumer society

	1972	1979	1985	1991	1996
Percentage of households in Britain with:					
Television	93	97	98	98	99
Video recorder	n/a	n/a	31	68	82
CD player	n/a	n/a	n/a	27	58
Home computer	n/a	n/a	13	21	27
Microwave oven	n/a	n/a	n/a	55	74
Deep freeze	n/a	40	66	83	91
Washing machine	66	74	81	87	90
Tumble drier	n/a	19	33	48	51
Dishwasher	n/a	3	6	14	20
Telephone	42	67	81	88	94
Central heating	37	55	69	82	88
Car or van	52	57	62	67	70

Source: Office for National Statistics, *Living in Britain*, 1996, table 3.20.

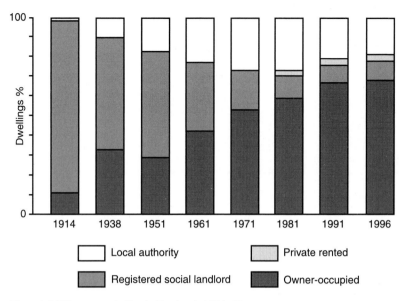

Figure A.2 Where people live in England, 1914–96

Source: Office for National Statistics, *Britain 1999*, © Crown copyright 1999, p. 346.

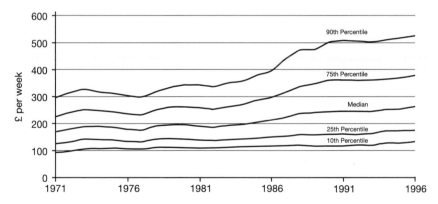

Figure A.3 High and low incomes in the United Kingdom. Average household disposable income has grown in real terms since 1970. At the same time the gap between those with high incomes (the higher percentiles) and those with low incomes (the lower percentiles) has also grown

Source: Office for National Statistics, *Social Trends*, © Crown copyright 1999, figure 5.16.

Note: The figure shows income before housing costs adjusted to January 1998 prices. The inderlying figures are adjusted to take account of different household sizes.

Table A.12 The distribution of wealth in the United Kingdom

	1976	1981	1986	1991	1994	1995
Marketable wealth						
% of wealth owned by:						
Most wealthy 1%	21	18	18	17	19	19
Most wealthy 5%	38	36	36	35	39	38
Most wealthy 10%	50	50	50	47	52	50
Most wealthy 25%	71	73	73	71	74	73
Most wealthy 50%	92	92	90	92	93	92
Total marketable wealth						
(£ billion)	280	565	955	1,711	1,950	2,033
Marketable wealth less value of dwellings						
% of wealthy owned by:						
Most wealthy 1%	29	26	25	29	29	27
Most wealthy 5%	47	45	46	51	53	51
Most wealthy 10%	57	56	58	64	66	64
Most wealthy 25%	73	74	75	80	83	81
Most wealthy 50%	88	87	89	93	94	93

Source: Office for National Statistics, *Social Trends*, © Crown copyright 1999, figure 5.25.

Table A.13 Economic activity and unemployment in the United Kingdom

	Activity rate		Unemployment rate	
	Men	*Women*	*Men*	*Women*
1988	88.6	70.3	9.1	8.5
1989	88.8	71.2	7.5	7.1
1990	88.7	71.6	7.1	6.6
1991	88.1	71.3	9.3	7.3
1992	86.7	70.9	11.7	7.5
1993	85.9	70.9	12.5	7.8
1994	85.6	70.9	11.6	7.5
1995	85.1	70.9	10.2	7.0
1996	85.0	71.4	9.8	6.5
1997	84.8	71.7	8.2	6.0
1998	84.3	71.9	6.9	5.5

Source: Office for National Statistics, *Labour Market Trends*, March 1999, table A.1.

Notes
Activity rate: Number in employment or unemployed as % of total working-age population.
Unemployment rate: % of economically active people who are unemployed on the ILO measure.

Table A.14 The pattern of working in the United Kingdom, 1998 (4th quarter)

	000s	*%*
Employees	23,486	86.8
Self-employed	3,277	12.1
Unpaid family workers	101	0.4
Government supported training and employment programmes	179	0.7
Total workers	27,044	100.0
of which		
full-time	20,320	75.1
part-time	6,718	24.8
workers with second job	1,194	4.4

Source: Office for National Statistics, *Labour Market Trends*, March 1999, table B.12.

Table A.15 A service economy: Employee jobs by industry in the United Kingdom, June 1998

	Employee jobs (000s)	*% of total*	*% change since 1988*
Agriculture and fishing	274	1.2	−18.5
Energy and water	222	1.0	−50.2
Manufacturing	4,081	17.6	−16.0
Construction	1,009	4.3	−7.5
Services	17,634	75.9	13.6
of which			
distribution, hotels, restaurants	5,338	23.0	17.3
transport and communications	1,381	5.9	4.4
banking, finance, insurance	4,071	17.5	28.4
public administration, education and health	5,823	25.1	4.3
other services	1,020	4.4	13.7
All jobs	*23,220*	*100.0*	*4.3*

Source: Office for National Statistics, *Britain 1999*, 1999, table 11.4.

Table A.16 Trade unions in the United Kingdom

	Number of trade unions	Membership (000s)
1971	525	11,135
1976	473	12,386
1981	414	12,106
1986	335	10,539
1991	275	9,585
1996	226	7,987

Source: Office for National Statistics, *Annual Abstract of Statistics.*

Figure A.4 Fewer strikes: Working days lost through industrial action in the United Kingdom, 1977–97

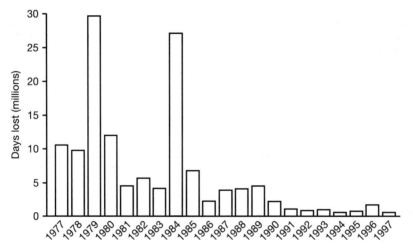

Source: Office for National Statistics, *Britain 1999,* © Crown copyright 1999, p. 162.

Table A.17 Rising crime: Notifiable crimes recorded by the police in England and Wales (000s)

Offence group	1987	1992	1997
Violence against the person	141	201.8	250.8
Sexual offences	25.2	29.5	33.2
Burglary	900.1	1,355.3	1,015.1
Robbery	32.6	52.9	63.1
Theft and handling stolen goods	2,052	2,851.6	2,165.0
Fraud and forgery	133	168.6	134.4
Criminal damage	589	892.6	877.0
Other	19.3	39.4	59.8
Total	*3,892.2*	*5,591.7*	*4,598.3*

Source: *Criminal Statistics England and Wales 1997* (Cm. 4162)

Table A.18 Membership of selected voluntary organisations in the United Kingdom, 1997

National Trust [a]	2,488,000
Royal Society for the Protection of Birds (RSPB)	1,007,000
Civic Trust [b]	330,000
The Wildlife Trusts [c]	310,000
World Wide Fund for Nature	241,000
National Trust for Scotland	228,000
Greenpeace	215,000
Woodland Trust	195,000
Ramblers Association	123,000
Friends of the Earth (FoE) [d]	110,000
Council for the Protection of Rural England	45,000

Source: Office for National Statistics, *Britain 1999*, © Crown copyright 1999, table 20.4.

Notes
[a] England, Wales and Northern Ireland only.
[b] Members of local amenity societies registered with the Civic Trust, November 1997.
[c] Includes the Royal Society for Nature Conservation (RSNC).
[d] FoE figure is for 1995.

Table A.19 Public spending, 1998–9

Government department	£ million	% of total	£ per head per week
Social Security	81,744	29.9	26.57
Environment, Transport & Regions	44,752	16.4	14.54
Health	37,643	13.8	12.23
Defence	22,549	8.3	7.33
Scotland	14,948	5.5	4.86
Education & Employment	14,179	5.2	4.61
Northern Ireland	8,548	3.1	2.78
Wales	7,113	2.6	2.31
Home Office	7,022	2.6	2.28
Agriculture, Fisheries, Food	3,420	1.3	1.11
Chancellor of Exchequer	3,193	1.2	1.04
Trade & Industry	2,748	1.0	0.89
Legal Departments	2,701	1.0	0.88
International Development	2,425	0.9	0.79
Cabinet Office	1,353	0.5	0.44
Foreign Office	1,119	0.4	0.36
Culture, Media & Sport	927	0.3	0.30
Other[a]	16,766	6.1	5.45
Total	*273,150*	*100.0*	*88.77*

Sources: HM Treasury, *Public Expenditure*, Cm. 4201, March 1999, table 1.12; Office for National Statistics, *Monthly Digest of Statistics*, March 1999.

Notes
There are several definitions of public spending. These figures show the public expenditure control total for 1998–9 (estimated outturn).
[a] European Communities, local authority self-financed expenditure, ECGD and allowance for shortfall.

Table A.20 Numbers of civil servants

1939	347,000
1944	1,164,000
1949	784,000
1954	751,000
1959	647,000
1964	658,000
1969	684,000
1974	712,000
1979	743,000
1984	634,000
1989	584,000
1994	561,000
1998	481,000

Note
The figures from 1974 onwards are on slightly different definitions. These had the effect of increasing the total by about 20,000 in 1974.

Source: *Civil Service Statistics*.

Appendix 4: Key sources – Politics on the web

This small selection of websites gives access to a vast amount of information on the political process in Britain. Some contain information in their own right while others provide links to further sites. Be aware that website addresses change – sometimes only slightly – from time to time.

Government departments

The CCTA Government Information Service homepage – http://www.open.gov.uk/ – contains links for all government departments, including Number 10 Downing Street, as well as many other *official bodies*, including HMSO, spending watchdogs, ombudsmen, inquiries and committees (including the Committee for Standards in Public Life), local authorities and assorted quangos.

The following types of material can be found using this site:

- *White papers* and most consultation (green) papers can be downloaded via the website of the publishing department. A wide range of general briefings and *technical documents* can also be found.
- *Press notices* are one of the best sources of information on recent policy developments. They can be accessed via departmental websites or via the Central Office of Information site.
- Recent *legislation* is now available on the internet. The website of Her Majesty's Stationery Office contains the text of public Acts of Parliament from 1996 onwards and secondary legislation (statutory instruments) from 1997 onwards. Beware – if legislation is amended by subsequent legislation, the Act or SI will remain on this site in its original form.

Official documents

http://www.official-documents.co.uk contains full version or summary of official documents published by The Stationery Office.

The UK Parliament

The parliamentary website – http://www.parliament.uk – contains a great deal of material on Parliament and the legislative process, including:

- *Hansard* for the Commons and Lords
- *Bills*: the text of current bills, and Hansard for the Commons committee stage of bills
- *Select Committee Reports*
- General *information* on Parliament, including an extensive series of factsheets, and details of parliamentary *helplines* for members of the public
- The *Weekly Information Bulletin*, which gives details of recent and forthcoming business in the House of Commons, including the progress of bills currently before Parliament. The *Sessional Information Digest* is an annual summary of such information.
- *Research papers* produced by the Commons library which give detailed background to major bills and other topics of current political interest.

Devolution

The devolved bodies in Scotland, Wales and Northern Ireland have all established their own websites:

- http://www.scottish.parliament.uk/
- http://www.assembly.wales.gov.uk/
- http://www.ni-assembly.gov.uk/index.htm

Pressure groups and political parties

The website for the BBC programme *On the Record* contains links for a large number of parties and pressure groups: http://www.bbc.co.uk/otr/politics.shtml

The European Union

The EU's official website – Europa – is at http://www.europa.eu.int/index-en.htm. As one would expect, it contains an enormous amount of information, including:

- Links to each of the *institutions* of the EU, including the European Parliament, the Commission, the Council of Ministers, and so on
- Information on *key issues* such as the euro and EU enlargement
- Electronic versions of *policy documents and legislation*.

News and comment

http://news.bbc.co.uk/ is an excellent, up-to-the-minute news service provided by the BBC.

Opinion polls

All of the main polling organisations have their own websites. MORI's site is a good one: www.mori.com/.

Index